WALKING THE CATHEDRAL CITIES OF ENGLAND

WALKING THE CATHEDRAL CITIES OF ENGLAND

TWENTY-EIGHT ORIGINAL WALKS
AND TOURS AROUND THE
CATHEDRALS AND CATHEDRAL
CITIES OF WESTERN
& EASTERN ENGLAND

ROWLAND MEAD

NEW
HOLLAND

First published in 2003 by
New Holland Publishers (UK) Ltd
London • Cape Town • Sydney • Auckland

Garfield House
86–88 Edgware Road
London W2 2EA
United Kingdom

80 McKenzie Street
Cape Town 8001
South Africa

14 Aquatic Drive
Frenchs Forest, NSW 2086
Australia

218 Lake Road
Northcote
Auckland
New Zealand

ISBN 1 84330 559 3

Publishing Manager: Jo Hemmings
Senior Editor: Kate Michell
Assistant Editor: Rose Hudson
Editors: Paul Barnett, Rowena Curtis, Pete Duncan
Cartographer: William Smuts

Printed

F
Spine: T
Back cover top: I   at Cana,
from the 1   d.

CONTENTS

INTRODUCTION

For many people, English cathedrals have a special fascination. They are undoubtedly the supreme expression of English architecture. In terms of enclosed space they were, until Victorian times, the largest buildings in the country. They are also extremely varied, both individually and in comparison with each other, lacking as they do the strict symmetry of the Classical style. Furthermore, English cathedrals often have as near neighbours the remains of their associated abbeys, and are usually surrounded by their host city's historic core, full of engrossing domestic architecture, ancient defensive walls and other sites of interest.

Numerous books have been written about the English cathedral, some emphasizing the architectural aspects and others of a more spiritual context. Most city authorities have produced a 'town trail' describing a route through the centre. This volume aims to combine these aspects on a regional basis. Each section begins by looking at the historical background of the cathedral and city. This is followed by a guided tour of the cathedral itself (with a plan for easy reference), concentrating on not just the architecture but also on relevant odd quirks and historical relics. Then there is a walking tour, beginning and ending at the cathedral, of the historic core of the city (again with a map). Options and alternative routes are supplied to suit the energy of the visitor and the time available. Possibilities for refreshment en route are suggested, with particular attention to historic pubs and old coaching inns, essential features of the English cathedral city.

ACKNOWLEDGEMENTS

I would like to thank a number of staff at New Holland for their help and expertise in producing the earlier editions of this book, including Charlotte Parry-Crooke, Tim Jollands, Rowena Curtis and Pete Duncan, all who have now moved on to other posts in the publishing world. More up-to-date thanks should go to Rose Hudson for guiding me through this present volume.

None of the cathedral authorities were contacted formally, but I am indebted to a vast number of guides and other staff, who often revealed some gems of information normally omitted from official brochures. Other useful material came from tourist information offices, where the staff were invariably cooperative and helpful, despite the fact that I often caught them at times when they were busy and harassed.

Last, but not least, my thanks to my wife for her encouragement and valuable theological knowledge. She uncomplainingly tested out the tours – in what often turned out to be vile weather. I could not have wished for a better companion with whom to visit our wonderful cathedral cities.

Rowland Mead
Shaldon, Devon

ENGLISH CATHEDRALS –
AN INTRODUCTION

A cathedral is a place of Christian worship that contains a *cathedra* – that is, a bishop's seat or throne. The *cathedra* was the bishop's symbol of authority; should the *cathedra* be moved, the cathedral building would have to be redesignated.

In medieval times, if a cathedral was attached to a monastery (a Norman innovation), the bishop had the further title of abbot, although the effective head of the monastery was its prior – an arrangement which often led to friction. Of the seventeen cathedrals in medieval England, eight were monastic, usually Benedictine (e.g., Canterbury, Ely and Winchester). Such cathedrals had a range of adjoining monastic buildings, usually on the south side, including a chapter house, dormitory, refectory, infirmary, hospital (or guest hall) and cloisters.

The other cathedrals were served by canons. There were two types of these: secular canons and canons regular, the latter working to fixed rules. The most important canons regular were the Augustinians, followers of the writings of St Augustine (d604); their liberal approach to life meant they had a much more workable relationship with the townspeople than did the monks.

The secular canons, on the other hand, were unhampered by rules and were generally free to live where they liked. They depended on a prebend or endowment (usually from a wealthy landowner), and were thus often known as prebendaries. This was, for example, the situation at Southwell, where many of the large houses around the cathedral were those provided for the prebendaries. The canons' function was to run the cathedral and its services, a role fulfilled by the dean and chapter today.

Newer Cathedrals

The cathedrals run by secular canons were collectively known after the Reformation as the Old Foundation. The five new sees created by Henry VIII – Oxford, Peterborough, Chester, Gloucester and Bristol – plus the surviving monastic cathedrals were the New Foundation. Confusingly, many of the secular cathedrals (e.g., Lincoln) have cloisters, although these were largely ornamental rather than practical.

During the Industrial Revolution people flocked from the land to the growing cities based on the coalfields in the Midlands and the north. This flow of population necessitated the setting up of a number of additional sees. New cathedrals were created, usually by upgrading existing parish churches – as at Manchester, Liverpool, Wakefield and elsewhere – but also from scratch, as at Truro. After World War II, some modern cathedrals were constructed: the one at Coventry replaced a building destroyed by enemy bombs, while that at Guildford was the product of an architectural competition.

Architectural Styles

The majority of English cathedrals are Gothic in style, but none has the purity of one specific period – indeed, it is often possible to find elements of Norman, Early English, Decorated and Perpendicular styles within a single cathedral.

It is frequently thought that English cathedral architecture originated in France and was brought over by the Normans, but this is an oversimplification: the Anglo-Saxons had imported the Norman style before the Conquest. Thereafter, English masons developed their own styles – for example, the Perpendicular, a style not seen among the French, who were then still experimenting with the Flamboyant, a development of the earlier Decorated style. Shape and form also differ between English and French cathedrals. The naves of French cathedrals soar to great heights, while English cathedrals tend to be long and low, with height gained by towers and spires. The extra length of English naves has two explanations. First, in monastic cathedrals the monks and townspeople were kept apart: the congregation occupied the nave and the monks the choir and presbytery, the two areas being separated by a *pulpitum* (screen). Second, the nave often had a non-religious use, such as the collection of tithes or the administration of justice, requiring a sizeable area. Another difference between English and French cathedrals can be found at the east ends. The French buildings are noted for their apse, a semi-circular structure within which was an ambulatory or processional way, often for pilgrims to pass by shrines. English cathedrals, on the other hand, are more likely to have a stepped or cliff-like east end, perhaps marked by a Lady Chapel.

Although one finds the occasional example of Anglo-Saxon work (such as Ripon's crypt), for convenience we can divide the medieval architectural styles into four.

Norman

The Norman style actually appeared (in parts of Westminster Abbey) during the reign of Edward the Confessor, but for simplicity's sake the start can be dated as 1066, at the beginning of the Norman Conquest. It lasted until approximately 1190. Known properly as Romanesque, it was common throughout Europe. In English cathedrals much of the Norman work has been replaced, but sufficient remains in buildings such as Durham, Ely, Gloucester and many others to recognise the essential elements. It was during the Norman period that the idea of three horizontal layers was introduced – the main arcade, the triforium (or tribune) and the clerestory – and their relative proportions are a key to the aesthetic appearance of the interior. The piers or pillars tend to be massive and cylindrical, with engaged shafts and occasionally, as at Durham, etched or chevron decoration. Arches are invariably rounded, sometimes with zigzag or dog-tooth mouldings. Sometimes, as at Ely, the arches interlock. Windows are small and narrow and splayed only on the inside. Roofs were initially wooden and highly decorated, although vaulting put in an appearance towards the end of the period, particularly in the aisles. Few Norman

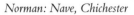

Norman: Nave, Chichester towers survive – they dropped like ninepins and were

Early English: North Transept, Salisbury

often replaced in later periods. Sculptural decoration was minimal, although exceptions are the west door at Rochester, the Prior's Door at Ely and the capitals in the crypt at Canterbury.

Early English

The Early English style marked the start of Gothic architecture and began in England around 1175, overlapping the end of the Norman period. It was to last until 1265. (It is interesting to note that the term 'Gothic' did not appear in the literature until the late 17th century). The Early English style had a lighter and more elegant appearance than the Norman. Pointed arches appeared and windows were tall and narrow, known as lancets after the surgeon's knife. Trefoils and plate tracery were used for the first time. Piers were often formed of columns with detached shafts (often of Purbeck Marble), united at the capitals, which frequently had stiff-leaved foliage. The Early English style probably first appeared in the choir at Lincoln and there are particularly fine examples to be seen at Exeter, Wells, the south Transept at York, Southwell and Peterborough.

Undoubtedly the most comprehensively Early English construction is at Salisbury, the English cathedral that comes nearest to having a single style; building started in 1220 and was more or less completed 38 years later.

Decorated

A further period of transition came with the Decorated style, which appeared *c*1250 and reached its zenith in the middle of the following century. (Architectural historians often divide the Decorated period into Geometrical or Early Decorated and Flowing or Late Decorated.) The style takes its name from the window tracery, which became extremely complex. The moulded stone mullions in the upper part of the windows formed graceful circles and other intricate designs. Piers came to have closely joined shafts, not detached as before, while capitals, bosses and other stonework were ornately carved with free-flowing foliage, animals and heads. All this work was expensive and labour-intensive, but this was no problem: it was a prosperous time and the Church was receiving considerable income from the land it owned. Examples of the Decorated style are plentiful in our cathedrals; there are particularly fine examples in the chapter houses at Southwell, Wells and Salisbury, in many parts of York Minster, in the Angel Choir at Lincoln and in the nave at Lichfield.

Decorated: Lady Chapel, Exeter

Perpendicular

The final stage of the Gothic, the Perpendicular, lasted 200 years, from 1350 to *c*1550. The Perpendicular, which has been described as the 'architecture of vertical lines', is best observed in window tracery, where the mullions carry straight on up to the head of the framework. The areas of glass became larger and the rectilinear spaces became more suitable for stained-glass renditions of stories and parables. Pillars were more elegant and led up to superb fan vaulting or the astonishing *pendant lierne* vault, such as that at Oxford. Rose windows appeared, usually in the transepts. Shallow panels in the solid masonry of walls were another hallmark of the period.

Perpendicular: Lady Chapel, Gloucester

The earliest extant Perpendicular cathedral window is probably that in the choir at Gloucester, but Southwell, Winchester and others have some striking west windows in this style. The crowning glory of the Perpendicular is to be found in Henry VII's Chapel at Westminster Abbey.

The subsequent Renaissance period saw a revival of the Classical and Roman styles of architecture. During this period – the 16th and 17th centuries – there was very little cathedral (or church) building in England, so the styles are little represented, the remarkable exception being St Paul's Cathedral. The huge Old St Paul's, a Gothic edifice, was destroyed in the Great Fire of 1666. The replacement – designed by Sir Christopher Wren (1632–1723) – with its massive dome, is totally unlike any other English cathedral.

The Gothic influence, however, would not go away. There was a strong revival of Neo-Gothic during Victorian times, often with unfortunate results; the replacement west front at St Alban's is one example.

Early Cathedral Life

The medieval English cathedral was a very different place from what we witness today. Before the Reformation the cathedral was often a very wealthy establishment, particularly if it had an important shrine and thus attracted pilgrims. It would be a riot of colour, with abundant statuary, a bejewelled and gilded altar, rich tapestries and paintings.

Life in a medieval monastery or cathedral might seem very harsh to us, but by comparison with the lot of most of the common folk of the time it was fairly comfortable. Each day a monk would have to spend about four hours in public worship, about four in study or private prayer and perhaps another six engaged in work for the benefit of the monastic community – cooking, perhaps, or the tending of vegetables. The abbot's rule was supreme within the community: he could be as totalitarian as any despot if he wished, although most abbots had more sense.

The day was divided up by acts of worship. With Matins immediately after midnight, Prime at sunrise, Terce at about 9am, High Mass at about 10am, Sext at noon, None in midafternoon, Vespers in the early evening and Compline at sunset – with other services thrown in on special occasions – the monks were not left much time for such activities as sleeping! In fact, they retired to their dormitories to sleep twice each night, between Compline and Matins and between Matins and Prime.

While some monks would live, grow old and die within a single monastery – this was the life of the Benedictines (followers of St Benedict of Nursia (*c*480–*c*547)) – members of many orders would frequently move from one to the next, preaching in towns and villages en route, helping the poor and needy, and living off alms. Such was the practice of, for example, the Dominicans (adherents of St Dominic (*c*1170–1221); called the Black Friars because of their garb), the Carmelites (gaining their name from Mount Carmel, France, where the order was founded; the White Friars) and the Franciscans (adherents of St Francis of Assisi (1181–1226); the Grey Friars). Members of military orders, such as the Knights Templar, were likewise unbound to a single monastery.

At the Reformation, Henry VIII's men plundered the sacred shrines of orders such as the Benedictines, smashed the statues and removed much of the plate, jewels and hangings. The monasteries were closed down and their stonework was often stolen by townspeople for building purposes. Further vandalism occurred during the Civil War, with soldiers often using cathedrals as barracks. Then followed ages of neglect. The Victorians strove to rectify this, not always happily. Nevertheless, our cathedrals still retain much of their ancient beauty and charm and few of us can remain unmoved by them.

Life Today in England's Cathedrals

Life in today's – Church of England – cathedrals is in some ways not so dissimilar from that of the medieval monastery. Although such activities as the tilling of fields have been superseded by their modern counterparts, the priests nevertheless still divide their time between religious and pastoral concerns – typically there are five services on a Sunday and two or three on each of the other days. Choral music remains an important aspect of cathedral life, with various first-rate choir schools attached to cathedrals.

Also unchanged since early times is the need to raise funds for the upkeep of the cathedral and other expenses involved in running it on a day-to-day basis. While large-scale benefactors play their part in this, the dean and chapter are also heavily reliant on contributions from the general public; thus, while it may grate on the sensibilities to be asked on visiting a cathedral for either an admission fee or a 'recommended donation' – which is very much the same thing – do bear in mind that without such measures the cathedral would very soon decline into the kind of rack and ruin that was probably its condition for centuries before the Victorian era.

With their many visitors, their shops, their information desks, their audiovisual displays and so forth, it might seem that today's cathedrals lack the stillness and tranquillity – the space for contemplation – that one might expect in a house of God. To a great extent this can be true, especially in such popular venues as St Paul's and Westminster Abbey. Yet even in such places, as one gazes in awe at a stained-glass window or steps for a moment into the cool silence of a side chapel, one can discover the transcendent peace that lies at the core of us all.

English Cathedrals in Historical Context

Rulers of England and the UK		Cathedral History	
Edwy	955–959	600–1000	Many English cathedrals, e.g. Canterbury and Winchester, had their foundation in Saxon times, often attached to monasteries.
Edgar	959–975		
Edward the Martyr	975–979		
Ethelred the Unready	979–1016		
Edmund Ironside	1016	1066	Norman Conquest. Many Saxon cathedrals demolished or rebuilt.
Canute	1016–1035		
Harold I	1035–1040	*c*1066–1190	Norman or Romanesque style of architecture, well exemplified in Durham and Ely cathedrals.
Hardicanute	1040–1042		
Edward the Confessor	1042–1066		
Harold II	1066		
William I (the Conqueror)	1066–1087	1170	Archbishop Thomas à Becket murdered in Canterbury Cathedral.
William II	1087–1100		
Henry I	1100–1135	*c*1190–1300	Early English style of architecture, seen, for instance, at Wells and Lincoln.
Stephen	1135–1154		
Henry II	1154–1189		
Richard I	1189–1199	*c*1250–1380	Decorated Gothic style of architecture, typified by Exeter and York.
John	1199–1216		
Henry III	1216–1272		
Edward I	1272–1307	*c*1350–1550	Perpendicular Gothic style of architecture, as seen at Gloucester.
Edward II	1307–1327		
Edward III	1327–1377	1532	Henry VIII begins the Reformation in England, separating the English church from Rome. Many statues and stained glass windows destroyed in the cathedrals.
Richard II	1377–1399		
Henry IV	1399–1413		
Henry V	1413–1422		
Henry VI	1422–1461		
Edward IV	1461–1483		
Edward V	1483	1536–1540	Dissolution of the Monasteries by Henry VIII. Many were refounded as cathedrals.
Richard III	1483–1485		
Henry VII	1485–1509		
Henry VIII	1509–1547	1642–1650	English Civil War. Troops used cathedrals as barracks, causing considerable damage.
Edward VI	1547–1553		
Mary I	1553–1558		
Elizabeth I	1558–1603	1666	Old St Paul's Cathedral burnt down in the Great Fire of London.
James I of England and IV of Scotland	1603–1625		
Charles I	1625–1649		
Oliver Cromwell, Lord Protector	1653–1658	17th century	English Renaissance style of architecture.
Richard Cromwell	1658–1659	1675–1710	St Paul's Cathedral rebuilt in Classical style
Charles II	1660–1685		
James II	1685–1688	18th century	Period of decay for most English cathedrals
William III and Mary II (Mary died 1694)	1689–1702		
Anne	1702–1714	19th century	Victorian times saw English cathedrals heavily restored, often badly.
George I	1714–1727		
George II	1727–1760	Late 19th century	Gothic revival. New cathedral built at Truro in this style.
George III	1760–1820		
George IV	1820–1830	1914–1918	World War I. English cathedrals largely unscathed.
William IV	1830–1837		
Victoria	1837–1901	1939–45	World War II. Many English cathedrals damaged in air raids, but only Coventry destroyed.
Edward VII	1901–1910		
George V	1910–1936		
Edward VIII	1936	1955–1962	Coventry Cathedral rebuilt in modern style.
George VI	1936–1952		
Elizabeth II	1952–		

CATHEDRAL ARCHITECTURE – GLOSSARY OF TERMS

APSE. A polygonal or semi-circular end to a cathedral chapel. It is usually vaulted.

ARCADE. A row of arches, usually between the nave and the aisles, supporting the main wall.

BALUSTER. A carved column supporting a handrail. A series of balusters is known as a balustrade.

BALL FLOWER. Stone ornament consisting of a globe shaped design with folded back petals, typical of the Decorated period.

BOSS. Located at the intersection of ribs in a vaulted roof. Usually carved with foliage or figures, it may be gilded or coloured.

BUTTRESS. A vertical area of stonework supporting a wall. An exterior buttress containing an arch is known as a 'flying buttress'.

CAPITAL. The moulded or carved block on the top of a column on which the superstructure rests. Often richly ornamented.

CHANCEL. The part of the cathedral east of the crossing.

CHANTRY. A small chapel within a cathedral, in which prayers were 'chanted'. Usually named after a donor.

CHAPTER HOUSE. An assembly room for meetings of the chapter, who are the governing body of the cathedral.

CHOIR. The part of the cathedral east of the screen and west of the presbytery, in which the service is sung.

CLERESTORY. An upper range of windows, below the eaves and above the aisled roof. Sometimes known as the 'clear storey' as distinct from the triforium or 'blind storey'.

CORBEL. A stone block projecting from a wall to provide horizontal support to various features. Often grotesquely carved.

CROSSING. The square space at the intersection of the nave and transepts, usually beneath the tower.

CRYPT. An underground chamber, usually vaulted, beneath the chancel. May contain an altar.

DIOCESE. The area under the jurisdiction of a bishop.

FAN VAULTING. A type of vault in which the ribs (which are decorative rather than structural) are of equal length and curvature. Typical of the Perpendicular period.

GALILEE. A chapel or porch at the west end of a cathedral, usually included in the processional route.

GARTH. The area enclosed by cloisters.

HAMMER BEAM. A horizontal beam projecting at right angles from the top of a wall providing support for a wooden roof.

LADY CHAPEL. A chapel dedicated to the Virgin Mary, usually located at the east end of the cathedral.

LANCET. A tall, narrow window with a pointed head and no tracery. Typical of the Early English period.

LANTERN. A tower with windows designed to give light to the crossing beneath.

LIERNE. Short vault ribs, which are purely decorative. Typical of the Perpendicular and Late Decorated periods.

MISERICORD. A bracket beneath a hinged seat in the choir stalls. When the seat was tipped up it gave some support during lengthy periods of standing. Often engagingly carved.

MULLION. A vertical stone bar sub-dividing a window into 'lights'

NAVE. The main body and western arm of a cathedral. May have aisles.

OGEE. A double S-curve found on arches and typical of the Late Decorated period.

PIER. A solid stone vertical support. May be carved or moulded.

PRESBYTERY. The area east of the choir where the high altar is located.

PULPITUM. A screen dividing the choir from the nave. The gallery or loft supported by the pulpitum often provided the location for the organ.

REBUS. A pictorial play on words often linked with the name of the bishop.

RETROCHOIR. In the eastern arm of the cathedral behind the high altar, but not including the lady chapel.

ROOD SCREEN. A screen, usually just west of the pulpitum and generally made of wood.

ROSE WINDOW. A circular window in which the tracery resembles a rose.

SANCTUARY. The area of the cathedral containing the high altar. Synonymous with the presbytery. In medieval times, fugitives from justice could shelter here after using the sanctuary knocker.

SEDILLA. A row of 3 canopied seats for the clergy on the south side of the chancel.

SPANDREL. The roughly triangular space between the outer curve of an arch and the mouldings enclosing it. Usually elaborately carved with, for example, foliage.

TIERCERON. A type of vaulting where minor ribs spring from the main rib and lead to the ridge rib.

TRACERY. Slender stone ornamental ribwork on the upper part of gothic windows. Also found on walls and screens.

TRANSEPT. The short arms running north–south in a cruciform church or cathedral.

TRIBUNE. A gallery extending along the roof of an aisle.

TRIFORIUM. An arcaded or walled passage at the intermediate level between the main arcade and the clerestory. Often known as the 'blind storey' because of its lack of windows and light. If there are windows, the term 'tribune' is preferable.

VAULT. Ceilings or roofs with load-bearing arches.

KEY TO MAPS

Each of the cathedral tours and city walks in this book is accompanied by a detailed map on which the route is shown in purple. Places of interest along the walks – such as churches, pubs and historic houses – are clearly identified. Opening times are listed chapter by chapter at the back of the book, starting on page 318.

The following is a key to symbols and abbreviations used on the maps:

Symbols

route of walk

railway line

major building

✝ church

public toilets

park

⊖ Underground

⇌ railway station

Abbreviations

APP	Approach	PDE	Parade
AVE	Avenue	PH	Public House
CLO	Close		(Pub)
COTTS	Cottages	PK	Park
CT	Court	PL	Place
DLR	Docklands	RD	Road
	Light	S	South
	Railway	SQ	Square
DRI	Drive	ST	Street
E	East	STN	Station
GDNS	Gardens	TER	Terrace
GRN	Green	UPR	Upper
GRO	Grove	VW	View
HO	House	W	West
LA	Lane	WD	Wood
LWR	Lower	WHF	Wharf
MS	Mews	WLK	Walk
MT	Mount	WY	Way
N	North		
PAS	Passage		

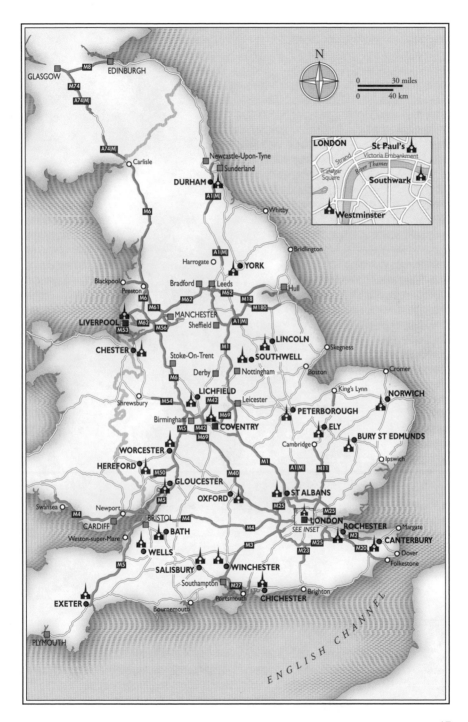

Chichester Cathedral with the Bishop's Palace in the foreground

WALKING THE CATHEDRAL CITIES OF WESTERN ENGLAND

EXETER

Access: The days when Exeter was out on a limb and a full day's drive from London and the Midlands are now fortunately over. The improved motorway and trunk road system ensures that Exeter can be reached from Birmingham via the M5 and from London via the M4 and M5 in about three hours. Coach services make full use of this accessibility: the National Express 501 Rapide service, for example, runs eight times a day to and from London. Exeter also has good train services connecting with London, the Midlands and the North; during the week there are 20 trains a day (including overnight sleepers) from London. Exeter Airport, some six miles (10km) to the east of the city, operates scheduled air services to cities including Belfast, Dublin, and Manchester.

Exeter has a long and fascinating history. The city was occupied by the Romans for almost four centuries, the most obvious reminder of those days being the city wall, probably built *c*AD200 and still largely intact today. The Romans named the settlement Isca Dumnoniorum. Excavations have revealed a mosaic pavement, a basilica and (in the cathedral close) a legionary bathhouse. The Romans eventually withdrew their legions in the 5th century.

It seems the first Christian community at Exeter dates back to the 7th century: St Boniface (680–755), the Saxon missionary to the Germans, received part of his education at a monastery here, and excavations have revealed the possible position of this building. Later a Saxon church stood to the west of the present cathedral. It was destroyed by the Danes in 1003 but rebuilt by King Canute (*c*995–1035) in 1019. Bishop Leofric, whose jurisdiction covered the whole of Devon and Cornwall, decided to move his seat from Crediton to Exeter in 1050, so this small Saxon church became a cathedral. King Edward the Confessor came in person to enthrone Leofric as the first Bishop of Exeter.

The Saxons here, as in many parts of Britain, resisted the Norman Conquest. The citizens of Exeter were under siege from William the Conqueror for nearly three weeks in 1068 before an honourable surrender was negotiated. The Normans then built Rougemont Castle to deter further Saxon insurrection. The 3rd Bishop of Exeter, William Warelwast (in office 1107–37), a nephew of the Conqueror, started to build the new cathedral of St Peter. This Norman work survives in the tower and in the base of the nave walls. Further development came at the end of the 13th century when, spurred on by news of the new cathedral at Salisbury, Bishop Bronescombe began a rebuilding in the Decorated style, adding a Lady Chapel (where he was buried) and the presbytery. His successors carried on the work into the quire and nave, the work being completed by the time of Bishop John Grandisson (1292–1369), probably by 1350.

During medieval times the city of Exeter developed as an important ecclesiastic centre. Within the city walls there were, in addition to the cathedral, 32 parish churches plus chapels and monasteries. Wealth at this time was largely based on the wool industry. Guilds flourished and were both numerous and powerful. The Guildhall and Tuckers' Hall date from this period.

At the cathedral, minor additions and developments continued, with the reconstruction of the chapter house and the building of various chantry chapels. Exeter suffered less than most cathedrals during the Reformation, but its cloisters were destroyed in the mid-17th century. At this time the cathedral was divided into two sections by a brick wall built over the Great Screen, with the Independents worshipping on one side and the Presbyterians on the other.

During the Tudor period Exeter was the sixth largest city in England, and it developed as an important trading centre. Many examples of Tudor domestic architecture can still be seen around the central area of the city, with the most famous illustration being Mol's Coffee House in the Cathedral Close. Famous sea captains like Hawkins, Drake, Frobisher and Raleigh were frequently seen around the city, which provided three ships to fight the Spanish Armada.

During the Civil War Exeter's loyalties were divided, and both Royalists and Parliamentarians occupied the city at various times, with more than one siege taking place. After the war the city soon recovered and prosperity resumed. In Georgian times development was largely outside the city walls and many distinguished crescents and terraces were built to house the burgeoning middle classes.

Lacking coal deposits, Exeter experienced a relative decline during the Industrial Revolution, but the Victorian era saw the expansion of the canal trade, the coming of the railways and the advent of horse-drawn trams. By 1860 the population had reached 50,000 and industries such as brewing, papermaking and printing had become established.

The cathedral had meanwhile been suffering from two centuries of neglect. The architect Sir George Gilbert Scott (1811–1878) began a major restoration in 1870. The stonework was cleaned, the Bishop's Throne was restored and the quire was transformed to match it. The outer bays of the organ screen were removed, as were the side walls of the quire, allowing a view into the quire from the nave.

The two world wars had little effect on Exeter until the night of May 3, 1942, when a German air raid, said to be in retaliation for an RAF raid on Lübeck, devastated the central part of the city: 156 people were killed, over 500 were injured and more than 1500 houses, many of historical and architectural importance, were completely destroyed. At the outbreak of World War II some of the cathedral's most valued treasures had been taken to a place of safety, and this precaution paid off when the cathedral received a direct hit during the Blitz. Luckily, although there was a considerable amount of damage, particularly to the quire, the main structure was unaffected. Recent years have seen a concentration on the cleaning of the stonework and the recolouring of the sculptures and monuments, so that the general impression today is of a cared-for and efficiently maintained cathedral.

These days Exeter is a thriving regional centre. Its university is popular and respected, while business and commerce prosper. Tourism has become increasingly important, with the cathedral a major magnet, attracting over 400,000 visitors annually.

TOUR OF THE CATHEDRAL

Start: The west front.
Finish: The chapter house.

The **West Front (1)** dates from the mid-14th century and is designed on three levels. The lower part consists of a screen of sculptured figures which make a fascinating study, although in many cases the statues are badly weathered. The second and third levels consist of windows in Decorated style with interesting tracery, but each in turn is partly obscured by the level below. The West Front has had considerable restoration in recent years.

If the initial exterior view is a little disappointing, the interior more than compensates. The **Nave (2)** is one of the delights of English cathedral architecture. Proportion is the key. The arcades have shafted pillars of unpolished Purbeck Marble that support moulded arches of Beer Limestone (from a quarry owned by the Dean and Chapter). Above is a narrow triforium, followed by a clerestory in which each bay is filled with a single large window containing complex tracery and which is largely responsible for the overall impression of light in the whole of the nave. Capping everything is the magnificent tierceron vaulting, probably the finest in Europe. Complementing this rich stonework are well coloured and gilded bosses and corbels. Look, in particular, for the boss depicting the murder of Thomas Becket, carved in 1340 and re-coloured in 1975. At the nave entrance we find the first two of many chapels. To the left, in the northwest corner, is the Chapel of St Edmund, which has links with the Devonshire Regiment. To the right is the Chapel of Bishop Grandisson, who completed the 14th-century redevelopments.

Now move to the **Font (3)**, which is made of Sicilian marble dating from 1687. The oak cover has eight inlaid figures of the apostles. The stem is modern. From the font there is a fine view of the **Minstrels' Gallery (4)**, the front of which contains angel figures playing medieval musical instruments; from left to right these are citole, bagpipes,

Sedilia, south side of Lady Chapel

recorder, fiddle, harp, trumpet, portative organ, gittern, shawm, tambourine and cymbals. The gallery is still used on occasions.

An Astronomical Clock

You now arrive at the **Great Screen (5)**, which was completed in 1325. It supports the organ, built by John Loosemore (*c*1613–1681) in 1665, and divides the nave from the quire. Along the top of the screen you can see a series of 17th-century paintings, while under the two side arches are the altars dedicated to St Mary and St Nicholas. Stepping into the **North Transept (6)** you find, dominating it, the orrery clock, probably dating from the late 15th century, although the dial at the top that records the minutes was added in 1760. The fleur-de-lys represents the sun and goes round a 24-hour dial, with midday at the top and midnight at the bottom. The moon's phases are shown and the day of the lunar month can be read from the inner ring. The gold ball in the centre represents the earth.

Walk along the north quire aisle and into the **Lady Chapel (7)**. Begun by Bishop Bronescombe around 1270, it has some splendid vaulting and a fine Decorated window. For a while it served as a library, but it was restored for worship in 1820 and is now used for daily services and private prayer. Don't miss the sedilia (tiered seats for the clergy) on the south side, or the dominating and beautifully gilded effigies of bishops Bronescombe and Stafford on either side of the entrance.

The Lady Chapel is flanked by two smaller chapels: to its north the Chapel of St Gabriel and to its south the Chapel of St Saviour (or Bishop Oldham's Chantry), which has a nice rebus (pictorial play on words) involving owls and dams.

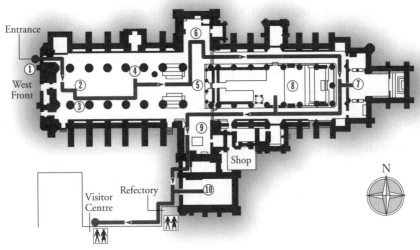

Key

1. West Front
2. Nave
3. Font
4. Minstrels' Gallery

5. Great Screen
6. North Transept
7. Lady Chapel
8. Quire

9. South Transept
10. Chapter House

From Quire to Chapter House

Move halfway down the south quire aisle and turn right into the **Quire (8)**, which is dominated by the Bishop's Throne, which is huge. This was made in 1312 using oak from the bishop's estates, and is considered one of the finest of its kind. It was dismantled during World War II and taken to safety, being returned during the postwar repairs. Next to the throne is the lectern, made of latten and probably dating from the early 16th century. The current quire stalls date from Sir George Gilbert Scott's renovations of 1870–77, but some of the old misericords were maintained. At the end of the quire is the Great East Window, one of the few examples of Perpendicular architecture in the cathedral; it replaced an earlier window whose stonework had decayed, but much of the original glass was retained.

Returning to the south quire aisle, note the Chapel of St James and St Thomas, destroyed by a bomb in 1942 and afterwards completely rebuilt.

Finally walk into the **South Transept (9)**. On your left is the Chapel of St John the Baptist. Next to the south wall is a monument to Sir John Gilbert, half-brother to Sir Walter Raleigh (1552–1618). Above the south transept is one of two Norman towers that contain the cathedral's bells – forming, it is claimed, the second heaviest ringing peal in England.

A door in the corner of the south transept leads to the **Chapter House (10)**. This was built in 1224 and underwent reconstruction in 1412. A further major renovation in 1969 enabled it to be used not only as the traditional meeting place for the clergy but also as an assembly room for concerts and other public functions.

Leaving via the chapter house door you find yourself in a courtyard, crossing which you can make your way back to the Cathedral Green.

WALKING TOUR FROM EXETER CATHEDRAL

This figure-of-eight walk looks at most of the historic features of Exeter's city centre, including parts of the old walls, the castle – which is built on Roman foundations – some old sandstone churches, historic inns, part of the riverside area and the postwar shopping centre, rebuilt after the 1942 Blitz.

Start and finish: The west front of the cathedral.
Length: 2½ miles (4km).
Time: 1½ hours, but longer if you visit the museum and churches.
Refreshments: A number of historic pubs and old coaching inns provide lunchtime sustenance. The following, all on the walking route, are of particular interest: the Ship Inn in St Martin's Lane, reputed to be a favourite of Drake; the Bishop Blaize Inn, the Prospect Inn and On the Waterfront, all close to the quayside; the White Hart Inn, Exeter's most famous coaching inn and full of atmosphere; and the Turk's Head in the High Street, where Dickens was a regular visitor. The cathedral's own refectory is highly recommended.

The cathedral stands by the **Cathedral Close (1)** amid a grassy area which was opened up by the demolition, in 1971, of the Church of St Mary Major. Look in the middle of the lawns for the **Statue of Richard Hooker (2)**; Hooker (*c*1554–1600) was a 16th-century ecclesiastical scholar, whose arguments prevented

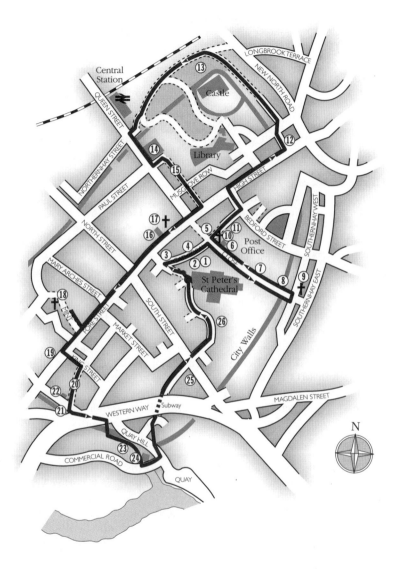

Key

1. Cathedral Close
2. Statue of Richard Hooker
3. Tinley's
4. Royal Clarence Hotel
5. Ship Inn
6. Mol's Coffee House
7. Bishop of Crediton's House
8. Burnet Patch Bridge
9. Southernhay
10. St Martin's Church
11. Ruins
12. Underground Passages
13. Northernhay Gardens
14. Royal Albert Museum
15. Gandy Street
16. Guildhall
17. Church of St Pancras
18. St Nicholas' Priory
19. Tuckers' Hall
20. Stepcote Hill
21. The House That Moved
22. St Marys Steps
23. Bishop Blaize Inn
24. Custom House
25. White Hart Inn
26. Bishop's Palace

the Church of England from becoming wholly puritan during the Reformation.

The Cathedral Close is bordered by a collection of historic buildings in a variety of styles. On the west side, next to the former Broadgate, is a building known as **Tinley's (3)**; once a hostel for travelling priests, it was a tearoom for decades until recently being converted into a restaurant.

Moving to the right along the close you come to the **Royal Clarence Hotel (4)**. Dating from 1769 and built in Georgian style, it gained its name from the Duchess of Clarence (later the wife of William IV), who stayed here on more than one occasion. Next to the Clarence is a narrow pedestrian alley, St Martin's Lane, in which stands the **Ship Inn (5)**. Claimed to have been a favourite watering-hole of Sir Francis Drake (*c*1540–1596), it also boasts a resident ghost.

A Historic Meeting Place

Move now to the north side of the close, to perhaps its most striking building (certainly its most photographed), **Mol's Coffee House (6)**. This is a stark black-and-white example of Tudor domestic architecture, bearing the date 1596; the top storey, with its Dutch gable, was added around 1885. The building gained its name from an Italian, Thomas Mol, who once lived here. In all probability it has never been a coffee house, but certainly it was a gentlemen's meeting place for the famous Devon sea dogs, among others. It is now occupied by Elands, a map and stationery business.

There follows a series of half-timbered and red sandstone buildings, now mainly offices. The most striking is the **Bishop of Crediton's House (7)**, notable for its magnificent carved oak doorway.

Carry on parallel to the cathedral until you reach the old city walls and pass under the **Burnet Patch Bridge (8)**; made of cast iron, this was built by Mayor Burnet Patch in 1814 to aid the regular inspection of the city walls.

You now reach **Southernhay (9)**, one of many elegant Georgian terraces in the central part of Exeter. The word 'hay', found as a suffix in several Exonian place names, means 'enclosure', and refers to developments outside the old city walls.

A Haven

Return now to the Cathedral Close. Keeping to the pavement, pass Mol's Coffee House on your right and leave the close at the northwest corner via Catherine Street, an alley between the SPCK Bookshop and **St Martin's Church (10)**. In medieval times there were as many as 32 parish churches in Exeter, and a number of these survive today. Built like most of the others in the local red sandstone, St Martin's dates from 1065, but was rebuilt in the 15th century. Should it be open, go inside: after the glories of the cathedral this much smaller, simpler church is a welcome oasis of tranquillity. Look for the chancel arch, the font, the Jacobean altar rails and the oak wagon roof. Externally, there is a fine Perpendicular window.

Proceeding along Catherine Street, note on the right a complex of **Ruins (11)**. These were once almshouses, in the middle of which was a small chapel. Excavations in 1987–8 revealed an early Roman fortress in the area and a house occupied by the cathedral's canons in medieval times; at Exeter the canons, whose work was to serve in the chantry chapels, were known as annuellars. The whole site was demolished by German bombers in 1942. A board recounts much of this history.

Ancient Water Supplies

You are now entering a part of the city that was rebuilt after World War II. Turn left at Bedford Street and then right into the pedestrianized (except for minibuses) High Street. At the side of Boots, turn down a small arcade.

After a few yards you'll find on the right what looks like a normal shop front but is in fact the entrance to the unique **Underground Passages (12)**, the city's most unusual attraction. These were built during the 14th century to carry fresh water from the springs of St Sidwella in two distinct systems, one serving the cathedral precincts and the other the nearby town. Visitors with claustrophobic tendencies might wish to give this diversion a miss, because the passages are extraordinarily cramped, but for anyone else the experience is a fascinating one.

Back Above Ground

After the underground passages you may well be in the mood for some fresh air! The well laid-out **Northernhay Gardens (13)**, claimed to be the oldest gardens in Britain, follow the line of the Roman walls and the ditch of Rougemont Castle. Little remains of the castle, which was erected by William the Conqueror and is now the site of the Crown Court, built in 1774 in the inner bailey.

Leave the gardens at the far end of Queen Street and turn left along the Victorian Gothic façade of the **Royal Albert Museum (14)**. Built between 1865 and 1869, this has a good collection of historical, ethnographic and industrial exhibits, plus silver, glass and china. There is also a small collection of the work of Devon artists.

Now take the road at the side of the museum into **Gandy Street (15)**. Once a dingy back lane, this now has thriving bistros, boutiques and specialist shops.

The far end of Gandy Street brings you back to the High Street. Turn right. A number of Tudor-aged buildings survived the Blitz, such as those occupied by Laura Ashley, Thornes (the chocolate makers), the Abbey National and the Turk's Head Inn. Next to the latter is the celebrated **Guildhall (16)**, believed to be the oldest municipal building in the country. Much of the present edifice dates from 1330, but there was almost certainly a Saxon building on the site. The Purbeck Stone portico is Tudor, and the attractive single-span wooden roof was installed around 1468. The imposing interior has been used for centuries as a meeting place and for civic ceremonies, as well as to house the municipal treasures.

At the rear of the Guildhall is a modern shopping centre; in the middle of all the concrete and glass is the tiny red sandstone **Church of St Pancras (17)**. Once derelict, it has now been restored and it has become fashionable for the mayor to adopt it as his or her parish church.

Down Fore Street

Return to the High Street and pass by yet another sandstone church, St Petrock's, to the traffic lights where Exeter's four main historic roads meet: High Street (which you're on), South Street (to your left), North Street (now a minor opening, to your right) and Fore Street (straight ahead). Go on down Fore Street and after 100yd (100m) or so turn right along a small alley called The Mint. At the end of this alley is **St Nicholas' Priory (18)**, founded in 1070 as a Benedictine daughter house of Battle Abbey in Sussex. In medieval times it is said to have entertained King John and other noble guests. Following the Dissolution of the Monasteries in 1536 only the guest wing survived. This was sold to the Mallet family, who were rich Elizabethan merchants. The city council purchased it for £850 in 1913 and has gradually restored it. Today the Priory is a museum where visitors can view the 17th-century furnishings, bells, clocks, tapestries and the pillars and vaulting of the Norman cellar.

Return to Fore Street, turn right and continue down the hill. After 50yd (50m) or so on the right you find the **Tuckers' Hall (19)**, an imposing sandstone building dating from 1471. This was the hall of the most powerful guild – the Company of Weavers, Fullers and Shearmen – when the city was an important centre for the production of woollen goods. Fullers, known also as Tuckers, had the job of removing the grease from the wool and there were many fulling mills along the River Exe. The Hall fell into disrepair during the 19th century, but has now been fully restored. It has some fine panelling and carving, plus a collection of weapons surviving from the days when the guild played its part in the defence of the city.

The House That Moved

Now cross Fore Street and proceed into King Street. A little way along, turn right into an unnamed road which becomes **Stepcote Hill (20)**. The hill has over 100 steps on each side for pedestrians, with a cobbled packhorse track in the centre. Its name derives from the Old English word for 'steep'. The West Gate to the city stood here until demolished in 1815. William of Orange marched his men through this gate when he entered the city in 1688.

At the foot of Stepcote Hill is an interesting collection of Tudor houses, with half-timbered work and jettied walls. The most famous of these is **The House That Moved (21)**. Once a merchant's house and reputed to be one of the oldest timber-framed houses in Europe, this was moved on rollers to its present site when a new inner relief road was built in 1961.

Among the Tudor houses is yet another small sandstone church, **St Mary Steps (22)**, founded in the 12th century and rebuilt in the 15th. When nearby St Mary Major was demolished its wooden screen was re-erected at St Mary Steps. The attractive east window is modern, but the font is almost certainly Norman. The church's main claim to fame, however, is its clock, sometimes known as the Matthew the Miller Clock after the central figure, although an alternative theory suggests this figure is actually Henry VIII. The clock, believed to have been erected in the 16th century, was restored in 1980. The figures 'perform' on the hour.

On the Waterfront

From Stepcote Hill, cross the inner relief road (Western Way) by the pedestrian crossing, turn left and, after a few yards, turn down some steps with blue railings. This route takes you over the city wall and down to the level of the quay. On the right is the **Bishop Blaize Inn (23)**, the first inn to be built (1327) outside the city walls. A plaque at the front of the inn tells the visitor that Blaize was a bishop who was martyred in the 4th century, having had his flesh torn with woolcombers' rakes; for this reason he was adopted as the patron saint of weavers.

Turn left and head for the waterside. The whole area, once a dangerous slum, has been redeveloped as a leisure and residential complex, mainly in a sympathetic way.

Buildings with historic or architectural interest have been carefully preserved, even though their use may have changed (note the bonded warehouses which are now discos and nightclubs!). The most impressive building is the **Custom House (24)**, an indication of Exeter's former maritime importance. Erected in 1681, it was one of the first brick buildings in the city. The arches over the ground-floor windows indicate there was once a colonnade here. A royal coat-of-arms in the roof pediment probably dates to the early 19th century. The two handsome cannon outside the Custom House came from a batch impounded in 1819 for non-payment of dues, having originally been bound for the Wellington Monument in Somerset.

Other buildings here include the tiny Wharfinger's Office, the Prospect Inn (excellent for lunches) and two huge five-storey warehouses (one in red sandstone, the other in white limestone) built in 1835. In one of these is On the Waterfront, a pizza restaurant with additional outside seating where you can watch boats, ducks, swans and moorhens pass by as you eat, all framed by an extremely pretty modern footbridge. Regrettably, the popular Maritime Museum on the far side of the river closed in the mid-1990s, although there are still boats you can explore; cross the river using either the footbridge or, for fun, the little hand-operated ferry.

To leave the waterside area, take the narrow lane opposite the Custom House and turn almost immediately right up a zigzag path by the multi-storey carpark and through a pedestrian tunnel (which bears one of several modern murals you'll have spotted around Exeter) under Western Way to emerge into Coombe Street. Pass behind the **White Hart Inn (25)**, the most famous of Exeter's coaching inns, to emerge on South Street.

Cross South Street and walk up the hill into Palace Gate. Ahead, through a gap in the stone wall, you can catch a glimpse of the **Bishop's Palace (26)**, where the cathedral library is located. This elegant building contrasts with the Cathedral Choir School on the other side of the road, which has a strong Victorian custodial look about it.

This brings you back to the Cathedral Close and the end of your walk.

The House That Moved

WELLS

Access: Despite being at the centre of a network of roads, Wells is rather remote from the main lines of communication. The nearest motorway is the M5, some 15 miles (25km) to the west, linking Wells with the Southwest and the Midlands. Some 20 miles (32km) to the north is the M4, which most visitors will use if driving from London. The nearest railway stations are at Frome and Bridgwater, while the closest international airport is at Bristol.

Set close to the rolling Mendip Hills, Wells is England's smallest cathedral city. It gained its name from the springs which rise near to the Bishop's Palace and which for centuries provided the town's inhabitants with reliable drinking water. A religious site developed close to these springs and Roman and Saxon burial places have been found nearby. Excavations in 1978 confirmed that a Saxon church was founded here by Aldhelm, Bishop of Sherborne, around AD705. In AD909 the diocese of Wells was set up and the church became the Cathedral of St Andrew. In 1088 the bishopric was moved to Bath and the Saxon cathedral was left to decay. The building was restored and enlarged by a later bishop, Robert of Lewes.

Robert's successor, Reginald de Bohun, decided to build a new church at Wells, and work started in 1180. The building was constructed in a cream-coloured limestone – the Inferior Oolite from Doulting, some eight miles (13km) from Wells. Work began on the quire and progressed along the nave. By 1239 enough had been completed for the building to be dedicated. Meanwhile, attempts were made to have the cathedral status restored and success came in 1245, when Bishop Roger became the Bishop of Bath and Wells, a title which remains to this day. Bath and Wells were joint cathedrals until Bath Abbey was dissolved during the Reformation. The town of Wells had by that time been granted its royal charter, King John giving it the status of a free borough.

The octagonal chapter house of the cathedral was completed in 1306, and later the quire was extended eastwards to join the Lady Chapel, which had begun life as a separate structure. Also in the 14th century there were elaborate plans to build a spectacular central tower and spire, but these were aborted when it was clear the foundations could not support the additional weight. The solution came in 1338–48 when master mason William Joy constructed the remarkable scissor arches to support the tower on three sides. The bells were removed, later in the century being installed in the purpose-built southwest tower.

Although Wells is not a monastic cathedral, it has a fine set of cloisters. These were the last part of the cathedral to be built, being completed in 1508 in Perpendicular style. The east cloister is the traditional entrance to the cathedral for the bishop from his palace. Built by Bishop Jocelyn in the 13th century, the palace has had numerous additions, including the Great Hall and chapel. Relations between the bishop and the townspeople were not always cordial and eventually a protective moat was built around the palace, with a drawbridge over the main gate. In an effort to appease the local people, Bishop Bekynton used the palace wells to provide a public water supply. Other bishops, such as Nicholas Bubwith (d1424) in the 15th century, provided almshouses for the poorer people in the town.

By the 14th century Wells was the largest town in Somerset, its wealth based on the textile industry. Unfortunately, during the Industrial Revolution industries such as this moved to the coalfields, and clothmaking collapsed. The up-side of this was that Wells was untouched by the grimier aspects of the Industrial Revolution. It survived as a market and ecclesiastical centre, attracting genteel society. Today it is a small regional centre with a growing tourist industry based around the cathedral, which in the view of many is the most attractive in the country.

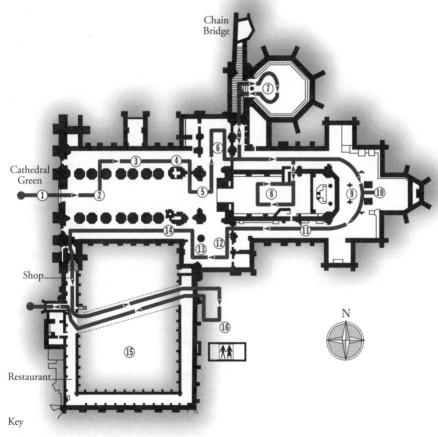

Key

1. West Front	7. Chapter House	13. Font
2. Nave	8. Quire	14. Sugar Chantry Chapel
3. North Porch	9. Retrochoir	15. Cloisters
4. Bubwith Chantry Chapel	10. Lady Chapel	16. Camery Gardens
5. Strainer Arches	11. Bekynton Chantry Chapel	
6. North Transept	12. South Transept	

TOUR OF THE CATHEDRAL
Start: The west front.
Finish: The cloisters.

The **West Front (1)** is best viewed from back across Cathedral Green. This is undoubtedly the finest west front in England. It is 147ft (44m) wide, so that it is as broad as it is high, and it resembles a huge and elaborate altar screen, complete with nearly 400 statues and three clearly defined horizontal architectural zones. Its buttresses and arcades cast strong shadows, so it does not have the flat appearance of other cathedral fronts such as those at Southwell and Winchester.

The sculptures represent a complete theological theme. The lowest zone (with many statues missing) concerns prophets and angels. Above this are biblical scenes. The central zone has martyred monarchs, saints and bishops, and then comes the Resurrection of the Dead. If you look next at the stepped gable in the centre, you can see that the lowest part shows the Nine Orders of Angels with, above this, the apostles. Finally, at the top, is Christ in Majesty, flanked by seraphim, dating from 1985 and replacing the rather battered medieval original. During recent restoration work, traces of medieval painting and gilding have been noted, so the west front must have once been even more impressive than it is today.

Step through the unremarkable west door and enter the cathedral. You are now in the **Nave (2)**. The vista in this part of the building is dominated by the massive strainer or scissor arches, but ignore these for now and concentrate on the main features of the nave. This was the earliest extant medieval building in England to have pointed arches used throughout. The scale here is modest, with the height from floor to vault only 67ft (20m), but the proportions are satisfying. Alec Clifton Taylor has described the piers as the most beautiful in England, and few would quarrel with this. Each pier is covered with some 24 slender shafts, while the stiff-leaved capitals and corbels are boldly presented, particularly towards the crossing, with heads and grotesques.

At the upper levels the nave is less impressive, with an arcade consisting of an unbroken line of small lancets below a rather plain clerestory. The simple vaulting reflects the curve of the strainer arches, and there is some recent painting of a delicate nature between the ribs.

Move across into the north aisle, pausing by the **North Porch (3)**. Dating from *c*1215, this is the main processional entrance into the cathedral and connects with the canons' quarters on the north side of Cathedral Green. Continue eastwards along the aisle until you reach, on your right, the first chantry chapel, the **Bubwith Chantry Chapel (4)**, dating from 1425. Bishop Nicholas Bubwith left his personal fortune to build the library over the east cloister and also set up almshouses in the town.

The Arches and the Chapter House
We now arrive at the crossing, which is dominated by the massive **Scissor (Strainer) Arches (5)**. The original central bell tower had a spire added in the early 14th century, but the foundations could not support this additional weight and the spire began to lean and crack. William Joy, the master mason at the time, devised a solution which is unique in English cathedrals. The scissor arches were built on three sides of the crossing, thereby bracing the tower. From the engineering point of view

they were a great success, but aesthetically they might be considered an ugly intrusion. It is difficult to be neutral about them: you must decide for yourself.

Now enter the **North Transept (6)**, one of the oldest parts of the cathedral. The astronomical clock you see here is the most ancient of any English cathedral, being first mentioned in 1392, and is the second oldest working clock in the country.

Climb the well worn sloping stairs towards the **Chapter House (7)**; the flight actually continues through to the Chain Bridge, but this section is rarely open. Pause to look at the stained glass, which is the oldest in the cathedral. Turn right into the chapter house itself, completed in 1319. Although unusual in being above ground level, it has the normal octagonal shape. The windows, with some excellent stained glass, are in Geometric Decorated style; and below them is an arcade with 51 stalls containing richly decorated canopies. An elegant central pillar leads up to some wonderful tierceron vaulting with carved foliage bosses. From the architectural point of view this is arguably the most beautiful of the English cathedral chapter houses.

The Cathedra and the Lady Chapel

Leave the chapter house and descend the steps back to the north transept and the crossing. Turn left here into the north quire aisle. Walk east and then turn right into the **Quire (8)**. This was the first part of the new cathedral to be built. Note that there is no triforium here, but the slender shafts give an impression of height. Also notice the unusual lierne vaulting, like a spider's web with lozenge-shaped intersections. The eastern aspect is dominated by the Decorated-style Jesse Window, dating from *c*1340 and sometimes called the Golden Window because of its colouring. At the east end of the quire is a 'Father' Willis organ, built in 1857. The wooden choir stalls go back to 1330 and have a fine collection of misericords – three of these have been mounted on the wall of the retrochoir. The *cathedra*, or Bishop's Throne, on the south side of the quire is of similar age to the stalls; it is unusual for its heavy stone door.

Return to the north quire aisle and turn right to the **Retrochoir (9)**. This part of the cathedral was completed in 1340 to link the quire with the Lady Chapel. Most experts feel this difficult task was sympathetically achieved. There are four chapels in this area – from north to south, Corpus Christi, St Stephen's, St John the Baptist's and St Katherine's – but none need detain you long. Spend your time instead looking at the **Lady Chapel (10)**. Originally octagonal in shape, this was separate from the main building until the retrochoir was built. The windows of the Lady Chapel have Reticulated Decorated tracery and their upper parts still have some of the original early-14th-century glass. The lower areas have a kaleidoscopic jumble of glass, broken during the Civil War. Don't miss the intricate 'starburst' lierne vaulting, which has some delicate modern decoration.

Leave the east end of the cathedral via the south quire aisle. Almost immediately on your right is the **Chantry Chapel of Bishop Bekynton (11)**. Built 15 years before his death and now surrounded by iron railings, the chapel contains Bekynton's Tomb, with two effigies, the upper one of the bishop in full regalia and the lower one of his cadaver. Bekynton, Bishop of Bath and Wells 1443–65, was also secretary to Henry VI and Lord Privy Seal. This important benefactor to both the cathedral and the town built the Chain Bridge, provided houses in the Market Place and supplied fresh water from St Andrew's Well for the populace.

The South Transept and the Cloisters

Turn left into the **South Transept (12)**. There are two more chapels on the east side, those of St Martin and St Calixtus, but the main item of interest is the Saxon **Font (13)**, the only item remaining from the Saxon building and the oldest feature of the present cathedral. Its rounded arches, now bare, once contained carvings of saints. The gilded oak cover of the font dates from *c*1635.

Before you leave the south transept take a look at the capitals on some of the pillars. These strong carvings have narrative themes. One shows a man with toothache – a recurring subject in the days when there were no real dentists! – and another depicts thieves taking fruit and being apprehended by the owner, seen delivering a hefty blow to one man's head.

Leave the transept and turn into the south nave aisle. On the right the beautifully carved **Bishop Sugar Chantry Chapel (14)** incorporates the pulpit. Both chapel and pulpit date from the 15th century.

At the end of the aisle, turn left through the shop into the **Cloisters (15)**. Built in the 13th century, they were enlarged two centuries later.

The Font at Wells

They enclose the Palm Churchyard and the entrance to Bishop Bekynton's conduit.

Cross the grass to the east cloister. Above this is the Cathedral Library, paid for by Bishop Bubwith; looking back across the cloisters you can see, above the west cloister, the Choir School set up by Bishop Bekynton around 1460.

Pass through the door in the east cloister and out into the **Camery Gardens (16)**. Here an information board shows where you can view the foundations of the Saxon Cathedral buildings; the Lady Chapel, Stillington's Chapel and much of the old cathedral can be clearly picked out.

Return through the cloisters and out onto Cathedral Green.

WALKING TOUR FROM WELLS CATHEDRAL

This circular walking tour takes a comprehensive look at the historic core of the city of Wells. It passes the ancient buildings around the cathedral close, including the Bishop's Palace and a number of gateways. The tour also looks at some of the city's old coaching inns, one of the most fascinating parish churches in the country and a wide range of domestic architecture.

Start: The west front of the cathedral.
Finish: The cathedral cloisters.
Length: 1½ miles (2km).

Time: About 1hr, but allow extra time if you want to visit the museum, parish church or Bishop's Palace.

Refreshments: There is a wonderful selection of old coaching inns which are full of character and offer lunchtime bar meals. There are three in Sadler Street – the Ancient Gate House, the Swan and the White Hart. In the High Street the best bet is the Star, while in the Market Place consider the 15th-century Crown Inn. Also recommended is the City Arms, once the town gaol, in Queen Street. All but the City Arms offer accommodation.

From the west front of the cathedral, head southwest to Market Place through **Penniless Porch (1)**, one of a number of ancient gateways leading to Cathedral Green. The porch was built in the time of Bishop Bekynton – his rebus may be seen on the north side – and got its name from beggars who congregated here, seeking alms from churchgoers. *Plus ça change* – today Penniless Porch is a favourite spot for buskers.

Continue along the north side of Market Place. On the pavement is a plaque measuring 22 feet 2½ inches (6.765m), the distance jumped by a local resident, Mary Bignall Rand, when she won the gold medal in the 1964 Olympic Games.

Turn right into **Sadler Street (2)**, which has a number of old coaching inns. The Swan goes back in the city's records to 1422, and was once the banqueting hall of the mayor; the present frontage is more modern. On the same side of the road is the half-timbered White Hart, while opposite is the Ancient Gate House Hotel, both likewise dating from the 15th century. The latter incorporates **Brown's Gate (3)**, which was used by vehicular traffic as late as 1965.

Step through Brown's Gate to Cathedral Green, which is an excellent spot from which to photograph the west front of the cathedral. Follow the road which runs along the north side of Cathedral Green; this road was once the main route through Wells for the stage coaches running from London to Exeter via Bath. On the left-hand side is a row of historic buildings, starting with the **Old Deanery (4)**, parts of which go back to the 15th century. The Dean now lives elsewhere and the building is used as the offices of the diocese. Some of its windows are believed to have been designed by Christopher Wren (1632–1723).

The next building is the **Wells Museum (5)**, which has displays on traditional lines, including sections on local archaeology and geology and the Local History Reference Library. The most bizarre exhibit is a stuffed swan, claimed to be the first of these birds to learn to ring the moat bell for food (see page 37).

Vicars Choral

You now approach the **Chain Gate and Bridge (6)**, built in the mid-15th century by Bishop Bekynton. The idea was to link the quarters of the Vicars Choral with the chapter house stairs, thereby keeping the choristers away from the temptations of the town. The gate probably gained its name from chains which at one time closed the entrance. Just to the right, on the north wall of the cathedral, is the external face of the cathedral clock. It dates from 1495 and shows two knights in armour who strike the bells at quarter-hourly intervals.

After passing through the Chain Gate, turn immediately left through an archway into **Vicars' Close (7)**. This delightful little cul-de-sac was built in 1363 in the time of Bishop Ralph of Shrewsbury as accommodation for the Vicars Choral. There were originally 42 small dwellings here, but after the Reformation the gentleman choristers were allowed to marry, so many of the dwellings were amalgamated to provide accommodation for families. The small walled front gardens were not originally part of the design. It seems the close was once a quadrangle which, it is claimed, provided a model for England's ancient universities. At the far end of the close is the **Vicars' Chapel and Library (8)**. The chapel was built *c*1400, in the time of Bishop Bubwith, but unfortunately is rarely open to visitors.

Almshouses and a Fine Church

On the right-hand side of the chapel some steps lead up to the road called North Liberty. Turn left here, noting the large houses of character, most of which are used by the Cathedral School. At the end of North Liberty, fork left to the head of Sadler Street. Here turn right into Chamberlain Street, with its varied range of domestic architecture. You are now entering the part of the city noted for its **Almshouses (9)**. On the right-hand side of Chamberlain Street are Harper's Almshouses, built from a bequest by Archibald Harper in 1711 for 'five poor decayed woolcombers'. Just past the junction with Priest Row are Bubwith's

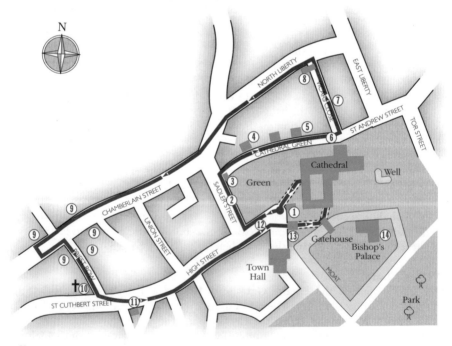

Key

1. Penniless Porch
2. Sadler Street
3. Brown's Gate
4. Old Deanery
5. Wells Museum

6. Chain Gate and Bridge
7. Vicars' Close
8. Vicars' Chapel and Library
9. Almshouses
10. St Cuthbert's Parish Church

11. City Arms
12. Market Place
13. Bishop's Eye Gateway
14. Bishop's Palace

Almshouses, provided in the early 15th century by Bishop Bubwith for poor men and women burgesses of the city. Turn down into Priest Row and on the left you find Llewellyn's Almshouses, which date from 1614. On the right is a complex of three further sets of almshouses, built at the bequests of Bishop Still, Bishop Wilkes and Walter Bricke, a wealthy draper.

At the end of Priest Row, on the right, is **St Cuthbert's Parish Church (10)**. The present building is almost certainly the fourth church to be built on the site. The original, probably a wooden Saxon church, was replaced by an 11th-century Norman building from which the piscina remains (in Tanner's Chapel in the south aisle). The third church was built in the middle of the 13th century in Early English style; several parts of it remain, such as the piers and arches in the present nave. Finally, a major renovation and extension took place in the 15th century in magnificent Perpendicular style. St Cuthbert's has some wonderful interior features, including a huge medieval door, a Jacobean pulpit, the Great Jesse Reredos, a marvellous 16th-century panelled ceiling in St Cuthbert's Chapel, some superb bosses and much more besides. Take time to appreciate this building – the largest parish church in Somerset.

Leave St Cuthbert's and swing round eastwards into the High Street, the main shopping thoroughfare. Immediately on your right, at the junction with Queen Street, is the **City Arms (11)**. This pink-washed stone-built pub was the city gaol from the time of Elizabeth I until the 19th century, and some of the cells still exist. Today a number of bars surround an attractive cobbled courtyard.

Proceeding up the High Street, note the water swilling down the gutters, part of the fresh-water system provided for the townsfolk from the wells near the Bishop's Palace.

The Market Place and Bishop's Palace

You now reach the **Market Place (12)**. This area is dominated by the Town Hall, which contains the Council Offices, the Law Courts and the Tourist Information Office. Note also the Gothic-style conduit, which in 1799 replaced an earlier one provided by Bishop Bekynton. Take a look at the two plaques on the wall of the Crown Hotel on the south side of the Market Place. One describes how an old Guildhall once stood in the Market Place and was the venue of the Bloody Assizes after the Monmouth Rebellion. The other marks the spot where William Penn (1644–1718), founder of Pennsylvania, preached to a crowd of 3000 in 1685.

Leave the Market Place via the **Bishop's Eye Gateway (13)**, to the right of the National Trust shop, one of four gateways built by Bishop Bekynton. This leads you to the **Bishop's Palace (14)**, the official residence of the Bishop of Bath and Wells. If it's open, do go in: this is the finest remaining example in England of a medieval bishop's palace. The building is surrounded by a sturdy wall and moat. Bishop Ralph of Shrewsbury built a gatehouse here with a drawbridge and portcullis, which were last used in 1831, when there were serious fears of riots over the Reform Bill. Look at the side of the gatehouse drawbridge, where there is a rope with a bell attached. Swans have learned to tug the rope when they wish to be fed. If time permits, take a stroll around the shady moat where a variety of waterfowl can be seen.

Leave the Bishop's Palace via the path opposite the gatehouse and follow the short route taken by countless bishops to their cathedral over the centuries until you reach a doorway giving access to the cathedral cloisters, where the tour concludes.

BATH

Access: There have always been important routeways west from London to the fashionable city of Bath. The A4 London–Bath road (the Great West Road) was a routeway even in pre-Roman times. Today motorists are more likely to use the fast M4, although speeds slow on the 12 miles (20km) from the motorway to the city. The nearby M5 provides links with the Southwest and the Midlands. The train from London's Paddington Station reaches Bath Spa Station in 1hr 10 minutes; the station is a short walk from the city centre. The nearest airport – at Bristol, west of Bath – deals mainly with charter flights; Heathrow Airport can be reached in about 2hr via the M4.

Bath owes its origins to the hot, mineral-rich springs that rise here. The first settlement may have been in Celtic times; legend has it that Prince Bladud cured his leprosy in the springs and perhaps gave the city its name. More historically certain is that there was an important Roman settlement here from AD43. The Romans built sophisticated hot baths, a temple to the goddess Minerva, numerous luxurious villas and formidable defensive walls. The Roman name for the town was Aquae Sulis.

When the Empire collapsed the baths went into decline, and the succeeding Saxon town centred instead on an important monastery, probably called St Peter's. It is known that King Offa (d796) of Mercia seized the monastery in 781. Interestingly, although Winchester had become the capital of the first united England, it was at Bath Abbey that Edgar the Peaceful (944–975) was crowned King of All England in 973.

After the Norman Conquest, John de Villula (d1122) was appointed bishop of nearby Wells, and two years later he transferred his seat to Bath. He immediately set about building a new cathedral. After de Villula's death the work continued, eventually being completed in 1170. This Norman building was almost twice the length of the present abbey. In 1244 it was decided that Bath and Wells should share cathedral status, and Roger of Salisbury became the first Bishop of Bath and Wells, a title which remains today. Later in the 13th century Bath's importance waned as subsequent bishops took up residence in Wells.

Meanwhile the monastery was going through hard times. The diminished number of monks found it impossible to maintain the cathedral, which gradually fell into ruins. Rescue came when in 1495 Oliver King was appointed Bishop of Bath and Wells. The story goes that he had a vision that left him in no doubt he should restore the abbey church. Work began in 1499, in the Perpendicular style. Magnificent though the new building was, it was on a relatively small scale – it could have fitted into the nave of the old cathedral. Within a few years the monastery had been dissolved in the Reformation, the see had been permanently relocated to Wells and the building had become Bath's parish church.

With the local wool trade languishing, Bath renewed its role as a spa town. This was stimulated in 1574 by a visit from Queen Elizabeth I, who granted the town a municipal charter. Later, Queen Anne was a frequent visitor, taking the waters to seek a cure for dropsy. As throughout history, society follows where royalty leads. Bath rapidly became a fashionable resort, its population increasing tenfold during the 18th century. The wealthy visitors expected more than health-giving waters, however. The Bath Improvement Act of 1789 provided the powers to redevelop the town. Three men led the move towards Bath's Golden Age: the city surveyor, Thomas Baldwin (1750–1820), the architect John Wood (1704–1754), later succeeded by his son, and the larger-than-life bon viveur Richard 'Beau' Nash (1674–1762). Elegant terraces and crescents appeared, built in the local honey-coloured Bath Stone, along with hotels, hospitals, theatres and casinos. Everyone of importance came here, often not only for the season but to live. Horatio Nelson (1758–1805), William Pitt the Elder (1708–1778), Thomas Gainsborough (1727–1788) and Jane Austen (1775–1817) were among many who had properties in Bath. A glance at the memorial tablets and stones in Bath Abbey reflects the importance of these times. This brilliant period also spawned the Bath bun, the Bath chair, Bath Oliver biscuits and the Sally Lunn bun.

By the mid-19th century, however, Bath was losing its pre-eminence. The railways had made seaside towns attractive and Bath, somewhat unjustly, gained the image of being a home for the elderly and the infirm. In response it did indeed develop into a genteel residential town, attractive to retirees. By the end of the 20th century, though, tourism was booming and visitors were attracted to the city again by its fine setting and its beautifully preserved buildings. Many people would consider that it has the most complete set of Georgian domestic architecture to be seen in the country, and this has encouraged its designation as a World Heritage City. Meanwhile the abbey and the nearby Roman Baths are on every visitor's itinerary, and provide a fascinating as well as an educational day out.

The central door on the West Front

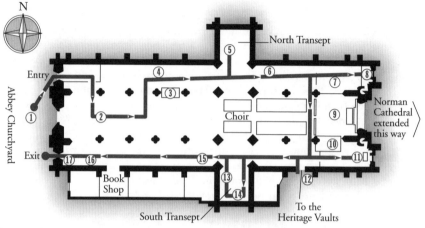

N

Abbey Churchyard

Entry

Exit

North Transept

Choir

Norman Cathedral extended this way

Book Shop

South Transept

To the Heritage Vaults

Key

1. West Front
2. Nave
3. Tomb of James Montagu
4. Memorial to Isaac Pitman
5. Organ Loft
6. Memorial to Admiral Arthur Philip
7. St Alphege Chapel

8. Edgar Window
9. Sanctuary
10. Chantry Chapel of Prior William Birde
11. Norman Chapel
12. Heritage Vaults
13. Waller Memorial
14. Jesse Window

15. Memorial tablet to Richard 'Beau' Nash
16. Memorial to William Bingham
17. Prior's Door

TOUR OF THE ABBEY

Start and finish: Abbey Churchyard, outside the abbey.

Stand outside the entrance to the Pump Room and the Roman Baths and look towards the abbey's **West Front (1)**. The view is dominated by the tall west window, built in Perpendicular style in the early years of the 16th century. On each side of the main window are 'ladders' on which angels ascend and descend, representing the dream experienced by Bishop Oliver King in which he was encouraged to build a new abbey church. Other details on the west front include the rebus of Oliver King (involving an olive tree and a crown), 16th-century statues of St Peter and St Paul and a late-19th-century effigy of Bishop King's patron, Henry VII.

The main central door on the west front, made of solid oak, contains the coats-of-arms of various members of the Montagu family. Enter the building, however, through the smaller northwest door. Proceed through a small foyer where you will be encouraged to pay a recommended entry fee. Move into the central aisle of the **Nave (2)**, where the character of the building can be appreciated. You will immediately be struck by the vast number of memorials – over 600 – and hardly a spare inch is not covered by a plaque or tablet. Of all England's cathedrals and abbeys, only Westminster can offer comparison. This position in the nave also gives good views of the almost identical east and west windows. The glass in both is Victorian, the west window depicting scenes from the Old Testament and the east window showing New Testament subjects.

Look next at the superb fan vaulting. In fact, only the vaulting in the east end is original. This was designed by the Vertue brothers, master masons to Henry VII. The vaulting in the nave is an accurate copy constructed as part of the Victorian restorations.

Memorials

Walk now into the north aisle, which is dominated by the **Tomb of James Montagu (3)**, Bishop of Bath and Wells 1608–16 and a great benefactor to the abbey. Montagu became bishop at a time when the abbey was in an appalling state of decay after the ravages of the Reformation. The story goes that on one particularly wet day he was in the roofless abbey with a friend, who complained about the lack of shelter: 'If it keeps us not safe from the waters above, how shall it save others from the fires beneath?' Montagu resolved to remedy the situation and spent £1000 of his own money to construct a wooden roof, which remained until the Victorians replaced wood with stone. Montagu went on to become Bishop of Winchester; his alabaster effigy shows the Blue Ribbon of the Garter, traditionally worn by holders of that post.

Among the many tablets on the wall of the aisle opposite the tomb is the **Memorial to Isaac Pitman (4)**. Pitman (1813–1897) did much to reform the spelling of the English language and, of course, invented Pitman Shorthand. Move into the north transept, where there is an audiovisual presentation on the life and work of the abbey. Note here the wooden spiral staircase to the **Organ Loft (5)**. The organ was rebuilt in 1996–7 by Klais of Bonn.

Proceed into the north choir aisle, where, immediately on the left, an Australian flag marks a tablet which is the **Memorial to Admiral Arthur Philip (6)**. Philip (1738–1814) founded the first penal settlement in Australia and was the first Governor of New South Wales. On retirement he lived in Bath until his death.

A Colourful Saint

Continue to the end of the aisle to reach the **St Alphege Chapel (7)**. Alphege or Aelfheah (954–1012) had a lively career. Born in Bath, he became a Benedictine monk here, eventually rising to be abbot. He went on to be Bishop of Winchester and then, in 1006, Archbishop of Canterbury. He was taken hostage by Danes at Greenwich and, when he refused to raise money for his release, was 'stoned' to death with ox bones. The chapel, a gift of the Friends of Bath Abbey, was dedicated in October 1997. Alphege's story is told in the embroidered triptych behind the altar. Note the cross made of copper from Zambia, denoting the link between the abbey and the church in that country. The font in the chapel dates from 1710. Look for the grating on the floor, through which there is a view of the floor and pillars of the old Norman cathedral.

At the end of the aisle is the **Edgar Window (8)**, the glass of which shows the crowning in Bath Abbey of King Edgar in 973. This ceremony joined Wessex and Mercia, so that Edgar became the first effective ruler of a united England. The ceremony, performed by the archbishops of Canterbury and York, remains the basis of coronation procedure to this day. Look for the nearby stone in the floor that marks the service attended by Queen Elizabeth II and Prince Philip in 1973 to celebrate the thousandth anniversary of Edgar's coronation.

Step round to the **Sanctuary (9)**. Above the high altar is the east window, whose Victorian glass was badly damaged during World War II. On either side of the window are some coats-of-arms from Stuart times. On the north side of the sanctuary is the large carved-oak chair occupied by the Bishop of Bath and Wells when he attends services in the abbey. Also on the north side is the **Chantry Chapel of Prior William Birde (10)**. After the death of Bishop Oliver King, Prior Birde completed the construction of the present abbey. Look for his rebus, often repeated among the detailed stonework, which involves a 'W' and a bird. The chapel is today reserved for private prayer.

Relics of Previous Abbeys

Walk to the eastern end of the south choir aisle, to the **Norman Chapel (11)**, named for a Norman arch into which is set a Perpendicular window. The original arch led into the south transept of the old Norman cathedral, which gives you some indication of how far past the east end of the present abbey church the older building stretched. The Norman Chapel contains a Book of Remembrance with the names of civilians and members of the armed forces killed during the bombing of the city during World War II.

Return westwards along the south choir aisle. A door on the left leads out to the **Heritage Vaults (12)**, opened to the public in 1994, and not to be missed. The structure of these goes back to 1499, but some of the artefacts on display are Saxon in origin, including a small 10th-century window, possibly from the original Saxon church. Other features of interest are a section of the floor of the monastery's cloisters and a scale model of the monastery and church as they were *c*1300.

Back in the abbey proper, continue along the south choir aisle and into the south transept, used for visiting exhibitions. Among the features of interest here is the **Waller Memorial (13)**, provided by Sir William Waller (*c*1597–1668) for his first wife Jane. Waller was a general on the Parliamentary side during the Civil War, and actually lost Bath to the Royalists (1643). His effigy was later damaged by Cavalier soldiers and was never repaired. He made provision to be buried here with his wife, but ended up in the Tothill Street Chapel in Westminster. Also of interest is the Victorian, but elegant, **Jesse Window (14)**, showing the descent of Our Lord from Jesse the father of David. Dating from 1872, it commemorates the return to health of the Prince of Wales, later Edward VII. (The Abbey has 52 windows with stained glass, occupying 80 per cent of the building's wall space.)

Turning into the south aisle, look immediately for the marble **Memorial Tablet to Richard 'Beau' Nash (15)**, who lies buried beneath the floor nearby. The flamboyant Nash was the self-proclaimed King of 18th-century Bath and the master of ceremonies of the spa's social life. Just past the bookshop is another interesting and more elaborate monument, the **Memorial to William Bingham (16)**; William Bingham (1752–1804), an influential US senator and financier, died during a visit to Bath. In the southwest corner of the south aisle you can see the outline of the **Prior's Door (17)**. Before the Dissolution of the monastery in 1539 this was the door through which the prior would leave for his lodgings, which overlooked the cloisters.

Leave the abbey through the southwest door of the west front to reach Abbey Churchyard once more.

WALKING TOUR FROM BATH ABBEY

This circular walk around the centre of Bath concentrates on the city's role as a fashionable resort and spa from Roman times to the days of 'Beau' Nash. It covers some outstanding domestic architecture, including the terraces of the Georgian and Regency periods, and looks at features which developed from this time of affluence in Bath's history, such as the Theatre Royal, the Assembly Rooms, the Guildhall and Pulteney Bridge.

Start and finish: The west front of the abbey, in Abbey Churchyard.
Length: 2½ miles (4km).
Time: 2hr, but allow longer if you want to visit the museums and the Roman Baths.
Refreshments: Many visitors will wish to have a meal in Sally Lunn's, claimed to be Bath's oldest house. There are a number of old inns of character, but they can be difficult to find. Try the Crystal Palace in Church Street, the Garrick's Head by the Theatre Royal, the Pig and Fiddle in Saracen Street, or the Saracen's Head in Milsom Street, said to be a favourite of Dickens and more or less unchanged since it was built in 1713. There is also a vast array of restaurants, wine bars and bistros.

Leave the west door of the abbey and head south between the Roman Baths and the abbey, passing the Tourist Information Office on the left. Walk down narrow, cobbled Church Street, passing the Crystal Palace pub on the right, and head into the square known as **Abbey Green (1)**. Recent excavations under the Crystal Palace have unearthed a number of skeletons, suggesting that this area might have been the monks' burial ground in monastic times. The area has even older associations, however, as the same excavations also revealed a Roman mosaic. Today the square is flanked by attractive Stuart houses and graced by a London plane tree 200 years old.

Leave Abbey Green eastwards along North Parade Passage. On the left is **Sally Lunn's Restaurant (2)**, an ancient house that once was part of the monastic buildings. It dates from 1482; Sally herself lived there at the bakery around 1680, producing her famous buns, modern versions of which are still on sale today. The building makes an excellent lunchtime stop not only for good food and ambience, but because of the delightful little museum in the cellar. This shows baking artefacts and ovens, plus a series of stone foundations of Roman, Saxon, Norman and medieval age. Indeed, excavations carried out in the 1980s suggest that there was a Roman guest house on the site.

Walk to the end of North Parade Passage and turn left into Terrace Walk. Cross the road towards the balustrades which mark the riverside Parade Gardens. Look left at a tree-lined square, **Orange Gardens (3)**, dominated on the left by the east front of the abbey and on the right by the rather ugly building which was once the Empire Hotel. The square was named after William of Orange, in honour of whose visit to Bath in 1734 Beau Nash erected an obelisk. Today the area around the obelisk is called Alkmaar Gardens, to mark the twinning of Bath with the Dutch town.

Continue walking along the edge of Parade Gardens. The road, known as Grand Parade, swings right towards the River Avon. Across the river is Bath Rugby Ground. Ahead, just past an attractive weir, is **Pulteney Bridge (4)**, designed by Robert Adam (1728–1792) in 1770 (his only work in Bath) and commissioned

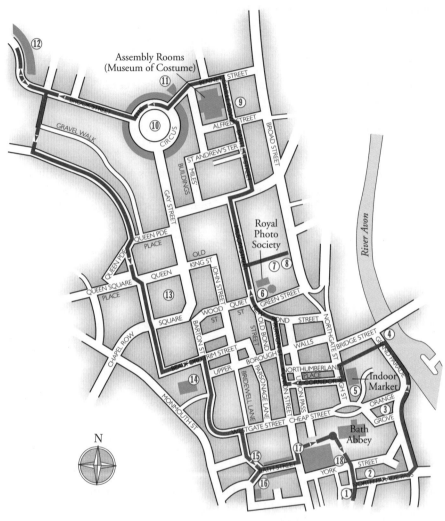

Assembly Rooms
(Museum of Costume)

Royal
Photo
Society

River Avon

Indoor
Market

Bath
Abbey

N

Key

1. Abbey Green
2. Sally Lunn's
3. Orange Gardens
4. Pulteney Bridge
5. Guildhall
6. Octagon

7. Shire's Yard
8. Postal Museum
9. Assembly Rooms
10. The Circus
11. Museum of East Asian Art
12. Royal Crescent

13. Queen Square
14. Theatre Royal
15. Cross Bath
16. Hot Bath
17. Pump Room
18. Roman Baths Museum

by the wealthy Sir William Pulteney (1684–1764), who was later to become Earl of Bath. Adam was clearly influenced by the Ponte Vecchio in Florence, as the bridge was originally lined with shops on both sides. It replaced a ferry and was planned to open up the eastern side of the city, where Pulteney had a large estate.

Traders

Just before the bridge, cross Grand Parade and walk through the indoor market, built on the site of a medieval slaughterhouse. It has a twelve-sided dome and a pillar known as the Nail; legend has it this was the spot where business was concluded, leading to the saying 'to pay on the nail'.

Emerge from the indoor market at the High Street. Immediately to the left is the **Guildhall (5)**, built by Thomas Baldwin (1750–1820) in the Adam style in 1766 and extended in Victorian times. Its notable Banqueting Room has a minstrels' gallery, magnificent fireplaces, portraits by Joshua Reynolds of George III and Queen Charlotte, and graceful chandeliers which, it is claimed, contain over 15,000 pieces of glass.

Cross the High Street and proceed along an arcade called The Corridor. You are now in the heart of Bath's pedestrianized shopping centre. Carry on until you reach Union Street. Turn right and walk on to where New Bond Street swings left into Milsom Street. This was Bath's fashionable shopping street during its Golden Age, the 1800s. On the right is the **Octagon (6)**, a former chapel and now the head-quarters of the Royal Photographic Society; it was here that Sir William Herschel (1738–1822) discovered the planet Uranus in 1781. A small museum has a Herschel exhibition, plus work by major photographers and classics from press photographs.

Next on the right is the entrance to **Shire's Yard (7)**, a development of over twenty shops on two levels around a courtyard. The area has changed little since the 1740s, when Alderman Walter Wiltshire ran a carting and carrying business from these premises, his carts taking 2½ days to reach London. One of Wiltshire's clients was Thomas Gainsborough, who lived in Bath at one time and who borrowed one of his horses for his famous painting *The Harvest Wagon*, which he gave to Wiltshire as a gift. At the far end of Shire's Yard is access to the **Postal Museum (8)**. It was from this building in 1840 that the letter bearing the first Penny Black was posted. The museum has a good collection of postal memorabilia, plus a full-size reconstruction of a Victorian post office.

Architectural Grandeur

Back in Milsom Street, continue to the junction with George Street. Turn right here and then left into Bartlett Street. This is Bath's antique quarter, with over 200 dealers plus shops where craftsmen such as goldsmiths can be seen at work.

Continue across Alfred Street and into Saville Row, where, on the left, are the **Assembly Rooms (9)**. Often claimed to be the finest suite of rooms in Europe, these were designed by John Wood the Younger (1728–1781) and opened in 1771. They became the centre for social life in the town, with dazzling balls and much gambling. Later they were a concert venue. The Assembly Rooms were restored in 1938, but badly damaged during World War II. After another restoration they reopened in 1963. Today, they house the Museum of Costume, depicting 400 years of fashion – there are some 200 dressed figures in period settings. Modern fashion is not forgotten, with an annual 'dress of the year'.

Leave the Assembly Rooms and walk along Bennett Street to **The Circus (10)**, designed by John Wood the Elder (1704–1754) and the first circular plan in the history of British urban architecture. The architect died shortly after the first foundation stone was laid in 1754, but the work was continued by his son. The houses are laid out in three sets of 33, interspersed with three equally spaced roads. Each house has three Classical columns, with Doric on the ground floor, Ionic on the middle floor and Corinthian on the top floor. A frieze above the Doric layer has a number of mystic symbols. Houses in The Circus were rented out during the 'season' and past residents (shown by wall plaques) have included William Pitt the Elder (1708–1778), David Livingstone (1813–1873), Robert Clive of India (1725–1774), William Makepeace Thackeray (1811–1863) and Thomas Gainsborough. In the early years of The Circus, the central space was occupied by a reservoir, which, being above the level of the basement kitchens, was able to provide a gravity-fed water supply. This area is now graced by a number of 200-year-old plane trees.

On the corner of The Circus and Bennett Street is the **Museum of East Asian Art (11)**, with artefacts from China, Japan, Korea and other countries, ranging in date from 5000BC to the 20th century. Leave The Circus from the west side, walking along Brock Street, where there are further examples of fine domestic architecture, with some interesting insurance company firemarks and ornate wrought-iron work.

You now reach one of England's most remarkable architectural features, **The Royal Crescent (12)**. Designed by John Wood the Elder and completed by his son between 1767 and 1775, the crescent comprises a semicircle of 30 houses with a frontage of Ionic columns, supporting a continuous cornice over 660ft (200m) long, all built in the honey-coloured Bath Stone. As in The Circus, the houses were often rented out for the 'season'. They are now largely privately occupied, although no. 1, once occupied by George III's son the Duke of York, has been preserved as a museum of 18th-century life. Period background music gives a lived-in feeling. The grassy space in front of The Royal Crescent features a ha-ha – a ditch constructed to keep cattle away from the houses.

Leave The Royal Crescent and walk southwards across the grass until you reach Royal Avenue. Turn left here (eastwards) through Royal Victoria Park. A jink in the road through Queen's Parade (the centre of the sedan-chair trade until that was superseded by the Bath chair) brings us to **Queen Square (13)**. Again we have John Wood to thank for this development: he built the square privately between 1729 and 1736, after the city authorities had rejected his plans, and himself lived in it, at no. 24, until his death. The square was named after Queen Caroline, the wife of George II. Famous residents have included Jane Austen (1775–1817), who lodged at no. 13. The obelisk in the centre of the square was provided by Beau Nash to celebrate the visit of Prince Frederick and his wife in 1738.

The Performing Arts

Leave Queen Square via Princes Street in the southwest corner. Swing left into Beauford Square and then right into Barton Street. Almost the whole of this block is taken up with the **Theatre Royal (14)**. One of the country's oldest theatres, this has seen many famous names perform on its stage over the last 350 years. Backstage tours are available on certain days.

On the south corner of the theatre is a bust of the 18th-century actor David Garrick, and nearby is the Garrick's Head pub. This building and part of the theatre were once the palatial home of Beau Nash, who lived there with his first mistress,

Fanny Murray. Later he lived with his second mistress, Joanna Popjoy, in a more modest nearby house, now a restaurant.

Hot Baths

From the Garrick's Head continue south along Sawclose, which swings round to the left into Westgate Street, the location of one of the gates in the old city walls. Turn immediately right down a paved path, St Michael's Place, past the Little Theatre Cinema on the right, to reach the area where the hot baths are located. This is the part of the city where the socialites gathered in the 1700s and 1800s to take and drink the waters.

Occupying a small triangle of land is **Cross Bath (15)**, probably named after the cross erected to commemorate the fact that the previously infertile Queen Mary, the wife of James II, conceived after taking the waters here. Cross Bath was a favourite of the nobility; the ladies, serenaded by musicians, would bathe alongside floating wooden trays that bore their cosmetics. A grille on the south side of the building looks across a steaming pool, giving a good idea of the ambience of those times.

Walk across the road to the building which contains **Hot Bath (16)**, designed by John Wood the Younger and a popular place for visiting royalty. Today, however, there is little to see here.

Leave the area eastwards along the colonnaded Bath Street, constructed by Baldwin in 1791 (he afterwards went bankrupt) and designed to provide a sheltered walkway for socialites as they moved between the baths. This brings you to the pedestrianized Stall Street.

Ahead is the **Pump Room (17)**, built by Baldwin in 1790 to replace an earlier building. It overlooked the Royal Bath and was a rendezvous for all who took the waters. It has 16 fluted columns and is lit by a huge chandelier. Other attractions are a bust of Beau Nash, two original sedan chairs and a tall clock, 10ft (3m) high, dating from 1709. The Pump Room remains a popular venue today, and you can drink the waters and/or other beverages while eating to the strains of the Pump Room Trio. Note the plaque on the exterior of the Pump Room which identifies Bath as a World Heritage Site.

Now turn into Abbey Churchyard (where the tour began). On the right is the entrance to the **Roman Baths Museum (18)**. By anyone's standards, this is one of the best museums in the country, containing the most comprehensive collection of Roman remains in Britain. Concealed for over 1000 years, the baths were rediscovered and excavated in the 19th century. Although the pillars and some of the statues are Victorian, one can still see the bases of the columns which supported the original roof. The ruin of the Roman Temple to Sulis Minerva can be seen, along with much of the pipe-work that supplied the water to the baths. The Roman remains are about 20ft (6m) below the present street level. The main Great Bath is 70ft (22m) long, 30ft (9m) wide and 5ft (1.5m) deep, and is still fed by the original Roman plumbing. The museum section shows some of the Roman artefacts discovered on the site, such as jewellery, carved inscriptions and coins, many of which were thrown into the sacred spring.

The Roman Baths, highly recommended, represent the conclusion of the walking tour.

SALISBURY

Access: Although not served by motorways, Salisbury is at the hub of a network of main roads. The A303, an important route from London to the West Country, runs just to the north (driving time from London about 2hr), while the A30, another key east–west link, passes through the city itself. Other main roads connect with Bath, Southampton, Portsmouth and Dorchester. Salisbury is a major stop on the London–West Country rail route from Waterloo. Regular coach services link with London, Southampton and Bristol. The nearest main international airports are at Gatwick and Heathrow, both of which can be reached by car and coach in under 2hr. There are ferry links from France through Southampton and Poole.

The story of Salisbury begins on a windswept hill known as Old Sarum, a couple of miles north of the present town. It was a hill fort in Iron Age times and later became the hub of a network of Roman roads; the Romans called the settlement Sorbiodunum. The Saxons in turn occupied the site, calling it Seares byrig; from the number of coins found it seems likely the Saxons had a mint here. William the Conqueror strengthened the defences of Old Sarum and built a military castle, and the Normans also united the dioceses of Sherborne and Ramsbury and built a new cathedral at Old Sarum, occupying a quarter of the space within the walls of the fortifications. Completed in 1092 by Bishop Osmund, the cathedral was badly damaged by lightning only a few days after its consecration.

Osmund's successor, Bishop Roger, immediately started on a new building. The foundations of this second Norman cathedral show that it was 317ft (96.6m) in length. By the early 13th century, however, there were plans to move the cathedral to a lowland site. The reasons are obvious: the site was bleak and lacked fresh water, and relations between the military and the clergy were often acrimonious – on one occasion the bishop and his clerics returned in the evening to find the gates locked against them and had to spend an uncomfortable night out in the open. Enough was enough and eventually, in 1219, Bishop Richard Poore obtained permission from the Pope to build a new cathedral in the valley nearby.

The foundation stone was laid in 1220. Along with the new cathedral, houses were built in what is now the Close for not only the bishop but the canons, other clergy and workmen. Poore also laid out the street pattern of New Sarum, or Salisbury, which received its Royal Charter in 1227 – although it was to remain under the control of the cathedral for another four centuries.

The construction of the new cathedral began at the east end with the Lady Chapel (now known as Trinity Chapel), under the supervision of the master mason Nicholas of Ely, helped by one of the canons, Elias de Dereham; Elias was one of Henry III's courtiers and had been present in 1215 at the sealing of the Magna Carta, one of the four original copies of which can be seen in Salisbury today. The building stone used for the cathedral was a cream limestone from Chilmark, some 12 miles (19km) west and, as with many cathedrals of this era, the limestone was set off by thin dark shafts of Purbeck Marble. On completion of the Lady Chapel, the bodies of three former bishops were brought down from Old Sarum and re-interred; they included Bishop Osmund, who was later canonized and whose shrine soon attracted pilgrims in large numbers.

By 1258 the nave, choir and transepts had been completed and the building was consecrated. The west front was finished c1265 and an enormous detached bell tower was built on the southwest side of the cathedral. The architectural style throughout was Early English, making Salisbury a rarity among English cathedrals. Only St Paul's in London can claim such devotion to one particular style.

Just two major additions were to come. Between 1285 and 1310 the magnificent tower and spire were constructed, rising to a height of 404ft (123m) – the tallest in England. The foundations were never designed to support such a structure, so drastic measures had to be taken to provide additional strength. Buttresses were built into the clerestory walls, plus external flying buttresses coming from the main aisles to the tower, while strainer arches were built in the choir aisles. These measures seem to have worked, as neither the spire nor the supporting pillars have moved since Wren's survey in 1668. The second addition was the construction of the cloisters, between 1240 and 1270. These were the first to appear in an English cathedral and are arguably still the best. Cloisters are normally associated with monastical cathedrals, but Salisbury has always been a secular establishment, so its cloisters were clearly built for their aesthetic value alone. Each cloister stretches for 140ft (42m), and the style is Geometric Decorated. Leading off the cloisters and in similar architectural style is the chapter house, built between 1263 and 1284.

There was often friction between the clergy and the citizens of Salisbury, and in 1327 the dean and chapter obtained a licence from Edward III to build a protective wall around the close. Permission was given to use stone from the Old Sarum cathedral, by now derelict. With the river on two sides and the new wall on the other two sides, the close became secure. The gates were locked at night and one, the North (or High Street) Gate, had a portcullis which could be dropped whenever the townsfolk were being particularly obstreperous.

In the Civil War both Royalists and Parliamentarian troops occupied the close at various times while fighting for control of the city. During this period Parliament appropriated the bishop's estate, which was later bought by the city authorities: the clergy had to suffer the indignity of seeing the Bishop's Palace being used as an inn.

Things returned to normal for both Close and cathedral after the Restoration in 1660. This coincided with the reign (1667–89) of the able and learned Bishop Seth Ward, previously Professor of Astronomy at Oxford. Salisbury attracted many intellectuals, such as Samuel Johnson (1709–1784), James Boswell (1740–1795) and Joshua Reynolds (1723–1792), while Sir Christopher Wren (1632–1723) influenced many of the new buildings now appearing in the Close. The city of Salisbury had meanwhile become increasingly prosperous, its wealth based on wool. The twice-weekly markets attracted people from far and wide, stimulating the growth of inns, many later to specialize in coaching. The road system, previously focusing on Old Sarum, was reorganized, and new bridges were built across the rivers.

By the mid-1700s the cathedral was in urgent need of repairs. Shute Barrington (1734–1826), bishop from 1782, arranged for the architect James Wyatt (1746–1813) to undertake renovations. Wyatt, who had studied in Italy and become the fashionable architect of the time, made a disastrous foray into cathedral work. His appalling alterations to Lichfield are well known, and his work at Salisbury was equally vandalous. On the credit side, he levelled and drained the churchyard and removed the ugly bell tower, but inside the cathedral he removed a number of chapels, stripped away much of the medieval glass, broke up and moved around a number of tombs, covered the medieval paintwork with limewash and scrapped the pulpitum, replacing it with an inferior screen. This was not a happy period for the cathedral!

Victorian renovations in cathedrals are generally not highly regarded, but Sir George Gilbert Scott's work at Salisbury at least repaired some of Wyatt's damage. Scott (1811–1878) strengthened the tower with iron bracing, provided replacement statues for the west front and revamped the choir. Wyatt's screen was replaced by an open metal one (since removed) designed by Francis Skidmore (1816–1896), and a new Minton floor was laid in the choir. Glass was reintroduced to many of the windows. The limewash, alas, could not be removed, and was painted over with the old designs.

Repair and restoration have continued ever since. In the 1950s it was found that the spire needed urgent attention and the top 30ft (9m) had to be completely rebuilt at a cost of £6½ million – a sum which most visitors would consider well worth spending. Between 1978 and 1983 the 15th-century library over the eastern cloister was restored. The 1980s saw the appearance of two notable works of art. In 1980 the Prisoners of Conscience window was unveiled; designed by Gabriel Loire of Chartres, it is of Impressionist design but is coloured in 13th-century style. And in 1982 Elisabeth Frink's remarkable bronze statue *Walking Madonna* was placed outside the north porch. In 1985 an Appeal was started to raise £6,500,000 for the repair and conservation of the spire, tower and West. Helped by funds from English Heritage, the work was completed in 2000, appropriately in time for the Millennium.

The city of Salisbury was largely unaffected by the Industrial Revolution. Today it is a regional centre and market town with industries largely of an agricultural and technological nature. Tourism is a major money-earner, and the cathedral and its tranquil close are a magnet for the many visitors from home and abroad.

TOUR OF THE CATHEDRAL

Start: Cathedral Close, near the path leading to the north porch.
Finish: The refectory and bookshop.

The tour begins by the **Statue of the Walking Madonna (1)**, close to the path leading to the north porch, which is the cathedral's main ceremonial entrance. This bronze sculpture by Elisabeth Frink (1930-1994) was completed in 1981 and put in place a year later.

Walk around the west front of the building. At the time of writing this was covered with scaffolding and plastic sheeting. The work, which is likely to take several more years, is concentrated on the statuary, which is badly eroded. (It is worth remembering that the cathedral's stonework has suffered more atmospheric pollution during the last 150 years than in the rest of its history.) Plans are also underway to restore the main west porch to the colours of medieval times.

Enter the cathedral via the southwest door, next to the cloister wall. You are obliged to pay a 'donation', the amount of which is detailed on a notice board; to all intents and purposes this is an entrance fee, with concessions for students and pensioners.

Pass into the **Nave (2)**. Despite the fact that you can see the whole length of the building (the choir screen has been removed), the general impression is of height rather than length. Simplicity, some would say severity, is the keynote of the architecture. The cathedral is mainly built of Chilmark Limestone, a white oolitic rock, and there is a strong contrast between this and the almost black shafts of Purbeck Marble (widely used in Early English architecture). The arches and capitals of the arcade are plain, while the triforium is rather squat, with its arches divided by trefoils. Above, the clerestory windows have triple lancets. The light-and-shade effect is pleasing, but the nave suffers through lacking its medieval glass, removed by Wyatt in the late 18th century.

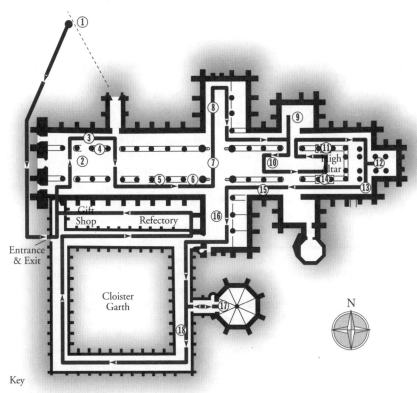

Key

1. Statue of the Walking Madonna
2. Nave
3. Medieval Clock
4. Tomb of William de Longespée the Younger
5. Tomb of St Osmund
6. Tomb of William de Longespée the Elder
7. Crossing
8. North Transept
9. Morning Chapel
10. Choir
11. Chantry Chapel of Edward Audley
12. Trinity Chapel
13. Tomb of the Earl of Hertford
14. Chantry Chapel of Walter, Lord Hungerford
15. Mompesson Tomb
16. South Transept
17. Chapter House
18. Cloisters

Walk across to the north aisle, where there is a **Medieval Clock (3)**. This was once positioned in the detached bell tower on the northwest side of the cathedral, but the tower was demolished by Wyatt in 1790. The clock, which has no face, dates from *c*1386 and is certainly the oldest working clock in England, if not the world.

Tombs and Monuments
The spaces between the arches of the nave are taken up with numerous tombs – some plain slabs, others with effigies, some of early bishops and brought from Old Sarum, others of local soldiers and statesmen. Unfortunately, most of the tombs were placed here by Wyatt, who in moving them from their previous positions in the cathedral apparently mixed up the effigies and put them on tombs to which they did not belong.

Three of the tombs are of particular interest. Close to the medieval clock is the **Tomb of William de Longespée (4)**. Son of the third Earl of Salisbury, de Longespée (*c*1212–1250), a general in the Crusades, was killed in the assault on Mansura. On the same slab is a small tomb, possibly of a 'boy bishop' who died in office. (Choristers used to elect one of their number to bear the title of 'bishop' from the Feast of St Nicholas on December 6 to the Feast of the Innocents on December 28). More probably it is an example of a heart burial, quite likely that of Richard Poore, bishop 1217–29 and founder of the cathedral.

Cross to the south aisle to find the **Tomb of St Osmund (5)**. St Osmund (d1099), second bishop of Old Sarum, was canonized in 1457. His remains were brought to the cathedral in 1226 and originally placed in a shrine in Trinity Chapel. The shrine was broken up in 1539 during the Reformation. The 'tomb' we see in the nave today may be part of the shrine. Finally, next to the crossing is the **Tomb of William de Longespée the Elder (6)**. De Longespée (1196–1226), third Earl of Salisbury, was a half-brother to King John, a witness to the signing of the Magna Carta (1215) and present at the laying of the cathedral's foundation stone in 1220.

Proceed to the **Crossing (7)**. The tower and spire (said to have a combined weight of 6400 tons) are supported by four Purbeck Marble pillars which have a decided bend. Hardly surprising, considering there is only 3ft (1m) of foundations! The tower has been subsequently supported by strainer arches, flying buttresses and interior stone buttresses. The vaulting of the crossing dates from 1480; its paintwork shows the royal arms of the time plus the arms of various bishops.

Move left into the **North Transept (8)**, dominated by three levels of Early English lancet windows. The stained glass, by Hemmings, dates from 1895, although 13th-century in style. Of the numerous monuments the most impressive is that of John Blythe, bishop 1494–9 and at one time Chancellor of Cambridge University. Along the east side of the transept a modern wooden screen conceals the Chapel of St Edmund of Abingdon and St Thomas of Canterbury. The triptych and altar front date from the late 19th century and were originally in the Trinity Chapel.

Leave the north transept and walk along the north choir aisle, turning left into the **Morning Chapel (9)**. The most interesting feature here is the monument to the artist Rex Whistler (1905–1944), which takes the form of a revolving glass prism. Engraved by his brother Laurence, the prism is set in a blue-and-gold lantern resting on a corbel of Purbeck Marble (from the same quarries as most of the cathedral's 13th-century stone). Alongside the monument are the remains of the stone pulpitum removed from the choir by Wyatt in the 18th century.

Choir and Chantry Chapels

Cross the north choir aisle and enter the **Choir (10)** – the archaic term 'quire' is often used at Salisbury. While the architecture of the choir is similar to that of the nave, the fabric owes much to the Victorian renovations. The canons' stalls, some of which have misericords, are 13th-century, but the rest of the stalls were added in the 19th century and the canopies in 1913–25. Sir George Gilbert Scott (1811–1878) provided the Bishop's Throne and the Willis organ (this replaced George III's organ, which was given to St Thomas's Church in the city). Scott was responsible also for the repainting of the vaulting in the medieval style, after being unable to remove Wyatt's coating of whitewash. Two of Scott's introductions have not survived – the Minton floor and an open metal screen by Skidmore. The new high altar, introduced in 1984 and made from stone from Old Sarum, is notable for its superb modern altar frontals. Note also the wall plaque commemorating the distribution of the Maundy Money by Queen Elizabeth II in April 1974.

Return to the north choir aisle. On the right is the delightful little **Chantry Chapel of Edward Audley (11)**. Audley was bishop 1502–24. The chapel is in Perpendicular style and retains some of its original colouring. The painting of the Virgin and Child comes from Florence, while the altar fabrics are modern.

On reaching the end of the aisle turn right into the open-plan **Trinity Chapel (12)**, formerly known as the Lady Chapel. This is the oldest part of the cathedral, and was the scene of the initial consecration in 1225 – note the consecration crosses on the wall on either side of the altar. The superb Early English architecture is graced by slender pillars of Purbeck Marble, leaving narrow side aisles with blind arcading. Dominating the chapel is the Prisoners of Conscience Window (1980) by Gabriel Loire of Chartres. People's opinions on the window differ enormously: to judge it fairly, view it in the morning when the suns streams in from the east; a wet afternoon produces an entirely different effect. To the left of the altar is the Prisoner of Conscience Candle, festooned in barbed wire. Before leaving Trinity Chapel, look for the 14th-century wooden Madonna and Child on the north wall.

Move now into the south choir aisle. At the east end is the resplendent **Tomb of the Earl of Hertford (13)**. Born Edward Seymour (1539–1621), the earl was the nephew of Jane Seymour (1509–1537), Queen of England. Beside him lies the effigy of his wife, Lady Catherine Grey (*c*1538–1568), sister of Lady Jane Grey (1537–1554), Queen of England for nine days in 1553 before being imprisoned and beheaded. Further down the aisle on the right, framed with iron railings, is the **Chantry Chapel of Walter, Lord Hungerford (14)**, who died in 1449. The chapel was restored in 1778 by the Earl of Radnor and removed from the nave to this position to be used as the Radnor family pew – you can see a line of seats inside.

Next, on the left, is the sumptuous **Mompesson Tomb (15)**, repainted in its original colours in 1964. A curiosity here is that the figures of Sir Richard

Mompesson (d1624) and his wife, Lady Katherine, face west rather than the usual east. This is explained by the fact that the tomb was originally on the north side of the cathedral.

Step now into the **South Transept (16)**, structurally a replica of the north transept. There are three chapels here. In the Chapel of St Margaret of Scotland the altar frontal is a 17th-century Spanish embroidery with scenes of the life of St Theresa of Avila; this is one of the treasures of the cathedral. In the Chapel of St Laurence – a deacon c258 and said to have been martyred in Rome on a gridiron – the altar top is 13th-century and the oldest in the cathedral. And finally, in the Chapel of St Michael the Archangel are regimental colours and books of remembrance.

The Chapter House and Cloisters
Leave the south transept by the door in the southwest corner. Go along the north cloister and turn left into the **Chapter House (17)**. Built 1263–84, this was clearly closely modelled on that in Westminster Abbey. It is octagonal with a slim central pier of Purbeck Marble leading up to fine fan vaulting, somewhat spoiled by insipid painted decoration. The windows are Geometric Decorated in style (almost all the original glass has gone), and below is blind arcading with stone benches. Notice the capitals on the wall shafts, where the carved foliage also reveals occasional birds, heads and animals. The spandrels of the arcade have a medieval stone-carved frieze showing scenes from the Old Testament – the stewards can provide a detailed list of the subjects. The overall effect is perhaps ruined by the Minton tiled floor, which seems totally out of place. There are displays of silverware and religious documents, and the chapter house also contains one of the four surviving originals of the Magna Carta (1215), written in Latin on vellum and running to about 3500 words.

Leave the chapter house and return to the **Cloisters (18)**. Completed c1340, these are the largest and, with the possible exception of Gloucester, the finest in England. The style is Early Geometric Decorated, matching the chapter house, and there is simple quadripartite vaulting. Salisbury was never a monastic cathedral, so monks never walked in contemplation here. In the cloister garth are two magnificent cedar trees, planted in 1837 to commemorate Queen Victoria's accession to the throne; superb though the trees are, many visitors feel they detract from the simple lines of the cloisters. A library built over the eastern cloister in 1445 contains many ancient manuscripts and early printed books, but is not open to the public without a special permit.

The exit from the cathedral is, in true modern commercial fashion, via the refectory and bookshop.

WALKING TOUR FROM SALISBURY CATHEDRAL
The tour begins in the Cathedral Close, arguably the finest of any English cathedral city, with its superb late-18th-century buildings, including two museums. You then leave the close via one of the gates in the wall and move into the city centre, with its ancient coaching inns, vibrant market and St Thomas's Church, undoubtedly one of the most interesting parish churches in the country. A short stretch of the River Avon follows before you return through another gate to the Cathedral Close.

Start and finish: The west front of the cathedral.

Length: 1½ miles (2.4km).

Time: The walk is on level ground throughout, so can be comfortably completed in well under an hour. Allow extra time if visiting the museums and St Thomas's Church.

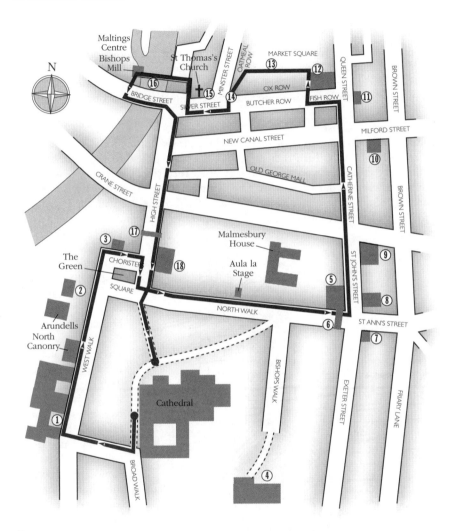

Key

1. The King's House
2. The Wardrobe
3. Mompesson House
4. Bishop's Palace
5. Malmesbury House
6. St Ann's Gate

7. The Old Bell Inn
8. The King's Arms
9. The White Hart
10. The Red Lion
11. House of John a'Porte
12. Guildhall

13. Market Place
14. Poultry Cross
15. St Thomas' Cross
16. City Mill
17. North (or High Street) Gate
18. Matrons' Collage

Refreshments: Light snacks are available in the cathedral refectory. There are no other food outlets in the close, except within the two museums. There is a wide selection of ancient inns on the walking route, many with coaching origins. These include: the Old Bell in St Ann's Street; the King's Arms and the White Hart Hotel in St John's Street; and the Red Lion Hotel in Milford Street. In summer the Bishop's Mill has some pleasant outdoor tables alongside the River Avon. Many of these hostelries offer accommodation.

The first part of the tour concentrates on the Cathedral Close, one of the most attractive in England. There are some superb examples of domestic architecture, particularly from the late 17th century. The size of the open space around the cathedral means that photographing England's tallest cathedral spire is not a problem.

The Cathedral Close

From the west front of the cathedral take the path south for about fifty yards until you reach Broad Walk. Turn right here and, the playing field to your left, stroll on another fifty yards until you arrive at West Walk. Turn right.

Immediately on your left now is **The King's House** (1), which has a long and interesting history. It was built by the Abbots of Sherbourne, but with the Dissolution of the Monasteries it fell into lay hands. The impressive oriel window was added in the late 15th century. In the early 17th century the owners played host to King James I on a number of occasions – hence the building's name. In the 19th century it was a school and then became a Diocesan Training College for schoolmistresses; the two sisters of Thomas Hardy (1840–1928) were students at the college. In 1980 The King's House became the home of the Salisbury and South Wiltshire Museum, which has won several awards for its innovative presentation.

The next building on the left is the Old Deanery, which

St Ann's Gate leading to the Cathedral Close

has a medieval hall. Pass the North Canonry to Arundells, for many years the home of Sir Edward Heath (b1916), the former prime minister. Set back from West Walk is the **Wardrobe (2)**, originally a 13th-century canonry, although with many later additions. It may have gained its name through being some sort of storehouse for the bishops. It was then a hall of residence for the training college before becoming the Museum of the Royal Gloucestershire, Berkshire and Wiltshire Regiment.

Proceed now into Choristers Square, which runs round a grassy area known as The Green. The most important building here is **Mompesson House (3)**, located on the north side. Built in the late 17th century by Sir Thomas Mompesson, MP for Salisbury, it was used between 1942 and 1946 as the official residence of the Bishop of Salisbury. It is now owned by the National Trust.

Leave Choristers Square and turn left along North Walk. On the left is the flint end of the former canonry, known as Aula le Stage, parts of which date from the 13th century. Next on the left is the former Salisbury Theological College; this closed in 1994 but still holds courses for external students.

From outside the college, look south along Bishop's Walk and in the distance you can see the gates leading to the **Bishop's Palace (4)**. Parts of the building go back to the consecration of the cathedral in 1225. It received considerable damage during the Civil War, but was restored in the late 17th century by Bishop Seth Ward (1617–1689) with the help of Christopher Wren (1632–1723). In 1947 the bishop moved into smaller premises and the palace was taken over by the Cathedral School. The grounds are private and the building is not normally open to the public.

Continue along North Walk towards St Ann's Gate. On the right, the brick Georgian building is the sixth-form block of Bishop Wordsworth School. On the left just before the gate is **Malmesbury House (5)**, another 13th-century canonry. It was enlarged in the 14th century and leased to the Harris family, one of whose descendants became the first Earl of Malmesbury. The façade of the building was added by Wren. Charles II and George Frederick Handel (1685–1759) were among the more illustrious visitors to the house.

You are now approaching **St Ann's Gate (6)**. The gate was built in the early 14th century, although the Vicars Choral Chapel above the arch was added later. St Ann's, like the other gates to the close, is still locked at 23:00 (which must have been very frustrating for the lady students at the training college!). It is thought that Handel made his first public performance in England in the room above St Ann's Gate.

Inns of Character

Pass through the gate and turn left. Pause for a moment to inspect the wall, which displays some carved stonework which came from the first cathedral at Old Sarum.

Turn left into St John's Street, which runs parallel to the wall of the close. This street is notable for its number of inns of character, many of which offer possibilities for a lunch stop. Opposite St Ann's Gate, on the corner of Exeter Street and St Ann's Road, is the **Old Bell Inn (7)**, which dates back to the 14th century. Heading into the city centre, you can see on the right of St John's Street the **King's Arms (8)**, a half-timbered coaching inn with a medieval atmosphere. Further along on the right, on the corner of Ivy Street and St John's Street, is the **White Hart Hotel (9)**: with its Classical façade, this was undoubtedly Salisbury's grandest coaching inn. Stagecoaches left for London at 22:00 nightly.

Carry on northwards as St John's Street merges into Catherine Street. A brief diversion to the right into Milford Street takes you to the **Red Lion Hotel (10)**, a half-timbered building of considerable character. The south wing was constructed between 1280 and 1320, reputedly to house men working on the cathedral. The main part of the Red Lion belongs to the 18th century, when it was a thriving coaching inn. From here a coach called the Salisbury Flying Machine left daily for London. Wander under the huge archway, designed to take the largest carriages, into the attractive courtyard with its models of red lions.

Return to Catherine Street and continue north into Queen Street. Immediately on the right is the **House of John a'Porte (11)** This magnificent half-timbered building with a double-jettied frontage was built in 1425 by John a'Porte, a wealthy wool merchant and several times Mayor of Salisbury. The ground floor is now a shop specializing in glass and china.

Cross the road and enter Fish Row. On the right is the **Guildhall (12)**, which houses the Tourist Information Office. In order to see the front of the building, turn down a small alleyway to the right, which brings you into the Market Place. The original Guildhall was burnt down in 1780 and the present building, with its Classical façade, was completed 15 years later. It was donated to the city by the Earl of Radnor.

The Market Place and St Thomas's Church

You now find yourself in the **Market Place (13)**. A market has been held here twice weekly since 1361, and this area has always been the hub of commercial activity in the city. Numerous inns lined the Market Place to provide accommodation for pilgrims visiting the Shrine of St Osmund; today only two of these inns remains, the rest having been converted to other uses.

Leave the Market Place in the southwest corner and come to the **Poultry Cross (14)**. The present Cross dates from the 15th century, replacing an earlier one which had stood on the site for over 200 years. It consists of six piers enclosing a central column. Above is a superstructure with flying buttresses surrounding a central spire topped with a cross. Farmers used to sell their wares beneath the Poultry Cross, which was also a popular venue for open-air sermons.

Leave the Poultry Cross westwards along Silver Street and turn right almost immediately along the alleyway leading to **St Thomas's Church (15)**. This must be one of the most fascinating parish churches in the country – it is an absolute gem and should not be missed. It dates back to *c*1220, but most of the building is 15th-century Perpendicular. There is a tremendous amount to see, including the Doom Painting over the chancel arch, a magnificent carved 'Somerset Angel' roof, a superb Lady Chapel with medieval murals, a Georgian organ presented to the cathedral by George III in 1792 and given to St Thomas's in 1877 – and much more. A small brochure giving full details of the church is well worth buying.

Leave St Thomas's Church and go straight ahead towards the Maltings Centre. After crossing the River Avon, turn immediately left under an arch and head towards the bridge, a few steps away. This gives you a superb view back towards the old **City Mill (16)**, which is mostly 17th-century in age, although the original mill is believed to be one of four Salisbury mills mentioned in the Domesday Book. It was used for grinding grain and for fulling cloth, while the associated buildings have at various times produced beer, tobacco and snuff. To the left is the Bishop's Mill, an old building which has been modernized and converted into a popular restaurant.

Walk back to Silver Street and turn right into High Street. Note on the left the modern Old George Shopping Mall, named after a coaching inn. Ahead is the **North Gate (17)** or High Street Gate, leading into the Cathedral Close. The North Gate, built 1327–42, is still locked between 23:00 and 06:00. For many years it had a portcullis which could be lowered if the townsfolk became rebellious, and the culprits could then be locked up in the small jail contained within the gate. Next to the gate is the porter's lodge – the job of porter was much sought after by royal servants in the Middle Ages.

Pass through the gate and immediately on the left is the **Matrons' College (18)**, founded in 1682 by Bishop Seth Ward to house ten widows of clergy – a function it still fulfils today. Note the coat-of-arms of Charles II above the main doorway.

You are now back in the Cathedral Close, where the tour concludes.

Most of St Thomas's is built in the Perpendicular style

WINCHESTER

Access: Winchester is linked by road to London via the M25 and the M3 (junctions 9–11). The A34 provides access to the Midlands. There are frequent railway connections with London Waterloo. The nearest airport is Southampton International, which has scheduled services to a number of European and British cities.

The Romans formed a settlement at the place where Winchester now stands. Called Venta Belgarum, it in due course became probably the country's fifth largest city. There is no evidence of Christianity in Roman Winchester; this had to wait until Anglo-Saxon times. In 635 Cenwahl built the Old Minster, which three decades later became a cathedral when the ecclesiastical centre of Wessex was transferred from Dorchester-on-Thames. Excavation work in the 1960s revealed the foundations of the Old Minster and these have been marked out in brick on the north side of the present cathedral.

The Anglo-Saxon city, known as Wintancaestre, was notable for two men, King Alfred and Bishop Swithun (St Swithin). Alfred the Great (*c*848–899), who made Winchester his capital city, was a noted scholar and statesman, and performed heroic deeds in protecting the city from the invading Danes, rebuilt the city walls and laid out the present street plan. When he died in 899 he was buried in the Old Minster, but his tomb was later transferred to the New Minster built by his son Edward the Elder (d924). The Old Minster thereafter became a Benedictine monastery, while Alfred's widow Ealhswith founded a nunnery called Nunnaminster, which later became St Mary's Abbey. As a result of all this Winchester became one of the most important ecclesiastical centres in Europe. Bishop Swithun (d862), for his part, probably built the city's bridge over the River Itchen. When his bones were exhumed in 971, to be placed in a shrine, it rained heavily for a considerable time, leading to the popular saying that, if it rains on St Swithin's Day, it will rain for the next forty days.

The Norman period brought notable changes to Winchester. The city, still capital of England, surrendered to William the Conqueror in November 1066, and after he was crowned later in the year he ordered the construction of a castle on the city's west side which was to become the seat of the early Norman kings. Four years later William appointed a Norman bishop, Wakelin, whose task was to build a new cathedral. Work began in 1079 and by 1093, when the first dedication took place, the east end, transepts, central tower and part of the nave were complete. The Old Minster was then demolished so that the nave could be finished. The Norman cathedral, now measuring 535ft (164m) in length, was the longest in Europe at the time. The only parts of it remaining today are the transepts and crypt.

In the early 13th century the east end of the cathedral was extended by a large retrochoir built in Early English style. It was once thought this was done to house the remains of St Swithun, which were attracting hordes of pilgrims, but in fact these remains were located on a feretory platform behind the high altar until shortly before the Reformation. During the early 14th century, the choir – located, unusually, underneath the crossing – was constructed and the presbytery arches were rebuilt. Attention then turned to the nave. Rebuilding work was started by Bishop Eddington and completed by probably the most famous Bishop of Winchester of all, William of Wykeham or Wickham (1324–1404), who founded Winchester College and New College, Oxford. The work, in Perpendicular style, started at the west front and proceeded eastwards. The existing Norman piers were encased by new stone and the entire nave was revaulted. Many of Winchester's chantry chapels also date from this period. The final major work on the cathedral came around 1500, when the eastern end of the Lady Chapel was rebuilt.

Up to now the cathedral had been the monastery church of St Swithun's Priory, but in 1539 the priory was officially dissolved, along with the other monastic foundations and friaries in the city. At the same time St Swithun's Shrine was destroyed. The prior became the first bishop, with a chapter of twelve canons. Further disruption came during the Civil War: the cathedral was twice entered by Parliamentary soldiers, who inflicted considerable damage before riding through the city brandishing their spoils.

By now the city of Winchester had lost much of its importance, political power having moved to London and ecclesiastical influence to Canterbury. There was little industry in the city and, by the late 18th century, it had become a residential town for the gentry. The coming of the railways in the mid-19th century, however, led to a new expansion and also brought in tourists for the first time.

During the early years of the 20th century it was realized that the walls of the east end of the cathedral were in danger of collapse, as the foundations were sub-siding into the marshy subsoil. Underpinning was obviously necessary. The work was carried out by a deep-sea diver named William Walker. Working six hours a day for five years in atrocious conditions, he eventually underpinned almost the whole cathedral by removing old logs and replacing them with sacks of cement concrete.

In 1993 a new Visitor Centre was opened by Her Majesty Queen Elizabeth II. It is located within an attractive walled garden and includes a restaurant and giftshop.

TOUR OF THE CATHEDRAL
Start and finish: The west door.

The **West Front (1)** is approached through an avenue of lime trees. Built in the time of Bishop Eddington, it is dominated by the elegant Perpendicular Window. Although it has been criticised by several architectural historians, you will probably be impressed by the window, particularly when you come to look at it from inside, where you'll be able to see that scraps of glass recovered after the vandalism of the Civil War have been used.

Step inside the building via the west door, to the left of which stairs lead to the treasury, housed in a Tudor gallery. Note here the 17th-century bronze statues of Charles I and James I.

Proceed to a position halfway down the **Nave (2)**. Largely built in the time of Bishop William of Wykeham, the nave is Perpendicular in style but, remarkably, was transformed from the original Norman without the latter being demolished: the pillars were simply encased in the later stonework, and much of the Norman masonry remains. The three storeys of the Norman nave were replaced by two storeys, enlarging the main arches and removing the triforium. The roof was completely revaulted in lierne style, with some superb bosses and corbels which you'll be able to see better if you've brought binoculars with you.

An Author's Tomb

Move into the north aisle and look for the simple slab on the floor marking the **Tomb of Jane Austen (3)**. Austen lived in the nearby village of Chawton, but died in the city at the age of 42; surprisingly, the inscription gives little indication that she was a writer! Close to her tomb is the Norman **Font (4)**. Made from black Tournai Marble, it is decorated with scenes and miracles from the life of St Nicholas, the Patron Saint of children. The end of the nave is terminated abruptly by the Victorian **Choir Screen (5)**, designed by Sir Gilbert Scott (1811–1878). Dark and spiky, it stands out irritatingly against the mellow cream-grey stonework of the nave. Turn now into the **North Transept (6)**, where you can see how the cathedral would have looked in Norman times. The transept was built between 1079 and 1093 out of limestone brought from the Isle of Wight. There are three equal levels, all with rounded arches – the main arcade, a triforium with each arch subdivided, and a clerestory. The flat wooden ceilings were added in Victorian times.

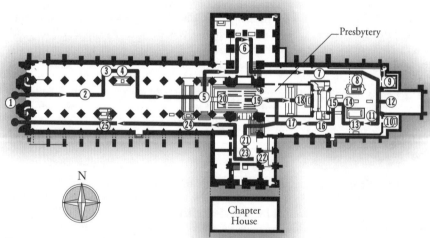

N

Key

1. West Front
2. Nave
3. Tomb of Jane Austen
4. Font
5. Choir Screen
6. North Transept
7. Bishop Gardiner's Chapel
8. Bishop Waynflete's Chapel
9. Guardian Angels Chapel
10. Bishop Langton's Chapel
11. Diver Statuette
12. Lady Chapel
13. Cardinal Beaufort's Chapel
14. Monument to St Swithun
15. Holy Hole
16. Bishop Fox's Chapel
17. Mortuary Chests
18. High Altar and Screen
19. Tomb of William Rufus
20. Choir
21. South Transept
22. Chapel of Prior Silkstede
23. Bishop Wilberforce's Memorial
24. Bishop Eddington's Chapel
25. William of Wykeham's Chapel

Chantry Chapels

Winchester is noted for its many chantry chapels, and you'll see the first examples in the north transept, with the Epiphany Chapel on the west side and the Holy Sepulchre Chapel, which has some interesting wall paintings, adjoining the choir.

Leave the transept and proceed into the north retrochoir aisle, passing the presbytery on your right. The retrochoir is the area where the more interesting chantry chapels are found. First on the right is **Bishop Gardiner's Chapel (7)**, showing a strange variety of styles. Stephen Gardiner (in office 1531–55) was the last Roman Catholic Bishop of Winchester. Next on the right is **Bishop Waynflete's Chapel (8)**; Waynflete was also a headmaster of Winchester College and founded Magdalen College, Oxford. At the east end of the cathedral the Lady Chapel is flanked by two more chapels. On the north side is the **Guardian Angels Chapel (9)**, named after the paintings of angels in the vaulting, and on the south side is **Bishop Langton's Chapel (10)**. Langton died of the plague in 1500, unfortunately just before he was to become Archbishop of Canterbury. Look for his rebus and note also the ceiling, which has been restored and painted to resemble its medieval appearance.

At the entrance to Bishop Langton's Chapel is the **Diver Statuette (11)**, made to commemorate the work of the deep-sea diver William Walker, who as we have seen saved the cathedral by underpinning the foundations. Unfortunately the statuette was modelled on the consultant engineer rather than on Walker himself!

The **Lady Chapel (12)** was built in two stages. The western end is 13th-century, and the chapel was extended eastwards around 1500 in Perpendicular style, a project funded by Elizabeth of York whose son, the unfortunate Prince Arthur (1486–1502), was christened here. Look for the rebuses in the vaulting of bishops Hunton and Silkstede. Murals from Silkstede's time show legends from the life of Our Lady.

Leave the East End and walk past **Cardinal Beaufort's Chantry Chapel (13)** – Beaufort was present at the trial of St Joan of Arc (*c*1412–1431), whose statue is outside the Lady Chapel, and is believed to have held the keys to her dungeon – and turn into the centre of the retrochoir, where there is a modern **Monument to St Swithun (14)** at the spot where his shrine finally stood. Earlier the saint's remains had been displayed on a feretory platform behind the high altar. Look for the **Holy Hole (15)** at the base of the rear of the altar which enabled pilgrims to crawl under the platform to get closer to the healing powers of the relics. This part of the retrochoir has some particularly fine 13th-century floor tiles.

Bones of Monarchs

Return to the south retrochoir aisle. Immediately to the left is **Bishop Fox's Chantry Chapel (16)**, beautifully carved in stone. His effigy is in the form of a cadaver; as the chapel was built before he died, there was plenty of time for him to be reminded of his own mortality! Further west, high on the screen, are the famous **Mortuary Chests (17)**, which contain the bones of many pre-Conquest bishops and monarchs, including possibly King Canute (*c*995–1035). Unfortunately, Cromwell's men rummaged through the chests, so the bones have become somewhat disordered.

Turn now into the presbytery, dating from the 14th century and the only part of the cathedral in Decorated style. Behind the **High Altar (18)** is the massive

15th-century Great Screen. The original statues on the screen were smashed during the Reformation, but the remains are on display in the Triforium Gallery Museum. The present statues were placed there in Victorian times. At the boundary of the presbytery and the choir is the so-styled **Tomb of William Rufus (19)**, although the ashes of this king are in fact among the bones in the mortuary chests. Son of William the Conqueror, the unpopular King William Rufus (*c*1087–1100) was killed by an arrow (possibly by his companion Walter Tirel) while hunting in the New Forest.

The **Choir (20)**, which is located under the central tower, is distinguished by its early-14th-century stalls, with their superb carving. Look for the heads of monkeys and other animals, plus a Green Man. There are over 60 misericords. Note, too, the Jacobean choir pulpit, given by Prior Silkstede around 1500.

An Angler and a Philanthropist's Son

Leave the choir and walk via the south retrochoir aisle to the **South Transept (21)**, which like the north transept is in Norman style. There are two chapels here, the more interesting being the **Chapel of Prior Silkstede (22)**, which, although Norman, was restructured by Silkstede in the early 16th century. The chapel has some interesting murals, but the important feature is the grave of Isaak Walton (1593–1683), author of *The Compleat Angler*, who died in Winchester's Cathedral Close in 1683. Walton was married twice, both to relatives of bishops. He spent much of his time in ecclesiastical circles, while fishing was just a pastime.

In the centre of the transept is **Bishop Wilberforce's Memorial (23)**. Samuel Wilberforce (1805–1873) was the son of William Wilberforce (1759–1833), the philanthropist who was prominent in abolishing the slave trade. The monument, which was designed by Sir George Gilbert Scott (1811–1878), shows the bishop's colourful effigy supported by six angels.

There are two more chantry chapels to see, and these are the oldest in the cathedral – fittingly they are named after the two men who between them remodelled the nave. At the eastern end of the south nave aisle is **Bishop Eddington's Chantry Chapel (24)**, which was meant to fit under the original Norman arcade, and **William of Wykeham's Chantry (25)**. Wykeham, in addition to his work as a bishop, founded Winchester College, whose former pupils are known as 'Wykehamists'.

From Wykeham's Chapel continue along the south nave aisle to the west door, where the tour concludes.

WALKING TOUR FROM WINCHESTER CATHEDRAL

The tour includes the Cathedral Close, parts of the pedestrianized shopping centre, some of the city's ancient monuments and a section of the Riverside Walk.

Start and finish: The west front of the cathedral.
Length: 1¾ miles (3.2km).
Time: 1½hr, though allow longer if you want to visit the museums and other buildings.
Refreshments: A number of ancient hostelries and coaching inns on or close to the walking route offer excellent pub lunches and bar meals. You might try: the Eclipse, on The Square, a half-timbered former rectory whose tables spill out onto the pavement in the summer; the Wykeham Arms, in Kingsgate Street, a pub close to

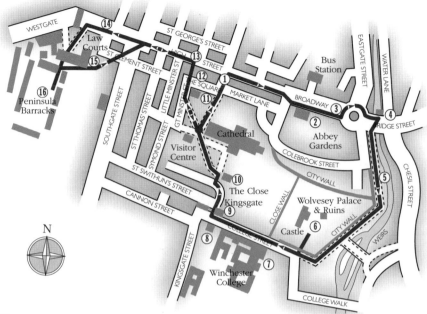

Key

1. High Street
2. Guildhall
3. Statue of King Alfred
4. City Mill
5. Riverside Walk
6. Wolvesey Castle

7. Winchester College
8. Jane Austen's House
9. Kingsgate
10. The Deanery
11. City Museum
12. The Eclipse

13. City Cross
14. Westgate
15. The Great Hall
16. Peninsula Barracks

Kingsgate and Winchester College and full of old school desks and other memorabilia from the college; the Hotel du Vin and Bistro (formerly the Southgate Hotel), in Southgate Street, a Georgian building close to the law courts; and the Old Market Tavern, in Market Lane, a traditional pub overlooking the cathedral.

Leave the west front of the cathedral and turn right, crossing the Cathedral Close, to arrive at the gap between The Square and Market Street. Pass through this gap to reach the pedestrianized **High Street (1)** where, despite some modern shop fronts, many of the buildings retain their ancient features and character. Turn right and proceed down the gentle hill. The High Street now widens out into The Broadway. On the right is the Victorian **Guildhall (2)**, whose green-roofed clock tower is a local landmark. The Guildhall is now used as a conference centre and has an art gallery; it is also the home of the Tourist Information Centre. Next door is the Abbey House, the official home of the Mayor of Winchester. Opposite the gardens of Abbey House is the imposing bronze **Statue of King Alfred (3)**, erected in 1901 on the millennial of his death. Standing on a plinth of Cornish granite, Alfred clasps a shield and raises his sword, staring resolutely up the High Street.

Along the Waterside

Continue past the statue until you reach the City Bridge. The first bridge here over the River Itchen was probably built by St Swithun; the present one dates from 1813. Cross the road carefully to the **City Mill (4)**, built in 1744 with the wheel restored in 1995. There were numerous mills along the River Itchen from medieval times onward. There is a speedy mill race to see, plus an attractive island garden. The City Mill is owned by the National Trust (which has a small giftshop on the premises), and part of the building acts as a Youth Hostel.

Leave the mill and return to the south side of City Bridge. Take the path between the river and the pub called Barringtons. You are now on the **Riverside Walk (5)**, locally known as Weirs Walk, which leads to the water meadows of the River Itchen and eventually to the Hospital of St Cross. The tour takes you along only a few hundred yards of the walk, but it shows some of the leats and mills of pre-Industrial Revolution times. To your right is a stretch of the old city walls, parts of which may date back as far as Roman times. After an area of public gardens, you come to a large mill which has been converted into accommodation, and shortly after this you should turn right into College Street.

The Castle and College

Behind the wall to the right are the remains of **Wolvesey Castle (6)**. There was a building here in Anglo-Saxon times, but the present ruins are of a 12th-century fortified palace constructed by various bishops. It was a popular residence for visiting royalty, and Henry V is believed to have received the French ambassador here before the invasion prior to Agincourt. Wolvesey Castle was almost entirely destroyed in the Civil War, when parliamentary troops captured the city. A few years later, Bishop Morley began to build a new palace in Baroque style. One wing of this building remains and is the residence of the present Bishop of Winchester.

Proceed further along College Street. Almost the whole of the left-hand side is occupied by **Winchester College (7)**. Founded by Bishop William of Wykeham in 1382 and designed by William Wynford – who was also responsible for the cathedral nave – the college was set up to train seventy scholars for the church. Their education was to be completed at New College, Oxford, also founded by Wykeham. Winchester College expanded considerably during the 19th century and is now one of the country's foremost public schools. The highlight is the College Chapel, where there is the tomb-effigy of William of Wykeham. The chapel tower is believed to have been designed by Sir Christopher Wren (1632–1723) in the 1680s.

Further left along College Street is **Jane Austen's House (8)**. In fact, the novelist lived here for only a few weeks before her death. Her main residence was in the village of Chawton, a few miles outside the city, but she had come to live in this modest yellow brick house to be near her doctor. At the end of College Street, turn right under **Kingsgate (9)**, one of two surviving city gates. Above the gateway is the tiny Church of St Swithun, still in use as a place of worship.

Carry on and pass through Priory Gateway into the Cathedral Close. Directly right is Cheyney Court, undoubtedly the most photographed house in the city. With yellow and black half-timbered work, it is partly built into the medieval walls and is festooned with wisteria in early summer. Once part of the Bishop of Winchester's courthouse, Cheyney Court was restored after damage in the Civil War.

Cheyney Court

Go left through the close. Ahead is **The Deanery (10)**, which was the Prior's House before the Dissolution of St Swithun's Priory. The distinctive 13th-century porch has three lancet-shaped arches. Attached is the 15th-century Prior's Hall, while to the southeast is the Pilgrims' Hall with one of the earliest surviving hammer-beam roofs.

Ancient and Modern

Take the pathway to the left of the Deanery, leading to the south side of the cathedral. The grassy area has a number of modern sculptures, mostly made of scrap iron.

You are now back at the west front of the Cathedral, where the second part of the walk starts. Take the path obliquely northwest across the grass through an avenue of lime trees to The Square. On the corner to the right is the **City Museum (11)**, a flint building with some interesting exhibits showing the archaeology and history of the Winchester area. Some fascinating Victorian shop interiors have also been recreated. Opposite the museum is a delightful little half-timbered pub, the **Eclipse (12)**, once the rectory of the old Church of St Lawrence.

Pass through the narrow end of Great Minster Street into the upper portion of the High Street. Immediately to the right is the **City Cross (13)**, also known as the Buttercross. Erected in the 15th century and restored in 1865, it is backed by ancient half-timbered houses with jettied walls and is roughly on the site of William the Conqueror's palace. Notice the nearby clock, jutting out over the High Street on an ornate wrought-iron frame; it was given to the city of Winchester in 1713.

State and Military History

Walk up the High Street to the **Westgate (14)**, one of four original gates in the city's walls. About six hundred years old, it stands on the site of an earlier Roman gateway and was well fortified in its time, with a portcullis (you can still see the grooves) and openings from where burning oil and missiles could be hurled at attackers. Note on the north side the two coats-of-arms – the royal arms and those of the City of Winchester. The Westgate became a debtors' prison in the 17th century. Today it houses a small museum displaying ancient weights and measures, plus a painted ceiling which came from Winchester College. There are superb views over the city from the roofwalk.

Pass through the Westgate's arch and turn immediately left into a large square surrounded by a complex of buildings, including the modern law courts. The most important building here is the **Great Hall (15)**, sometimes known as the Castle Hall because it is part of the complex of castle buildings built originally by the Conqueror – although the Great Hall itself in fact belongs to the rebuilding period of Henry III in the early 13th century. It is considered the finest medieval hall in the country after Westminster. Once a royal residence, it suffered from a serious fire in 1302, after which monarchs preferred to stay at nearby Wolvesey Castle. Following the Civil War the hall was used for the administration of justice: the infamous Judge George Jeffreys (1648–1689) often sat here, and Sir Walter Raleigh (1552–1618) was condemned to death here in 1602. It was a county court until the 1970s, when the new law courts were built.

The star exhibit in the Great Hall is the Round Table, which is mounted on the west wall. Measuring some 18ft (5.5m) across, the table shows King Arthur in Tudor clothing and has the names of his knights around the edge.

Behind the Great Hall is Queen Eleanor's Garden, said to be a faithful representation of a medieval garden. On the southeast side of the Great Hall are some excavations of William the Conqueror's castle, which have excellent viewing platforms and information panels.

To the west of the Great Hall, and approached via Queen Eleanor's Garden, is the **Peninsula Barracks (16)**, the home of no fewer than five regimental museums including that of the Gurkhas. Winchester has always been a garrison town, and several centuries of military tradition are on display in the museums. Return to the Westgate and walk back down the High Street. Turn right at the City Cross through a narrow passageway past the City Museum, and return to the west front of the cathedral, where the tour concludes.

College Street from Kingsgate

CHICHESTER

Access: Chichester is some five miles (8km) from the coast (it is often claimed Chichester has the only English cathedral that can be seen from the sea). The A27, which becomes the M27 to the west of Chichester, is the main east–west coastal road in Southeast England. A number of other main roads lead to the city from the north and south. There are coach services to London. The main south coast railway line from Brighton to Southampton runs through the city, with the station located on the south side of the ring road. There are twice-hourly services to London Victoria and hourly services to London Waterloo. The nearest international airport is London Gatwick, with which Chichester is connected by coach. Ferry services from the continent arrive at Portsmouth, some 12 miles (19km) to the west.

Although there were certainly Bronze Age people living in the area, Chichester's history really begins with the Romans. Around AD40, the Romans established a strategic base at Fishbourne, near one of the arms of Chichester harbour. Within a few years they formed a settlement, Noviomagnus, at Chichester itself. Walls of earth and timber were built around the town and the cross-like street plan that survives to the present day was laid out. Roman roads radiated out from Noviomagnus, including Stane Street, which ran northeast to Londinium.

The Romans left around AD410 and there gradually followed a large-scale settlement of people from Lower Saxony. Among these immigrants was a chieftain whose son Cissa is believed to have given his name to the present-day town – 'Chichester' can be parsed as 'Cissa's fortified place'. The Saxons increasingly suffered from Viking raids, and in the 9th century the original Roman walls were rebuilt as part of King Alfred's scheme to construct a chain of fortified towns. The Saxons, under Saint Wilfrid or Wilfrith (634–709), a former Bishop of York in exile, built a small cathedral at Selsey to the south.

Following the Conquest, William I decreed that all bishoprics should be in large centres of population, so in 1075 the Selsey see was moved to Chichester. In 1100, work on a new cathedral began under Bishop Ralph de Luffa. Enough of the building was completed by 1108 for it to be consecrated. Despite delays caused by fires, much of the building had been completed (in Romanesque style) by 1123. In the 12th century another fire destroyed the wooden roof. Bishop Seffrid (in office 1180–1204) rebuilt it with stone vaulting and added a clerestory. The ubiquitous Purbeck Marble, in the form of shafts, was also introduced at this time, along with flying buttresses on the exterior.

The 13th century saw the addition of a number of chapels and porches in the nave aisles, mainly in Early English style. These made it one of the widest English cathedrals at this time. This century was also important for the episcopate of Richard of Wych – later to become St Richard of Chichester. His shrine attracted pilgrims in large numbers. During the 14th century, the Lady Chapel was extended with three more bays and the quire was laid out in much the form we see today.

The 15th century was marked by the addition of the somewhat asymmetrical cloisters and the completion of the bell tower – the only remaining detached example among English cathedrals. John Arundel (in office 1459–78) was responsible for the stone quire screen or pulpitum.

The Reformation proved an eventful time for Chichester. The cathedral was perhaps fortunate in having as bishop Robert Sherburne (in office 1508–36), who had been secretary to Henry VII and was very much a 'political' bishop. He accepted Henry VIII's changes to the religious system and followed a practical and accommodating course. As a result Chichester did not suffer the damage which many other English cathedrals received during the Reformation, although the Shrine of St Richard was a notable casualty.

The city of Chichester had become a thriving market town meanwhile, its prosperity being based largely on the wool trade, with needlemaking another important local industry. During the Civil War most of the local traders and merchants supported the Parliamentarians, while the religious elements were staunchly Royalist. Parliamentarians besieged the city for several days in 1642 before the Royalists surrendered. At this time, street markets were held on Wednesdays and Saturdays, with livestock an important trade. The Sloe Fair, dating from 1107, was also a popular event.

Like so many others around the country, Chichester Cathedral had suffered from centuries of decay and neglect. It had to wait until the more prosperous Victorian times for extensive restoration. Additional problems were caused by the fall of the spire in 1861, when the eroded stonework and structural weaknesses became obvious. The initial reconstruction of the spire was carried out by Sir George Gilbert Scott (1811–1878), and his work set the pattern for the continual restoration up to the present day.

One remarkable feature of Chichester Cathedral is the way in which modern works of art have been incorporated into the building in complete harmony with the medieval architecture. These include the font (1983), Graham Sutherland's painting *Noli me Tangere*, Skelton's statue of *Our Lady and the Holy Child*, the John Piper tapestry (1966) behind the high altar, the Anglo-German tapestry (1985) at the location of the Shrine of St Richard, and the modern glass of the Marc Chagall window (1978).

TOUR OF THE CATHEDRAL

Start: The west front.
Finish: The font and west door.

The **West Front (1)** is marked by its two squat towers. The northwest tower collapsed in 1635 and was not rebuilt until 1901. Further away to the northwest is the detached bell tower, the only one still remaining at any English cathedral. Dating from the first decade of the 15th century, it has three stages and is capped with an octagonal lantern; it is 120ft (36.5m) in height, matching the elevation of the two west towers. The ground floor is occupied by the cathedral giftshop.

Enter the cathedral through the much altered and renovated west door. On the right is a welcome desk; although there is no pressure to make a donation, you will probably wish to do so.

Step forward into the **Nave (2)**. This fine Romanesque structure clearly owes much to Winchester. It was begun in 1114, but the vaulting and much of the facing were introduced only after a serious fire in 1187. It is of unusual proportions, with the clerestory and triforium of greater combined depth than the arcade. The latter has massive multiform piers with vertical engaged shafts. The main arches of the triforium enclose smaller twin arches (as at Winchester). The clerestory, which was added a century after the rest of the nave, leads up to simple vaulting. There are double aisles on each side of the nave.

Turn back to the northwest corner of the nave to find **St Michael's Chapel (3)**, the Sailors' Chapel, dedicated in 1956 to men from Sussex who had lost their lives at sea during World War II. Note the ship's bell from HMS *Sussex*, above which is the Royal Yacht Squadron burgee flown by Sir Francis Chichester (1901–1972) when he sailed around the world in *Gypsy Moth* in 1966–7.

Leave the chapel and walk along the north aisle. Turn into the side aisle, where, on the left, is the memorial **Statue of William Huskisson (4)**. Huskisson was MP for Chichester and worked to promote the construction of the Wey and Arun Canal, but is probably best remembered as the first prominent person to be killed by a train. He was knocked down in 1830 on the day the Manchester and Liverpool Railway was opened.

Famous Sons and Daughters

Return to the north aisle and proceed eastwards. On the left is the **Arundel Tomb (5)**. The effigies are almost certainly that of Richard Fitzalan (*c*1307–1376), 13th Earl of Arundel, and his wife Eleanor. They were originally buried in the chapter house of Lewes Priory, but were brought here after the Dissolution. The lady's crossed legs and the pair's joined hands are unusual. It was once thought that the hands were linked during the Victorian restoration, but recent research has shown this feature to be original – one of the earliest examples of this concession, permitted when the husband was a knight rather than a civilian. Another unusual monument can be seen on the right of the aisle. This is the **Monument to Joan de Vere (6)**. Joan (d1293) was the daughter of Robert de Vere, Earl of Oxford. The monument is probably the first in England to show 'weepers' – figures of mourning – along the side of the tomb. John Flaxman thought it the finest medieval effigy in England.

To the right is the pulpitum or **Bell-Arundel Screen (7)**. Erected by John Arundel (in office 1459–78), it originally had two chapels within its outer arches and virtually cut off the quire from the nave. The screen was taken down in 1859, which was timely as the spire collapsed the following year and this event would undoubtedly have destroyed it. After restoration it was eventually re-erected in 1961 as a memorial to George Bell (in office 1929–58).

Walk under the screen, noting the sturdy vaulting and strong bosses, and move into the **Quire (8)**, which lies, unusually, wholly beneath the crossing. Largely 14th-century in age, the stalls, canopies and arches are original, but needed restoration after the fall of the spire. The stalls contain a fine set of misericords dating from 1330.

The Arts, Ancient and Modern

Return through the screen and enter the north transept. There are two features here of particular note. Set in the floor is the **Memorial to Gustav Holst (9)**. A simple plaque covers the ashes of the composer (1874–1934), who had strong connections with the city. The north wall of the transept is largely covered with 16th-century **Lambert Barnard Paintings (10)**. In the form of panelled medallions, the paintings show the heads of the bishops of Chichester from St Wilfred to Robert Sherburne. The latter, it must be surmised, probably commissioned the work, as it is his face which appears on all the bishops' heads!

Leave the transept and walk along the north quire aisle. Immediately on the left is the **Treasury (11)**. Entry is via a turnstile and there is a modest admission fee. The Treasury, which occupies the former Chapel of the Four Virgins, contains the usual collection of silverware, from both the cathedral and churches within the diocese. Of particular interest are various rings and crozier heads discovered in bishops' tombs during the repair work in the 19th century.

Cross the aisle and turn right into the presbytery. Dominating this area of the cathedral is the **John Piper Tapestry (12)**. Designed by John Piper (1903–1992) in 1966, it was woven by Pinton Frères at Felletin in France. Its vivid modern colours illustrate the theme of the Holy Trinity. The high altar in front of the tapestry is of simple modern design, using contrasting limestones, and is the work of Robert Potter.

Return to the north quire aisle. Note on the left the **Memorial to Edward Storey (13)**. Storey (in office 1478–1503) gave the city its Market Cross and provided the endowment for the Prebendal School, still attended by the cathedral's choristers. At the end of the aisle is the **Chapel of St John the Baptist (14)**. The highlight of this rather uninspiring chapel is the reredos, which takes the form of a painting (1984), the work of Patrick Procktor, that shows scenes from the life of St John the Baptist and was clearly inspired by the painting by Nicholas Poussin (1594–1665). There is little stained glass of note at Chichester (the medieval glass was presumably lost during the Reformation), so it is pleasing to see the modern glass in the window next to the Chapel of St John the Baptist. This was designed by Marc Chagall (1887–1985) and made by Charles of Marq at Rheims. It was unveiled by the Duchess of Kent in 1978.

Move across into the retrochoir, where on the right (west) is the **Anglo-German Tapestry (15)**. Designed by Ursula Benker-Schirmer in 1985, it was woven in Marktredwitz in Bavaria and at West Dean College to the north of Chichester. The largely abstract design purports to show the life of St Richard of Chichester, whose shrine was located in the area of the platform in front of the tapestry. Bishop George Bell's ashes are also interred here. The platform has a modern Purbeck Marble altar, designed by Robert Potter. The candle ornaments are the work of Geoffrey Clarke.

Turn in the opposite direction and walk into the **Lady Chapel (16)**. Originally, the chapel had only two bays, but a further three were added around 1300, with the windows in Decorated style. Note Lambert Barnard's ceiling decoration, at one time probably found throughout the cathedral. Attached to a pier on the north side of the chapel is a modern (1988) sculpture of Our Lady and the Holy Child by John Skelton.

Leave the Lady Chapel and the retroquire and move into the south quire aisle. At the extreme east end is the **Chapel of St Mary Magdelene (17)**. Behind the simple altar is another of the cathedral's modern treasures, the painting *Noli me Tangere* ('Touch me Not') by Graham Sutherland (1903–1980). It shows Christ

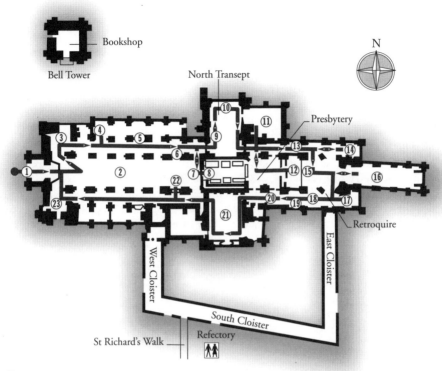

Bookshop

Bell Tower

North Transept

N

Presbytery

Retroquire

West Cloister

East Cloister

South Cloister

St Richard's Walk

Refectory

Key

1. West Front
2. Nave
3. St Michael's (Sailors') Chapel
4. Statue of William Huskisson
5. Arundel Tomb
6. Monument to Joan de Vere
7. Bell-Arundel Screen
8. Quire

9. Memorial to Gustav Holst
10. Lambert Barnard Paintings
11. Treasury
12. John Piper Tapestry
13. Memorial to Edward Storey
14. Chapel of St John the Baptist
15. Anglo-German Tapestry
16. Lady Chapel

17. Chapel of St Mary Magdlene
18. Roman Mosaic
19. 12th-Century stone carvings
20. Memorial to Robert Sherburne
21. South Transept
22. Pulpit
23. Font

appearing to Mary Magdalene after the Resurrection. The setting is Sutherland's own garden in the South of France. Further along the south quire aisle are some railings surrounding a glass panel which reveals a **Roman Mosaic (18)** from the 2nd century. It was part of the floor of a house which extended under the cathedral walls and out into the precincts and was possibly one of the major public buildings of Roman Chichester. The mosaic is made up of fragments of chalk, limestone and brick and can be illuminated by inserting a coin.

We now come to two of the most important artistic treasures in the cathedral, the **12th-Century Stone Carvings (19)** which are attached to the wall of the aisle. One shows *Christ Arriving at Bethany and Being Greeted by Mary and Martha* while the other depicts *The Raising of Lazarus*. They are thought to date from *c*1125 and may originally have formed part of a screen. These Romanesque sculptures were probably once highly coloured, and it is believed the eyes used to contain jewels.

A Reforming Bishop

Further along the aisle on the south side is the **Memorial to Robert Sherburne (20)**, bishop from 1508 until his death in 1536. This political, reforming bishop has been referred to as the 'second founder of the cathedral', and he certainly left his mark in a number of ways.

Next step into the **South Transept (21)**, where the dominating features are two more Lambert Barnard paintings, dating from the 16th century. One panel shows King Caedwalla of Wessex granting St Wilfred land on which to build a cathedral. The second depicts Henry VIII giving an assurance to the ubiquitous Sherburne that he had the right to the bishopric.

Walk into the south aisle. On the right is another of Chichester's modern additions, the **Pulpit (22)**. This was designed by Robert Potter and Geoffrey Clarke in 1966 and is made of stone-faced reinforced concrete, aluminium and leather-covered wood. Further along the aisle are two side chapels, the Chapel of St Clement and the Chapel of St George. The latter is the memorial chapel of the Royal Sussex Regiment.

Finally you come to one of the most attractive features of the cathedral, the modern **Font (23)**. It was designed by John Skelton in 1983 and is made of polyphant stone from Cornwall, with the bowl of beaten copper. On the wall behind, a miniature version acts as a sconce, and beside it is a painting by Hans Feibusch (1898–1998), *The Baptism of Christ* (1951), one of the earliest of the modern additions to the cathedral.

The tour concludes here – exit by the west door.

WALKING TOUR FROM CHICHESTER CATHEDRAL

The tour begins by exploring the cathedral precincts, including the cloisters and two ancient gateways. You then move into the historic core of the city, where there is a variety of interesting domestic architecture, particularly in the area called The Pallants. A short stretch of the city walls is walked before you return along an old Roman street to the City Cross and the cathedral. Less mobile visitors will appreciate the walk being almost entirely on the flat.

Start and finish: The west front of the cathedral.
Length: 1½ miles (2.4km).
Time: Little over an hour, but allow extra time to visit the Pallant House Gallery and the City Museum.
Refreshments: The cathedral's refectory (closed Sundays) is just off the south cloister, and tables spill out into the walled garden during the summer months. Near the cathedral, in South Street, is the Medieval Crypt Restaurant. Pubs with atmosphere are thin on the ground, but try the White Horse in South Street (which claims to be Chichester's oldest pub), the Hole in the Wall Tavern in St Martin's Street (off East Street) and the Dolphin and Anchor in West Street, opposite the cathedral, which also offers accommodation.

From the west front of the cathedral take the path southwards (i.e., in the opposite direction to the bell tower); the buildings of the Prebendal School are on the right.

Swing around to the left, parallel to the south side of the cathedral; there is a good view of some of the recent restorations to the stonework.

Pass through a gateway into the **Cloisters (1)**. Built *c*1400, these were extensively restored in Victorian times. They do not form a perfect square: if they did they wouldn't fit into the shape left by the nave and the south transept. Chichester was never a monastic cathedral, so monks never strolled these cloisters in contemplation. The architecture is simple and the roof is wooden, made of Irish oak.

The west cloister leads to **St Richard's Porch (2)**, which has a double-arched entrance supported by thin Purbeck marble columns. Between the arches is a statue of St Richard dating from 1894. The south doorway beyond has some dogtooth ornamentation; this and the vaulting above are in Early English style.

Return to the south cloister and leave the area via a doorway to St Richard's Walk, which has some interesting Georgian-fronted houses. This leads to Canon Lane, with the 18th-century Deanery immediately opposite. (Look back from the end of St Richard's Walk for a superb view of the cathedral.) Walk briefly to the right, towards **Palace Gateway (3)**. This dates from the 14th century and was the gatehouse for the Bishop's Palace. Through the gateway and immediately to the right there is a view of the brick- and flint-built Bishop's Palace. Parts of the building date back to the 13th century; it is now largely used by the Prebendal School.

Return to Canon Lane and head towards the east end. Note on the left **Vicars' Close (4)**, a terrace of four 15th-century houses, once occupied by the Vicars Choral; the hall at the end of the path was once their refectory. Vicars' Close was initially a square, but the original rears of the houses to the right were converted to shops in South Street and this side blocked off with a wall. Return to Canon Lane and walk through **Canon Gate (5)**. This flint-built gatehouse was constructed in the 15th century, but had extensive renovation in 1894.

The Pallants

You are now in South Street. Turn left and walk towards the city centre. Note on the left the Medieval Crypt, now a restaurant. Most of the buildings on this side of the road are still owned by the Church Commissioners. Opposite is the White Horse Inn, which dates from 1416 and claims to be the oldest pub in the city. Cross South Street and take the narrow road – West Pallant – at the side of the White Horse.

You are now approaching the area known as **The Pallants (6)**. Four roads – North, South, East and West Pallant – form a cross. The name comes from the fact that the Archbishop of Canterbury once had a palantine, or exclusive jurisdiction here over this area. The Pallants have some delightful Georgian domestic architecture, with former wealthy merchants' house alongside those of artisans. Some of the larger buildings have now become offices and it is interesting to see how the smaller houses have been gentrified in recent years – indeed, The Pallants remains a very desirable place to live. As you walk along West Pallant, note on your left the redundant Church of All Saints, which dates back to the 13th century.

West Pallant leads to the crossroads in the centre of The Pallants, and here you find **Pallant House (7)**, claimed to be one of the finest Queen Anne houses in the England. Built in 1712 for Henry Peckham, a wealthy local wine merchant, it is now home to a good collection of porcelain, sculpture and paintings, mainly of the British

Modern School, including works by Sutherland, Moore, Piper and Nash. The rooms have been faithfully restored, each reflecting a different period in the house's history, and a peaceful walled garden in formal Georgian style can be enjoyed at the rear. The stone birds on the front gateway are dodos.

Leave The Pallants via East Pallant, turning left into Baffin's Lane. At the end of the lane, fronting East Street, is the former **Corn Exchange (8)**, with its imposing

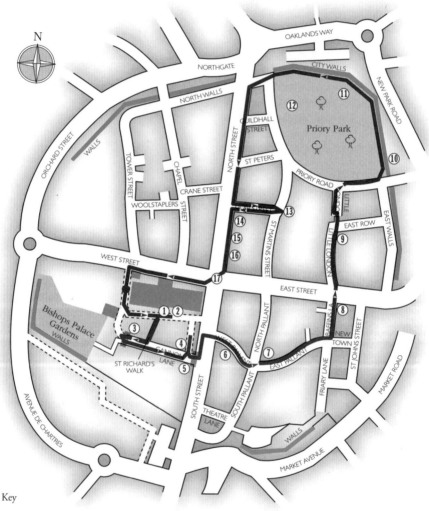

Key

1. Cloisters
2. St Richard's Porch
3. Palace Gateway
4. Vicars' Close
5. Canon Gate
6. The Pallants

7. Pallant House
8. Corn Exchange
9. City Museum
10. City Walls
11. Castle Mound
12. Franciscan Friary

13. St Mary's Hospital
14. Council Chamber
15. Butter Market
16. St Olave's Church
17. Market Cross

Classical frontage. This has a fascinating history. Built in 1830, it was first used for the auctioning of corn and later became a popular theatre, before hosting the city's first moving-picture show in 1896. It remained a cinema until 1980, and is now, regrettably, a branch of a fast-food chain.

Cross East Street and turn into Little London. There are various fanciful suggestions – generally linked to royalty – as to how the street got its name, but none quite rings true. On the right, on the corner of East Row, is the **City Museum (9)**, housed in a former 18th-century granary; on its outer wall there is an iron

The Canon Gate

hoist which was used to lift sacks of grain to the upper floors. The museum displays objects and artefacts from the Chichester area from prehistoric times to the present day.

City Defences

Continue along Little London until you reach Priory Road: Priory Park lies ahead. Turn right and walk up onto the **City Walls (10)**, first built by the Romans during the 2nd century AD. Originally made of earth, they were later faced with flint and mortar. Most of the walls survive; they can be traced for 1½ miles (2.4km) and enclose 101 acres (41 hectares) of the city. They were last used for defence in 1642, when the city was besieged by Cromwell's army during the Civil War.

Turn left and walk around the walls in an anticlockwise direction, following the edge of Priory Park. There are two main features in the park. In the northern corner is the shrub-covered **Castle Mound (11)**, once the site of a wooden Norman castle, destroyed in 1217. Nearby are the remains of the 13th-century **Franciscan Friary (12)**. All that is left of the Grey Friars is the chancel of the monastic church. This building, which stands isolated in the park, became the Guildhall and is now the Guildhall Museum. Its displays mainly concern the history of the city and Priory Park.

Leave the City Walls at what was the site of the North Gate. If you're keen to see the rest of the walls, there's a useful brochure available from the Tourist Information Centre in South Street.

Now turn left into North Street and head back towards the city centre. The pedestrianized North Street is full of interest. On the left, make a brief detour along Lion Street. This shortly leads to St Martins Square, on the far side of which is **St Mary's Hospital (13)**. The hospital dates back to 1269, later becoming an almshouse administered by the cathedral chapter, and this is still its function. At the east end of the building is a chapel where residents are obliged to attend a daily service.

Justice and Trade

Return along Lion Street to North Street. Immediately on the left is the **Council Chamber (14)**. This brick building has a Classical façade with Ionic columns and dates back to 1731, the Assembly Rooms being added at the rear some fifty years later – these were used as a courthouse until 1940. Set into the wall to the left of the main entrance is the Neptune and Minerva Stone. This slab was found nearby in 1723 and is believed to have come from a Roman temple on the site.

A few steps along from the Council Chamber is the Market House or **Butter Market (15)**, built in 1807, probably to a design by Nash, in an effort to introduce hygiene and order to market days. Thenceforth, all fresh food had to be sold under the cover of the Butter Market. It now has two storeys of specialist shops and stalls.

On the left, further towards the town centre, is the tiny **St Olave's Church (16)**, now an SPCK shop. This church has Saxon origins; it is older than the cathedral and thought to be dedicated to King Olaf Haraldsson (995–1030), Patron Saint of Norway, canonized in 1164. The church may have been built by Scandinavian merchants, who traded with the city. It had some extensive Victorian restoration, but there is still lots of Saxon work to see.

The city centre is reached at the **Market Cross (17)**, the focal point of the Roman street plan. The Cross was built by Bishop Storey in 1501 as a place for local citizens to sell their goods. He also founded the Prebendal School where the cathedral choristers are still educated.

Proceed into West Street, where the cathedral – and the end of your walk – can be seen on the left.

The Bishop's Palace with the Cathedral in the background

OXFORD

Access: Oxford lies in the Vale of Oxford at the confluence of the Thames and the Cherwell. It is 40 miles (65km) by road from London, from which it is easily reached by the M25 and the M40. (Drivers are advised to use the 'Park and Ride' system.) The Oxford Bus Company runs frequent coach services to London's Victoria Coach Station. Trains run hourly (more frequently at busy times) from London's Paddington station. Airports within reach include Luton, Birmingham, Heathrow and Gatwick. The CityLink coach service runs regularly to both Heathrow and Gatwick, while National Express operates six services a day to Birmingham Airport.

There is evidence of Bronze Age and Iron Age settlement in the Oxford area, but its low-lying surroundings were not attractive to the Romans. At the fall of the Roman Empire, however, Roman soldiers settled in the region to become farmers. By Anglo-Saxon times the Thames had become a strategic boundary between the kingdoms of Wessex and Mercia. It is believed that around AD730 St Frideswide (d *c*735) founded the first abbey on the present site of Christ Church, and the original town clustered around the building. Frideswide was to become the Patron Saint of Oxford.

Shortly after the Norman Conquest a castle was built on the western side of the town. Early in the next century, the convent was reformed to become an Augustinian priory. The present Christ Church was begun by Prior Robert of Cricklade around 1150, and within eighty years a spire and a Lady Chapel had been completed and the chapter house rebuilt. Not until 1500, however, was the roof vaulted.

Meanwhile the town was attracting scholars from all over the country and indeed from Europe. By the 13th century much of the teaching was being carried out by friars, and students were living in halls around the town. Powerful bishop-philanthropists began to establish colleges, which initially catered only for graduates. In 1379 New College was founded and immediately accepted undergraduates, which was the start of the gradual move in influence from the academic halls to the colleges.

By 1400 Oxford had a population of 6000, making it one of the largest towns in the country. Water mills had been built along the rivers, and industries such as cloth- and leathermaking had developed, while the growing university also provided much employment. The year 1478 was marked by the first book to be printed in the town, and the first library appeared ten years later.

In 1525 Cardinal Thomas Wolsey (*c*1475–1530) founded Cardinal's College on the site of St Frideswide's Monastery, but when Wolsey fell from grace in 1529 Henry VIII took over the half-finished college and it was renamed King Henry VIII's College. The Reformation (and the consequent Dissolution of the Monasteries) was a crucial time for Oxford, but Henry decided to retain the colleges and use them to educate his supporters. The diocese of Oxford was created in 1542 and Christ Church – as King Henry VIII's College was now known – became, uniquely, both a cathedral and a college. The mid-1500s also saw the Protestant

Martyrs – Thomas Cranmer (1489–1556), Hugh Latimer (*c*1485–1555) and Nicholas Ridley (*c*1500–1555) – burnt at the stake in Oxford at what is now Broad Street. Later in the century Elizabeth I visited the city, which was expanding considerably along with the university.

During the Civil War Oxford was a Royalist centre, and Charles I used the city as his headquarters for four years. In 1646, however, Oxford was besieged by the Parliamentary army of General Thomas Fairfax (1612–1671). Charles fled in disguise and shortly afterwards the city surrendered. Thereafter Oxford continued to expand: the Botanic Gardens, the Sheldonian Theatre (designed by a young Christopher Wren) and the Ashmolean Museum date from this period. At Christ Church, Tom Quad was completed with canons' houses instead of Wolsey's proposed chapel and cloisters, while Wren's Tom Tower, with its ogee capping, also appeared.

In 1748 the Radcliffe Camera was built, and the remainder of the century saw some startling changes. In 1771 the Pavement Commission was set up, and as a result much of the medieval town was destroyed. Roads were widened and the Magdalen Bridge was constructed. The year 1790 saw the coming of the Oxford Canal; this brought coal from the Midlands and for the next half-century Oxford was a busy inland port. When the railway came in 1844 much of the canal trade disappeared, but today the canal is popular with leisure traffic. In 1879 Oxford's first two female colleges, Lady Margaret Hall and Somerville, were opened.

The Victorian period in Britain saw many cathedrals subject to restoration, which was often unfortunate. The Christ Church renovations, however, carried out by Sir George Gilbert Scott (1811–1878) in the 1870s, were largely undertaken in a sympathetic way. The neo-Norman windows at the east end belong to this period, as do the chancel stalls and the wrought-iron screens. G.F. Bodley (1827–1907) designed an ornate bell tower, but the Governing Body had second thoughts and it was never completed. The bells were rehung, rather inappropriately, under the hall stairs.

In 1913 William Morris (1877–1963) built his car factory at Cowley on the outskirts of Oxford. This was to become the major employer in the city for the rest of the century. Morris became Lord Nuffield and was an important benefactor to the university, particularly in the sciences and medicine.

Oxford suffered minimal damage during the two world wars, and also survived the proposal to build a link road across Christ Church Meadow – an outrageous scheme which was fortunately thrown out. The postwar period saw a number of additions to the Christ Church site. In 1967, the Picture Gallery was opened in the Deanery Garden. This award-winning building has an important collection of Old Masters, along with special exhibitions of contemporary art. The following year saw the opening of Blue Boar Quad, close to Blue Boar Street. Finally, in 1986, St Aldgate's Quad was built on the far side of St Aldgate's Road.

Today, Christ Church finds itself in a unique position. It is Oxford's largest and wealthiest college and also a cathedral – but one of England's smallest cathedrals in what is the country's largest diocese. Another interesting quirk is that four of its canons are also professors – all of which adds to the fascination of this building, which attracts nearly a quarter of a million visitors annually.

TOUR OF THE CATHEDRAL
Start: Meadow Buildings.
Finish: The west door.

Approach Christ Church from the city centre along St Aldgate's, but do not enter via the gateway under Tom Tower. Carry on to the end of the building and turn left at the path which leads to Christ Church Meadow. Just inside the gateway is probably the only spot to get a decent photograph of the exterior of the cathedral.

Carry on to Meadow Buildings. Halfway along the buildings is the porch where entrance is gained to the cathedral and other areas of Christ Church, and where you'll need to pay your admission fee. Follow the path round to the left and turn under an archway which leads to the **Cloisters (1)**. These were built in the 15th century along with the former refectory on the south side and the dormitory to the east. The cathedral occupies the north side, but the western side of the cloisters was destroyed by Wolsey, who planned more magnificent ones around Tom Quad.

Halfway along the east side of the cloisters (to the right) is the 13th-century

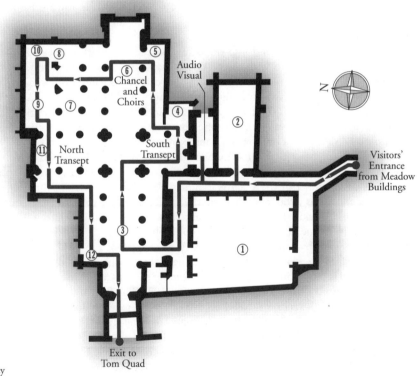

Key

1. Cloisters	5. St Catherine Window	9. Latin Chapel
2. Chapter House	6. Chancel	10. St Frideswide Window
3. Nave	7. Lady Chapel	11. St Michael Window
4. Becket Window	8. Shrine of St Frideswide	12. Jonah Window

Chapter House (2), which also functions today as a souvenir shop and the treasury. Unfortunately, the paraphernalia of the shop distracts from the essential simplicity of the Early English architecture, with its lancet windows showing detached shafts and stiff-leaved foliage in the spandrels. The chapter house has some interesting stained glass, dating from between the 15th and 17th centuries. Note also the unusual roof bosses. There is an audiovisual presentation in the room next to the chapter house.

Inside the Cathedral
Leave the chapter house and move round the north side of the cloisters to enter the southwest corner of the cathedral. On reaching the **Nave (3)** one is immediately struck by the small size of this area – but remember that Wolsey demolished the three western bays of the priory church to accommodate his Great Quadrangle. An unusual feature is that the pews in the nave face inwards, no doubt because the cathedral is also the college chapel. Note the curious double arches of the Norman arcade – probably a device for suggesting greater height, but not a successful feature. The pulpit is Jacobean. Nearby is the bust of Dean Henry Aldrich (1647–1710), the noted scholar and architect, while on a pillar close to the vice-chancellor's stall is the memorial to Bishop George Berkeley (1685–1753), after whom the Californian town is named.

Great Windows
Move along the south aisle and into the barely perceptible south transept. The east side of this area is taken up with the St Lucy Chapel, where one finds the **Becket Window (4)**. This, the oldest window in the cathedral, dates from *c*1320. The central panel of stained glass shows the martyrdom of Archbishop Thomas à Becket (*c*1118–1170), murdered in Canterbury Cathedral in 1170, although the original face of Becket is missing: it was removed after the Reformation, Becket having been posthumously declared a traitor. The removal of the face was not the act of vandalism you might at first think, because it allowed the authorities to save the window as a whole. Also in this area are a number of memorials to Cavalier supporters of Charles I in the Civil War, plus the unmarked graves of three of the king's young cousins who also died in the conflict. Note, too, the flags of the Oxfordshire and Buckinghamshire Regiment; these date from the Crimean War and World War I. In the nearby aisle is the tomb of Robert King (d1557), first Bishop of Oxford and before that last Abbot of Osney Abbey, suppressed in 1542.

Walk back into the main body of the building and turn right along the south choir aisle. At the end is the Military Chapel, which features the **St Catherine Window (5)**, designed by Edward Burne-Jones (1833–1898) in 1878. The face of the central figure, Saint Catherine of Alexandria, is based on that of Edith Liddell, whose sister Alice was the inspiration for Lewis Carroll's *Alice's Adventures in Wonderland* (1865).

You now enter the **Chancel (6)**, which includes the choir. This is the area of the cathedral which all serious students of architecture come to see. The attraction is the pendant lierne vault, which dates from the end of the 15th century, replacing the original Norman timber roof; its designer, William Orchard, did much work at the Divinity School. Each bay has a star pattern of strong lierne ribs with a series of pendant lanterns which seem to defy gravity and which were a daring design for that period of architecture. Closer inspection shows they are supported by moulded ribs which form a series of arches. The vaulting makes an elegant contrast to the simple Norman arches below. The eastern end of the chancel was rebuilt by Scott in the 1870s. The reredos behind the high altar is attributed to Bodley and includes the figures of four saints.

St Frideswide's Shrine

Move now to the north side of the cathedral, where there are two parallel chapels. The first is the 13th-century **Lady Chapel (7)**. The most significant feature here is the **Shrine of St Frideswide (8)**, built in 1289 to house the relics of the Anglo-Saxon princess who founded the original monastery on the site of Christ Church and who is now the Patron Saint of Oxford. The shrine, originally brightly painted, was destroyed at the Reformation and the saint's remains buried nearby. The shattered stonework of the shrine was recovered in the 19th century and reassembled, although the original silk canopy has been lost. Opposite the shrine is a large wooden structure which was probably a watching loft to guard the relics from visiting pilgrims. The only other watching loft existing in an English cathedral is at St Albans.

The second chapel is the **Latin Chapel (9)**, built in 1330, which gained its name from the services, traditionally said in Latin until 1861. Today the chapel is used for private prayer. On the far side of the Latin Chapel are windows with 14th-century glass, while on the south side are three tombs dating from the same period: of Lady Elizabeth Montacute, a benefactor of the original monastery; of Alexander de Sutton, a 13th-century prior of the Augustinian Monastery of St Frideswide; and of an unknown knight of the 14th century – whoever he was, he was a huge man for his day, measuring 6ft 6in (2m) tall! The feature of interest in the Latin Chapel, however, is the **St Frideswide Window (10)**, designed by Burne-Jones in 1858 and considered one of his best works. The lower windows depict the life of St Frideswide, while a roundel at the top shows a boat carrying the saint to Heaven.

Step now through the north transept, where the only item of interest is the dominating **St Michael Window (11)**, made by Clayton and Bell in the early 19th century. The glass shows St Michael (and his angels) fighting a dragon. Carry on into the north aisle, at the end of which is the altogether more interesting **Jonah Window (12)**, made by the Dutchman Abraham van Linge around 1630. The figure of Jonah, shown surveying the city of Ninevah, is made of traditional stained glass, but the remainder of the window has been produced by painting the glass with coloured ground glass mixed with oil and water – a technique later to become quite common.

Leave the cathedral by the west door, which leads out into Tom Quad.

WALKING TOUR FROM CHRIST CHURCH CATHEDRAL

The tour is in two parts. The first is a short walk around Christ Church, Oxford's most interesting and prestigious college. The longer second part is a circular walk which takes in some other well-known Oxford colleges, such as Merton, Magdalen, Hertford and Trinity, along with notable city features like the Radcliffe Camera, the Bodleian Library and the Sheldonian Theatre. The tour also includes a section of Christ Church Meadow and the Botanical Gardens. Oxford is so full of fascination that half a dozen similarly intriguing walks could be made, but this tour probably contains the most interesting features of the city for those with limited time.

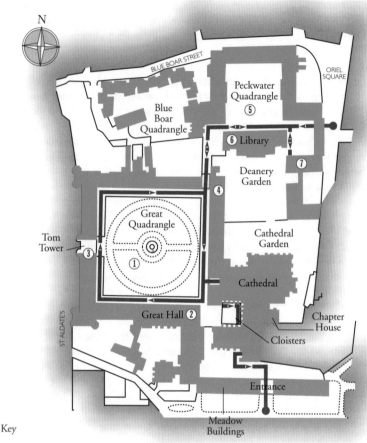

N

BLUE BOAR STREET

ORIEL SQUARE

Peckwater Quadrangle
⑤

Blue Boar Quadrangle

⑥ Library

⑦

Deanery Garden

④

Great Quadrangle
◎
①

Tom Tower
③

Cathedral Garden

ST ALDATES

Cathedral

Great Hall ②

Chapter House

Cloisters

Entrance

Meadow Buildings

Key

1. Great Quadrangle
2. Great Hall
3. Tom Tower

4. Deanery
5. Peckwater Quadrangle
6. Library

7. Picture Gallery

Start (shorter walk): The west front of the Cathedral.
Finish (shorter walk): The cathedral entrance.
Start (longer walk): The west front of the Cathedral.
Finish (longer walk): The Carfax Tower.
Total length: 2½ miles (4km).
Total time: 1½ hours, but allow longer for visits to museums, gardens and churches.
Refreshments: You are quite spoilt for choice at lunchtime in Oxford, with a vast range of bistros, wine bars and ancient inns. Popular student pubs include the 16th-century Turf Tavern, off Holywell Street, the King's Arms, on the corner of Holywell Street and Parks Road, the Golden Cross, in the nicely restored Golden Cross Yard and the 15th-century Chequers Inn, in the High Street.
Note: The Oxford colleges are private, working institutions. Do not wander around them without permission. Most are closed during the morning, while some will

accept visitors only if they are accompanied by the official blue-badged guides. Some colleges, such as Christ Church, charge for entry. Always check at the porter's lodge to ascertain the conditions of entry.

AROUND CHRIST CHURCH

Leave the cathedral via the West Door to the **Great Quadrangle (1)** or, as it's usually known, Tom Quad. This was the brainchild of Cardinal Thomas Wolsey, who from humble beginnings became a student at Magdalen College before rising to become Archbishop of Canterbury and Chancellor of England. He decided to found a new college in Oxford, and the project was started in 1525. Four years later, however, he fell from grace and all work ceased. It was the next century before work recommenced and the north side of the quad was completed. The Great Quadrangle is the largest in Oxford; to accommodate it Wolsey had to demolish the three westernmost bays of the cathedral nave. He had intended that the quad should be cloistered; although this plan never came to fruition, the arches can be seen set into the walls. Note the small pond in the centre of the Great Quadrangle containing the Statue of Mercury. The water in the pond was intended for use in fighting fires.

Walk clockwise around the quad. Almost immediately on the left is a doorway, with stairs leading to the **Great Hall (2)**. When climbing the stairs, note the fan vaulted ceiling, which spreads from a single elegant column. The vaulting was constructed in 1640 during the time of Dean Samuel Fell. From the landing, enter the hall, which is the biggest in Oxford. It has a superb black-and-gilded hammer-beam roof, and both the walls and the ceiling sport literally hundreds of coats-of-arms. The walls are festooned with paintings of former alumni of Christ Church, including six prime ministers and other notables such as William Penn (1644–1718), W.H. Auden (1907–1973), John Locke (1632–1704) and Charles Dodgson (1832–1898), better known as Lewis Carroll. The hall is used daily for dining by the junior and senior members of the college.

Descend the stairs and return to the Great Quadrangle. Turn left and continue around the quad in a clockwise direction. In the middle of the west side is the main entrance to the quad, capped by one of Oxford's best known landmarks, **Tom Tower (3)**. The tower dates from 1681 and was designed by Christopher Wren (1632–1723). Its bell, known as Great Tom and said to weigh seven tons, came from Osney Abbey, destroyed at the Dissolution. Great Tom is so-named not after Thomas Wolsey but after Thomas à Becket. At 21:05 each evening the bell rings 101 times, once for each member of the original college. This is done by 'Oxford time', five minutes behind GMT – the city being five minutes west of Greenwich!

Continue around the north side of the quad (completed in the 17th century) until you reach the northeast corner. This is occupied by the **Deanery (4)**, which has a fine castellated parapet. The dean of the cathedral also governs the college. It was in this building that Charles I lived during much of the Civil War.

Lesser Quads

Pass through the archway and walk on into **Peckwater Quadrangle (5)**, built during the 17th-century expansion of the college on the site of the medieval Peckwater Inn. The quad's design was the work of Dean Aldrich, said to have been a disciple of Wren. One of the buildings around the quad is the **Library (6)**, completed in

1772; its style, unlike that of the rest of the quad, is Classical, with strong Corinthian columns supporting a massive cornice and balustrade. The upper floor of the library is one of the most beautiful places in the city; its shelves and columns are made of dark Norwegian oak, capped by a delightful pink-and-white stucco ceiling. But you will have to take my word for this: the library is not open to visitors.

Move along the front of the library into the small, cobbled Canterbury Quad. This was the site of Canterbury College, demolished when Wolsey redesigned the area. On the right of the quad is the **Picture Gallery (7)**. Christ Church is the only Oxford College to have an important collection of Old Master paintings: there are works here by Frans Hals (*c*1580–1666), Tintoretto (*c*1518–1594), Anthony Van Dyck (1599–1641), Michelangelo (1475–1564) and Raphael (1483–1520).

If you don't wish to take the longer walk, exit via Canterbury Quad into Orion Square, which leads northwards into the High Street. Otherwise, return to the cathedral entrance in Meadow Buildings via Peckwater Quadrangle, the Great Quadrangle and the cathedral cloisters.

BEYOND CHRIST CHURCH

Leave the cathedral entrance at Meadow Buildings and turn left along Broad Walk towards **Christ Church Meadow (8)**. Today the Meadow is largely given over to playing fields, which lead down to the River Cherwell, a popular punting venue. A recent proposal to build a relief road across the Meadow was sensibly thrown out.

After following Broad Walk for a few yards, turn left and follow the wall northwards. Halfway along the path is a gate in the wall which gives good views towards the east end of the cathedral. Carry on to the end of the path to an iron 'kissing gate' that leads to a track between Merton and Corpus Christi colleges. Do not go through this gate, but turn right here along the path called Dead Man's Walk. The wall to your left marks the southern boundary of the grounds of **Merton College (9)**. Founded in 1264, Merton is almost certainly the oldest of the Oxford colleges in terms of both statutes and buildings, such as the medieval library. You cannot enter Merton from Christ Church Meadow. Continue along Dead Man's Walk to the cottages at the end of the wall. Look for the plaque in the wall marking where James Sadler (1753–1828), England's first aeronaut, made an ascent in a fire balloon on October 4 1784, landing safely near Woodeaton.

The Botanical Gardens and Magdalen College

At the cottages turn left and head towards the iron gateway. Pass through the gate and walk north along Rose Lane to its end, where it meets High Street. Turn right and enter the **Botanic Gardens (10)**, which are fronted by an attractive parterre. The oldest in the country, they were founded in 1621 by Henry Danvers as a physic garden for the School of Medicine, and renamed the Botanic Gardens in 1784. The gardens were the original home of Oxford Ragwort, a yellow flowering plant which 'escaped', spread all over the country, and is now regarded as a troublesome weed.

Leave the Botanic Gardens and turn right to **Magdalen Bridge (11)** which spans the River Cherwell. This part of the river is popular for punting in the summer, and here is as good a place as any if you wish to try your hand at this tricky art. There has been a bridge here since 1004, when the original wooden structure was built. The first stone bridge appeared five centuries later, and was replaced by a drawbridge during the Civil War. The present bridge dates from 1772, when it

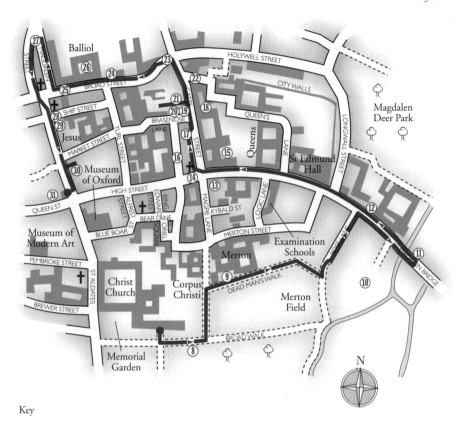

Key

formed part of the Pavement Commission's road-improvement schemes.

Across the road and adjacent to the bridge is **Magdalen College (12)**. Pronounced 'maudlin', the college was founded in 1485 by William Waynflete, Bishop of Winchester. Located outside the city's old walls, Magdalen College had room to spread and it has a sizeable deer park stretching along the Cherwell's water meadows. The deer were introduced in the 18th century to supply venison for the college. Note the dominating tower, which dates from 1505; choristers sing a Latin grace from the top of it each May Day morning, and it was used as a lookout point by the Royalists during the Civil War. The High Street frontage of Magdalen College features a superb range of gargoyles located just above the first floor windows. If you're allowed into the college, try to see the two delightful quadrangles and the chapel, which dates back to 1480.

University College and the University Church of St Mary the Virgin

Continue west along the High Street towards the town centre. The architecture here is magnificent – it led Nikolaus Pevsner to describe this as 'one of the world's greatest streets'. To the left is **University College (13)**, another to stake a claim to be the oldest college in Oxford. None of the original 13th-century buildings remain, however, as much of the college was rebuilt in the 17th century. There are two fine quadrangles to see, the Front Quad and the Radcliffe Quad, both almost identical in design, and also some statues of note: Queen Anne and Queen Mary adorn the Gate Towers, while the Front Quad has a statue of the unpopular James II (one of only two in the country). Elsewhere, a small dome covers the monument to the poet Percy Bysshe Shelley (1792–1822), expelled from University College for writing what were considered revolutionary pamphlets.

Cross the High Street opposite St Mary's Church and go through the narrow entrance to Catte Street. Turn immediately left before reaching the Radcliffe Camera and enter the **University Church of St Mary the Virgin (14)**. This church is full of interest and should not be missed. Pass through the shop to the nave, which is 15th-century Perpendicular in style. The Oxford Martyrs – Latimer, Ridley and Cranmer – were tried here for heresy before being burnt at the stake in Broad Street; the pillar opposite the pulpit was partly cut away so a wooden platform could be installed for Cranmer's trial. John Wesley (1703–1791) preached many a sermon from the pulpit before leaving to found the Methodist Church. John Henry Newman (1801–1890) was vicar here 1828–43 before converting to Catholicism and eventually becoming a cardinal. Another significant preacher was John Keble (1792–1866), whose sermon in 1833 launched the Oxford Movement. Certainly the galleries on the east and west walls help to form an auditorium worthy of the preaching of such men.

The oldest part of the church is the Adam de Brone Chapel, dating from 1328. De Brone was Rector of St Mary's and founder of what was later to become Oriel College. Note his tomb, made of Purbeck Marble and recently restored by Oriel.

Two other parts of St Mary's should not be missed. The Coffee Shop is in fact the old convocation house, built in 1320, in which for two centuries university meetings and ceremonies were held. And finally, do climb the 127 steps of the tower. The view from its parapet of the city's 'dreaming spires' is undoubtedly the best available.

Scholars and the Stage

Step out from St Mary's into Radcliffe Square. To the right is **All Souls College (15)**, the only Oxford college with no students – only graduate research Fellows. It was founded in 1473 by Henry Chichele, Archbishop of Canterbury. The main attractions are the North Quad, designed by Nicholas Hawksmoor (1661–1736), the Codrington Library, built with the proceeds of the sugar trade, and the chapel, which has a screen designed by Wren. Wren was also responsible for the attractive sundial in the quad. On the other side of Radcliffe Square is **Brasenose College (16)**. The name comes from the 'brazen nose' door knocker once attached to the main gate. At one stage it was stolen, and on recovery it was resited in the main hall. The quad dates from 1516 and features another interesting sundial.

Dominating the square is the circular **Radcliffe Camera (17)**. This Classical building surmounted by a dome was the idea of Hawksmoor and designed by James

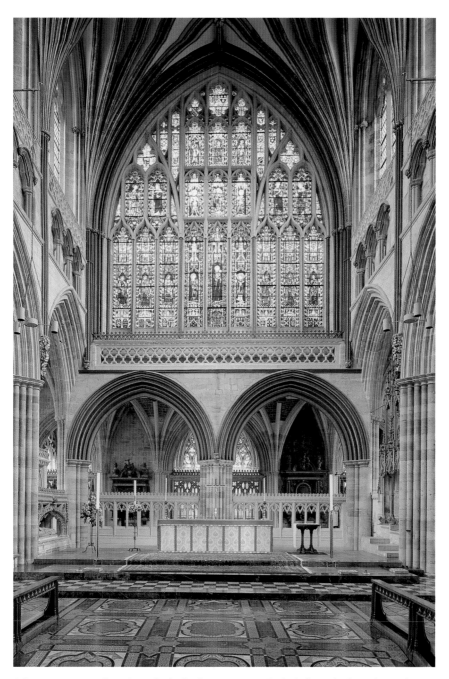

The great east window above the high altar in Exeter Cathedral was built in the 14th century, but received new Perpendicular tracery and stained glass in 1390.

Detail of the c1320 star vault in the Lady chapel at Wells Cathedral. In the centre is the figure of Christ in Glory supported by four angels.

Bishop Oliver King's new west front (early 1500s), Bath Abbey. It features climbing ladders to heaven on the stair turrets.

The 14th-century strainer arches in the eastern crossing at Salisbury Cathedral. Through them, one can see the tombs of the two bishops who built the tower and spire.

A view of the interior of Winchester Cathedral. Thetis Blacker's vibrant and detailed modern batik banners decorate the nave all the way down to the choir screen.

Chichester Cathedral from the southeast, with the Lady Chapel on the right. The cathedral has copper roofs (a cheap alternative to lead), hence their green tinge.

The fine pendant vault in the choir at Christ Church, Oxford, with Sir George Gilbert Scott's Norman-style rose east window, c 1875.

Above: *The north aisle of the crypt at Winchester Cathedral is a wonderfully eerie location for Anthony Gormley's contemporary sculpture* Sound II, *particularly when flooded.*

Above: *The ornate pulpitum screen at Chichester Cathedral, created between 1318 and 1325 (although the two openings to the choir stalls appeared only in the 1870s).*

Gibbs (1545–1754). It was completed in 1749 and named after Dr James Radcliffe (1689–1716), physician to William III. Radcliffe left £40,000 in his will for the construction of a library, and the building originally housed scientific books; it is now a reading room of the larger Bodleian Library. The Radcliffe Camera (the word means 'vaulted chamber') is not open to the public.

Pass to the right of Radcliffe Camera along Catte Street. On your right is **Hertford College (18)**, which had the distinction of being closed down in 1805 for lack of students; it was refounded in 1874. Opposite Hertford is a small square, to the south of which is the **Bodleian Library (19)**. A small opening leads into the Old Schools Quadrangle, which is built in Jacobean-Gothic style. Note the gate tower, known as the Tower of the Five Orders, which was supposedly designed to introduce students to the five orders of Classical architecture: Doric, Tuscan, Ionic, Corinthian and Composite. The library was founded by Thomas Bodley (1545–1613), who donated the initial 2000 books and made a deal with the Stationers' Company in 1610 that they would send the library a copy of every book published. It is still purely a reading library: no books can be borrowed.

Also in the complex of buildings here is the **Divinity School (20)**, entered through the doors behind the Earl of Pembroke's statue. Work began on this building in 1426 and took sixty years to complete, but the result is the finest interior in Oxford. The main attraction is the pendant lierne vaulted ceiling, with sculptured figures and 455 carved bosses. It is no surprise to learn that the architect was William Orchard, responsible for the similar ceiling in the chancel of Christ Church Cathedral.

Housed above the Divinity School is Duke Humphrey's Library, which contains a collection of manuscripts donated by Humphrey, Duke of Gloucester, in 1440. Note the sturdy beamed ceiling.

Nearby is the **Sheldonian Theatre (21)**. Described as a 'roofed-over Roman theatre', the Sheldonian is used for concerts, lectures and degree ceremonies. It was one of the first buildings designed by a youthful Christopher Wren, then still a professor of astronomy in Oxford. One of its main attractions is the flat painted ceiling. You can climb into the cupola for excellent views over the city.

Trinity and Balliol Colleges

Return to Catte Street and the junction with New College Lane, which is straddled by the **Bridge of Sighs (22)**, linking the two parts of Hertford College. The bridge was clearly inspired by the Venetian original. Continue to the end of Catte Street, where you find the junction with Broad Street, Holywell Street and Parks Road. Note on the corner the King's Arms, a popular student pub. Turn left here and proceed along Broad Street. On the right is the **New Bodleian Library (23)**, which was opened in 1930 to take the increased amount of books being published. It is connected to the old library and the Radcliffe Camera by a system of underground passages.

The next group of buildings on the right (north) side of Broad Street form **Trinity College (24)**. The original college buildings here were set up by a group of monks from Durham in 1286 but were closed down in the Reformation. The college was refounded as Trinity College by Thomas Pope (c1507–1559) in 1555.

Trinity has a Baroque chapel with limewood carvings attributed to Grinling Gibbons (1648–1721), plus some extensive gardens.

Broad Street now widens out. This was the site of the Horse Fair in the Middle Ages and the place where the Oxford Martyrs – bishops Latimer, Ridley and Cranmer – were burnt at the stake in 1555, the spot being marked by a cross. The south side of Broad Street is distinguished by a row of attractive coloured-wash buildings, among which is **The Oxford Story (25)**, a museum which describes the history of the university. Visitors go first to a 'common room', thence being whisked through the ages on a motorized desk with a headset commentary.

On the other side of Broad Street is **Balliol College (26)**, yet another claimant to the title of Oxford's oldest college. It was set up in 1263 by John de Balliol or Baliol (d1269), reputedly as a penance for insulting the Bishop of Durham. Most of its present buildings are Victorian, however, including its uninspiring little chapel. It is well known for producing politicians; alumni have included Harold Macmillan (1894–1986), Edward Heath (b1916) and Lord Jenkins of Hillhead (1920–2003).

You now reach the city centre and the main shopping area. To the right, St Giles splits into two around the Church of St Mary Magdalen. Take the right-hand arm. After about fifty yards you find on the left the **Martyrs' Memorial (27)**, erected in 1841 in memory of the Oxford Martyrs.

Return to the road junction along the left-hand arm and continue across into Cornmarket Street. Shortly you'll see to your left the **Church of St Michael-at-the-Northgate (28)**. Its late-Saxon tower – the oldest stone building in the city – was used as a lookout point. The tower was connected to the old North Gate – removed by the Pavement Commission in the late 18th century – by the Bocardo Prison, where the three bishops were held before their martyrdom.

The church itself has a number of interesting features. The window above the altar has some stained-glass medallions dating from 1290, almost certainly the oldest examples of stained glass in Oxford. The font is late-14th-century, and it is claimed that William Shakespeare (1564–1616) stood by it when acting as godfather to a Cornmarket innkeeper's child. Note also the 15th-century pulpit, from which Wesley preached a sermon in 1726. Entry to the church is free, but there is a charge to climb the tower, from where there are good views of the city's roofscapes.

You are now at Ship Street where, on the corner, is the former **Ship Inn (29)**, a picturesque half-timbered Tudor building with jettied walls. It was recently restored by Jesus College and is now partially occupied by Laura Ashley. Further along on the left, Market Street leads to the **Covered Market (30)**, yet another feature established by the Pavement Commission. It is full of atmosphere, with butchers, delicatessens and other food outlets alongside florists, boutiques and other specialist shops.

You finally arrive at the end of Cornmarket Street, at the crossroads known as the Carfax, overlooked by the **Carfax Tower (31)**. This is all that remains of the Church of St Martin's, demolished in 1896 as part of the Pavement Commission's road-widening plans. On the east side of the tower is a splendid clock, with quarterboys striking the two bells at fifteen-minute intervals. There are excellent views of the city from the top of the tower.

The walk ends at this point, some three hundred yards from Christ Church, where it began.

GLOUCESTER

Access: Road links are good. The city is less than 5 miles (8km) from the M5, leading to the Midlands and the Southwest, while the M4, which connects with London, is a 30-minute drive to the south. National Express coach services link with many parts of the country, and seats may be booked through the Tourist Information Office. Rail links are also excellent: trains from Paddington take under 2hr, and there are also direct services to Bristol, Bath, South Wales and the Midlands. The nearest international airport, at Bristol, deals mainly with charter flights.

Although there is evidence of Iron Age occupation in the area, Gloucester's significant history begins with the Romans, who built a fortress, Gleven, around AD48 at Kingsholm to guard what was then the lowest crossing point of the River Severn. Twenty years later a new fortress was built on what is now the modern city centre. The main Roman legions withdrew from Britain around AD400, to be replaced by the Saxons, who took Gloucester in 577. The city declined during the next three centuries, despite the founding of St Peter's Abbey on the present cathedral's site. The 10th century was better, due to the patronage of Aethelflaeda or Ethelflaed (d*c*917), daughter of King Alfred. In 1058 the Benedictines again rebuilt St Peter's Abbey.

William the Conqueror built the first castle at Gloucester in 1068. Fifty years later his son, Henry I, built a second castle on the site of the modern prison. In 1072 Serlo, the first Norman abbot, was appointed to the rather moribund abbey. A man of great energy and foresight, he began to build a new abbey church in 1089, the foundation stone being laid by Robert Bishop of Hereford. By 1100 the whole of the east end was completed and the church was dedicated. Serlo's successor built the nave and the cloisters, and the Norman abbey church was complete by 1126.

There was some minor rebuilding in Early English and Decorated style, and then a major reconstruction in the 14th century, financed by a rather macabre source. In 1327, the unfortunate King Edward II was murdered in Berkeley Castle. He was buried in the north choir aisle of Gloucester's Abbey Church. His son, Edward III, provided funds to transform the area around the tomb. These funds were augmented by the contributions of the pilgrims who flocked to the site. The result was one of the finest Perpendicular sections of any English cathedral and – largely due to the influx of pilgrims – the city of Gloucester became the 15th wealthiest town in the country.

Work began on the south transept in 1331, followed by the complete remodelling of the choir and presbytery. Although the Norman aisles and galleries were retained, the Perpendicular panelling gives a cage-like effect. Above, clerestory windows and a lierne vault were added. The east end was graced with a superb window, probably the largest in Medieval Europe. Attention turned in 1360 to the north transept and then in the latter part of the 14th century to the cloister, with its magnificent fan vaulting. The following century saw the addition of the superb Perpendicular tower. The rebuilding work on the cathedral was completed with the Lady Chapel, again in the Perpendicular style.

Meanwhile, Richard III had granted the city of Gloucester a town council and the county of Gloucestershire had been established. Carmelite, Franciscan and Dominican friaries had also been established in the city, although these were soon to be suppressed. During the Reformation, in 1539, St Peter's Abbey was dissolved by Henry VIII. Three years later the Abbey Church became a cathedral in its own right. Although some of the monastic buildings and various statues and other furnishings were destroyed, the cathedral survived the Reformation in reasonable condition.

Gloucester saw a considerable amount of action during the Civil War. The city was a Parliamentarian stronghold and in 1643 Charles I and 30,000 men besieged it for over a month. They eventually ended the siege when a Parliamentary force marched in from London. After the Restoration, Charles II took his revenge by knocking down the defensive walls and reducing the boundaries of the city.

The 18th century was largely a period of stagnation for the cathedral – although the city was thriving, thanks to its agriculture-based industries. This century saw the birth in Gloucester of three famous men – George Whitefield (1714–1770), the charismatic evangelist; Robert Raikes (1735–1811), the prison reformer and pioneer of Sunday Schools; and John Stafford Smith (1750–1836), who did the arrangement of a traditional English tune that Francis Scott Key (1779–1843) put words to for the US national song, *The Star-Spangled Banner*.

The 19th century saw the opening of the Gloucester and Berkeley Canal, which enabled small ships to avoid the sand banks of the Severn and stimulated an important transhipment trade in the port. Life improved in the city with the introduction of public baths, electric lighting and horse-drawn trams. This was also a time for major restoration at the cathedral, the work being largely carried out by F.S. Waller (1842–1923) and Sir George Gilbert Scott (1811–1878). The choir and presbytery were paved; the choir sub-stalls and Bishop's Throne were introduced; and a new high altar reredos designed. A considerable amount of Victorian glass appeared, mainly by Charles Eamer Kempe (1837–1907) and Christopher Whall.

Gloucester continued to develop in the 20th century, and by the 1990s had over 100,000 inhabitants. By the middle of the century, the city's docks were in terminal decline and many surrounding buildings were derelict. In the 1980s an innovative plan was devised to revive the area. The city council started the ball rolling by moving its administration to the docks and the remaining warehouses were soon converted to museums, galleries and restaurants. Gloucester Docks is now a major tourist attraction. In recent years, Gloucester Cathedral has been the location for the BBC series of Joanna Trollope's *The Choir* and two *Harry Potter* films. (Potter fans can access www.gloucestercathedral.uk.com/2001/hpotter.asp.) In 1989, a 900th anniversary appeal was launched for the restoration of the tower, which was completed in 1994. The year 2000 marked the 900th anniversary of the consecration of St Peter's Abbey.

TOUR OF THE CATHEDRAL
Start: The south porch.
Finish: The cloisters.

Enter the cathedral via the south porch, with its recently restored stonework and ancient wooden door. Proceed past the bookshop to the west end of the nave, where there is the alabaster **Statue of Edward Jenner (1)**, the Gloucestershire man who discovered the technique of vaccination against smallpox. Jenner (1749–1823) figured on one of the Royal Mail's special stamps in the lead-up to the Millennium.

Now look at the **Nave (2)**. The first impression most visitors have on entering Gloucester Cathedral is of the simplicity and severity of the massive Norman columns – in surprising contrast with the almost entirely Perpendicular style of the exterior. Above the cylindrical columns are simple arches with chevron and dogtooth decoration. At the middle level is a tiny double-arched triforium. The proportions are not aesthetically pleasing. The original wooden Norman roof was replaced in 1242 by stone vaulting which springs from the base of the triforium.

Turn to face the west end. The window, in Perpendicular style, was constructed in the early 15th century, but the glass is Victorian. It shows biblical events including the birth of Jesus, at the centre of the window, and Moses at the Red Sea.

The Great and the Good

Walk to the south nave aisle, where you see the first of over four hundred memorial tablets and plaques to the great and good of Gloucester. The majority are of little interest, but a few will be picked out on the tour. Halfway along the aisle is the **Raikes Memorial (3)**

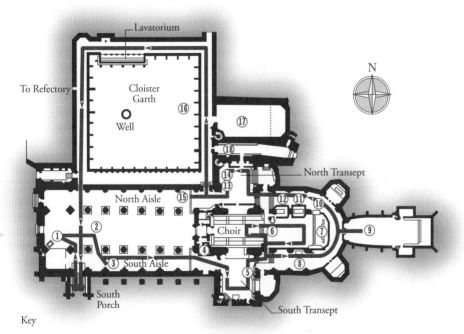

Key

1. Statue of Edward Jenner
2. Nave
3. Raikes Memorial
4. Seabroke Chantry Chapel
5. Mason's Bracket
6. Quire
7. East Window

8. Effigy of Robert, Duke of Normandy
9. Lady Chapel
10. Effigy of Osric
11. Tomb of Edward II
12. Effigy of William Parker
13. Bower Monument

14. Gloucester Cathedral Exhibition
15. Machen Memorial
16. Cloisters
17. Chapter House
18. Treasury

– a testament not to the founder of the Sunday Schools but to his younger brother, the Reverend Richard Raikes (c1743–1823). The memorial was designed by Thomas Rickman, who is credited with devising the terms 'Early English', 'Decorated' and 'Perpendicular' to describe the different styles of Gothic architecture. Nearby a Victorian stained-glass window shows the coronation of the boy king Henry III, crowned here in 1216 at age nine – the only English king since the Norman Conquest not to be crowned at Westminster Abbey.

Continue to the end of the aisle. On the left is the delightful little **Seabroke Chantry Chapel (4)**. Thomas Seabroke was Abbot of St Peters 1450–57. In addition to his alabaster effigy, there is an interesting hanging pyx which would have held communion bread and wine.

Move into the south transept, where there are two chapels – the Chapel of St John the Baptist, located behind the choir stalls, and, on the east side of the transept, St Andrew's Chapel, now used by scouts and guides. There are two items of interest in the transept itself:

The Mason's Bracket in the south transept

the huge buttress crossing the Perpendicular tracery on the east side and designed to support the old Norman tower; and the **Mason's Bracket (5)** on the west wall. Made of stone, this L-shaped monument is thought to have been made by the master mason in memory of an apprentice who fell to his death from the cathedral roof. Nearby is the entrance to the crypt, which is not usually open to visitors.

The Quire and Lady Chapel

Leave the south transept and walk eastwards, turning left into the **Quire (6)**. You now see a complete change from what has been on view before. Here we have archetypal Perpendicular architecture, the earliest in any English cathedral. The work started in the 1330s after the abbot of the time acquired the remains of the murdered King Edward II. Encouraged by his son, Edward III, and helped by the money from pilgrims who flocked to the dead king's shrine, the abbot completely remodelled the east end of the building to provide what was effectively a royal chapel within a medieval monastic church. Look first at the choir itself, which retains some of the monastic stalls, some with excellent misericords. At the west end you can admire the finely carved and decorated organ case, dating from 1665.

Turn now to the east to fully appreciate the Perpendicular architecture. It is clear that a cage-like structure masks the Norman work, which can still be seen in the aisles. The proportions here are pleasing, with a large tribune gallery topped with a massive clerestory allowing light to flood in. The imposing **East Window (7)** is almost certainly the largest cathedral window in England – it's as big as a vertical tennis court! Dating from *c*1350, it includes most of its original glass. Close inspection shows that it is not in fact flat but has two slanting 'wings', like those of a gigantic triptych. The window is said to commemorate those who fought with Edward III at the Battle of Crécy (1346). The floor of the presbytery was retiled in Victorian times, but near the high altar the steps contain a wide range of 14th-century tiles. Finally, look up at the superb lierne vaulting, showing a network of struts, three of which run parallel along the highest area. There are numerous gilded bosses, mostly foliated, but over the high altar you can see a series of angelic musicians. Few people leave this part of the cathedral without experiencing a feeling of uplift at its beauty.

Step back into the south choir aisle, now in effect the south ambulatory. Immediately on your right is a large semicircular cope chest, which dates from the 1500s. Opposite is one of the oldest memorials in the cathedral, the **Effigy of Robert, Duke of Normandy (8)**. Made of wood, it dates from *c*1260. Robert (*c*1054–1134), Duke of Normandy, the eldest son of William the Conqueror, had hoped to succeed him but was imprisoned at Cardiff Castle by his brother, Henry, so that his younger brother, William Rufus (c1056–1100), became king. Robert died at Cardiff in 1134 and is probably buried in the chapter house.

Pass the south ambulatory chapel on the right and head into the **Lady Chapel (9)**. Built 1457–99, this occupies the site of the apsidal chapel of the earlier Norman church. Built once more in Perpendicular style, it was the last major work during the time of the abbey. There is also some fine lierne vaulting to be seen, echoing that in the quire. The Lady Chapel is unusual in that it has two chantry chapels (with singing galleries above), like mini-transepts. Behind the altar is a stone reredos, which must have been an impressive sight in its time, although most of the statuary has been destroyed and the three main niches are now filled with modern tapestries.

Turn back towards the west to see the gallery above the entrance vestibule. Beneath the gallery is an ancient lead font mounted on a modern concrete plinth. The font dates from *c*1140 and came from a church in the Wye Valley. There are two monuments of note. On the north wall is the effigy to Elizabeth Williams, who died in 1622, while on the opposite wall is that of her sister Margery. Both died in childbirth, always a danger in those days. They were the daughters of Miles Smith, Bishop of Gloucester 1612–24, who played an important part in the translation of the King James Bible.

Memories of Famous Men

Leave the Lady Chapel and walk along the north ambulatory, passing on the right the War Memorial Chapel of St Edmund and St Edward. On the left are three of the most important monuments in the cathedral. First is the **Effigy of Osric (10)**. Osric, Prince of Mercia, founded St Peter's Abbey in 681. On his death he was buried in the abbey church, but his remains have been moved several times. His effigy, which holds a model of the abbey, has occupied this position since 1530. On the wall next to the effigy is a glass case containing the Carne Cross, carved by Lt.-Col. James Power Carne VC (1906–1986), commander of the 'Glorious Gloucesters', while he was a prisoner during the Korean War.

You next reach the **Tomb of Edward II (11)**. The alabaster tomb, with its soaring pinnacles, was ordered by Edward III in memory of his father, murdered in

Berkeley Castle in 1327. Edward II, despite the picture of him we might gain from Marlowe's play, was at the time thought to have been a good king, and the tomb soon attracted pilgrims in large numbers. Note the recesses cut into the adjacent pillars to allow pilgrims to walk around the tomb.

The third memorial of this trio is the **Effigy of William Parker (12)**, the last Abbot of St Peter's. The chantry was built during his lifetime, but the stone chest does not in fact contain his remains – their actual whereabouts is a mystery.

Step past St Paul's Chapel (on the right) and into the north transept. Look on the west wall for the **Bower Monument (13)**. This unusual wooden monument shows John and Ann Bower along with their seven daughters and nine sons (boys on the left, girls on the right). Above are shields with the children's names. Some names are repeated or have a shield that is painted black, suggesting that many of the children died while young. John Bower (d1615) was an apothecary. There is an ironic inscription on the canopy: 'Vayne Vanytie, all is Vayne.'

A door in the corner of the north transept leads up narrow stairs to the **Gloucester Cathedral Exhibition (14)**. This stretches around the tribune gallery and includes the 'whispering gallery', a stone passageway which runs behind the east window. The exhibition traces the history of the cathedral from the building of the monastery by Osric in Saxon times up to the present day. There is a small charge for this exhibition, which is highly recommended, particularly for the views it gives of the east window and looking down into the choir.

Returning to ground level, turn briefly into the north nave aisle where, on the right, is another monument from the same historical period as the Bower Memorial: the **Machen Memorial (15)**. It shows the figures of Thomas and Christian Machen kneeling before their prayer books. Below are the 'weepers' of their thirteen children – seven boys on the left and six girls on the right. Some of the figures are half-sized, and it is assumed these represent children who died in infancy. Machen (d1615) was an ex-mayor of Gloucester. The Machen and Bower memorials have many similarities, and the two men may have known each other well.

Cloisters and Chapter House

Go back towards the north transept and walk out into the **Cloisters (16)**, built 1351–1412. The cloisters formed a square walkway which connected the various monastic buildings – such as chapter house, dormitory, refectory and infirmary – so that the monks could reach them under cover. They also provided an opportunity for study and contemplation – look for the recesses (carrels) where the monks could work. The north cloister has a well preserved lavatorium, a long stone trough where the monks could wash. The water came from a well that you can still see in the cloister garth. Opposite the lavatorium is another recess, an open cupboard for storing towels. The Gloucester cloisters are noted for their splendid fan vaulting, the first to appear in any English cathedral and later widely copied.

Just off the east cloister is the **Chapter House (17)**, where the monks met daily to discuss business and read from the rule of St Benedict. It is highly probable that the chapter house was the site where William the Conqueror's Christmas Council ordered the Domesday Survey. Alongside the chapter house is an alleyway (slype) which the monks used as a locutorium, a place where they could relax their rule of silence. This area is now the cathedral's **Treasury (18)**.

The tour concludes at the cloisters. Leave by the southwest or southeast doors or the refectory in the west cloister.

WALKING TOUR FROM GLOUCESTER CATHEDRAL

The walk first circumnavigates the cathedral and views some of the old buildings and gates dating back to the days of the abbey. It then follows part of the Via Sacra, the old Roman walls, before arriving at Gloucester Docks. Although commercial water traffic has more or less ceased, the leisure industry has taken over the docks, making them a major tourist attraction. The return route to the cathedral passes by the remains of two of the city's ancient friaries.

Start and finish: The south porch of the cathedral.
Length: 2 miles (3.3km).
Time: Under 1hr, but you will probably wish to visit at least some of the many churches and museums along the route.
Refreshments: The excellent cathedral refectory is to the west of the cloisters. Plenty of city-centre pubs offer bar meals, but some are pretty rough inside: choose with care! The Fountain Inn in Westgate, first licensed in 1216, can certainly be relied upon. The New Inn in Northgate has a galleried courtyard; it was built around 1450 to accommodate pilgrims visiting the grave of Edward II. Other old inns include The Fleece and Dick Whittington's, both in Westgate. The more up-market New County Hotel in Southgate Street also provides accommodation.

Standing at the south porch of the cathedral you are on the cathedral close, known as **College Green (1)** because, after the Dissolution in 1541, the cathedral came under the jurisdiction of a college of clergy. Walk past the west front of the cathedral and the War Memorial and over Lower College Green to **St Mary's Gate (2)**. The arch dates from the 13th century and was the main entrance to the abbey. It is said that the room over the arch was a viewing place when Bishop John Hooper (1495–1555) was burnt at the stake in 1555. A fine range of houses to the south of the gate includes the monastic almonry and granary.

Turn right and pass under the 14th-century inner gate of the monastery to reach **Miller's Green (3)**, the monastery's inner courtyard. If you're interested in domestic architecture you'll be fascinated by the schoolmaster's house, the old mill, the organist's house and the deanery. The most important, however, is the **Parliament Room (4)**, a half-timbered house resting on a 13th-century stone undercroft. This was almost certainly the monastery guest hall, and derives its later name from the fact that Richard II summoned parliament here in 1378. He had just introduced the unpopular poll tax and was too scared to hold the parliament in London!

Leave Miller's Green via the alleyway past Little Cloister House, which has an interesting timber supported window. Ahead are the remains of the abbey **Infirmary (5)**. After the Dissolution, this building quickly became derelict; the arches and the west wall are all that is left today. Nearby were the monastery's herb garden and vineyard. You have from here a good opportunity to view the external features of the east end of the cathedral and appreciate the fine Perpendicular

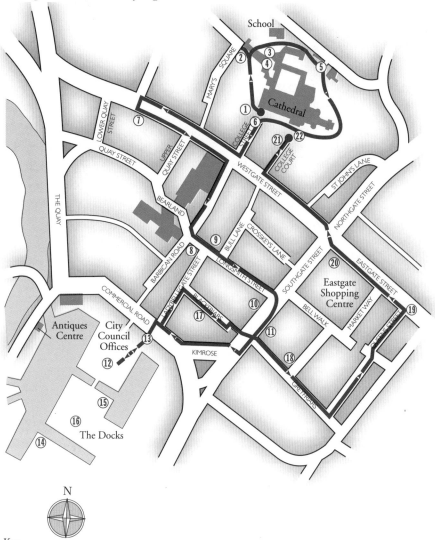

Key

1. College Green
2. St Mary's Gate
3. Miller's Green
4. Parliament Room
5. Infirmary
6. King Edward's Gate
7. Folk Museum
8. Transport Museum
9. Ladybellegate House
10. Golden Cross Inn
11. Church of St Mary de Crypt
12. Gloucester Docks
13. Soldiers of Gloucester Museum
14. National Waterways Museum
15. Museum of Advertising and Packaging
16. Mariners' Church
17. Blackfriars Friary
18. Greyfriars Friary
19. East Gate Viewing Chamber
20. St Michaels Tower
21. House of the Tailor of Gloucester
22. St Michael's Gate

St Mary's Gate

architecture, particularly that of the tower, built in the time of Abbot Seabroke. Take the path around the east end and back to the south porch.

Harsh Discipline

From here leave the Cathedral Close by **King Edward's Gate (6)**, the place where King Edward's body was received. Little of the gateway remains today except part of the west tower, upon which the arms of Osric, the founder of the abbey, may be seen. The wrought-iron gates were added in 1989.

Move into the short College Street and turn right into Westgate Street. A few yards along on the left you find the monolithic Shire Hall, built in 1815. Almost opposite is the redundant Church of St Nicholas, with its curiously shaped leaning spire. On the other side of the road is the **Folk Museum (7)**, located in a range of half-timbered and Jacobean houses. It is thought that the main house was the place where Bishop John Hooper spent his last night in 1555 before being burnt at the stake. The buildings housed a pin factory in the 18th and 19th centuries. Today there are displays showing local crafts and industries plus mock-ups of a dairy, an ironmonger's shop and wheelwright's and carpenter's workshops. The top floor features a Victorian schoolroom, where visiting schoolchildren are obliged to dress up in period clothes and experience the harsh discipline of those times!

Leave the museum and return along Westgate Street towards the city centre. On passing the Shire Hall, turn immediately right into Berkeley Street. This is part of the Via Sacra, which follows the route of the old city walls. Turn left on reaching Longsmith Street. Opposite is the small **Transport Museum (8)**, which is housed in the old fire station and will not be a high priority for those with limited time. On the north side of Longsmith Street is **Ladybellgate House (9)**, a superb Georgian townhouse dating from 1705. The Raikes family lived here for a number of years. The building is now the offices of a firm of solicitors.

Continue along Longsmith Street until you reach Southgate Street, and turn right. Immediately to your right is another Raikes house: the **Golden Cross Inn (10)**, a half-timbered 16th-century building with a double-jettied wall. There are more connections with Robert Raikes across the road at the **Church of St Mary de Crypt (11)**, where the Sunday School stalwart is buried. This is one of Gloucester's oldest churches, with Norman origins, having been founded about 1100, although all the windows are Perpendicular in style. There are a number of medieval wall paintings and some interesting brasses. George Whitfield, the rousing 18th-century preacher, gave his first sermon here. Regrettably, the church is often closed to visitors.

Gloucester Docks

Towards the end of Southgate Street, fork right via Kimrose Way into Commercial Road. At the pedestrian crossing, walk over to the building labelled 'Custom House'. An alleyway to the left of the building leads down to **Gloucester Docks (12)**. The River Severn, with its sandbanks and rocks, was never easy to navigate, and in 1793 an Act of Parliament gave permission for the construction of a canal to link Gloucester with Berkeley. In 1812 it was decided to end the canal at Sharpness, and shortly afterwards the dock basins at Gloucester were opened. A local rail company terminated its railroad at the docks, enabling the transhipment of goods, and by 1820 the canal was linked with the national network, thereby connecting Gloucester with London and the Midlands. The docks dealt initially with products such as corn and timber and prosperity seemed assured. Unfortunately, the growth of the railways and the development of ports downstream, such as Avonmouth, led to a gradual decline. By the 1970s the docks were almost derelict, so the City Council decided to move its administration to the docks, acquiring several warehouses. Soon various leisure and retail outlets moved in. Some of the warehouses, named after the companies who originally owned them, have been converted into imaginative museums. The Docks soon became hugely popular with tourists and has appeared in many films.

The Custom House, when viewed from the Docks, is seen to be the **Soldiers of Gloucester Museum (13)**. Displays follow in the footsteps of the Gloucester regiments in their campaigns over the past three centuries, with lifelike models of World War I trenches, guns, medals and other souvenirs. The **National Waterways Museum (14)**, based in Llanthony Warehouse, is also a must. This presents a vibrant display of the history of our canals and waterways, with models and audiovisual displays, and provides an insight into the life of those who worked on the canals. There are several historic boats in the neighbouring docks. The museum runs boat trips using the *Queen Boadicea II*, a small ship which was present at the Dunkirk evacuations.

The Albert Warehouse houses the Robert Opie Collection at the **Museum of Advertising and Packaging (15)**. Claimed to be the only museum of its type in the world, this displays products and packaging from the Victorian era to the present day. And don't miss the delightful little Victorian **Mariners' Church (16)**, built for the sailors and dock workers, but also popular with townsfolk. There is also an antiques centre, pubs, eating places and specialist shops. Tourists often spend the whole day here!

Returning to the Cathedral

Leave Gloucester Docks by the same route as you entered – the alleyway at the side of the Soldiers of Gloucester Museum. This brings you back to Commercial Road. Go over the pedestrian crossing and walk up Ladybellgate Street. Turn right into Blackfriars. On the right is the **Blackfriars Friary (17)**, said to be the most complete of its type in the country. It was founded in 1239 and at its height accommodated 30–40 friars. After the Dissolution in 1539 the site was bought by a wealthy local clothier, Thomas Bell, who converted the cloisters into his workshop and the church into his mansion. Blackfriars is not normally open to the public.

Continue to the end of Blackfriars, which leads to Southgate Street. Note the pin-like bollards – a reference to one of Gloucester's industries. Cross over the road and take the path at the side of St Mary de Crypt Church. Pass the Music and Drama Library on the left and keep going until you reach a gap in the stone wall that leads into the ruins of **Greyfriars Friary (18)**. This Franciscan friary church was founded *c*1231 by Thomas Berkeley, but only parts of the nave and north aisle remain and nothing of the other friary buildings. After the Dissolution in the 16th century the church was converted into tenements and workshops.

Continue to the end of Greyfriars and reach the stone-built public library. Turn left along Constitution Walk at the back of the library to go through part of the modern Eastgate Shopping Centre to Eastgate Street. Immediately on your right you'll see the concrete and glass cover of the **East Gate Viewing Chamber (19)**, entry to which is from Queen's Walk. There are good views from here of the medieval walls and the city's East Gate. The original Roman gate was made of wood, part of a fortress built in AD68, but it changed greatly over the years. The view shows one of two towers that date from *c*1230 and a B-shaped gateway. There was evidently a moat, crossed by a drawbridge, and a horsepool, built *c*1550 to wash horses and swell timber in carts, plus a toilet dated *c*1700. The tower served at various times as a prison, a school and a house.

Turn left and walk along Eastgate Street to the central crossroads (The Cross), which is dominated by **St Michael's Tower (20)**, where you can see the arms of Richard III, who granted the city its charter in 1483. The arms were unveiled by the Duke of Gloucester in 1983 to commemorate five centuries of city status. The tower is all that remains of the medieval St Michael's Church.

Cross over into Westgate Street, then, shortly after, turn right along the narrow College Court. On the left is the House of the Tailor of Gloucester (21). Beatrix Potter (1866–1943) modelled the tailor's house in her classic *The Tailor of Gloucester* (1903) on this small building. Since 1979 it has been a giftshop and museum owned by Frederick Warne, her publishers. Potter fans will be in their element here. Younger visitors will love the moving tableau of mice at work on the mayor's coat!

At the end of College Court is the minute St Michael's Gate (22), probably the route taken by pilgrims visiting the tomb of Edward II. Pass through the gateway and back into the Cathedral Close, where the walk ends.

HEREFORD

Access: Hereford can easily be reached by road: the nearest motorways are the M50 to the southeast and the M6 to the east. It is 135 miles (220km) from London, a journey which can be achieved in 3hr. National Express coaches run from London. Hereford can also be reached from Paddington by rail. The nearest international airport is at Birmingham, some 58 miles (93km) to the east.

Hereford is located on the north bank of the River Wye at a traditional early fording point. Its role in defending Saxon territory against the Celts meant that armies often occupied the town; the name 'Hereford' means 'army ford'. Its strategic importance in Saxon times meant a number of Saxon kings came to the town, and some had their coins minted here. This was also the time when the first Hereford Castle was built, although the Normans later built a larger structure on the site. The Saxons also built the first cathedral at Hereford, probably of wood, in AD676. A later stone cathedral was destroyed by Welsh invaders in 1055. When Offa, King of Mercia, had Ethelbert, King of the East Angles, killed, Ethelbert was buried at Hereford, and his remains have always attracted pilgrims to the cathedral.

Following the Conquest, the first Norman bishops began rebuilding the cathedral, starting in 1080 under Bishop de Losinga (in office 1079–95) and his successor Raynhelm (in office 1095–1107). The oldest parts of the cathedral are accordingly in the Norman style. The cathedral went through bad times during the reign of the unfortunate King Stephen in the 12th century, but things picked up during the early 13th century, when the Lady Chapel and the crypt beneath it were completed in Early English style. The north transept was built later in the century by Bishop Aquablanca (in office 1240–1268) and reflects the work which was going on at Westminster Abbey at that time. The 13th century was also important for the relic known as the Mappa Mundi, the cathedral's greatest treasure. This pictorial map of the world dates from 1290 and was probably brought to the cathedral to support the canonization of Bishop Thomas Cantalupe (in office 1275–82). By the end of this century, however, the city of Hereford was losing its importance as a military centre following the conquest of Wales by Edward I.

During the 15th century there were a number of additions to the cathedral in Perpendicular style, including the cloisters, the great west window and some chantry chapels. Hereford Cathedral suffered badly during the Reformation, with a series of reforming bishops who made sure that the building was despoiled of many of its treasures. During the Civil War, both the bishop and the citizens supported the Royalist cause. Despite being taken and retaken, the city suffered little damage until it was besieged in 1645 by Lord Leven and a Scottish army, great damage then being done. The Scots were eventually driven away by the army of Charles I, but later the city was taken again, apparently due to the treachery of its governor, one Colonel Birch. This time the cathedral was ransacked: brasses destroyed, windows smashed and the library pillaged. The courageous dean of the time is said to have preached to the soldiers, condemning their sacrilege. Although they levelled their muskets at him, he was, remarkably, not killed.

By the end of the 18th century the cathedral was in an appalling condition and the architect James Wyatt (1746-1813) was called in to undertake restoration. Although he was highly regarded, he was an unfortunate choice, as several other cathedrals found to their cost. He built a new west front, shortened the nave, removed the Norman triforium and clerestory and used plaster unsparingly. The Victorians continued the restoration, directed mainly by N.J. Cottingham (1823–1854), who provided the reredos behind the high altar, the choir floor and pew ends and the replica Norman arch. Sir George Gilbert Scott (1811–1878) designed an inappropriate metal screen between the crossing and the choir; this has recently been removed for 'restoration', but thankfully will not return. The Victorians also provided a considerable amount of stained glass of mixed quality. Overall it would be fair to say that the changes made here by the Victorians are not as objectionable as in many other cathedrals. Today, the cathedral has a friendly, welcoming ambience and attracts over 200,000 visitors annually, many attracted by the Mappa Mundi and the remarkable Chained Library.

The city, meanwhile, has maintained much of its market-town atmosphere. It has avoided the heavy industrial development which many places attracted during Victorian times. Its industries, such as cidermaking, are light, being mainly connected to farming. It has also developed as a tourist centre, being a gateway to the Welsh mountains and the Wye Valley. The Three Choirs Festival is based at Hereford every third year.

TOUR OF THE CATHEDRAL
Start: The north porch.
Finish: Chapter House Yard.
Hereford does not have a ceremonial entrance on its west front, which was redesigned in the early 20th century. Enter the cathedral via the **North Porch (1)**, which is sometimes known as the Booth Porch, after Bishop Charles Booth (d1535), and dates from 1519. Once a chantry chapel, approached by a spiral staircase, this occupied the space above the porch. Note the porch's superb modern iron gates.

Proceed into the cathedral and turn immediately left to find the **Memorial to Bishop Booth (2)**, set into the north aisle wall. The ornately painted and gilded tomb is protected by heavy iron railings. Booth was the last medieval bishop of Hereford, dying in 1535, immediately before the Reformation.

Step from here into the centre of the **Nave (3)**. The massive piers and arches are Norman and were built around 1100. The arches are decorated with chevron designs, each one being subtly different. The triforium and clerestory levels date from Wyatt's work at the end of the 18th century, and you may feel that the two styles do not sit comfortably together. Walk across to the southwest corner of the nave, where there are a number of items of interest. Between the piers is the alabaster **Effigy of Sir Richard Pembridge (4)**. Pembridge fought at Poitiers (1356) and was one of the first Knights of the Garter – note the garter on his left leg. His right leg is a Victorian replacement for an earlier wooden one, itself a substitute. Nearby is the late-Norman **Font (5)**, the sides of which have carvings of the apostles, their faces erased during the Reformation. The circular, mosaic-topped base is Victorian.

In the corner of the aisle is normally kept a **Mobile Organ (6)**, which can be trundled around the cathedral on its wheeled platform; its main use is during the

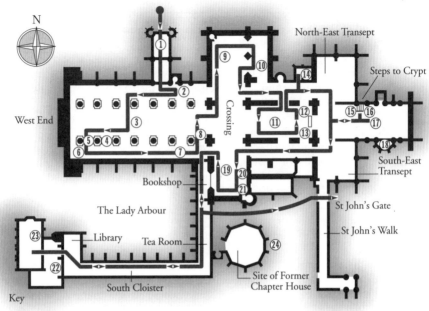

Key

1. North Porch
2. Memorial to Bishop Booth
3. Nave
4. Effigy of Sir Richard Pembridge
5. Font
6. Mobile Organ
7. North Aisle
8. Corona
9. North Transept
10. Shrine of St Thomas Cantalupe
11. Choir
12. King Stephen's Chair
13. Ethelbert's Statue
14. Stanbury Chantry Chapel
15. Crypt
16. Facsimile of Mappa Mundi
17. Lady Chapel
18. Audley Chantry
19. South Transept
20. John Piper Tapestries
21. Denton Tomb
22. Mappa Mundi
23. Chained Library
24. Chapter House Yard

Three Choirs Festival. There are two other organs in the cathedral: the main 'Father' Willis organ in the choir and one in the Lady Chapel's chantry.

Proceed east along the **North Aisle (7)**. There are two stone effigies set into the wall of Thomas de Pembridge, treasurer of the cathedral in the mid-14th century, and Stephen de Ledbury, dean of the cathedral at about the same time. This brings you to the beautifully carved Jacobean pulpit (the base and steps are modern).

Cross in front of the pulpit. Dominating the crossing to the right is the **Corona (8)**, a modern wrought-iron crown which hangs above the nave altar. The chevron design matches the decoration on the nave's Norman arches. Proceed to the north aisle and on into the **North Transept (9)**. This was built by Bishop Peter Aquablanca *c*1250 and is of an unusual Geometrical Decorated design, with almost pointed, triangular arches, reminiscent of work at Westminster Abbey; this replaced the original Norman design, which can still be seen in the south transept. The transept also has a number of monuments to bishops, the most interesting of which is the alabaster bust of Bishop Field, who came to Hereford after being bishop successively of Llandaff and St David's and who died in office in 1636. In the corner of the north transept is the **Shrine of St Thomas Cantalupe (10)**, which dates from 1287. The lower part of the shrine, which is made of Purbeck Marble, shows 15 Knights Templar; the bishop was a Provincial Grand Master of this order. He was also the last Englishmen to be canonized before the Reformation. His shrine attracted many pilgrims and was the source of much revenue for the cathedral. Walk into the north choir aisle, where on the right you see a showcase depicting the last journey of St Thomas. Opposite is the tomb of Bishop Aquablanca.

Two Thrones

Continue along the aisle and turn into the **Choir (11)**, which is full of interest. The main arches and the triforium are Norman, but the clerestory and vaulting are Early English, dating from *c*1250. The choir stalls and canopies are richly carved in the Decorated style and have a good collection of misericords. The Bishop's Throne dates from the same period. The other 'chair' of interest is **King Stephen's Chair (12)**, on which Stephen is supposed to have sat during his visit to the cathedral in 1142. If this were true – and it is doubtful – then it would be one of the oldest pieces of furniture in the country. Elizabeth II has used the chair on two recent visits.

Statue of St Ethelbert

Elsewhere in the choir, the high altar reredos, the flooring and the mock Norman arch were the work of N.J. Cottingham during the Victorian restorations. The wooden woodpecker plaque on the organ casing reflects the fact that the restoration of the organ was sponsored by Bulmers, the local cidermaker, whose emblem is a woodpecker. Before you leave the choir area, inspect the Victorian tiled floor in front of the high altar. One of the tiles shows the rather gory death of St Ethelbert, the cathedral's patron, murdered in 794 on the orders of King Offa of Mercia. **Ethelbert's Statue (13)**, minus hands and facial features, can be found nearby, against the wall to the right of the high altar.

Return to the north choir aisle, where on the north side is one of the most delightful parts of the cathedral – the **Stanbury Chantry Chapel (14)**. John Stanbury (in office 1453–74) was originally a Carmelite friar before becoming confessor to Henry VI. He was thereafter the first Provost of Eton, then Bishop of Hereford. His chantry chapel, built in the 1470s, is in an ornate Perpendicular style, with intricate wall carving and some superb fan vaulting. It is rare to get so close to such fine vaulting, so enjoy the detail. The 20th-century glass (paid for by Eton College) shows scenes from Stanbury's life. Note that the impression of Hereford Cathedral shows the tower capped by the wooden spire removed in 1790. The chapel also has a finely carved wooden triptych above the altar. (During Lent all the cathedral's triptychs are folded up.)

You are now approaching the east end of the cathedral, which once had an apsidal end. This was replaced by two shallow transepts, an ambulatory (sometimes referred to as the retrochoir) and the Lady Chapel. The whole area is in Transitional or Early English style. To the left of the entrance to the Lady Chapel are stairs leading down to the **Crypt (15)**; said to be the only example of a cathedral crypt built later than the 11th century, this is today used for private prayer. Apparently it was at one time called 'Golgotha', as it was used as a charnel house. There are few features of interest in the crypt, but don't miss the tomb at the west end, which in place of effigies on the top has the incumbents' figures etched on the lid.

Tombs and Effigies

Climb the steps back to the Lady Chapel, where there is a **Facsimile of the Mappa Mundi (16)**. It's worth spending some time looking at this, as it is considerably easier to decipher than the original. Head next into the **Lady Chapel (17)**. This and the crypt below were built in Early English style around 1225, but suffered considerable alteration in Victorian times, and all the stained glass dates from this era. The Lady Chapel once contained the Shrine of St Thomas and until the 19th century was the home of the Chained Library. On the north wall is an intricately painted and gilded tomb, believed to be that of Peter de Grandisson. Nearby, kept behind glass because of its fragility, is a Victorian tapestry altar frontal designed by Sir George Gilbert Scott and made in Belgium.

On the south side of the Lady Chapel is the two-storey **Audley Chantry (18)**. Erected by Bishop Edmund Audley (in office 1492–1502), it contains the cathedral's third organ. It is separated from the Lady Chapel by a fine decorated screen bearing the painted figures of numerous saints. Audley was successively Bishop of Rochester, Hereford and Salisbury, and it was while he was at Hereford that he had the chantry built. He later had another one constructed at Salisbury, where he is buried.

Leave the east end and turn into the south choir aisle, where there are identical effigies of four medieval bishops. Their probable names are shown on the wall, but it is not accurately known which effigy is of which bishop.

You next reach the **South Transept (19)**, which has a variety of architectural styles. The north wall is pure Norman, with five tiers of rounded arches of varying size. In the three largest arches in the second tier are the **John Piper Tapestries (20)**. These show three trees from the Bible: the Tree of Knowledge of Good and Evil (note Adam and Eve), the Tree of the Cross and the Tree of Life. In the southeast corner of the transept is the **Denton Tomb (21)**, dating from 1566, which shows the effigies of Sir Alexander Denton, his wife Elizabeth and their infant child. Both the south and west walls of the transept have large Perpendicular windows, and the vaulting also dates from this period. The west wall of the transept has two interesting items – a Norman fireplace (the only other known example is at Durham) and a triptych from Hereford's twin town of Nuremberg.

The Mappa Mundi and the Chained Library

Leave the south transept, turn left and go through the cathedral shop and the tearoom, both located in the east cloister. Turn into the south cloister, at the end of which is the New Library Building. An entrance fee (with concessions) is required here to see the Mappa Mundi and the Chained Library Exhibition. The New Library Building was opened by Queen Elizabeth II in 1996 and was given the Building of the Year Award in 1997.

The **Mappa Mundi (22)** dates from the end of the 13th century and is believed to be the work of Richard of Haldingham, a canon at the cathedral. It is a map of the world as conceived in the Middle Ages, with the Mediterranean Sea and Jerusalem at the centre and England and Wales near the lower left-hand edge. The imagery is fascinating: the Garden of Eden is complete with Adam, Eve and an apple tree; Babylon is marked by the Tower of Babel; and Lot's wife stands by the shore of the Dead Sea. There is much more to see, including a whole range of strange animals with a dodgy distribution – for example, a monkey inhabits Norway!

The **Chained Library (23)** is a rich collection of medieval manuscripts from both England and abroad. There are nearly 1500 books with chains attached in what is probably the largest such collection in the world. The practice of chaining came about because during the Middle Ages and even in the Renaissance books were rare and their readers not necessarily honest. The exhibition, which uses models and computer technology, is an essential part of a visit to Hereford Cathedral.

Return through the cloisters to the tearoom, and move outside into **Chapter House Yard (24)**. The chapter house, which was a fine 14th-century building, was unfortunately pulled down *c*1715, and all that remain are the stone foundations, including the bases of the buttresses – excellent seating when people overflow from the tearoom on warm summer days.

Leave the yard through St John's Gate. On the right is St John's Walk, a covered way with carved roof beams that led to the College of the Vicars Choral. Here the tour ends.

WALKING TOUR FROM HEREFORD CATHEDRAL

The tour begins in the Cathedral Close and proceeds down to the Wye Bridge and a riverside walk. You cross the river to see the site of Hereford Castle before going on into the heart of the city, with its superb domestic architecture, ancient parish churches and pedestrianized shopping areas. There is an optional extension of the walk to the Cider Museum to get a flavour, as it were, of the area's main industry.

Start and finish: The north porch of the cathedral.
Length: 2 miles (3.2km), plus a 1 mile (1.6km) for the diversion to the Cider Museum.
Time: A little over 1hr, but add time if you want to visits the museums.
Refreshments: The small cathedral tearoom only serves light snacks. There are plenty of ancient inns en route, many with coaching origins. However, although interesting from the exterior, some can be rough inside. At the top of the range is the Green Dragon Hotel in Broad Street, whence coaches once left for London. Other possibilities are the Orange Tree Inn in King Street and the Grapes Tavern in Capuchin Lane. There is a unique 'community' restaurant in the nave of All Saints' Church.

The tour begins in the **Cathedral Close (1)**, a grassy area with mature trees which is well used by visitors and the citizens of Hereford. It was open land in medieval days, when it was the site of St Ethelbert's Fair, and it was the city's only graveyard until 1791. It is said that at one time pigs roamed here at will, occasionally digging up bodies, so the cathedral authorities had to enclose the site. Here you have a good opportunity to look at the external features of the cathedral. Dominating the exterior is the magnificent tower, which has much in common with those of the neighbouring cathedrals of Gloucester and Worcester. The tower dates from *c*1300 and is Decorated in style, with a profusion of ball flower decoration. You don't have to look closely to see that much of the pink sandstone of the cathedral's exterior is in bad condition, and the cathedral's stone masons are kept very busy. You can watch them working in their small yard between the north and northeast transepts.

Leave the close from the west side and walk into Broad Street. Ahead is the **City Art Gallery, Museum and Library (2)**. This multi-purpose building was constructed in 1874 and extended early in the 20th century. It has a good archaeological section and changing exhibitions of art and sculpture. Opposite the museum notice the Roman Catholic **Church of St Francis Xavier (3)**. This ochre-coloured church has a Classical frontage and was one of the first post-Reformation Catholic churches to be built in the country.

By the River

Walk south towards the Tourist Information Office and turn right along King Street to its junction with Bridge Street. At this point, in the middle of the road, once stood St Nicholas' Church, but in the early years of the 19th century it was removed stone by stone to a new home in Victoria Street. Walk down Bridge Street towards the River Wye and **Wye Bridge (4)**. In Roman times there was a ford just to the east, and later a wooden bridge. The present stone bridge, with its elegant arches and pedestrian refuge places, dates from the late 15th century.

At the far side of the bridge, take the steps down past the Bridge Inn to **Bishop's Meadow (5)**. This recreational area, once owned by the cathedral authorities, was eventually given to the city. A shady riverside walk gives views across the Wye towards the cathedral, with the Bishop's Palace to the left and the College of Vicars Choral to the right. Some of the dead trees along the walk have been imaginatively carved by local artists. Cross over the river via **Victoria Footbridge (6)**; this suspension bridge, replacing a ferry, was built to celebrate Queen Victoria's Diamond Jubilee in 1897.

From Castle Green to the Old House

After crossing the bridge, climb the steps up to the left to reach **Castle Green (7)**. This open space was once the castle bailey. In the centre of the green is a local version of Nelson's Column – Nelson was a frequent visitor to Hereford.

Walk round the edge of the green, passing some public toilets on the left. On the right is Castle Pool, all that remains of the castle moat. The first castle on this site was Saxon, dating from 1052. It was later strengthened by the Normans. Behind the pool is the back of St Ethelbert's Almshouses (see below).

Turn back to the left along Castle Hill. On the left is a grassy area, Redcliffe Gardens. This was the site of the castle keep, demolished in the 17th century. At the southern end of the gardens is Castle Cliffe, once the castle's watergate. At the end of Castle Hill is a water fountain set into the wall. This is the site of **St Ethelbert's Well (8)**, once renowned for its healing waters. Above the fountain there is a much eroded stone head, believed to have once been in the cathedral.

Turn right into Quay Street; the Cathedral School occupies most of the buildings to both right and left. At the end of Quay Street, turn right into Castle Street. On the right you can see the front of St Ethelbert's Almshouses. The present buildings date from 1805, but there were almshouses here bearing this name centuries earlier.

Now swing left into St Ethelbert Street, where there are some impressive houses, mainly in Georgian style and many with wrought-iron balconies. Turn left again into the broad St Owen Street. Halfway along on the left is the **Town Hall (9)**. This

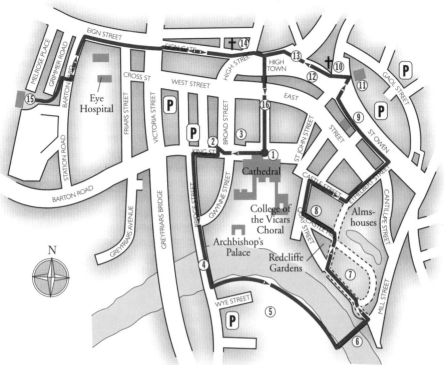

Key

1. Cathedral Close
2. City Art Gallery, Museum and Library
3. Church of St Francis Xavier
4. Wye Bridge
5. Bishop's Meadow
6. Victoria Footbridge
7. Castle Green
8. St Ethelbert's Well
9. Town Hall
10. St Peter's Church
11. Shire Hall
12. The Old House
13. Market Place
14. All Saints' Church
15. Cider Museum
16. Church Street

somewhat imposing building, completed in 1904 in Edwardian Baroque style, contains the council chamber, the mayor's parlour and many of the city's civic treasures and regalia.

You now reach St Peter's Square, named after the 11th-century **St Peter's Church (10)**, the oldest church in the city. Built in the traditional pink sandstone, the church has a prominent spire, but the overall effect is spoiled at the front by a sheltered walkway that looks like a glass conservatory. Opposite is the **Shire Hall (11)**. Built in Classical style, it was designed by Sir Robert Smirke (1781–1867), also responsible for the British Museum in London. Outside the Shire Hall is a statue of Sir George Cornewall Lewis, MP for the city in the mid-19th century.

Walking to the left of St Peter's Church, you now approach the heart of the city, known as Hightown. Immediately ahead is the **Old House (12)**. This half-timbered, three-storied building with jettied walls dates from 1621 and has a profusion of latticed windows and carved gables. Over the main door is the coat-of-arms of the Butchers' Guild. The Old House is the last remaining building in a terraced row of butchers' shops (shambles) which once stood here – this is why the jettied walls are found on only three sides. The building has had a variety of uses in its long history, being by turns a fish shop, a saddlery, a hardware store and a bank before being handed over to the city authorities, who have converted it into a highly atmospheric museum. Apart from the furniture and other artefacts, which go back to the 16th century, there is a most informative and interesting display about the effect the Civil War had on Hereford.

Commerce and Spirit

You have now reached the bustling **Market Place (13)**. There has been a market here since Norman times. The large timber-framed Guildhall was demolished in 1862 because of its ruinous condition, but you can still see its position marked out by a line of coloured bricks set into the pavement.

Go to the end of the Market Place, cross the High Street and walk along the pedestrianized Eign Gate. Immediately on your right is **All Saints' Church (14)**. There has been a church here since *c*1200, the present building dating from 1330. The top third of its dominating, slightly crooked, spire was rebuilt in 1994, but the whole is still slightly out of kilter. Step inside for a real surprise: the whole of the west end of the nave and its gallery have been converted into a highly popular restaurant. The rest of this parish church is full of interest. There is a fine hammer-beam roof, a pulpit dating back to 1621 and a Queen Anne reredos in the Chapel of St Anthony. Don't miss the font, which is claimed to be as old as the church itself. The actor David Garrick (1717–1779) was baptised here.

The Cider Museum

From All Saints' Church there is an optional excursion to the Cider Museum. Walk to the end of Eign Gate and take the pedestrian subway under Victoria Street to emerge in Eign Street. Pass the Eye Hospital on the left. At the traffic lights, turn left along Barton Road. Almost immediately cross Barton Road by the pedestrian crossing into Grimmer Road. The **Cider Museum (15)** is signposted just a few yards away. The museum has a reconstructed farm ciderhouse with some of the presses and other equipment from past centuries, plus the traditional 'tack' of the travelling cidermaker. The cellars can be visited, as can the distillery, which makes fortified products such as cider champagne, cider liqueurs and cider brandy. You can taste the cider, and a giftshop sells cider and other items.

Return by the same route to All Saints' Church to resume the main tour. Leave the Market Square on the south side by a narrow alley known as Capuchin Lane. This crosses East Street, widens, and becomes known as **Church Street (16)**. On the corner is the Grapes Tavern; here, in the 18th century, the 'London Letter' was read to the eager citizens. Church Street is full of specialist shops and restored half-timbered buildings. A number of plaques on the walls above the shops show historical items of interest. One indicates the house where Roger Kemble (1721–1802) was born: he was the father of a theatrical family that included Sarah Siddons (1755–1831). As you near the cathedral, another plaque points out a house containing a medieval hall, the former home of the cathedral organist Dr Sinclair, an associate of Elgar. Finally, don't miss Capuchin Yard, a small alleyway devoted mainly to craft workshops.

Church Street leads back to the Cathedral Close and the end of the tour.

WORCESTER

Access: Worcester is located close to the M5 and therefore has good road links via the motorway system to all parts of the country. The city is 113 miles (181km) from London, 27 miles (43km) from Birmingham and 111 miles (178km) from Manchester; leave the M5 at junction 7. Parking in Worcester is not usually a problem: the nearest carparks to the cathedral are in Copenhagen Street and King Street. National Express coaches stop on the outskirts of Worcester, with scheduled local bus services to the city centre. There are regular trains from London Paddington to Shrub Hill Station Worcester, the journey taking 2½ hours. Trains from Birmingham arrive at Foregate Street Station. The nearest airport is at Birmingham. Coaches from London Heathrow Airport run twice daily.

Worcester was an important Roman town, protected by an earth embankment. It appears that towards the end of the Roman occupation Christianity had made an impact – certainly two graves recently discovered beneath the undercroft of College Hall suggest a Christian burial. In Anglo-Saxon times a diocese of Worcester was created, sometime towards the end of the 7th century. The first bishop was called Bosel and his simple cathedral was dedicated to St Peter. In 971 Bishop Oswald founded a Benedictine monastery on the site. He built a new church to replace the old one and dedicated it to St Mary. Oswald died in 992 and was later canonized. His shrine became a place of pilgrimage.

The year 1062 saw the appointment of Wulfstan as prior and bishop. Four years later came the Norman Conquest, but the able Wulfstan proved acceptable to King William and kept his positions. He decided to build a new cathedral in the Romanesque style, and a start was made with the crypt in 1084; this remains the largest Norman crypt in England. Above the crypt the east end of the cathedral was completed within five years. The design was typified by alternating bands of white limestone and green sandstone – a pattern which can be seen today in the chapter house. Wulfstan was likewise canonized after his death, and this meant pilgrims had a second shrine to visit. In 1216, King John was buried in the cathedral, as stipulated in his will, attracting to his tomb yet further visitors. The pilgrims' offerings were an important revenue in the continual restoration of the Norman cathedral.

Changes came with the appointment in the 1220s of Bishop William de Blois. He built a Lady Chapel at the east end in Early English style. The effect was obviously pleasing, because de Blois and his successors, bishops Cantelupe and Gifford, continued the process in the rest of the cathedral, gradually replacing Wulfstan's Romanesque with Gothic work as far as the crossing. In 1317 Bishop Thomas de Cobham started on the nave. There was evidently a gap in the work, probably coinciding with the Black Death, with the result that the nave was completed in Decorated and Perpendicular styles. All that remained was the construction of the tower, the revaulting of the nave and the building of the north porch. By the end of the 14th century the cathedral was to all events and purposes the building we see today.

The monastery, meanwhile, was also thriving. Monastic buildings included the infirmary, refectory, dormitory and, of course, the cloisters. When Prince Arthur (1486–1502), the brother of Henry VIII, died in 1502 at Ludlow Castle, he was buried in the cathedral, and an imposing chantry, just to the right of the high altar, was constructed to house his tomb. This represented what was to be the pinnacle of the monastery's influence: changes were soon to come.

At the Reformation Henry VIII dissolved the monastery (1540). The cathedral was refounded and the prior, Henry Holbeach, became the first dean. Regrettably, the shrines of Oswald and Wulfstan were destroyed and the whereabouts of the saints' bodies remains unknown. Considerable damage was also done to statues and other fittings and stained glass.

As with many cathedral cities, Worcester saw plenty of action during the Civil War, which both started and ended here. There was a skirmish between Cavaliers and Roundheads at Powick Bridge in 1642, while the Battle of Worcester in 1651 was the decisive action of the campaign, resulting in the rout of the Royalist army and the flight of the future Charles II to France. Cromwell's troops were billeted in the nave of the cathedral for some time, inflicting predictable damage.

The 17th century saw the cathedral in a sad state of repair and, although there was some restoration work done in the 18th century, it was piecemeal and of poor quality. It was left to the Victorians to save the fabric of the cathedral. The soft pink sandstone of which most of it is constructed was severely eroded in places and much needed to be replaced. Work at Worcester started in 1854, with Sir George Gilbert Scott (1811–1878) playing an important role. Much Victorian glass appeared, along with the west door, the Bishop's Throne, the nave pulpit, the high altar reredos and the vault paintings. One of Scott's better moves was to remove the organ (and its screen) from the west end of the choir and replace it with a light screen, thus allowing uninterrupted views along the length of the cathedral. Whether it was wise to relocate the organ screen in the south transept is debatable. Perhaps it is charitable to say that, despite the controversial nature of the work, Worcester Cathedral provides an excellent opportunity to study the full range of Victorian sculpture, glass and artwork.

The city of Worcester also developed during Victorian times, with the railways gradually replacing the canal as the main means of moving both freight and passengers. The Industrial Revolution did not bring the ugly development found in many cities in the Midlands and the North. Worcester developed light industries based around agriculture plus specialist glove and pottery making. Fortunately the two world wars inflicted little damage on either the city or its cathedral. The second half of the 20th century saw the coming of the motorways, allowing tourists, the modern pilgrims, even easier access to the city and its cathedral. Some 300,000 visitors come annually to Worcester Cathedral, their contributions helping the ongoing fight to maintain the fabric of this magnificent building. The 1990s were a cause of some celebration for Worcester, as 1992 was the Millennium of St Oswald and 1995 was the 900th anniversary of St Wulfstan.

TOUR OF THE CATHEDRAL

Start: The north porch.
Finish: The east cloister and College Green.

Enter via the north porch and move towards the west end. On the right is a simple **Wall Plaque to Edward Elgar (1)**. Above is the Elgar Window, based on the poem *The Dream of Gerontius* (1865) by Cardinal John Henry Newman (1801–1890). Sir Edward Elgar (1857–1934), a local man, was organist at the local Roman Catholic church but had many links with the cathedral.

It is often suggested that, to appreciate the architectural features of Worcester's **Nave (2)**, the visitor should stand near the second pier on the south side. All the features west of here are in the Transitional Norman style, while to the east the architecture is Perpendicular and Decorated. The proportions of the various levels are pleasing. The triforium is of particular interest. Each bay has a pair of arches, with sculptures filling the tympanum. The shafts are of Purbeck Marble. Just behind is a subsidiary arcade with smaller and lower arches, a pattern which continues in the east end of the cathedral. The glass in the west window is Victorian and shows the story of the Creation.

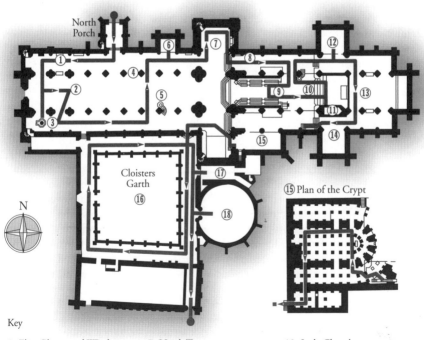

Key

1. Elgar Plaque and Window
2. Nave
3. Font
4. Beauchamp Tomb
5. Pulpit
6. Jesus Chapel
7. North Transept
8. Oriel Window
9. Quire
10. Tomb of King John
11. Chantry of Prince Arthur
12. St George's Chapel
13. Lady Chapel
14. Dean's Chapel
15. Crypt
16. Cloisters
17. Slype
18. Chapter House

Walk across to the southwest corner of the nave, where, in the aisle, is the **Font (3)**. This is remarkable for its extraordinary wooden and gilded cover which soars away to the roof and has doors at its lower end giving access to the font itself. Only the Victorians could have designed something as extraordinary as this!

Move along the nave eastwards and cross over to a gap in the pews to the north side, where you find one of the more interesting of the many memorials in the cathedral. This is the **Beauchamp Tomb (4)**, bearing effigies of Sir John Beauchamp and his wife. Beauchamp was a favourite of Richard II, but fell foul of the Merciless Parliament in 1388 and was executed. The heads of him and his wife rest on black swans. Over to the right is Scott's ornate marble **Pulpit (5)**; this would no doubt be admirable for a Methodist chapel, but in a Gothic cathedral it stands out like a sore thumb. Move to the left for a quick look into the 14th-century **Jesus Chapel (6)**, reserved for private prayer and once the baptistry. The ornately carved oak reredos that dominates the chapel dates from 1899.

Walk round into the **North Transept (7)**, which is festooned with monuments to the great and good of the city. The most distinctive is the white marble monument to John Hough, Bishop of Worcester 1717–43. He was a Fellow of Magdalen College, Oxford and was elected President by the Fellows in 1687, but then dismissed by James II's Commissioner, who required a Roman Catholic president. The Magdalen scene is depicted on the memorial.

Leave the transept and walk along the north quire aisle. On the left is a small **Oriel Window (8)**, which was part of the sacrist's house built on the outside of the cathedral wall. The window enabled the sacrist to watch over the pilgrims visiting the shrines in the sanctuary.

The Quire and Altar

Turn right into the **Quire (9)**. This area of the cathedral dates from the early 13th century and is in Early English style. Note the pointed arches, the slender Purbeck Marble pillars, the bold carving on the capitals and the sculptures in the spandrels of the triforium. Some of these carvings were restored in Victorian times, but the majority are 13th-century. Turn to the choir stalls. The back rows on each side date from the 14th century and have a superb collection of 37 carved misericords. Move into the sanctuary, dominated by the over-ornate Victorian marble reredos showing Christ in Majesty seated between the four evangelists. Far more pleasing is the modern altar-front collage tapestry showing the cathedral and nearby buildings reflected in the River Severn. Look up at the vaulting. The painting was designed by Sir George Gilbert Scott based on 13th-century originals. If you've been to Salisbury and Winchester cathedrals you'll see the similarities.

Immediately in front of the altar is the **Tomb of King John (10)**. A friend of Wulfstan, John left a codicil to his will expressing his wish to be buried at Worcester. The marble top of the tomb is the lid of the original coffin, while the base dates from the 15th century. This is claimed to be the earliest extant royal effigy in the country.

To the right of the sanctuary is the magnificent stone **Chantry of Prince Arthur (11)**. Arthur, the elder brother of Henry VIII, had just married Catherine of Aragon when he died, aged 15, at Ludlow Castle. (Catherine went on to marry Henry.) His body was brought with great pomp to Worcester, where a long series of funeral services was held involving three bishops, eight abbots and the Prior of Worcester. The chantry, which contains Arthur's tomb, has some superb vaulting and imagery. It is believed to have been built by masons from Westminster Abbey, where they were working on a chapel for Henry VII. A good view of the chantry can also be had from the south choir aisle.

Chapels

Return to the north aisle. On the left stands **St George's Chapel (12)**, the chapel of the Royal Worcestershire Regiment. It has a number of military memorials, including one to the World War I chaplain G.A. Studdert Kennedy (1883–1929), better known as 'Woodbine Willie'. Note the exterior stone screen, which dates from the 15th century and which occupied a place behind the high altar until the Victorian renovations. Opposite the chapel is a stretch of wall with some faintly discernible medieval paintings. Covered with limewash during the Puritan regime, these were exposed during the Victorian renovations and left in pre-restoration condition to show the previous state of the cathedral. There are two tombs beneath the wall paintings; although the incumbents cannot be identified, the ball flower decoration on the arch of the eastern tomb is *c*1320.

We have now reached the east end of the cathedral, dominated by the **Lady Chapel (13)**. Apart from the stained glass and the roof decoration, the chapel is much as it was when built by Bishop de Blois in the early 13th century. It is typically Early English in style with pointed lancet windows and free use of Purbeck Marble shafts; the carved scenes in the spandrels are an important feature. The two tombs at the sides of its entrance are those of bishops de Blois (in office 1218–36) and Cantelupe (in office 1237–66), who were responsible for the reconstruction of the east end of the cathedral.

Leave the Lady Chapel and walk back along the south side of the cathedral. To the right is the **Dean's Chapel (14)** or southeast transept, where there are a number of examples of the original 13th-century sculpture in the spandrels. The tomb in the centre of the chapel is that of Sir Griffith Ryce, standard-bearer to Prince Arthur. Note the similarities between the tombs of Ryce, King John and Prince Arthur. Also in the southeast transept, in a glass recess in the west wall, is a triptych of Our Lady and the Holy Child, made of Derbyshire alabaster in the late 15th century and thought to be by Sir W. St John Hope. From this position it is possible to view the exterior of Arthur's Chantry, decorated with a number of heraldic devices and the pomegranate, symbol of the city of Granada, Catherine of Aragon's home. The tombs beneath the chantry, believed to be those of Bishop Gifford (in office 1267–1301) and Lady Gifford, were already in position when the chantry was constructed over them.

Crypt and Cloisters

Take the steps down into the **Crypt (15)**. The oldest part of the cathedral, built by Wulfstan 1084–9, this is the largest Norman crypt in England – and was once even larger, before the eastern end was filled in to support the new choir above. The crypt

Ruins of the monastery Guesten House

is a good example of the strong but simple Romanesque architecture. It is believed the columns were re-used from an earlier building. The crypt is regularly used for exhibitions; at the time of writing there were displays on Oswald, Wulfstan and the Worcester Pilgrim.

Leave the crypt by the exit stairs to the south transept. This area is almost entirely filled with the organ case, once at the west end of the choir but placed here by Scott during the Victorian restoration, reportedly against his better judgement. From the transept turn into the **Cloisters (16)**, built during the 14th and 15th centuries and once at the core of the monastic community. All four cloister walks have items of interest. The west walk has a lavatorium (washing place) for the monks; the doors leading to their dormitory have now been filled in with stone. In the east walk is a row of five bells of various sizes, all that remain of the original peal of eight bells; the oldest dates back to 1374. The space behind the bells once contained cupboards for the monks' books as they worked at desks in the spaces by the windows. The cloisters have a fine range of bosses in the vaulting. Finally, note the attractive cloister garth or garden, which contains the types of herb which the monks would have grown; there are also a few gravestones, but these would not have been there in monastic times – monks were usually buried on the west side of their church, but at Worcester many of the graves were removed so the Lady Chapel could be built. The bones were transferred to a specially built charnel house, probably near the north porch.

From the east cloister look into the **Slype (17)**. This narrow passage led from the cloisters to the cemetery and was the place where the monks were allowed to converse. Note the walls, into which small arches and pillars are set; they probably came from the earlier Saxon cathedral. The slype is now the cathedral tearoom.

Also on the side of the east cloister is the **Chapter House (18)**, where the monastic community held its daily meetings. This was built in the early 12th century with alternating bands of green sandstone and white limestone set against interlocking arches (it is possible that much of the early Norman cathedral was in this style). The upper part of the building, including the windows, dates from the late 14th century and is in Perpendicular style. The vaulting is supported by a slender pillar. This chapter house is claimed to be the earliest of any English cathedral. A curiosity is that, although the building is circular inside, the exterior is decagonal because of the wall-strengthening in the 14th century.

Leave the cathedral by the east cloister and the passage which runs past the end of the monks' refectory (now the King's School Hall). This leads you to College Green, on the south side of the cathedral, and the end of the tour.

WALKING TOUR FROM WORCESTER CATHEDRAL

The tour begins and ends in the monastic surroundings of the cathedral. The Royal Worcester Porcelain Factory gives a glimpse of one of the city's most important industries before you move on to look at Worcester's role in the Civil War. The tour then proceeds into the largely pedestrianized city centre, with its wealth of well preserved historic buildings. Waterways are represented by the River Severn and the Worcester and Birmingham Canal.

Start: The south side of the cathedral, at the cloister entrance.
Finish: The north porch of the cathedral.
Length: 1½ miles (2.6km).
Time: Just over 1hr, but you will probably want to visit one or more of the museums.
Refreshments: The cathedral tea room is small and offers only a limited range of snacks, but plenty of historic pubs in the city centre offer good lunchtime food, including the King Charles II Restaurant in New Street, the Salmon's Leap opposite the Royal Worcester works, Ye Olde Talbot Hotel and the Cardinal's Hat (*c*1482), both in Friar Street, and the Old Pheasant and the Swan With Two Necks, both in New Street. An unusual eatery is RSVP in the redundant St Nicholas Church, which has been converted into a trendy café-bar.

College Green (1) is Worcester's version of a cathedral close; it gained its name at the time of the Dissolution, when the administration of the cathedral was taken over by a college of the dean and canons. Some of the buildings are used by the King's School. Leave the green by the archway under **Edgar Tower (2)**; this pink sandstone structure was built in the 13th century on the orders of King John and was the main entrance to the monastery. Passing through the arch, pause to look at the huge wooden gates, which it is believed are the originals.

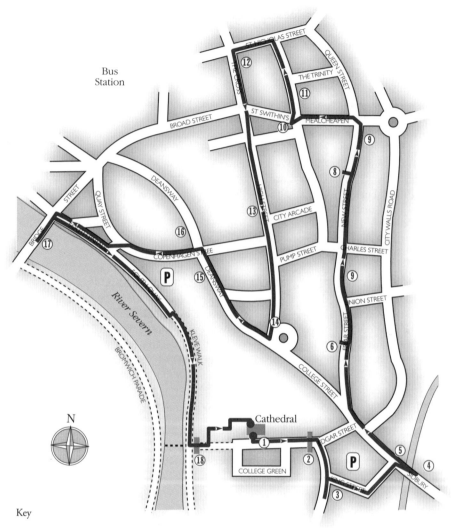

Key

1. College Green
2. Edgar Tower
3. Royal Worcester Pocelain Works
4. The Commandery
5. Worcester and Birmingham Canal
6. Museum of Local Life
7. The Greyfriars
8. Reindeer Court Shopping Centre
9. King Charles Restaurant
10. St Swithan's Church
11. Queen Elizabeth's House
12. Church of St Nicholas
13. Guildhall
14. Statue of Sir Edward Elgar
15. St Alban's Church
16. St Andrew's Spire
17. Worcester Bridge
18. Watergate

From Edgar Tower, turn right past the King's School Tuck Shop and proceed down Severn Street. On the left, just past the junction with King Street, is the **Royal Worcester Porcelain Company (3)**. The firm was founded in 1751 by Dr John Wall and gained its first Royal Warrant in 1789 from George III. Today the company's china and porcelain are world famous, and there is much here to see.

Royal Connections

Head back towards the cathedral, turning right almost immediately along King Street, which skirts around the carpark to the road called Sidbury. Cross Sidbury with care and head for the half-timbered building known as the **Commandery (4)**. This dates largely from the 15th century and was founded as the Hospital of St Wulfstan. After the Reformation it was in the hands of the Wylde family. In more recent years it served as a college for the blind and then a printing works, before being purchased by the City Council in 1977. It now houses a museum, the Civil War Centre. The entrance is deceptively small, the museum in fact being a rambling complex of buildings with oak-panelled rooms where audiovisuals are used to tell the tale of the Civil War. The Commandery was the Royalist headquarters at the Battle of Worcester in 1651, and just outside the building was the Sidbury Gate, which was stormed by the Parliamentarian forces. The Royalists were overwhelmed and Charles II subsequently had to flee for his life to France. The Commandery has a giftshop and a popular canal-side restaurant.

Alongside the Commandery is Sidbury Bridge, which crosses the **Worcester and Birmingham Canal (5)**. One of the locks is just below the bridge. The canal was built in the 18th century and was busy with freight until the railways came onto the scene. It is 30 miles (50km) long and has five tunnels and 58 locks, which are narrow and only one gate wide.

Continue towards the city centre, forking right into Friar Street. This pedestrianized street has a wealth of ancient buildings, many half-timbered. A good example can be seen immediately on the left – the **Museum of Local Life (6)**. The building dates from the 16th century and has a post and pan and a fine jettied wall. The museum reflects the social life and history of Worcester, particularly over the last two centuries. Further along Friar Street, on the right, is another half-timbered building, **The Greyfriars (7)**, now owned by the National Trust. Built in 1480 with early-17th- and late-18th-century additions, it was rescued from demolition during World War II and has been carefully restored.

Friar Street progresses into New Street. On the left is the imaginative **Reindeer Court Shopping Centre (8)**, which has many small specialist shops and restaurants. The main entrance is through an old 16th-century coaching inn, The Reindeer, originally called The Rayned Deer. Continue along New Street until on the right you see the **King Charles II Restaurant (9)**. This and the florist's shop around the corner date from 1577 and comprise the building in which King Charles II stayed before evading Cromwell's soldiers.

You have now reached the Cornmarket, a small square which once contained the city's stocks. Turn left into Mealcheapen Street, where at the end is the plain wall of **St Swithun's Church (10)**. Now redundant, this 18th-century church is looked after by the Churches Conservation Trust. It is normally closed, but if you would like to look inside you can ask for keys at the Tourist Information Centre in the Guildhall.

Now turn right into Trinity Street. On the right is a simple half-timbered building with a large balcony, **Queen Elizabeth's House (11)**; from here Queen

Elizabeth I is reputed to have addressed the citizens of Worcester when she visited the city in 1575. At the end of Trinity Street, turn left into St Nicholas Street and then left again into The Cross. This was the point where the four main roads of the city met, a prime position – as shown by the imposing bank frontages. Also prominent here is the redundant **Church of St Nicholas (12)**, dating from the 18th century but built on the site of an earlier church. Today it has been converted into an imaginative café-bar, RSVP: the stained-glass windows and pulpit have been retained among the tables, while the font forms a flower-covered centrepiece. This place is proving a popular watering hole.

A Many-Faceted City

Wander down the pedestrianized High Street. On the right is the impressive frontage of the Queen Anne-style **Guildhall (13)**. Dating from 1724, with major renovations in 1870, this was the site of the City Assizes for over two centuries. You are free to look around and perhaps take tea in the first-floor Assembly Room. Note the exterior, showing the city's coat-of-arms, with the motto 'City Faithful in War and Peace' – you'll recall that Worcester supported the Royalists during the Civil War. The statues of Charles I and Charles II can be seen on either side of the main door. The Guildhall is also the site of the helpful Tourist Information Centre.

Continue to the end of the High Street, marked by the **Statue of Sir Edward Elgar (14)**. Facing the cathedral, the statue was unveiled by Prince Charles in 1981. Elgar spent much of his childhood in the family music shop, marked by a blue plaque on the wall just a few yards from the statue. Regarded as one of the great English composers, Elgar was also an organist, violinist and teacher. Although a Roman Catholic, he had many connections with the cathedral and was closely associated with the Three Choirs Festival. His birthplace, at Lower Broadheath, some three miles (5km) from the centre of Worcester, is open to the public.

Turn right into Deansway and walk down to the junction with Copenhagen Street. Look across the road to the modern college, sandwiched between two churches. On the left is the minute **St Alban's Church (15)**, built of pink sandstone and dating from the 12th century. It has joined the ranks of Worcester's many redundant churches and today is a day-care centre for the homeless. On the right is the 246ft (75m) **St Andrew's Spire (16)**, all that remains of the church of the same name, which was demolished in 1940. Known during the prime of the Worcester glove industry as 'The Glover's Needle', the spire is surrounded by attractive gardens.

Cross Deansway by the pedestrian crossing and walk down Copenhagen Street to the River Severn. Turn right along South Parade to **Worcester Bridge (17)**. There has been a bridge here since 1313. The present structure was built in 1781 and widened in the 1930s. Worcestershire County Cricket Ground lies just beyond the bridge, and the racecourse is a few hundred yards upstream. From here you get magnificent views of the cathedral.

Return along South Parade to the riverside thoroughfare called Kleve Walk, after one of Worcester's twinned towns. Follow Kleve Walk for about two hundred yards until you reach the **Watergate (18)**, which was the westerly entrance to the monastery and the traditional landing-point for the ferry across the River Severn; the ferrymen lived in the house above the gate. Note the wall on the right, which has a series of plaques showing the height the river has reached at various times. The Severn carries away most of the rain that falls on the highlands of Central Wales and is thus prone to flooding – flood waters have even stopped play at the cricket ground!

Pass through the Watergate. The path straight ahead up the hill takes you directly back to College Green, but for a more interesting route to the cathedral turn left and head through the gardens towards some ruins. These turn out to be the reredorter, the drainage conduit from the monks' toilets in the old dormitory (dorter). Climb the steps past the west window of the cathedral, with its rose window, and proceed along the north side of the building to the North Door, where the tour ends.

Courtyard of the Commandery Museum

COVENTRY

Access: The M6 motorway runs just to the north of the city, giving easy connections to the M5, the M42, the M69, the M1 and the M54. Coach services use these routes for speedy links with many parts of the country. Coventry is also on one of the busiest railway lines in England. The nearest international airports are at Birmingham, ten miles (16km) to the west, and East Midlands, at Castle Donnington, 45 miles (60km) to the northeast. There is also a canal basin close to the city centre, although the waterway is now almost entirely confined to leisure traffic. Coventry has a park-and-ride system. There are plenty of carparks between the inner ring road and the city centre, and visitors to the cathedral will not find parking a problem.

There is no archaeological evidence of Roman occupation in the area which is now central Coventry. It is known that Saint Osburga founded a nunnery here some time in the 7th century; this was destroyed in 1016, when Mercia was in revolt against King Canute (*c*995–1035). In 1043 Edward the Confessor granted a charter to Earl Leofric (d1057) and his wife Godiva (*c*1040–1080) to set up a Benedictine monastery at Coventry – this is the Godiva whom legend says rode naked through the streets in an attempt to save the citizens from unfair taxation. The priory flourished and, as was often the case in those days, a settlement grew around it. After the Conquest the Norman earls of Chester played an important part in encouraging the growth of the town. They built a motte and bailey castle in the late 11th century, later demolishing it to accommodate a new street plan. The monks, meanwhile, having built their priory and church, constructed two parish churches for the townsfolk: Holy Trinity Church was completed in 1113 and St Michael's Parish Church in 1145. The three church spires were to be the town's most notable landmarks for centuries. At the end of the 11th century, the priory church was designated a cathedral and the diocese of Coventry and Lichfield set up.

Over the next three centuries Coventry's prosperity was based on the textile industry, particularly wool-making, with leather- and glassmaking also important. By the mid-14th century it was the fourth largest town in England (after London, Bristol and York), and the rich merchants constructed some magnificent houses, a few of which remain today, plus the superb St Mary's Guildhall (1342). It was during this period that St Michael's Parish Church was rebuilt in Perpendicular style.

This prosperity did not last. The wool trade was already declining when Henry VIII dissolved the priory in 1538. The monastic buildings went into private hands before gradually falling into decay as the stonework was removed for other building projects. The see of Coventry and Lichfield was transferred at this time to Lichfield.

After the lean years, Coventry's second period of economic growth came with the Industrial Revolution. Progress was led by the watch- and clockmaking industry, which employed over 2000 people and set the town on the way to becoming a notable centre of engineering. The manufacture of cycles was followed by that of motorbikes and then, as the 20th century evolved, the making of cars. An important landmark was 1918, when the diocese of Coventry was founded, with St Michael's Parish Church becoming the city's second cathedral.

The two World Wars saw Coventry's factories making planes, vehicles and munitions, work which attracted people from far and wide and doubled the city's population. Coventry's factories, however, were a prime target for German bombers during World War II, and St Michael's Cathedral was to suffer too. On the night of November 14 1941, Luftwaffe bombs destroyed much of Coventry's city centre; 568 lives were lost and there were hundreds of injuries. The cathedral suffered several direct hits and the wooden roof soon fell. The local fire brigade could not cope, and the cathedral officials were reduced to saving what valuable artefacts they could. Remarkably, the tower and spire remained unscathed among the ruins, along with the nave walls, crypt and south porch.

The following day it was agreed that the cathedral would be rebuilt. Sir Giles Gilbert Scott submitted designs, but it was soon realized that it would be too expensive to renovate the existing building. A competition was held to design a new cathedral, and 219 plans were submitted. The winner, although his nontraditional design was not universally popular, was Basil Spence (1907–1976), then a little-known architect, Work began on the new cathedral in 1955 and the foundation stone was laid by Queen Elizabeth II a year later.

In May 1962, in the presence of the Queen, the new Coventry Cathedral was consecrated. A Visitor Centre was opened in 1984; here high-technology audiovisual material tells the story of Coventry, concentrating on the theme of reconciliation. The cathedral celebrated its Silver Jubilee in 1987.

TOUR OF THE CATHEDRALS

Start (old cathedral): St Michael's Porch.
Finish (old cathedral): The north door.
Start (new cathedral): Priory Street by St Michael's Steps.
Finish (new cathedral): Exit door in southwest corner.

Before touring the two buildings, it is crucial to understand the rationale behind Spence's design for the new cathedral. His approach was always to consider the ruins of the old cathedral and the new cathedral as a single entity, with St Michael's Porch providing the physical link: the old building would signify crucifixion and sacrifice, the new cathedral resurrection. The common theme throughout is reconciliation.

THE OLD CATHEDRAL

Though razed in 1940, the old cathedral, remains consecrated ground and, indeed, services still take place in the crypt chapels and at the Altar of Reconciliation. The ruins form a shell of pink sandstone walls with Perpendicular windows that lack, of course, their glass. The nave pillars are mere stumps, interspersed with seats. The tower, with its tall spire, has remarkably remained intact.

Enter the ruins from the north door via St Michael's Porch and what are known as the Queen's Steps. Turn right and note the plaque on the wall telling something of the history of the building. One fascinating point here is that the iron struts introduced to strengthen the tie beams of the wooden roof twisted in the heat of

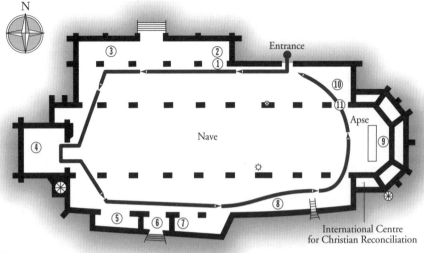

N

Entrance

Apse

Nave

International Centre
for Christian Reconciliation

Key

1. Statue of Reconciliation
2. Girdlers' Chapel
3. Smiths' Chapel
4. Tower
5. Dyers' Chapel

6. Bishop Haigh's Memorial
   Chapel
7. Cappers' Room
8. Ecce Homo
9. Altar of Reconciliation

10. Drapers' Chapel
11. Effigy of Bishop Yeatman-Biggs

the fire caused by the incendiary bombs and were responsible for bringing down much of the upper masonry. Further on the right is the **Statue of Reconciliation (1)** by Josefina de Vasconcellos, showing two kneeling figures. It was made by the artist when she was 90 and given to the cathedral by Richard Branson in 1995 to mark the 50th anniversary of the end of World War II.

You then come to the first of numerous guild chapels around the nave aisles; they show the strength of the woollen craft industries in the city in the 1300s and 1400s. The chapels were primarily chantries where masses were sung for deceased members, but were used also as meeting places for the conduct of the guilds' affairs. They had private entrances and were not open to the public. The guilds paid for chantry priests; in 1522 there were six of these. By the end of the 16th century, however, the guild chapels and all their possessions had passed to the city authorities. The chapels are marked by 'hallowing places' depicted on engraved plaques. Immediately behind the Statue of Reconciliation is the **Girdlers' Chapel (2)**, and this is followed shortly afterwards by the remains of the **Smiths' Chapel (3)**.

Step across to the **Tower (4)**, built between 1373 and 1394. The spire, added in 1433, is at 294ft (90m) the third highest in England (after Salisbury and Norwich). Built on unstable ground, the tower was in bad shape by the time it was comprehensively restored in 1895, using red sandstone from the Runcorn quarries. The spire, one of three to grace the central Coventry skyline over the centuries, would have been immediately recognizable by the four flying arches at the junction of spire and tower. Also distinctive are the statues of the Botoner family, generous

14th-century benefactors. The tower's twelve bells were rehung in 1987 to celebrate the cathedral's Silver Jubilee, and were rung for the first time when Coventry City won the FA Cup Final. It is possible to climb the tower for marvellous views over the city, but be warned: there are 180 steps, and they're steep.

Now proceed along the south side of the ruins. First you find the **Dyers' Chapel (5)**, which still contains one rather decrepit monument. Next is the enclosed **Bishop Haigh's Memorial Chapel (6)**, claimed to be one of the oldest parts of the building and named after the bishop at the time of the destruction; it is known also as the Chapel of Resurrection. Above Bishop Haigh's Chapel is the **Cappers' Room (7)**, the only above-ground guild chapel to have survived. It is still used for meetings.

Further along the south side is the *Ecce Homo* **(8)**, a statue carved by Sir Jacob Epstein (1880–1959) in 1934–5 from a block of Subiaco marble. It was presented to the cathedral by Lady Epstein in 1969. The *Ecce Homo* represents Christ on trial before Pilate, with his hands bound and the crown of thorns on his head.

You now approach the sanctuary and the east end of the ruins. In the southeast corner is the place where the old organ used to be, and just past here is the International Centre for Christian Reconciliation. The east end is in the form of an apse, with fine Perpendicular windows. In its centre is the **Altar of Reconciliation (9)**, topped by the Charred Cross. When the cathedral burned in 1940, two of the roof beams fell in the form of a cross. An altar was hastily built from broken masonry and the charred cross placed upon it. The carved words 'Father Forgive' form an important part of the Coventry Litany of Reconciliation, a prayer based on the Seven Deadly Sins.

Turn back now to the south side to the last guild chapel, the **Drapers' Chapel (10)**. The feature here is the bronze **Effigy of Bishop Yeatman-Biggs (11)**; he was bishop when the See of Coventry was revived in 1918. The swastika on his mitre reminds us that this was a symbol of good luck long before the Nazis adopted it.

Leave the ruins through the north door. You can either go straight on to the new cathedral or go round the ruins anticlockwise via Cuckoo Lane and Bayley Lane to Priory Street, and start the second part of the walk from there.

THE NEW CATHEDRAL

Bear in mind that the new building is aligned north–south, instead of the traditional east–west, so the normal directional terms used in other cathedrals do not apply. All the features described have a symbolism and meaning, and the theme of reconciliation is continued from the old building.

From Priory Street, with the university to your east, approach the main entrance by climbing St Michael's Steps. This is a good position to appreciate the exterior of the building, which is predominantly constructed of pink Hollington Sandstone with, in places, a contrast provided by blue-green Lakeland Stone. On the right of the steps is the huge bronze **Sculpture of St Michael and the Devil (12)**, the last of Epstein's religious works. The sculpture suggests that good will always triumph over spiritual guilt and evil.

Climb the steps to St Michael's Porch. Pause to look at the south end of the cathedral, which is in reality a **Glass Screen (13)**, the work of John Hutton (b1906). In many of the panels the glass has been incised with figures of angels, apostles, saints, prophets and patriarchs. As well as providing a link between the old and new cathedrals, the screen allows a view through to the nave, showing that the building is open to the world rather than cut off from the wider community.

Step into the building, noting the cherubs on the door handles – more of Epstein's work. At the information desk to the right the friendly staff will suggest a donation for the upkeep of the cathedral. Turn back to face the glass screen, which may well give a different impression when seen from the interior of the building, particularly if the sunlight is streaming in from the south.

Depictions of Christ

Move across to the circular **Chapel of Unity (14)** in the southwest corner. On the right of the entrance is a collage showing in pictorial form the diocese of Coventry, while opposite is a sculpture by Helen Huntingdon-Jennings of the head of the crucified Christ, made from the metal of a crashed car. Entering the chapel, you are immediately struck by the mosaic floor, which shows the continents and the symbols of the four gospels; designed by Einar Forseth, it was a gift from the people of Sweden. There is a simple central glass altar, below which a dove can be seen in the mosaic. Above the altar is a tall cross, painted black to reflect the fact that the 'church' is still not united. The narrow windows were designed by Margaret Traherne and given by German Christians.

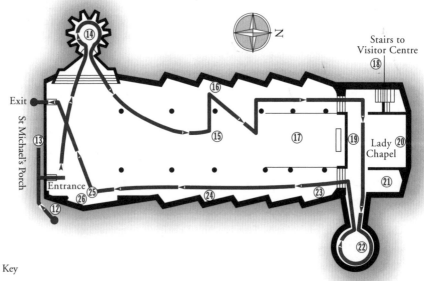

Key

12. Sculpture of St Michael and the Devil
13. Glass Screen
14. Chapel of Unity
15. Nave
16. Tablets of the Word
17. Chancel
18. Visitor Centre
19. High Altar
20. Sutherland's Tapestry of Christ
21. Chapel of Christ in Gethsemane
22. Chapel of Christ the Servant
23. The Plumb Line and the City
24. Nave Windows
25. Font
26. Baptistry Window

Walk back into the **Nave (15)**. This is a good spot to take a long-distance view of the Sutherland tapestry, which will be examined more closely later. As you look north, the zigzag roughcast walls and the slim concrete pillars give an impression of height, but in fact the walls are a mere 70ft (22m) high. The south-facing lower parts of the walls are distinguished by eight **Tablets of the Word (16)**. They contain New Testament texts and were inscribed by Ralph Beyer in uneven lettering to emphasize that they are the work of man, rather than machine, and that man is still dependent on the primitive truths of the church.

Move along the nave to the **Chancel (17)**. The stalls for the canons and choir have a canopy of spikes, resembling thorns or birds in flight, which tower up above the Provost's stall and the bishop's *cathedra*. Note, too, the modern organ console. In front of the stalls are the pulpit and lectern, designed by Basil Spence. Both the eagle on the lectern and the crucifix on the pulpit are the work of Dame Elisabeth Frink (1930-1994).

Walk to the left (north) side of the chancel to find a wooden Norwegian organ, a gift to the Coventry Song School. Ahead, steps lead down to the **Visitor Centre (18)** in the undercroft. The complex also includes the Song School, lecture hall, broadcasting studio, restaurant and shop. The Visitor Centre opened in 1984 and uses high technology in its audiovisual presentation to tell the story of Coventry Cathedral.

Geoffrey Clarke's High Altar Cross

From the top of the Visitor Centre steps, turn right behind the **High Altar (19)**. A simple concrete affair, the altar is flanked by six tall pottery candles, while surmounting it is Geoffrey Clarke's abstract cross. Made of gilded silver, it contains in its centre the original cross of nails from the old cathedral.

Turn now in the opposite direction, towards the Lady Chapel, to view **Sutherland's Tapestry of Christ (20)**. This is a neck-craning exercise, because the tapestry, which replaces the traditional east window, measures 74ft (23m) by 38ft (12m). Designed by Graham Sutherland (1903–1980), it was made in France by Pinton Frères and paid for by an anonymous resident of Coventry. The tapestry shows a huge seated figure of Christ wearing a carpenter's apron. Note the normal sized human being between his feet. On either side are the four traditional symbols of the evangelists, Matthew, Mark, Luke and John, while to his right the Devil is shown being thrown down into Hell. At the base is the crucifixion scene. Sutherland's original plans and paintings of the tapestry can be seen in the undercroft and in the Herbert Art Gallery (see page 133). The tapestry dominates the cathedral and is undoubtedly its most precious asset.

Places of Strength

Move past the Lady Chapel to the delightful little **Chapel of Christ in Gethsemane (21)**. When Jesus went to the Garden of Gethsemane to pray on the night before his crucifixion he was visited by an angel, who brought him strength. Here in Coventry this chapel is today used for private prayer and meditation. The gold-and-grey mural behind the simple altar shows an angel holding the cup of suffering. The metal screen enclosing the chapel represents the crown of thorns and was made by the Royal Engineers.

Walk up the sloping corridor into the **Chapel of Christ the Servant (22)** or, as it is often known, the Chapel of Industry. This circular chapel, designed by Basil Spence, has clear glass windows through which you can see many of the buildings of central Coventry; the idea is that the cathedral is part of the wider city community and that worship and life in general are closely entwined. In the centre of the chapel is a stone base bearing the words 'I AM AMONG YOU AS ONE THAT SERVES', and above this is an oak altar table inlaid with boxwood. Both were the work of apprentices at the city's technology college. Rising above the altar is a white aluminium cross enveloped by a crown of thorns made by Geoffrey Clarke.

Return now to the nave. Immediately on the left is a sculpture entitled *The Plumb Line and the City* **(23)**, made in 1971 by Clarke FitzGerald from Cincinatti. Composed of a collage of metal items, the 'city' contains factories, churches, schools, office blocks, cars, etc. The symbolism of the plumb line, based on *Amos* 7:8, poses the question: are the inhabitants of the city upright or not?

From this point you can view the **Nave Windows (24)**, not visible when you were walking in the opposite direction. There are five windows on each side of the nave. Their modern stained glass – by Lawrence Lee, Keith New and Geoffrey Clarke – depicts human life through the stages of Birth, Youth, Maturity, Old Age and Resurrection. The windows are 70ft (22m) high. Their angled south-facing position ensures maximum light and they look quite stunning on days when the sun is streaming through.

Walk finally to the southeast corner of the cathedral. Backed by the baptistry window, the **Font (25)** is a rough three-ton boulder from the Valley of Barakat, near Bethlehem. A scallop-shaped basin has been hollowed out on the top. The whole thing is mounted on a black marble base. Behind the font is the massive, curved **Baptistry Window (26)**, designed by John Piper (1903–1992) and made by Patrick Reyntiens. The window, 81ft (24.6m) high and 51ft (15.5m) across and stretching from floor to ceiling, contains 195 panels of brilliantly coloured glass, mainly deep blue and red on the outside and merging to a sunburst of white and yellow in the centre. The symbolism is of baptism. This is regarded by experts as possibly the greatest stained-glass window in the country.

Leave the cathedral by the exit door in the southwest corner.

WALKING TOUR FROM THE CATHEDRALS

Unfortunately, much of the historic core of Coventry was destroyed in the Blitz, but enough remains to offer an interesting walk. This short circular tour includes historic features such as the remains of the priory, some fine Elizabethan houses, a medieval guildhall and some remnants of the city walls, with gates at each end, plus one of the most interesting parish churches in the country. There are two museums to see – the Herbert Art Gallery and Museum and the superb Museum of British Road Transport. The tour ends at the Tourist Information Office, under which is the city's only medieval vaulted cellar open to the public.

Start: St Michael's Porch, between the old and new cathedrals.
Finish: The Tourist Information Centre in Priory Street.
Length: 1½ miles (2km).
Time: Under 1hr, but allow considerably more time if visiting the Transport Museum, the Herbert Gallery and Holy Trinity Church.
Refreshments: Benedict's Coffee Shop in the cathedral's Visitor Centre is worth a visit. Of the numerous pubs in the city centre along the walking route, few can be recommended for lunch apart from the old half-timbered Golden Cross on the corner of Hay Lane and, opposite, the modern Newt and Cucumber.

Leave St Michael's Porch, which links the two cathedrals, and head northwest past the circular exterior of the Chapel of Unity to the end of **Priory Row (1)**, where there is a range of domestic buildings from various architectural periods. No 11, the Provost's House (or Gorton House), is an early-18th-century town house with a brick frontage and pillars in the Ionic style. It was severely damaged during World War II but has been faithfully restored. Nos 9–10, today part of the Coventry International Studies Centre, are early-

16th-century houses, Priory Row

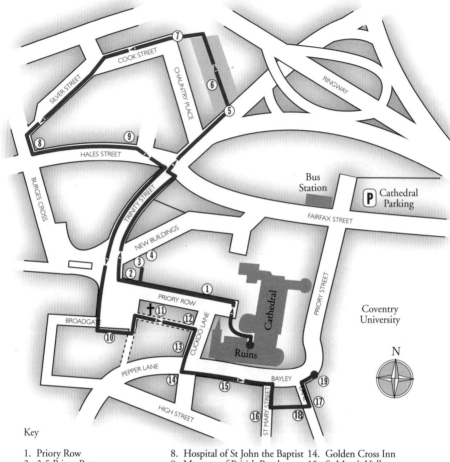

Key

1. Priory Row
2. 3-5 Priory Row
3. Blue Coat School
4. New Buildings
5. Swanswell Gate
6. Lady Herbert's Garden
7. Cook Street Gate
8. Hospital of St John the Baptist
9. Museum of British Road Transport
10. Statue of Lady Godiva
11. Holy Trinity Church
12. Coventry Cross
13. County Hall
14. Golden Cross Inn
15. St Mary's Hall
16. Council House
17. Herbert Art Gallery and Museum
18. Drapers' Hall
19. Tourist Information Office

19th-century town houses; their cellars are possibly part of the priory foundations and are some 30ft (9m) below the present street level. No 7, now the office of the Friends of Coventry Cathedral, was built around 1800; John Gulson, a mayor of the town and a public benefactor, lived here between 1835 and 1904.

Walk to the end of Priory Row. Just before the half-timbered house, an alleyway leads to the right. Beneath the railings, there is an excellent view of the foundations of what is believed to be west front of the Benedictine Priory Church built by Leofric and Godiva, and this Saxon couple are thought to be buried nearby. Excavations have shown that the east end of the church was near the present-day cathedral Visitor Centre, so the building would have been larger than either Holy Trinity, St Michael's or the modern cathedral. The priory was demolished during the Reformation, although the central tower remained. On the other side of Priory Row you can view the exterior of Holy Trinity Church, the red sandstone of the tower contrasting with the cream limestone of the nave.

You now reach **3–5 Priory Row (2)**, a collection of half-timbered buildings dating from the late 16th or early 17th century. They form one of only three surviving double-jettied buildings in the city. The alleyway to the right, parallel with the foundations, leads to the **Blue Coat School (3)**, opened as a charity school in 1714 and rebuilt on the same site in 1856–7 in the style of a French château. It was during these 19th-century renovations that the foundations of the priory were discovered. The Blue Coat School closed in 1940.

Quiet Places

Return to Priory Row. Turn right and right again into Trinity Street. Shortly on the right are the **New Buildings (4)**, a four-storey industrial site dating from 1849–50 and originally a steam-powered ribbonmaking factory. When this industry declined, John Gulson bought the building, which thereafter had a number of uses, including being used as a 'Ragged School' for poor children.

Cross Trinity Street at the traffic lights and head towards the Art Deco Hippodrome with its peeling paintwork. Cross Hales Street and, shortly along on the left, come to the only surviving stretch of the city's medieval walls, largely demolished in the 1660s on the orders of Charles II. At the southern end of the wall is the pink sandstone **Swanswell Gate (5)**, believed to date from the mid-15th century and probably the main gate into St Mary's Priory – it led in the other direction to the priory's fishpools. In the early years of the 20th century the gate was used as a residence, but in 1931 it was given to the city by Sir Alfred Herbert, a wealthy local industrialist, and carefully restored the following year.

Turn under the arch of the gate and enter **Lady Herbert's Garden (6)**. This was created in the 1930s as a memorial to Lady Herbert, Sir Alfred's second wife. With a pond and some exotic shrubs, it makes a peaceful change from the hustle and bustle of the city centre. Follow the right-hand path parallel to the old city wall until, at the top of the gardens, you reach **Cook Street Gate (7)**, a second survivor of the original twelve town gates. Believed to have been completed around 1385, it was largely derelict during the 19th century. It was given to the city in 1913 by Colonel W. F. Wyley, a local mayor and alderman, and restored after the end of World War I. A scheduled ancient monument, it still has road traffic running under it.

Pass through the gateway and walk down Cook Street and via Silver Street to Bishop Street. Turn left here and, on the corner of Hales Street, you find the **Hospital of St John the Baptist (8)**. This was founded in 1340, and its buildings once extended across what is now Hales Street. All that remains today is the 14th-century church that replaced the hospital's original chapel. The hospital was dissolved, along with monasteries, in the mid-16th century. In 1557 the building was converted into a 'Free Grammar School', which remained here until Victorian times, when it moved to Warwick Road; it is now known somewhat ironically as the Henry VIII School.

Road Transport

Continue along Hales Street until you see, on the left on the corner of St Agnes Lane, the **Museum of British Road Transport (9)**. Don't be put off by the rather unprepossessing exterior: this is a wonderland of cycles, motorbikes, cars and commercial vehicles, from 'penny farthings' to Thrust, the holder of the world land-speed record. The amazing thing is that the vast majority of the exhibits were built in the Coventry area, a fact that brings home to you the former importance of the city's engineering and metalworking trades. There are also mock-ups of Victorian shops and a rather alarming 'experience' of what it was like to be in the Coventry Blitz.

Leave the museum and turn right, back up Trinity Street, into the modern town centre, rebuilt after the wartime destruction. Carry on into Broadgate, where you will see the huge canopy covering the **Statue of Lady Godiva (10)**. Legend has it that Lady Godiva rode naked through the streets of Coventry in protest at the taxes her husband Leofric had imposed on the townspeople. Most averted their eyes but, of course, not Peeping Tom. The bronze statue, the work of Sir William Reid Dick (1879–1961), was unveiled in 1949.

Church and Tavern

Leave the modern Broadgate and go back to **Holy Trinity Church (11)**. This is one of the most interesting parish churches in the country. A church stood on this site as early as 1113, built by the Benedictine monks for their tenants, but this was destroyed by fire in 1250. The oldest part of the present building is the 13th-century north porch. There is a priest's room above the door, which was probably the main exit to the priory. In the Middle Ages the church had fifteen chapels; few of these remain, although the Tanners' Chapel on the north side has a medieval piscina. The south side of the nave has some stone seats (for the weakest to go to the wall). Holy Trinity has some interesting stained glass, both old and modern; there is some particularly good modern glass in the Great West Window by Hugh Easton. Other items of interest include the pulpit, dating from *c*1470 (the foliage beneath contains carved heads of, possibly, Henry VI and Queen Margaret of Anjou), the eagle lectern and the font (both 15th-century).

Exit from Holy Trinity and go along the alleyway called Trinity Churchyard to the right of the building. At the end is the **Coventry Cross (12)**. The present cross is a replica of the original, erected in 1541 in Broadgate but demolished in the 18th century. With four tiers and surrounded by a flight of four steps, the new cross was unveiled in 1976.

Turn right at the cross and go along the short Cuckoo Lane. Immediately on the right is the old **County Hall (13)**, a solid stone building in Classical style built in the 18th century and probably the city's only public building of this period to survive. Its rear was once the town gaol. The last public execution in Coventry took place in the street outside County Hall in 1849.

Next on the right is the **Golden Cross Inn (14)**, a 15th-century half-timbered building with double-jettied walls. It was comprehensively restored in the 19th century. Inside it there is a dragon beam in the ground-floor ceiling. Turn left past the modern Newt and Cucumber pub into Bayley Lane, believed to have been named after the motte and bailey of the Earl of Chester's castle, pulled down in the mid-12th century; the lane probably ran along the side of the castle's ditch. On the left are the walls of the ruined second cathedral, while on the right are a series of ancient buildings: first is a half-timbered house with jettied walls on brick foundations, probably dating from *c*1500. Note the elaborate carving on the beams.

Civic Buildings

You now come to **St Mary's Guildhall (15)**, on your right, justifiably claimed to be one of the finest medieval guildhalls in the country. It was built *c*1340 and probably included parts of a 12th-century castle in the south wall. Built for the Trinity guild, it in due course became the first seat of local government in the town. At first-floor level is the stunning Great Hall, which has a late-14th-century wooden roof. Below is a large vaulted undercroft. Set in the walls is a tower in which, it is claimed, Mary Queen of Scots was once imprisoned.

Now turn right along the narrow St Mary's Street. On the right is the **Council House (16)**, with its main frontage on the High Street. It was built 1913–17 and few would consider it an architectural gem; its main point of interest is the clock tower on the corner, featuring a number of statues including portrayals of Leofric and Godiva.

Halfway along St Mary's Street, turn left through some small gardens that contain an outdoor exhibition showing the history of the Bayley Lane area from the 11th century to the present. This part of the city was the centre of the wool industry, and many of the wealthy merchants, particularly drapers, had their homes here. Coventry cloth was famous for both its quality and its colour – a blue dye which never faded (hence the term 'true blue'). Later, when the woollen industry declined, so did the Bayley Street area. Much of it was destroyed during World War II.

Cross the road to the **Herbert Art Gallery and Museum (17)**. Named after Sir Alfred Herbert, the museum opened in 1959. Many of its exhibits relate to the Coventry area and include the drawings for Sutherland's cathedral tapestry. The gallery has works by L.S. Lowry (1887–1976) and Henry Moore (1898–1986).

Opposite the museum is the **Drapers' Hall (18)**, the headquarters for centuries of the Drapers' Guild. The present building, probably the third on the site, can hardly be called distinguished. It was built in 1832 and has a Greek Revival stone frontage, whose symmetry has been ruined by later alterations. The arms of the Drapers' Company can be seen over the upper corners. The rest of the exterior of the hall is of dull Midlands brick.

On the same side of the road as the museum is a Peace Garden, opened in 1990 on the 50th anniversary of the Blitz which destroyed the cathedral. The main feature is a Peace Stone, which has lines pointing to Coventry's twin towns (there are 28 of them!).

Nearby is our last port of call, the **Tourist Information Office (19)**, located in a modern building (opened 1990) erected over a 14th-century vaulted cellar, which is open to the public and can be reached down a flight of steps. The cellar measures 22ft (6.7m) long and 11½ft (3.5m) wide, in two nearly square bays. The ceiling has simple groyne ribs in the local red sandstone. In one of the bays is a display case showing some of the artefacts found during excavations, including cow-horns, clay pipes, ceramics and tiles.

Return to street level, where, opposite the cathedral, the tour concludes.

LICHFIELD

Access: The A38 and A5 trunk roads link the city to the Midlands motorway network, including the M42, M40, M6 and M1. Lichfield is fortunate in having two railway stations: trains from London Euston call at Lichfield Trent Valley, while trains from Birmingham run to both this station and Lichfield City. The nearest airports are Birmingham International and East Midlands, both within a 45min drive.

Archaeological evidence suggests there were settlements in the area in prehistoric and Celtic times. Later, during the Roman occupation of Britain, two roads crossed some two miles (3km) southwest of the present city: Ryknild Street (the present A38) and Watling Street (the present A5). At this point the Romans built a posting station, known as Letocetum ('Wall Village'), which became a military base. The site has been excavated to reveal the remains of a fort, baths, granary and an inn.

The story of Lichfield Cathedral begins with St Chad (d672). He was a pupil of St Aidan at Lindisfarne before being appointed Bishop of Mercia in 669. He immediately moved the see from Repton to Lichfield, where there was already a small church called St Mary's. Chad was not to last long in the post, however: he died three years later, being initially buried near St Mary's Church. Pilgrims flocked to his grave after miracles were reported. A new cathedral of St Peter was built to house his shrine, while pilgrims also visited St Chad's Well, about half a mile to the east.

The Saxon church was quickly replaced after the Conquest by a new cathedral in Norman style. Begun in 1085, the building was further expanded in the 12th century under the leadership of Bishop de Clinton, who was to die during the Second Crusade in 1148. The Norman cathedral must have been unsatisfactory, because in 1195, work began to replace it with a new building in Gothic style; nothing remains of the Norman cathedral except a few foundations discovered during excavations in the area of the present-day choir, but, almost certainly, St Chad's Shrine would have been placed behind the high altar. The transepts (in Early English style) of its replacement and St Chad's Head Chapel were completed by 1240 and the chapter house nine years later. Then came the nave, in Geometric Decorated Gothic, and by 1327 the west front was finished. The Lady Chapel followed between 1330 and 1340, so that by the end of the 14th century the cathedral was more or less complete. This was to be the Golden Age of Lichfield Cathedral, and the town itself became an important ecclesiastic centre. The cathedral and its close had been surrounded by sturdy sandstone walls in Bishop de Clinton's time, but this was not to work in the cathedral's favour in the centuries to come.

Always a secular establishment never attached to a monastery, Lichfield survived the Reformation relatively well. However, it did not escape unscathed, as Henry VIII's commissioners destroyed the Shrine of St Chad and removed the relics along with other treasures. Many statues were smashed, although structurally the fabric survived.

During the Civil War Lichfield suffered more than any other English cathedral. The sandstone walls and sturdy gates made the close an ideal fortress, and it was soon occupied by Royalist forces. However, in March 1643 the Roundheads, despite the death of their leader Lord Brooke (1611–1643), took the close. It was recovered by the Royalists one month later, Prince Rupert (1619–1682) firing cannons from the mound to the north of the cathedral. In 1643, it was taken back by the Roundheads, whose soldiers wreaked havoc in the cathedral, smashing statues, looting tombs and defacing monuments. There was very little stained glass left intact and the central spire had already been felled by cannonballs.

After things had quietened down with the Restoration, Bishop Hackett (d1669) set about the process of rebuilding the spire and patching up the rest of the damage done. For two centuries, nevertheless, Lichfield Cathedral was a pale shadow of its former greatness. In 1788 James Wyatt (1746–1813) began alterations: admittedly he saved the nave from falling down by removing much of the heavy vaulting and replacing it with lighter plaster, but many of his renovations and changes can in retrospect be considered nothing but disastrous. His most appalling alteration was to block up the arches of the choir aisles to create what has been described as a 'church within a church'.

The city of Lichfield, meanwhile, had become a thriving place. Its citizens of the time included the writer and lexicographer Samuel Johnson (1709–1784), the actor David Garrick (1717–1779) and the inventor Erasmus Darwin (1731–1802).

By the 19th century the Industrial Revolution was well under way. Despite coal deposits in the nearby South Staffordshire coalfield, Lichfield did not become a place of heavy industry like many of its neighbours – rather, it maintained its position as a prosperous market town and ecclesiastic centre. The middle part of the century saw the start of Sir George Gilbert Scott's restorations to the cathedral. Many Victorian renovations to English cathedrals are regarded as little more than vandalism, but Scott's work at Lichfield was done sympathetically and went a long way towards returning the cathedral to its medieval splendour. He redeemed Wyatt's insensitive work in the choir, which he provided with a colourful Minton tiled floor and an attractive metal screen linking it to the nave; he also restored the statues on the west front and St Chad's Head Chapel in the south aisle. Although the Victorian glass is not particularly distinguished, the early years of the century saw the introduction to the Lady Chapel of superb 16th-century stained glass from the suppressed convent of Herckenrode in Belgium. In the Close, the episcopal palace at last had a bishop in residence. George Selwyn (in office 1867–78) extended the building, and it is now the choir school.

Lichfield and its cathedral were largely unscathed during the two world wars, and today the cathedral has resumed its medieval role as a meeting place and venue for the local community. Foremost is the annual July International Festival of music, drama and entertainment. The building is in good shape thanks to a rolling maintenance programme.

TOUR OF THE CATHEDRAL
Start: The Cathedral Close.
Finish: The west end.

The **West Front (1)** is best viewed from halfway across the Cathedral Close. From here you can see the three spires (the main central spire and the two western ones), collectively known as the Ladies of the Vale. The stonework on the west front is the same as on the rest of the building – pink sandstone to which a residue of industrial pollution gives a curious mottled effect.

You will be immediately struck by the large number of statues on the west front: there are over a hundred, all but three being Victorian replacements. Central, high above the main door, is Jesus; this figure replaced that of Charles II, now found by the south transept door. The other statues, found in five rows, represent Saxon and Norman kings, early bishops, apostles and missionaries. The middle row includes a statue of Queen Victoria sculpted by her daughter Princess Louise. Artistically the statues have little merit – Alec Clifton Taylor observed in connection with the identical fussy little curls on each statue that they might pass as 'an advertisement for a local hairdresser'.

The architecture is more interesting. The two spires merge via heavily crocketed ornamentation into the towers, which in turn lose their identity within the five ranks of statues. The central window at the third level is in Geometrical Decorated style, a pattern repeated around the ground-level doors. A curious feature is the way the horizontal layers 'wrap around' the side of the west front; this in fact helps relieve the general flatness of this part of the building.

Enter the cathedral through the southwest door. Proceed into the **Nave (2)**. This is short, with only seven bays, and low – a mere 57ft (17.4m) from floor to vault – but the proportions are very satisfying. The arcade takes up 50 per cent of the height, with the rest being equally divided between the triforium and the clerestory. The vaulting, mainly in wood and plaster, is of the tierceron type. The style throughout the nave is Geometric Decorated. Of particular interest are the thin triple-attached shafts that sweep right up from floor to vault, taking the eye to the unique triforium windows which are in the form of curved triangles containing three circles filled with a trefoil. They look equally effective on the outside of the building. The trefoil pattern is repeated in the spandrels of the arcade. Note, too, the well carved oak-leaved capitals on the arcade's main pillars (which lean inwards rather alarmingly). Looking back to the west end, you can see the modern gallery, built by the Friends of Lichfield Cathedral.

Move over to the **North Aisle (3)**. Here there is blind arcading and, below that, stone seating where, in the days when the congregation stood in the nave, 'the weakest went to the wall'. Here also we see the first of many monuments in the cathedral – in this case brass wall plaques in memory of those who fell while serving in the South Staffordshire Regiment.

Walk ahead to the **Crossing (4)**, beneath the central tower. Dominating this area is the unusual choir screen: made of metal, it is painted and gilded. It was designed by Francis Skidmore (1816–1896) and erected during Sir George Gilbert Scott's renovations. The screen is complemented by the pulpit, made of similar materials.

Cross to the **North Transept (5)**. Of various undistinguished monuments here the most important is in the northwest corner: the remains of the 15th-century stone monument to Dean Haywood, which was smashed during the Civil War. Also in the transept is the 19th-century marble font, carved with biblical scenes. On the north side of the transept is the St Stephen's Chapel, which has a number of memorial tablets to former organists.

The Lichfield Gospels

Proceed now into the north choir aisle and turn left into a **Vestibule (6)** which leads to the chapter house. The vestibule has finely carved double arcading, below which is a medieval pedilavium, where feet were washed. Note, too, the vaulting, with stone infilling and impressive bosses. At the far end of the vestibule is a modern memorial bust of Bishop Edward Woods (1877–1953) by Jacob Epstein (1880–1959).

The **Chapter House (7)** dates from 1249 and is an elongated octagon vaulted from a central pier. The architecture is Early English. Note the stained glass in Kempe's window showing the life of St Chad. The main interest here, however, is the display on the Lichfield Gospels. Probably dating from around 730, they spent some time in Wales, but have been at Lichfield since the 10th century. Remarkably, they survived the desecrations of the Civil War, when they were protected by the Duchess of Somerset. The illuminated Gospels are written in Latin; there were once all four gospels, but only *Matthew, Mark* and part of *Luke* remain. Outstanding is the marvellous 'carpet page', whose design is based on the cross. The style is similar to that of the Lindisfarne Gospels and the Book of Kells at Trinity College, Dublin. The pages of the Gospels are made of vellum. The scribe's name is not known, but he was almost certainly a monk who devoted his life to the project.

The cathedral library, above the chapter house, is not normally open to the public.

The Retrochoir and Lady Chapel

Return via the vestibule to the main body of the cathedral and proceed along the north choir aisle. At the far end are memorials to the 19th-century bishops Lonsdale and Ryder. Turn right here into the **Retrochoir (8)**, where there is a tablet in the floor marking the place where St Chad's Shrine once stood. The shrine was provided by Bishop Langton in the 14th century at a cost of £2000, but

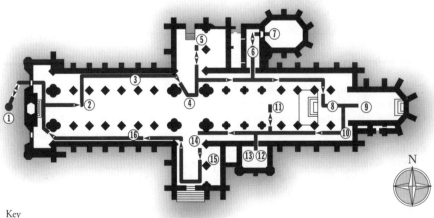

Key

1. West Front	7. Chapter House	13. St Chad's Head Chapel
2. Nave	8. Retrochoir	14. South Transept
3. North Aisle	9. Lady Chapel	15. St Michael's Chapel
4. Crossing	10. The Sleeping Children	16. South Aisle
5. North Transept	11. Choir and Presbytery	
6. Vestibule	12. Consistory Court	

was destroyed during the Reformation. Behind the tablet is the effigy of Bishop George Selwyn (in office 1867–78), who became the first bishop of New Zealand. Tiles around the tomb depict his work in that country.

Step into the **Lady Chapel (9)**, arguably the most impressive part of the cathedral. It follows the same height as the choir, but without, of course, the aisles. With its tall, narrow windows and angled east end, it has a distinctly continental feel about it. Set between the windows are statues of angels, each beneath a crocketed canopy; these are Victorian replacements, the originals having been destroyed during the Reformation. Blind arcading runs beneath the windows. Behind the altar is a gilded reredos, carved in Oberammergau. The main delight of the Lady Chapel, however, is undoubtedly the 16th-century stained glass brought from the suppressed convent of Herckenrode in Flanders by Sir Brooke Boothby (1744–1824) in 1803.

The Sleeping Children

From the Lady Chapel, move into the south choir aisle. Immediately on the left is the cathedral's most notable monument, **The Sleeping Children (10)**, an alabaster carving by Sir Francis Chantrey (1781–1841), who was also responsible for the Bishop Ryder Monument in the north choir aisle. Dating from 1817, the sculpture shows two young sisters, Ellen-Jane and Marianne, a cathedral prebendary's daughters who died in childhood. Nearby is a medieval piscina with traces of a mural, thought to date from around 1400. The south choir aisle is notable also for its collection of tombs and monuments of former bishops. Look for, successively, Bishop Hackett (d1669), who restored the cathedral after the ravages of the Civil War, Bishop de Langton (d1321), who built the Lady Chapel, and Bishop Patteshall (d1245), plus a number of lesser-known deans and archdeacons.

Halfway along the north choir aisle, turn right into the **Choir and Presbytery (11)**. To the right, the high altar is made of local stone, with the reredos of alabaster. The sedilia was put together in the 19th century using medieval stone. The choir was also revamped by Scott in the 19th century, reversing Wyatt's earlier meddling. Note the superb Minton tiled floor, with its roundels showing scenes from the life of St Chad. Behind the choir stalls are a series of shields. Finally, on the south side, is the richly carved Bishop's Throne.

Consistory Court and St Chad's Head Chapel

Return to the north choir aisle. Immediately on the left is the old **Consistory Court (12)**, now the cathedral treasury, containing robes, vestments and silverware. There is, unusually, some stunning modern silverware dating from the early 1990s, the Lang Lichfield Silver Collection, named after Dean Lang (in office 1980–94). Also on display are reproductions of the pendants which pilgrims would buy after visiting St Chad's Shrine or the Holy Well. A door in the wall leads to the Duckitt, which was the original, and more secure, treasury. On the west side of the room are some wooden seats, believed to be the original chairs in which the bishop sat during court hearings.

Now take the stairs up into the 13th-century **St Chad's Head Chapel (13)**. The head of St Chad, covered in gold leaf, was shown to pilgrims passing through the gallery outside the chapel. The gallery, incidentally, gives fine views of the Minton tiled floor in the presbytery. The chapel itself has robust sandstone vaulting.

Descend the stairs and return to the aisle. Move into the **South Transept (14)**, where there is a return to the Early English style of architecture – this is the oldest part of the cathedral. Look at the nearest pillar of the crossing, where there is a rummer, an early-18th-century bottle used to measure out the daily 2½-pint (1.4l) ration of ale for the adult members of the choir (or Vicars Choral).

On the east side of the transept is **St Michael's Chapel (15)**, which contains the colours of the South Staffordshire Regiment along with a Book of Remembrance. The chapel also has memorials to local notables Samuel Johnson and David Garrick. The windows of the chapel display a few fragments of medieval glass which survived the destruction of the Civil War.

Leave the south transept and walk down the **South Aisle (16)**. Of interest here is the second window on the left, which tells the story of David and Goliath, reminding us that, in times when most of the congregation could not read, the stained glass was relied upon to tell the Bible stories. Further along the aisle are some unusual wall monuments which have traces of medieval paintwork.

The tour concludes at the west end of the cathedral.

WALKING TOUR FROM LICHFIELD CATHEDRAL

The walk begins in the Cathedral Close, where a number of fine buildings may be seen and there is also the opportunity to inspect the external features of the cathedral. The walk continues into the city centre, following the grid pattern of roads established by Bishop de Clinton in the 12th century. You are treated to a wide range of domestic architecture, and the walk has many literary associations. The three museums en route are well worth a visit, as are some of the city's old coaching inns.

Start and finish: The west front of the cathedral.
Length: 1 mile (1.6km). The walk is almost entirely on flat land.
Time: 45 minutes, but allow extra time for the museums.
Refreshments: Bird Street has three famous old coaching inns – The Swan, The George and The King's Head – which have plenty of atmosphere and serve excellent lunches. Nearer the cathedral, the Angel Croft Hotel provides good bar meals. There are a number of bistros and coffee shops in the pedestrianized part of the city.

The **Cathedral Close (1)** was originally laid out by Bishop de Clinton (in office 1129–48) in the 12th century, when it was surrounded by a ditch; a sturdy stone wall followed. These defences led to the close being used as a fortress during the Civil War, when it was subjected to three sieges. As a result many of the medieval buildings were destroyed and in due course Parliament ordered the wall to be pulled down so that the cathedral could never again be a Royalist stronghold. Most of the present buildings were constructed in the 17th and 18th centuries, but behind their façades there are often medieval cores.

A Circumnavigation of the Cathedral

Immediately to the left of the west front, on the south side of the close at no 21, is the modest **Bishop's House (2)**, which has been the residence of the Bishop of

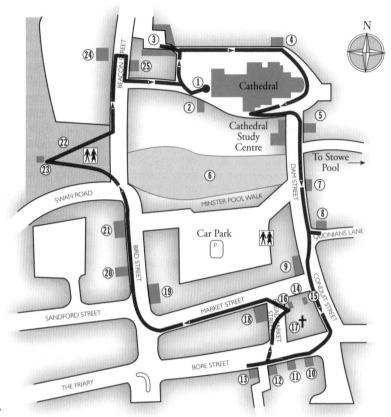

Key

1. Cathedral Close
2. Bishop's House
3. Vicars' Close
4. Old Bishop's Palace
5. St Mary's House
6. Minster Pool
7. Brooke House
8. Quonians Lane
9. Corn Exchange and
   Market Hall

10. Five Gables
11. Guildhall
12. Donegal House
13. Tudor Cafe
14. Market Place
15. Statue of Boswell
16. Statue of Johnson
17. St Mary's Church
18. Samuel Johnson
    Birthplace Museum

19. The George
20. The King's Head
21. The Swan
22. Beacon Park
23. Statue of John Smith
24. Angel Croft Hotel
25. Erasmus Darwin Museum

Lichfield only since 1954. The house was rebuilt in the 1790s, but its interior has some medieval remains, probably of a canon's house.

Head now to the northwest corner of the close, past an old pump, part of a water supply system which dates back to the 12th century – probably one of the first examples of a piped water supply in England. Walk down a narrow alleyway into **Vicars' Close (3)**, a grassy square surrounded by recently restored half-timbered buildings. This was the northern of two courtyards built to provide accommodation for the Vicars Choral, the adult members of the cathedral choir. Returning to the close, note the terrace of houses at the west end. These buildings were once part of the southern courtyard of Vicars' Close and originally their frontages faced inwards to the close, but by the end of the 18th century they had reversed their orientation to face the cathedral.

Walk along the north side of the close, where there is a range of 17th- and 18th-century buildings, including the school house and the deanery. One half-timbered building, apparently used as a garage, shows the remains of a cruck framework. At the far end is the **Old Bishop's Palace (4)**, built in 1687 to replace an earlier medieval building. Surprisingly, few bishops chose to live in the close, and this palace was often rented out; one of its famous tenants was Anna Seward (1742–1809), the poet. Bishop Selwyn, in the 1860s, was the first bishop to live in the palace, and the east and west wings were added during his occupancy. Selwyn's widow lived in Selwyn House at the east end of the close, from where there is a view over Stowe Pool.

The walk along the north side of the close gives you an opportunity to view some of the external features of the cathedral, including the flying buttresses which support the tilting pillars of the nave, the trefoiled windows of the clerestory, the beautifully carved north transept doorway and the 'continental' look of the Lady Chapel – note the double line of statues between the chapel's windows.

Walk further round to the south side of the cathedral, where on the corner of the south transept is a much-eroded statue of Charles II. This once occupied a key position on the west front, but was removed during the 19th-century restorations. After the ravages of the Civil War, Charles gave money and timber to help repair the cathedral. Note, too, the carving on the south transept door, with its seven bishops.

Domestic Architecture

Leave the Cathedral Close by the southeast corner. On the right is the Visitors' Study Centre and on the left is **St Mary's House (5)**, once the vicarage for St Mary's

Half-timbered buildings in Vicars' Close

Church in the city centre and now the diocesan office. St Mary's House embraces part of the old stone walls of the close, including a corner turret. The path at the side of the house gives views of some of the blocked arrowslits. Archaeological research has shown this was the site of a huge stone gatehouse destroyed in the 18th century.

Head now along the pedestrianized Dam Street, named after the embankment which blocked the stream to form **Minster Pool (6)**, now a pleasant lake containing a selection of wildfowl. Minster Pool was originally one of three lakes, but the upper pool has been drained and is now Museum Gardens. The lower and larger lake, to the east, is Stowe Pool.

Continue towards the city centre along Dam Street, where there is a variety of domestic architecture to be seen. Note on the left the Georgian **Brooke House (7)**, where a plaque notes that Lord Brooke (1611–1664), a leader of the Parliamentary forces in the Civil War, received his fatal wound on this spot. The shot was fired from the battlements of the steeple by the deaf Royalist John Dyott. Further along Dam Street, make a short diversion into **Quonians Lane (8)**, where immediately on the left is a half-timbered house of the type which would have housed an artisan in medieval times. There is some interesting stone carving on the wall.

Pass the Market Place (see below) to the right as Dam Street merges into Conduit Street. Above the shop fronts to the right you see the **Corn Exchange and Market Hall (9)**, built in 1849. The arcaded ground-floor area once contained a poultry market and a buttery; the arcades were filled in with shops in the 1970s. Ahead is the impressive frontage of Boots the Chemists: although it appears to be of some antiquity, it actually dates from the early years of the 20th century.

Turn right into Bore Street to find many of the more interesting and historic houses in the city. First on the left is **Five Gables (10)**, a half-timbered building probably dating from the late 16th century. It displays some intricate carving and herringbone pattern work. Next on the left is the **Guildhall (11)**, largely in Gothic style, constructed 1846–8 by the Trustees of Lichfield Conduit Lands, although parts of it go back to the early 15th century. It was not the first guildhall in the city, however; there is believed to have been one by 1387, in the time of Richard II. Guilds have always been powerful in Lichfield, particularly the religious Guild of St Mary, founded by Bishop Langton in 1295, which ruled the city for two centuries until it was dissolved in 1548.

Now you come to **Donegal House (12)**, a Georgian town house built for the Robinson family in 1730. A plaque outside the building states that it was given to the manor, aldermen and citizens of the city by Mrs M.A. Swinfen-Broun of Swinton Hall, Lichfield, in 1928. The ground floor is presently occupied by the helpful Tourist Information Centre. It is worth walking up the stairs to the first floor to view the Sketchbook Exhibition, where a number of the panelled rooms have been used to depict such topics as 'The Life of a Georgian Lady' and the work of various tradesmen such as millers, carpenters and scribes. The rooms have informative illustrative plaques, while waxwork models dressed in the clothing of the time add a lifelike touch.

To the right of Donegal House is the **Tudor Café (13)**, a 16th-century half-timbered building with jettied walls. The timberwork is in a variety of styles – post and pan, square, herringbone and, in the gables, patterned. The large amount of expensive wood in the building suggests the original owner was one of the more affluent members of Lichfield society. At the side of the Tudor Café is Tudor Row, a narrow alleyway leading to some small specialist shops.

Johnson and Boswell

Cross Bore Street and head along the short Breadmarket Street into the **Market Place (14)**. A market has been held here since 1153, when King Stephen granted Bishop Durdent, also Lord of the Manor of Lichfield, the right to hold a Sunday market. Since then this area has always been the centre of city life, whether for trade, socializing, public meetings or watching people being burnt at the stake (look at the plaques on the side of St Mary's Church for further gory details).

There are two statues of note in the Market Place. On the east side is the **Statue of Boswell (15)**. James Boswell was an associate of Samuel Johnson during the latter's London days, and they remained firm friends. Boswell's masterpiece was *The Life of Samuel Johnson* (1791), described by Macauley as 'the greatest biography in the English language'. Johnson often brought Boswell to Lichfield to experience country life at its best. At the opposite end of the Market Place is the **Statue of Johnson (16)**, which fittingly looks across the road to his birthplace and museum.

Do not leave the Market Place without visiting **St Mary's Church (17)**. There has been a church on this site since the 9th century and the present building is the fourth to be constructed here. Sadly, this parish church is now redundant and has been converted into a sort of civic centre and tourist attraction. The small Dyott Chapel has been retained as a place of worship, and elsewhere on the ground floor is an Old Peoples' Day Centre and an attractive coffee shop. The whole of the nave has been given a mezzanine level and this houses the Heritage Centre, which boasts audiovisual displays, dioramas and models describing the history and development of Lichfield. A metal spiral staircase leads up to a viewing platform on the tower, where you can enjoy superb vistas over the city's rooftops and away to the spires of the cathedral.

Cross Breadmarket Street to the **Samuel Johnson Birthplace Museum (18)**. Johnson was born in this building in 1709, the son of a bookseller. He was educated at a local Dame School before going on to Lichfield Grammar School, followed by a short spell at Pembroke College, Oxford, before lack of funds forced him to leave. For a brief period he ran a school just outside Lichfield, where one of his pupils was David Garrick. Johnson later moved to London, where he was to make his reputation. He wrote the first dictionary of the English language plus other works of literature and was the central figure in a group of the leading writers and scholars of his day. He made many return visits to Lichfield before his death in London in 1784. His birthplace is now a museum. In the basement is a mock-up of the 18th-century kitchen with the precocious nine-year-old Johnson reading the ghost scene from Shakespeare's *Hamlet*. Other rooms are devoted to 'Johnson and his Century' and 'London Life'.

Coaching Inns

Leave the Johnson Museum and turn left along Market Street, where there is a fascinating mixture of ancient and modern shop fronts, inns, bistros, and occasional Georgian and Tudor buildings. At the end of Market Street turn right into Bird Street. This Georgian road is notable for its former coaching inns. The heyday of the coaching inn was from the end of the 18th century to about 1840, when the railways took over the trade. In 1831 it is recorded that 31 coaches a day passed through Lichfield to such destinations as Birmingham, Liverpool and London, plus three Royal Mail routes to Chester, Liverpool and Sheffield. The first of these coaching inns you come across, on the right hand side of Bird Street, is the **The George (19)**. It retains its Regency ballroom, with ships' timbers in the ceiling. The Irish dramatist George Farquahar (1678–1707) was billeted at the George in 1704, and it was here that he wrote *The Recruiting Officer* and *The Beaux' Stratagem*. Opposite the George is the **The King's Head (20)**, which is full of military history and memorabilia. A plaque on the wall outside records that in 1705 Colonel Luke Lillington raised a Regiment of Foot here – this was later to become the South Staffordshire Regiment. Further along, on the left, is the **The Swan (21)**, the oldest surviving inn in the city, probably dating to the 15th century. Famous visitors have included Johnson, Boswell and Elias Ashmole (1617–1692), the scholar who founded the Ashmolean Museum in Oxford. Another, perhaps less welcome, visitor is the resident ghost – an apparently friendly White Lady. The Swan and the George were not only coaching but political rivals, with the Tory headquarters at the Swan and Whigs drinking at the George. Presumably neutrals went to the King's Head!

Continue along Bird Street until you see Minster Pool on the right. Underneath the road are the foundations of a medieval bridge. Turn into **Beacon Park (22)** on the other side of the road. Here there are two statues of note, one of King Edward VII, erected in 1908, and the other, on the far side of the gardens, the **Statue of John Edward Smith, Captain of the *Titanic* (23)**. The statue was unveiled in 1914 and attracted little interest until the 1990s, when James Cameron's film *Titanic* was released. Now the statue attracts hordes of camera-wielding visitors, much to the wry amusement of locals. Smith, who went down with his ship, was actually born in Hanley and has no connection at all with Lichfield, so after the success of the film Hanley suggested the statue should go there . . . an offer the Lichfield authorities politely refused! The statue was the work of Kathleen, Lady Scott, whose first husband was Robert Falcon Scott (1868–1912) – Scott of the Antarctic.

Leave the Museum Gardens and turn left along Beacon Street (known until Georgian times as Bacon Street and famous for its brothels). On the left is the **Angel Croft Hotel (24)**, a Georgian building whose 18th-century railings have survived various war efforts. Opposite is the **Erasmus Darwin Centre (25)**, which opened in April 1999. Erasmus Darwin (1731–1802), the grandfather of Charles Darwin (1809–1882), was a remarkable man in his own right. A well liked local doctor, he was also a philosopher, inventor, poet and botanist. He was a friend of the potter Josiah Wedgwood (1730–1795) and introduced the inventors Matthew Boulton (1728–1809) and James Watt (1736–1819) to each other, possibly in this house, which was his home between 1758 and 1781.

Walk along the side of the Darwin Museum, past the remains of the old West Gate and back into the Cathedral Close, where the tour concludes.

CHESTER

Access: Chester is well placed to take advantage of both the north–south and cross-Pennine motorways, while the A55 expressway leads to North Wales and Holyhead (for ferries from Ireland). London is 188 miles (302km) and Birmingham 85 miles (136km) away. National Express provides coach links with many other towns and cities. There are good rail links with the rest of the country: trains from London Euston take 2½ hours. The nearest international airport is at Manchester, a 45min motorway drive to the northeast.

Chester's history begins with the Romans, who in AD79 built a fortress on a low sandstone plateau within a meander of the River Dee and constructed the original city walls. They named the fortress Deva (after the river), and its main purpose was to act as a military base for operations against the Welsh. The site of the fortress was superb – the river was on three sides and it could be forded and later bridged – and, since the Dee was deeper in those days, sea-going ships could easily reach the site. The fortress became one of three main Roman garrisons in Britain and is thought to have housed up to 6000 troops, being particularly associated with Agricola's 20th Valeria Vatrix Legion. Deva had the typical rectangular shape of a Roman fort, and the Roman street plan is still largely in place today. The Via Principalis (now Eastgate and Watergate streets) ran east–west and the Via Decumana (now Northgate Street) and the Via Praetoria (now Bridge Street) north–south.

By AD383 the Romans had withdrawn from the area, but the site was probably never completely deserted. Some 500 years later the Saxons, under Aethelflaeda or Ethelflaed (d.c917), a daughter of King Alfred, refortified Deva and extended the walls to counter the Welsh and the Vikings. Cestre, as it was now known, became a busy port. Aethelflaeda, meanwhile, had dedicated a church to St Werburgh. An Irish–Norse community had also established itself and was involved in the tanning of hides in the riverside area. Chester was sufficiently important to have its own mint and in AD937 received a visit from King Edgar (the first King of All England), who was rowed along the river by eight Celtic kings as a sign of their allegiance.

After the Conquest, William built a castle at Chester as part of his campaign to control the north of the country. He installed his nephew, Hugh Lupus, the Wolf, as Earl of Chester; this title remains today and is automatically given to the eldest son of the monarch. After subduing the local inhabitants, Hugh converted the Saxon minster into a Benedictine abbey with the help of Anselm, the Abbot of Bec in Normandy. Over the next 150 years the monks pulled down the Saxon building and replaced it with a Norman-style church; there are a few remains today of this Norman building in the north transept of the current cathedral. Later, the monks were dissatisfied with the heavy Norman architecture and began to replace it piece by piece with a lighter, more elegant, Gothic-style building. They had just completed this church when Henry VIII dissolved the monastery in 1540. A year later Henry declared the abbey church a cathedral and created the diocese of Chester. The last abbot, Thomas Clark, became the first dean.

By this time the Dee had silted up and Chester was finding it difficult to maintain its prosperity as a port. It had further problems during the Civil War. The city supported the Royalist cause and the citizens were under siege by the Parliamentarians for over a year before being starved into submission. By the end of the century, however, Chester was once more thriving: it became an important regional centre and its industries supplied many of the goods required for the North American colonies.

In the early 18th century, with the turnpike system coming into being, Chester became an important coaching centre. With this came the growth of inns – some 150 are known to have been licensed at this time. Elegant Georgian houses were built, such as those in Abbey Square, while the old medieval gateways were replaced by modern arches. The riverside area, known as The Groves, became a well used promenade for local people. Across the Dee, the silted-up Roman harbour was now used as a popular racecourse. Chester was also becoming a prestigious resort for the gentry. In addition, the city linked up with the national canal network, the Chester Canal joining with the Shropshire Union System. For the cathedral, however, these were hard times, with the fabric and exterior stonework in bad condition.

The Victorian era was significant for both city and cathedral. Chester continued to prosper and, mercifully, did not attract the heavy industry of many of its northern neighbours. Medieval Revival was the name of the game and many of Chester's black-and-white half-timbered buildings are not in fact Elizabethan but Victorian. The city fathers made sure that The Rows – the lines of shops at both ground and first-floor level – were preserved and extended. The city walls, too, were maintained; today Chester is the only English town with a complete circuit of medieval walls. The railway came to Chester in 1840, with links to Crewe and Birkenhead. A new road led from the General Railway Station to the newly built Grosvenor Bridge, making the first change to the medieval road pattern; this was the largest stone single-span bridge in the world. Another innovation was the new suspension bridge from The Groves to the west bank of the Dee, opened by the youthful Princess Victoria. Towards the end of the century the Eastgate Clock was erected to celebrate the same Victoria's Diamond Jubilee.

It was the Victorians who saved the cathedral from ruin. The restoration, as for many other English cathedrals, was in the hands of Sir George Gilbert Scott (1811–1878), and as usual his schemes were controversial. His renovations were mainly to the floors and ceilings, but much of the stained glass dates from his time, as do the mosaics on the wall of the north nave aisle. At the end of the 20th century, new stained glass was introduced in the nave, while the undercroft (previously the monks' wine cellar) has been developed as an informative exhibition centre.

Today, the cathedral looks in good condition, although the exterior stonework needs constant attention. Fortunately, the thousands of tourists who visit Chester annually regard the cathedral as an essential port of call and contribute generously.

TOUR OF THE CATHEDRAL
Start and finish: The northwest porch.

Enter the cathedral through the door at the northern corner of the west front.

Proceed past a small area called the Abbot's Passage, built in the 12th century to provide a route for the abbot to step into the cathedral; today it contains a continuous video presentation describing the history of the cathedral.

Walk into the **Undercroft (1)**, which has some sturdy vaulting and was the cellar of the monastery. After being a workshop for many years, it was converted into a permanent exhibition centre in 1992.

Pass briefly into the southwest corner of the cloisters before entering the **Nave (2)**. This is small – only six bays long – and was built between 1360 and 1490; the architectural styles show the south side was completed before the north side, and there have been a number of additions over the last 150 years, with the Victorians adding the pulpit and lectern, plus the line of mosaics on the north aisle wall. These mosaics show scenes from the lives of Abraham, Moses, David and Elijah. The south aisle wall, in contrast, is covered with memorial tablets mainly from the 18th and 19th centuries. From here there is a good view of the west window, whose glass was installed in 1961. Figures represented include the Holy Family, Queen Aethelflaeda and saints Werburgh, Chad, Aidan, Oswald and Wilfred.

Continuity and Change

Carry on to the west end where, in the northwest corner, you find the **Baptistry (3)**, located in the base of a tower which the monks never got around to building. The font was brought from Venice in 1885, and some authorities think it was originally a Roman well head. In the opposite corner of the west end is the **Consistory Court (4)**, which dates from 1636 and is the oldest complete example of an ecclesiastical courtroom in England.

Walk along to the south nave aisle to inspect the **Westminster Windows (5)**, given to the cathedral in 1992 by the sixth Duke of Westminster in memory of his parents and to mark the cathedral's ninth centenary. They have the theme of continuity and change.

At the end of the aisle, turn into massive **South Transept (6)**, which is almost as large as the nave. It dates from 1350 and acted as the parish church of St Oswald; it was partitioned off from the main church until the parishioners moved out in 1881.

There are four chapels on the east side of the transept. The first is the Chapel of St Mary Magdalene of the Ascension, also known as the Children's Chapel. The second, and most interesting, is the Chapel of St Oswald. Note the carved wooden reredos, designed by Charles Eamer Kempe (1837–1907) and carved in Oberammergau. It shows Oswald, King of Northumbria (c605–642), leading his soldiers in prayer before battle against King Caedwalla. Next comes the Chapel of St George, the Regimental Chapel of the Cheshire Regiment, and finally there is the Chapel of Sts Nicholas and Leonard.

On the west side of the transept is the impressive **Westminster Memorial (7)**, in remembrance of Hugh Lupus Grosvenor (1825–1899), first Duke of Westminster. The memorial is surrounded by ornate wrought-iron railings. Note the four dogs in the corners – they are of a rare old breed known as the Talbot.

Move towards the crossing and approach the **HMS *Chester* Memorial (8)**. The ensigns remind us that this was the ship on which the teenage Jack Cornwell (1900–1916) died winning the VC at the Battle of Jutland. Walk under the tower and towards the **North Transept (9)**. The view is dominated by the organ, which was

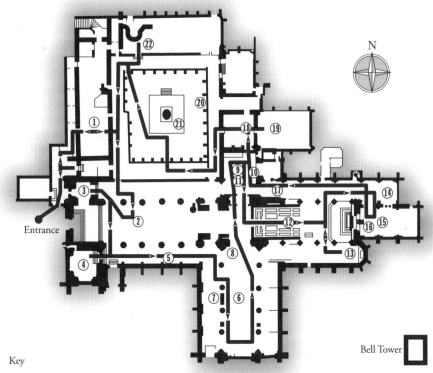

N

Key

1. Undercroft	9. North Transept	17. North Quire Aisle
2. Nave	10. Cobweb Picture	18. Vestibule
3. Baptistry	11. Memorial to John Pearson	19. Chapter House
4. Consistory Court	12. Quire	20. Cloisters
5. Westminster Windows	13. Chapel of St Erasmus	21. Cloister Garden
6. South Transept	14. St Werburgh's Chapel	22. Refectory
7. Westminster Memorial	15. Lady Chapel	
8. HMS *Chester* Memorial	16. Shrine of St Werburgh	

moved there by Scott during the 19th-century renovations. From an architectural point of view, the north transept is one of the most fascinating parts of the cathedral. There is a large Norman arch (*c*1100) on the east side and above it, at triforium level, a line of smaller Norman arches, giving an indication of the appearance of the cathedral before the monks introduced the Gothic style. Also in this area of the transept, placed in a wall niche, is the **Cobweb Picture (10)**. It shows Our Lady and the Holy Child painted on the net of a caterpillar – a common Tyrolean artform in the 19th century. Nearby is the imposing **Memorial to John Pearson (11)**, built in the 19th century to remember Bishop Pearson of Chester (in office 1673–86), the author of a well-known book on the Apostles' Creed.

From Quire to Chapter House

Walk back to the crossing and turn left into the **Quire (12)**. If you've been thinking the cathedral is so far rather dull, this impression will immediately change: the quire stalls and canopies are without doubt the best in the country. The quire itself was built 1280–1300 and is believed to have been the work of Richard of Chester, military engineer to Edward I. The stalls date from *c*1380 and are carved in Baltic Oak. The delicately carved canopies are individual in design. Immediately below is a line of corbels, while under the seats are some forty misericords treating both religious and secular topics. There are also some unusual bench ends, including a Tree of Jesse on the Dean's stall. Other carvings include a pelican, the so-called Chester Pilgrim and a variety of animals and grotesque figures. Scott's 19th-century additions to the quire fit in rather well: they include a carved wooden rood screen which matches the canopies, a superb tiled floor, the painted wooden ceiling and the Italian mosaic reredos behind the high altar. A modern altar front is based on the eucharistic symbols of bread and wine.

The Chester Pilgrim

Leave the quire to the right of the high altar to look briefly at the **Chapel of St Erasmus (13)**, a semicircular apse at the east end of the south aisle. The chapel has Victorian glass and a painted, vaulted ceiling. It is reserved for private prayer.

Return through the quire to the north aisle. Turn right. At the end of the aisle is **St Werburgh's Chapel (14)**, whose altar is believed to have been built from the remains of the original high altar, which was in the quire until 1876. Look at the floor by the altar: lines indicate the original east end of the Norman church. Werburgh (d*c*700) was the daughter of Wulfere of Mercia. About 675 she became a nun in the monastery at Ely founded by her aunt, St Etheldreda or Aethelthryth (*c*630–*c*679). Later she was made abbess of a convent in Mercia and became noted for her holy life. She was buried at Hanbury in Staffordshire, where numerous miracles occurred at her tomb. In the early 10th century her relics were brought to the Saxon minster at Chester.

Move next into the **Lady Chapel (15)**, built between 1250 and 1275 in Early English style, with some striking lancet windows. Note also the three large bosses in the roof, which show (from east to west) the Trinity, the Virgin and Child and the Martyrdom of St Thomas à Becket. The painted ceiling, the stained glass and the tiled floor are all Victorian. At the rear of the Lady Chapel is the early-14th-century **Shrine of St Werburgh (16)**. This was badly damaged at the Dissolution of the Monasteries and the relics removed, but was restored in the 19th century. On one of the corners there's a charming little carving of a dog scratching its ear.

Return to the **North Quire Aisle (17)** and walk back towards the crossing. On the left are some fragments of the 12th-century abbey church, later used for the foundations of the present quire. The remains, which came to light during the Victorian renovations, include a column, a capital and some medieval tiles. The stone screen behind is part of the pulpitum that divided quire from nave until 1875.

From the north transept, move into the **Vestibule (18)**, originally a waiting area for townspeople who wished to see the abbot, who would receive them in the chapter house. Six medieval abbots are buried here among the fine columns.

Next you come to the **Chapter House (19)**, built 1225–50 as a place for the monks to discuss daily business and hear a chapter from the Rule of St Benedict. The founder of the abbey, Hugh Lupus, is buried here. The rectangular chapter house retains its original stone vaulting (the only example in the cathedral) and has over twenty tall lancet windows.

The Cloisters

Leave the chapter house and proceed via the vestibule to the **Cloisters (20)**. Originally built in the 12th century, these were redesigned in the 16th century and restored by Sir Giles Gilbert Scott, a grandson of Sir George, in 1911–13. The cloister roofs have simple rib vaulting and bosses. The windows were added in the 1920s. Most visitors are entranced by the **Cloister Garden (21)**. In the centre is a deep-set pond, once the abbey well. It contains a sculpture entitled *Water of Life* by Stephen Broadbent, representing the story of Jesus and the Woman of Samaria. Around the pond are seats set among trees which came from the Holy Land. The south cloister has a number of slabs and tombs – one may relate to the 13th-century abbot Simon Ripley and another could be that of Richard of Bec (d1116), who came to England in 1092 as clerk to St Anselm and the following year was appointed the first abbot of the new monastery. His coffin is very large – the internal space is about 6ft 6in (2m) long – which suggests Abbot Richard was abnormally tall for the time.

The north cloister has a lavatorium, where monks washed before proceeding to the **Refectory (22)** which, appropriately, is today the cathedral restaurant. This is undoubtedly the most awe-inspiring of any cathedral eating place in the country. It was built in the 13th century and subsequently enlarged to take about forty monks and their frequent guests. While they ate in silence, one of the brothers read to them from the stone pulpit halfway up the south wall. Other features of interest for modern diners are the 17th-century tapestry on the west wall, the heraldic paintings on the north wall showing the arms of the earls of Chester and the modern (1939) hammer-beam roof.

Leave the refectory and return via the shop and the undercroft to the northwest porch, where the tour concludes.

WALKING TOUR FROM CHESTER CATHEDRAL

After you've had a look at the environs of the cathedral, the walk continues with a complete circuit of the city's walls, with short detours to view other attractions. At the end of this circuit the route moves into the city centre so that you can look at the unique double-layered shopping walks known as The Rows, set among ornate half-timbered buildings.

Start and finish: The west front of the cathedral.

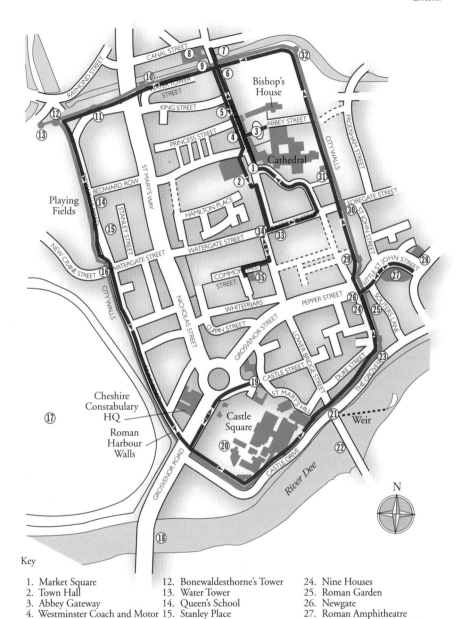

Key

1. Market Square
2. Town Hall
3. Abbey Gateway
4. Westminster Coach and Motor
   Car Works
5. Pied Bull Inn
6. Northgate
7. Shropshire Union Canal
8. Bluecoat School
9. Bridge of Sighs
10. St Morgan's Mount
11. Pemberton's Parlour
12. Bonewaldesthorne's Tower
13. Water Tower
14. Queen's School
15. Stanley Place
16. Watergate
17. Roodee Racecourse
18. Grosvenor Bridge
19. Grosvenor Museum
20. Chester Castle
21. Bridgegate
22. Old Dee Bridge
23. Recorder's Steps
24. Nine Houses
25. Roman Garden
26. Newgate
27. Roman Amphitheatre
28. Chester Visitor & Craft Centre
29. Thimbleby's Tower
30. Eastgate
31. Bell Tower
32. King Charles' Tower
33. The Rows
34. High Cross
35. Deva Roman Experience

Length: 3 miles (4.8km), with the circuit of the walls alone being 2 miles (3.2km).
Time: The walls walk takes up to 2hr, but allow longer for detours. Add a further
45 minutes for the walk into the city centre.
Refreshments: The cathedral refectory can be highly recommended for its space,
ambience and food. On the walls walk there is a group of excellent pubs
approximately halfway round the circuit. These include the 16th-century Bear and
Billet, close to the Bridgegate, the Albion in Bridge Street and the Off the Wall next
to Newgate. The Pied Bull Inn in Northgate Street is an archetypal coaching inn,
while in the town centre there are numerous inns with atmosphere, including many
adjacent to the High Cross.

Leave the west front of the cathedral and head along St Werburgh Street to the
Market Square (1). In the centre of the square is an attractive modern sculpture
by Stephen Broadbent, *A Celebration of Chester*; the three entwined figures represent
protection, industry and thanksgiving. A few yards away to the north are other
examples of stonework, in this case a group of Roman pillars and capitals.
Dominating the square is the imposing **Town Hall (2)**, built 1865–9 and opened
by Edward, Prince of Wales, later Edward VII. The building replaced the previous
town hall, known as the Exchange, burnt down in 1862, and is constructed of bands
of red and grey sandstone; its massive tower reaches 160ft (48.7m). which is higher
than the cathedral tower. Spend a moment to look inside the building, because the
waiting hall and staircase, just inside, are its finest features. The building's southeast
corner houses the Tourist Information Centre, which incorporates a wall built of
Roman masonry, possibly from the praetorium, the fortress's main building.

Cross Northgate Street to **Abbey Gateway (3)**, which was the main entrance
to St Werburgh's Abbey. The gateway was built in red sandstone in the 14th
century, but the upper storey was rebuilt at the end of the 18th. As you pass through
the gateway look up at the sturdy vaulting and bosses.

You now arrive in Abbey Square, which was at one time surrounded by the
medieval monastery's kitchens, bakery, brewery and other buildings. These have all
been replaced by attractive Georgian houses, including the Bishop's House in the
northeast corner. The pillar in the centre of the square is said to have come from the
old Exchange. Note the cobbled surface of the square and the lines of flat stones
('wheelers') designed to make the passage of carriages more comfortable.

Return to Northgate Street. Immediately opposite is the former **Westminster
Coach and Motor Car Works (4)** with its arched Edwardian façade. This
elegant building has been converted into the city library. Further along on the same
side of the street is the **Pied Bull Inn (5)**. As the Bull Mansion this was the
residence of Chester's recorder in the 17th century. It was refronted in the 18th
century and became an important coaching inn (notice the distances to major
cities shown on the wall). George Borrow (1803–1881) stayed here en route to
write his *Wild Wales* (1862).

The tour now arrives at the **Northgate (6)**, a main entrance – the Porta
Decumana – to the Roman city. Until 1807 Northgate was also the city jail. Like
the rest of the city's medieval gates, it was replaced in the early 19th century with
an archway. Step briefly through the gateway and stand on the bridge which

Gloucester Cathedral as seen from the northwest corner of the cloister, with its late 15th-century, 225-foot-high crossing tower. The chapter house is on the left.

Hereford Cathedral, viewed from the southeast. On the front left is the vicars' covered walkway. The 14th-century tower behind is covered in ballflower.

King John's tomb, which presides over the early 13th-century presbytery in Worcester Cathedral. Note the late Victorian high altar, marble screen and floor tiles.

Coventry Cathedral boasts the largest tapestry in the world. Made by Graham Sutherland, it hangs on the north wall and dominates the sanctuary and choir.

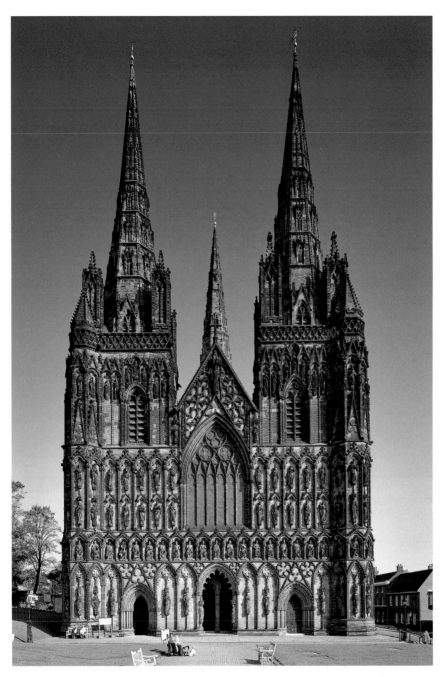

The 13th-century west front of Lichfield Cathedral. The lower part is one large image screen, and the towers and spire were added in the 14th century.

Chester Cathedral as seen from the southwest. The pinnacles, flying buttresses and turrets date from Sir George Gilbert Scott's 19th-century restoration.

Liverpool has the largest cathedral in Britain; it is also one of the largest in the world. This is the view through the nave bridge to the choir and high altar.

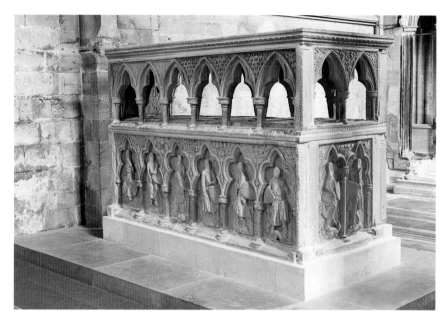

Above: *The shrine of St Thomas Cantilupe (1275–82), the last Englishman to be canonized before the Reformation, in the north transept of Hereford Cathedral.*

Above: *The breathtaking, intricate fan vaulting and stained-glass windows of the east walk of the great cloister at Gloucester Cathedral.*

crosses the **Shropshire Union Canal (7)**. Cut deeply into the local sandstone, the canal was opened in 1775 and provided a link between the Cheshire salt mines and the Midlands canal system.

The building next to the canal is the **Bluecoat School (8)**, which was built as a charity school in 1717 in an attempt, it is said, to combat the debauchery of the children of the city. There is a statue of a Bluecoat schoolboy over the main door. The school closed in 1949. Linking the school to the walls on the other side of the canal is the **Bridge of Sighs (9)**, across which condemned men were led from the jail to the Bluecoat School chapel for their last rites. It once had tall railings to stop the prisoners making their bid for freedom by jumping into the canal.

Around the Walls

Return to the Northgate, turn right and climb the steps up to the walls. Our route takes us in an anticlockwise circuit. The path runs downhill, parallel with the canal, to **Morgan's Mount (10)**, a square watchtower named after the commander of a gun battery during the siege of Chester in the Civil War. The walls were first built by the Romans as turf ramparts, later faced with stone. The Saxons strengthened and extended the walls down to the River Dee, and by the Middle Ages there were many towers, bastions and spurs. After damage during the Civil War, the walls were repaired and they became a popular venue for promenading during Victorian times. Today, Chester is the only English city whose walls survive in their entirety.

The Roman walls turned left here, but the course changed when the Saxons extended the fortifications down to the river. The path now crosses the inner ring road, on the other side of which is **Pemberton's Parlour (11)**, the remains of a round tower badly damaged in the Civil War. It was named for an 18th-century mayor of the city; it is known also as Goblin Tower, after a ropemaker who worked here.

Walk on to **Bonewaldesthorne's Tower (12)**, which marks the northwest corner of the walls. The waters of the River Dee once ran beneath the walls here, but after the river silted up and changed its course it was necessary to build the **Water Tower (13)** on the end of a spur. The tower did not hold water, as the name might imply, but was built to protect shipping in the nearby quays.

The path now drops down to street level, in City Walls Road. On your left here is the **Queen's School (14)**, which occupies the site of the former city gaol, closed in 1872. Presumably the pupils make the obvious jokes about the building's former use. The area in front of the present school was used for public executions. Also on the left is **Stanley Place (15)**, a small tree-lined square of Georgian houses. Cloth was sold for many years at the Linen Hall, which used to stand at the eastern end of the square.

You now reach the **Watergate (16)**. The original narrow gate was a place where tolls were charged for goods coming into the city from the river. The old Watergate was replaced in 1788 with the present arch. The path again returns to street level in Nuns Road. The 12th-century Benedictine nunnery of St Mary's stood here, while there were also Franciscan and Dominican friaries in the vicinity. To the right there are fine views of Chester's **Roodee Racecourse (17)**, claimed to be the oldest in the country. It is on the site of the Roman harbour, and a Roman quay can be identified beneath the walls. The unusual name comes from the Saxon *rood* (cross) and *eye* (island), the whole meaning 'the island with the cross'. From the walls you can just pick out the stump of a cross in the centre of the course. The walls also afford free viewing during the flat-racing season! You can see the track is an unusual shape: it is almost perfectly oval, with no finishing straight.

Grosvenor Bridge (18) is visible through the trees to your right. It was opened in 1832 by Princess Victoria, and at that time was the largest single-span stone bridge in the world. You can make detour here, following Grosvenor Road up to the roundabout and **Grosvenor Museum (19)**. This has displays of art, archaeology and natural history. Don't miss the Charles Darwin Natural History Gallery, the award-winning Roman Stones Gallery and the mock-up of a Georgian house.

Back on the walls, you are now approaching **Chester Castle (20)**, which in medieval times guarded the port and river crossing. Between 1788 and 1822 the site was redeveloped, leaving only Agricola's Tower. Much of the rest of the area has Greek Revival buildings, such as County Hall, the Museum of the Cheshire Regiment, the law courts and the local police headquarters. The riverside area beneath the city walls at this point was where leatherworkers (skinners) plied their trade. Famed for its obnoxious smells, the industry could not be tolerated in the city. The area can be pretty smelly today when the tide is out – the mangrove-like willows contain a good collection of supermarket trolleys, beer cans and other garbage.

On the left is the impressive balustraded **Bridgegate (21)**. The medieval Bridgegate (or Welshgate, as it was sometimes called) was heavily fortified and guarded the old Dee bridge. The gateway was badly damaged during the Civil War siege and was eventually replaced with the present structure in 1782.

Walk across the road to view the **Old Dee Bridge (22)**. This was built of stone in the 14th century after a number of earlier wooden bridges had been destroyed during floods. Until the 19th century it was the only crossing into Wales, and at the far end of the bridge was another gate, complete with portcullis and drawbridge. On the upstream side of the bridge is a weir, and the head of water created once powered numerous water wheels for grinding corn and fulling cloth.

Return to the walls. A little along on the right are the **Recorder's Steps (23)**, a recorder being a local 18th-century official. The steps provide a detour down to The Groves, a shady riverside area where boats can be hired.

The main walls path now swings north, running parallel with Park Street. On the left are the **Nine Houses (24)**, half-timbered almshouses provided for the local poor and needy; only six of the nine remain. On the other side of the wall is the **Roman Garden (25)**, where, among the greenery, a collection of Roman masonry has been assembled and a hypocaust put together. Modern 'Romans' in authentic costume can be seen guiding parties of children through this aspect of their history.

You next reach **Newgate (26)**, installed in 1938 alongside the old Wolfgate, named for Hugh Lupus. In a local story about the gate, a 16th-century alderman's daughter eloped through the gate at night on horseback, and the livid alderma persuaded the city authorities thereafter to have the gate permanently closed – clearly a local version of the saying 'to lock the stable door after the horse has bolted'!

A short diversion from Newgate takes you to the **Roman Amphitheatre (27)**, discovered in 1928 and excavated during the 1960s. The excavations revealed that this was the largest stone amphitheatre the Romans built in Britain, with its seating capacity of 7000. It would have been used for military training and ceremonies plus other, doubtless more bloodthirsty, activities. Across the road is the **Chester Visitor and Craft Centre (28)**, housed in a former Victorian school. A video show can be seen along with a life-sized reconstruction of The Rows with local craftsmen at work as in Victorian times. There is a restaurant and a Tourist Information Centre.

Return to Newgate and head north. After a short distance you come across the ruined **Thimbleby's Tower (29)**, probably named after Lady Mary Thimbleby, buried in the nearby St Michael's Church. The upper part of the tower was destroyed during the Civil War and the lower part is preserved under the wall of the walkway.

You now reach **Eastgate (30)**, capped by the highly photogenic Victorian clock. The present Eastgate was erected in 1769, replacing a medieval gate believed to have had traces of Roman arches in its stonework. Eastgate was the main Roman ceremonial entrance to the fortress, Eastgate Street being the eastern section of the Via Principalis. The clock was put up in 1897 to celebrate Queen Victoria's Diamond Jubilee. From here there are fine views into the heart of Chester's shopping area.

Continue along the walls towards the cathedral. On the left is the cathedral's modern free-standing **Bell Tower (31)**, completed in 1975 and claimed to be the first independent cathedral tower to be constructed in Europe since the 15th century. Further along on the left is the Deanery Field, where archaeologists have discovered the foundations of a Roman legion barracks.

The northeast corner of the walls circuit is marked by **King Charles' Tower (32)**, from where, it is believed, Charles I watched in 1645 as his forces were defeated by the Parliamentarians at nearby Rowton Moor.

The route now runs westwards along the walls, parallel to the Shropshire Union Canal, back to the Northgate, where you first joined the walls.

Back to the City Centre

Head along Northgate Street, past the Town Hall, into the area known as **The Rows (33)**. These are basically a series of covered galleries above street-level shops and probably date back to the 13th century. They are best seen in Watergate, Eastgate and Bridge Street, with a shorter section surviving in Northgate Street. A lot of the buildings are ornately half-timbered, with the upper floors being jettied and supported by pillars down to ground level. Many are, however, not as old as they look: the whole area received considerable renovation in Victorian times as part of the Gothic Revival. Nevertheless, the area is unique in Britain and is enjoyed by thousands of visitors annually, who come both to shop and to soak up the atmosphere.

In the centre of The Rows is the **High Cross (34)**, the battered old market cross where merchants struck bargains. Here, during the summer months, the town crier issues proclamations each day between Tuesday and Saturday at noon and 14:00.

A short detour from the High Cross along Bridge Street, Commonhall Street and Pierpoint Lane leads to an unusual museum, the **Dewa Roman Experience (35)**. Dewa, it is claimed, is the way Deva was pronounced in Roman times. You can sail back in time on a mock-up Roman Galley and walk through a typical Roman-era street, complete with sounds, sights and smells of Roman Chester.

Return to the High Cross and walk along Eastgate Street. In the near distance is a fine view of Eastgate and its clock. Turn left into St Werburgh Street, which brings you back to the cathedral and the end of the walk.

LIVERPOOL

Access: Liverpool is easily accessible by road, rail, air and sea. Visitors arriving by car should use the motorway system leaving the M6 via the M56 or M62. National Express run coach services to Liverpool from all the major cities in UK. Virgin run regular rail services from London Euston to Liverpool Lime Street, the journey taking under three hours. Liverpool airport is at Speke, some 7 miles (11km) from the city centre. Ferry services run to Liverpool from the Isle of Man, Belfast and Dublin.

The city of Liverpool takes its name from a tidal inlet that once stretched from the present Albert Dock to what is now the entrance to the Mersey Tunnel. The 'Liver' prefix probably comes from the Danish *lithe* or inlet. In the 12th and 13th centuries the settlement consisted of the church of St Nicholas, a substantial castle built by King John and a few surrounding streets occupied by no more than 500 people.

During the Civil War (1642–1648) the castle was completely destroyed by Royalist soldiers. In the succeeding years Liverpool grew in importance, helped by the discovery of local rock salt and coal. Its influence as a port also increased as the river at Chester silted up and trade with North America developed. Liverpool was heavily involved in the notorious slave trade. A 'triangle' of trade saw manufactured goods bound for West Africa, where slaves were taken on board for the West Indies and the southern part of the United States. Sugar and rum were then brought back to Liverpool. The slave trade was abolished in 1807, but by then the port had established trading links worldwide and it grew to be the country's second largest port. The first enclosed dock appeared in 1715 and further docks quickly spread along the waterfront. This was a time of considerable wealth for Liverpool and by the end of the 18th century the town had a population of over 50,000. Fine new buildings were constructed with the profits from the cotton trade. A landmark was the opening of the world's first passenger railway line, which ran from Manchester to Liverpool's Lime Street station.

Liverpool became an important port for immigration and emigration. Thousands left for a new life in Canada, America and Australia, while many Irish people settled in the city following the potato famine in the 1840s. The huge new transatlantic liners became a common sight in the port and firms such as Cunard and White Star set up their headquarters in Liverpool.

In 1890, Liverpool gained the status of a city and became the centre of a new diocese. The first bishop used St Peter's Church as his cathedral, but it soon became clear that this was inadequate. The second bishop, Francis Chevasse, and the Earl of Derby set up a committee that invited architects to submit plans for a new cathedral. The winning design was that of Sir Giles Gilbert Scott (1880–1960), the grandson of Sir George Gilbert Scott who had carried out a massive amount of restoration work on English cathedrals during Victorian times. Only 22 at the time, Giles was also, ironically, a Roman Catholic. It became his lifetime's work and he died before the building was completed. In 1904 the foundation stone was laid by

King Edward VII. Built of local sandstone, the cathedral took 74 years to finish and was finally dedicated in 1978 in the presence of Queen Elizabeth II. It is the largest Anglican Cathedral in the world.

Meanwhile, the city of Liverpool was experiencing mixed fortunes during the 20th century. Despite being a key port in both world wars, the city, the port and its ships suffered badly. As one of the most strategic places in the country, Liverpool was heavily bombed in 1941. The result was 4000 dead and more than 10,000 homes destroyed. Fortunately the half-finished cathedral remained unscathed. The city received further blows in the post war years. The textile industry declined in the face of cheaper competition from abroad, while Britain's entry into Europe meant that Liverpool's links with the Commonwealth were no longer so important. Liverpool found itself on the wrong side of the country to develop trade with Europe. The docks were saved from terminal decline by the development of deepwater facilities downstream at Gladstone and Royal Seaforth docks.

The end of the 20th century, however, showed a distinct revival in Liverpool's fortunes. The fields of art, entertainment and sport thrived, while the resilience and humour of its people refused to die. The Beatles phenomena put the city back on the map. The docks area was re-developed, with museums, restaurants, retails outlets and art galleries. Light industry has been attracted to the area. The two universities are popular with students. Above all, Liverpool has become the centre of a thriving tourist industry, in which its two cathedrals form important attractions.

TOUR OF THE ANGLICAN CATHEDRAL
Start and finish: The west front of the cathedral.

The cathedral is located on St James' Mount to the east of the city centre. Built almost entirely of the local pink sandstone, its statistics are impressive:

Length = 619ft (187m)
Area = 104,275 sq ft (9687m²)
Height of tower = 331ft (101m)
Nave vault = 120ft (36.5m)
Bells = Highest and heaviest ringing peal of bells in the world
Organ = 9765 pipes, making it the largest church organ

Not surprisingly, Liverpool Cathedral is the largest in Britain and the biggest Anglican cathedral in the world. The plan of the cathedral is in the form of a double-armed cross. In other words it has four transepts, and this plan has been adopted as the logo of the cathedral. It is aligned differently to other English cathedrals (except Coventry), as the nave runs north–south instead of the usual east–west, so that, for instance, there is a an east and a west transept and north and south ends. To save confusion, however, the usual liturgical directions will be used here with inverted commas.

The tour begins outside the '**West' Front (1).** Note the outcrops of local sandstone to the right, while to the left is a deep gully, which was once a quarry. It later became a graveyard. When the cemetery closed in the mid-1930s, it was estimated that there were over 57,000 bodies there. Included amongst their number was William Huskisson MP, the first man to be killed by a train (at the opening of the Liverpool–Manchester railway). The ground in front of the west porch contains

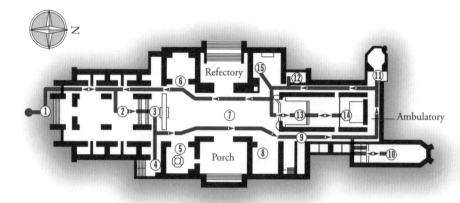

Key

1. 'West' Front
2. Nave
3. Dulverton Bridge
4. Lift to Tower
5. Baptistry

6. Visitor Centre
7. Central Space
8. 'Eastern' Transept
9. 'South' Choir Aisle
10. Lady Chapel

11. Chapter House
12. Holy Spirit Chapel
13. Choir
14. High Altar
15. War Memorial Chapel

a small plaque marking the burial place of Sir Giles Gilbert Scott and his wife. Look now towards the West Front, which is dominated by *The Welcoming Christ*, a sculpture by Dame Elizabeth Frink, who died shortly after it was dedicated in 1994.

Enter the cathedral by the glass door on the left hand side of the main porch. Walk along to the reception desk. There is no entrance fee but you will be gently encouraged to make a donation. Move from here into the **Nave (2)**, where the massive dimensions of the cathedral can be appreciated. Look towards the 'West' End and the tall west window, which covers an area of 16,000 sq ft (1468m²). The stained glass commemorates those who made a contribution to the building of the cathedral. Turning in the other direction, there is a unique feature, the **Dulverton Bridge (3),** which completely spans the nave.

Turn through an arch on the 'south' side of the nave, where to every visitors' surprise is an old-fashioned red telephone box. This was also designed by Sir Giles Gilbert Scott, so we have Scott's smallest structure sitting within his largest building! This is also the point where a lift leaves on the first stage of a journey to the top of the **Tower (4).** There are three stages to this climb. The first stage is by lift, followed by a walk along a corridor to the next lift and finally a climb of just over 100 steps to the top. There is plenty of opportunity to pause and view the massive interior of the tower, which is built not of stone, but brick and concrete. Also to be seen are the cathedral bells, the heaviest in the world. Emerging at the top of the tower, you are met by magnificent views over the city and the River Mersey. On a fine day with good visibility, Blackpool Tower and even the Lake District can be picked out. There is a small admission fee to the tower and tickets may be purchased in the bookshop.

We are now in the 'western' transept. To the 'south' is the **Baptistry (5).** The font is made from French marble and its 12 sides show figures representing the Apostles. The font's cover or baldachino is 39ft (12m) high and made of gilded oak. Note the font's surround, which represents the sea with fish swimming around. This symbolises the Israelites' passage from slavery in Egypt through the Red Sea to a new life. Move to the far side of the transept where you will find the **Visitor Centre (6).** Here is the cathedral shop which leads into the refectory. Above the shop is a hanging sculpture, the *Spirit of Liverpool*, in the form of sails meant to symbolize the seafaring traditions of the city. Note the subtle change of lighting every hour.

Walk now into the area known simply as the **Central Space (7)**, which lies directly under the tower. This huge area can accommodate several thousand people, so it can be put to a variety of uses, including concerts, plays, graduation ceremonies and festivals as well as cathedral functions. At the front of the steps of the Rankin Porch lies the Hillsborough Memorial Stone which remembers the Liverpool football fans who lost their lives at the FA Cup semi-final in 1989. On the floor in the middle of the Central Space is a circular marble memorial to Sir Giles Gilbert Scott, the architect who designed the cathedral.

The tour now reaches the '**Eastern' Transept (8).** Note the plaque in the paving, commemorating the consecration of the eastern transepts and the chancel of the unfinished cathedral in 1924 in the presence of Queen Mary and King George V. Move across the right-hand transept, where there is a monument to the Earl of Derby. The Stanley family, the Earls of Derby, have been influential in the Liverpool area since the 12th century. The famous horse race gets its name from this family and although now run at Epsom, it was originally run at Wallasey on the other side of the Mersey.

Proceed now along the **'South' Choir Aisle (9)**, where immediately on the right, set into the wall, is the Foundation Stone laid in 1904 by King Edward VII. Close to the stone is a model of one of Scott's early designs for the cathedral, which shows twin towers instead of the present single tower. As we move along the aisle, note the memorials and relief plaques to former bishops and deans, including Frederick Dwelly, the first Dean and Francis Chevasse, the second bishop. Those memorials in relief, along with many other works in the cathedral, have been carved by Liverpool's Edward Carter Preston.

On the right of the aisle, steps lead down to the **Lady Chapel (10).** This was the first part of the cathedral to be completed, being consecrated in 1910. Indeed it acted as the cathedral until the High Altar was consecrated in 1924. Take the upper steps first, which lead to a gallery giving a fine overall view of the chapel. Then take the lower steps into the chapel, where it is immediately obvious that it is far more elaborately decorated than the rest of the cathedral. Right round the chapel between the points of the arches and the triforium is a continuous text in gothic script. Many of the stained-glass windows of the Lady Chapel show women of significance from the bible and important Liverpool women who were missionaries or who worked with the poor of the city. Dominating the 'east' end of the chapel is a reredos in the form of a triptych. It was carved by G. W. Wilson to Scott's design. The side panels are fairly plain, but the central panel is elaborately carved and gilded. It shows the Nativity scene and Christ's Baptism in the Jordan. On the left of the altar is a statue of the Virgin Mary by Giovanni della Robbia, the 15th-century Italian sculptor. Before leaving the Lady Chapel, take a look at the entrance area where there is a bronze entitled *Redemption* by the Liverpool sculptor Arthur Dooley, backed by a superb modern embroidery by Ann McTavish.

Return to the 'South' Choir Aisle. At the end of the aisle by the votive candles is a maquette of Frink's *The Welcoming Christ.* Turn now into the ambulatory, where at the far end we reach the **Chapter House (11).** Compared with the size of the cathedral, the octagonal Chapter House appears tiny. It was built with donations from local lodges of Freemasons. There is a simple wooden altar backed by a modern painting by Craigie Aitchison entitled *Calvary 1998.* The Chapter house is usually closed to visitors, but most of the features can be seen through the wrought iron gates.

Walk along the 'North' Choir Aisle, pausing at the **Holy Spirit Chapel (12)**, which is reserved for quiet meditation and prayer. Note to the right of the altar an aumbry, where the Sacrament is reserved. There is a superb alabaster reredos showing Christ (in relief) praying by the Sea of Galilee.

Our tour has now returned to the Eastern Crossing. Move into the **Choir (13)**, with the pulpit to the left and the lectern to the right. Behind the choir stalls are two murals by Christopher Le Brun based on the parables of the Prodigal Son and the Good Samaritan. High above the choir is the organ, which is believed to be the largest in Britain. Proceed towards the **High Altar (14)**, noting on the right the massive stone-built *cathedra* or Bishops' Throne. As there is no barrier between the choir and the nave, the High Altar is visible from the full length of the cathedral. The simple altar is backed by magnificent carved sandstone reredos full of gilt work. Immediately above the altar is a representation of the Last Supper, while higher up is a Crucifixion scene. Note also the wooden altar rail, which has 10 beautifully carved figures, each representing one of the Ten Commandants.

Leave the choir and return to the Eastern Crossing. Step into the **War Memorial Chapel (15)** There is a cenotaph with an illuminated Book of Remembrance listing over 40,000 war-dead. Included among these names is Noel Chevasse, son of the second bishop, who during World War I was awarded two V.C's and a Military Cross for his gallantry – the only member of the armed forces to have been awarded such accolades. His bust can be seen on the east side of the transept. Also on show is the ship's bell from HMS *Liverpool,* which acts as a memorial to those who lost their lives in the Battle of the Atlantic.

Return now to the north nave aisle and the west end of the cathedral, where the tour concludes.

Memorial to Bishop Chevasse

WALKING TOUR FROM THE ANGLICAN CATHEDRAL

The tour begins in the religious and academic part of the city, before moving down into the commercial area with its imposing public architecture. The Cavern area, made famous by the Beatles, is visited, before going on to the River Mersey and the revitalised port area. There are art galleries and museums en route, so it is worth buying a National Museums and Galleries on Merseyside Pass (NMGM). For the cost of visiting one museum you can visit the rest for free, the pass being valid for one year.

Start and finish: The tour begins at the west front of the Anglican Cathedral and ends at Lime Street Station.
Length: 4 miles (6.5km)
Time: Allow at least half a day for the tour, so that the Roman Catholic Cathedral and a selection of the museums can be visited.

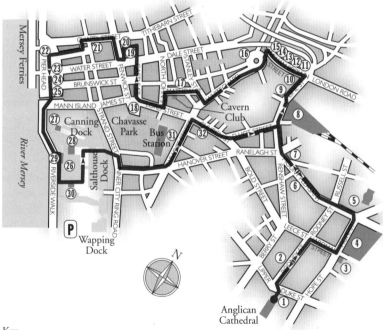

Key

1. Oratory
2. Rodney Street
3. Philharmonic Hall
4. Universities
5. R.C. Metropolitan Cathedral
6. Roscoe Memorial Garden
7. Britannia Adelphi Hotel
8. Lime Street Railway Station
9. St George's Hall
10. Wellington Column
11. Lancashire County Sessions House

12. Walker Art Gallery
13. Picton Reading Room and Hornby Library
14. Liverpool Museum
15. Mountford Building
16. Entrance to Mersey Tunnel
17. Beatles Area
18. Derby Square
19. Town Hall
20. Western Approaches Museum
21. Church of Our Lady and St Nicholas

22. Pier Head
23. Royal Liver Building
24. Cunard Building
25. Port of Liverpool Building
26. Albert Dock Area
27. Museum of Liverpool Life
28. Merseyside Maritime Museum
29. Tate Gallery
30. Beatles Story Museum
31. Paradise Street
32. Church Street

Refreshments: The refectory at the Anglican Cathedral has won Egon Ronay awards and is highly recommended. There are also a number of eating outlets in the Albert Dock area, including Taste at the Tate Gallery. There are a number of Victorian and Irish-style pubs in the city centre.

Leave the West Front of the Cathedral, noting on the right the building looking like a miniature Greek Doric temple. This is the **Oratory (1)**, the mortuary chapel for the nearby St James's cemetery. Designed by John Foster junior, it dates from 1829.

Notable Streets and Famous Addresses

Walk down the cathedral steps, cross Upper Duke Street and proceed along **Rodney Street (2)**. This is probably the most famous residential street in the city and many well-known figures have lived in these elegant Georgian terraced houses. The first house was built in 1783, one year after Admiral Rodney's famous naval victory. William Gladstone (1809–1898), four times Prime Minister, was born at no. 62. Lytton Strachey (1880–1932), one of the Bloomsbury Group of authors, who lectured for a while at Liverpool University, lived at no. 80. Arthur Clough (1819–1861) the poet, was born at no. 74, while no. 54 was the home of Dr. W.H. Duncan, who was Liverpool's first Medical Officer for Health in the mid-19th century. This was the first post of its kind to be set up anywhere in Britain, but made necessary by the poor health and appalling housing conditions of Liverpool's working classes. No. 11 was the birthplace of the author Nicholas Monsarrat (1910–1979), who wrote the classic *The Cruel Sea*. Few people live permanently in Rodney Street today, however. Most of the houses are used by professional firms. There is a sprinkling of architects and accountants, but the overwhelming majority are medical consultants – Liverpool's version of Harley Street.

Turn right at the traffic lights and continue to the right up Hardman Street to the next set of traffic lights. On the corner is the **Philharmonic Hall (3)**, home of the Liverpool Philharmonic Orchestra, the only orchestra in the country to own its own concert hall. The original hall on this site burnt down in 1933 and the present building dates from 1939. Its architectural style is officially 'Dutch impressionist', but there is more than a hint of Art Deco around. Opposite is the Philharmonic pub. The interior is one of the most ornate in the country and it is well worth having a quick glance inside.

We are now on Hope Street, the appropriately named road that links the two cathedrals. This area is also the academic centre of the city. Liverpool not only has two cathedrals but also boasts two **Universities (4)**, which makes for a lively atmosphere with many student bars and eating houses. Liverpool University was founded in the 19th century, while the John Moores University is of more recent origin, having developed from Liverpool Polytechnic. It also swallowed up the School of Art (where John Lennon and his wife Cynthia were students) and the Liverpool Institute (attended by Paul McCartney and George Harrison).

Ahead, and dominating the skyline, is the **Liverpool Roman Catholic Metropolitan Cathedral (5)**, which is located on the site of one of the largest workhouses which ever existed in England. The need for a Catholic cathedral became obvious in the second half of the 19th century, when the Catholic population of Liverpool increased dramatically following the Irish potato famine. The land was eventually bought in 1930 and Sir Edwin Lutyens (1869–1944) was commissioned to design a cathedral. Had his plans been completed, the building would have been the largest cathedral in the world, but because of the intervention of the World War II only the crypt was built. It was soon clear that Lutyens scheme was far too expensive and in 1959 a competition was held to design a new, more modest cathedral. Sir Frank Gibberd (1908–1984) won the competition with a spectacular design. (It is an interesting thought that the designer of the Anglican Cathedral was a Catholic and the designer of the Roman Catholic Cathedral was a Protestant!). Work started in the early 1960s and was completed within four and a half years.

Affectionately known as 'Paddy's Wigwam', the cathedral is circular in shape and built of modern materials such as concrete and glass. It is crowned by a cylindrical lantern of glass. The cathedral is notable for the marvellous modern stained glass, causing changing shafts of colour to pierce the interior like laser beams. The visitor will also be impressed by some superb work by contemporary artists such as Elizabeth Frink, John Piper and Patrick Reyntiens.

The interior design is fascinating. The High Altar, pulpit and choir are in the centre. The main aisle runs around the outside, flanked by 12 side chapels, interspersed by bronze Stations of the Cross designed and made by Liverpool artist Sean Rice. If you wish to see Lutyens' crypt, contact an attendant.

Leave the cathedral and walk down Mount Pleasant towards the city centre. Near the bottom of the hill on the left is the **Roscoe Memorial Garden (6)**, which occupies the graveyard of an old Unitarian chapel. The Garden is named after William Roscoe (1753–1831) a well-known social reformer in the city who attended the chapel. In its centre is a monument with eight Doric columns. Look for the Spanish tiles from Seville which are a monument to Joseph Blanco White (1775–1846), a Spanish priest and political exile, who spent the last six years of his life in Liverpool. He was a noted poet, who wrote in both Spanish and English. On the opposite side of Mount Pleasant is the massive **Britannia Adelphi Hotel (7),** built in 1912 to accommodate passengers overnight before or after their transatlantic trips by liner. Once used by royalty and presidents, it was considered to be one of the most luxurious hotels in the world, but today its grandeur has somewhat faded. A rather bizarre event occurred at the Adelphi in 1954, when Roy Rogers, the American cowboy film star, was a guest. He rode his horse Trigger up the steps of the hotel and into the foyer, both later appearing at a first floor balcony!

A Neo-Classical Extravaganza

The tour now enters Lime Street. On the right is **Lime Street Railway Station (8)**, terminus for trains from London. Built on the site of old lime kilns, it was also the terminus of the Liverpool and Manchester Railway which opened in 1830. Cross Lime Street by subway or at the traffic lights to **St George's Hall (9)**. By any standards, this must be one of the most impressive public buildings in the country, if not the world. It was designed in neo-classical style by Harvey Lonsdale Elmes and incorporated a concert hall and the assize courts. The hall was completed in 1854. The exterior features a vast array of Corinthian columns, plus a cenotaph and equestrian statues of Queen Victoria and Prince Albert. There are further statues and monuments, this time to the great and good of Liverpool, in St George's Gardens on the far side of the building. To the north of St George's Hall is the imposing **Wellington Column (10)**, which was inaugurated in 1863. The base of the column lists Wellington's campaigns and victories. Wellington's statue at the top of the column is cast in metal from guns captured at Waterloo. The column is 132ft (40m) high and nicely balances the modern Radio Tower in the city centre. Next to the column is a delightful fountain donated to the city by a former mayor in 1887.

Opposite the column is a string of further public buildings in matching neo-Classical style. First comes the former **Lancashire County Sessions House (11)**, which dates from 1887. Next is the **Walker Art Gallery (12)**, completed in the same year. It was sponsored by Sir Andrew Barclay Walker, a wealthy local brewer, after a disappointing public response for funds There are a number of friezes on the exterior of the building depicting Liverpool life. Look also for the Britannia look-alike in the portico – she carries a ship's propeller and is seated on a bale of cotton. The Walker Gallery is acknowledged to have one of the best collections of paintings and sculptures outside London.

The next neo-Classical building is the **Picton Reading Room and Hornby Library (13).** The circular reading room was opened in 1879 and is based on the design of the British Museum Reading Room. Alongside is the **Liverpool Museum (14)**, which was designed by Thomas Allom and opened in 1860. The displays are on three floors. The first floor deals with archaeology, concentrating on ancient Egypt and Greece. The second floor contains the Natural History section and has a comprehensive collection of geological specimens, including, inevitably, dinosaurs. The top floor appeals most of all to youngsters, concentrating on space and the universe, with a wealth of hands-on opportunities. The final building in this superb neo-Classical range is the **Mountford Building (15),** which opened in 1902 and is now part of John Moores University.

Immediately opposite the Mountford building is the entrance to the **Mersey Tunnel (16)** which links Liverpool with the Wirral on the far side of the Mersey estuary. Work started on the tunnel in 1925 and it was finally opened by King George V in 1934. It is 2.13 miles (3.4km) long and at its lowest point it is 33ft (10m) below the riverbed. The entrance to the tunnel is in Portland stone, decorated with Egyptian Art Deco designs.

Cross the busy junction via the pedestrian crossing and proceed along Whitechapel. This road follows the line of the tidal creek that was known as the Pool, long since filled in and built over. Proceed along Whitechapel until Stanley Street appears on the right. A statue of *Eleanor Rigby* sculptured by Tommy Steele used to stand on the right hand side of the road, but at the time of writing this area was being re-developed and the statue may well move to another location.

Turn left into Matthew Street, which could be described as the birthplace of the **Beatles (17)** phenomena. On the right is the Grapes pub, which was one of the 'fab four's' haunts, while on the left is the famous Cavern Club where the Beatles made their name. Other pop musicians who performed here included Gerry and the Pacemakers, the Searchers and P. J. Proby. The Cavern Club was demolished in 1973 to allow an underground railway to be built, but it has been faithfully rebuilt under the Cavern Walks shopping centre. Some hotels in the city provide vouchers to visit the Cavern. Look for the statue of John Lennon which lounges in a doorway on the right hand side of the street.

At the end of Matthew Street turn left and walk to Lord Street. Turn right here and proceed to **Derby Square (18)**, which lies on the site of the Liverpool Castle that was badly damaged in the Civil War and eventually demolished in 1721. The Square is dominated by the Statue of Queen Victoria, unveiled in 1906 by her daughter Princess Louise (who apparently was not enamoured with the representation of her mother). Turn right into Castle Street. We are now entering the financial area of the city, and imposing Victorian bank frontages can be seen on either side of the street. The road plan in this area of the city has changed little since the streets were laid out in the 13th century and it is often said that 'the history of Castle Street is the history of Liverpool'.

At the end of Castle Street is the magnificent **Town Hall (19)**, completed in 1754 and the last work of John Wood the Elder of Bath (1704–1754). It was badly damaged by fire in 1795 and was later reconstructed by James Wyatt (1746–1813) (the same man who was responsible for some disastrous 'improvements' to cathedrals). He added an impressive dome and the two-storey Corinthian portico. The Town Hall was badly damaged during World War II, but was quickly restored.

Walk around the back of the Town Hall into the space known as Exchange Flags (just to the right was the site of the old Liverpool Stock Exchange). Dominating this area is the Nelson Monument, which was almost certainly the first outdoor public sculpture erected in the city. Walk down the other side of the Town Hall to Water Street, where imposing banks and insurance companies line the pavements. Turn almost immediately right in Rumford Street. Shortly on the right is Derby House, now the **Western Approaches Museum (20)**. It was here in the basement that the Battle of the Atlantic was directed during World War II. Because of its strategic position, Liverpool received more attention from enemy bombs than any city outside London.

Now turn left and head down Chapel Street towards the river. On the left is the **Church of Our Lady and St Nicholas (21)**, which acts as Liverpool's parish church. It is often known as the 'Sailors Church' and was for centuries a landmark for ships. It dates from the 13th century, but

Church of Our Lady and St Nicholas, the city's parish church

little of the structure remains from these times. The old tower fell in 1810 and killed 25 worshippers. It was replaced five years later. The nave was destroyed during the World War II and rebuilt in the 1950s. There is an impressive metal sculpture on the Chapel Street side of the church showing *Christ Upon an Ass* by Brian Burgess.

Old Docks and New Tourism

Ahead is the road known as The Strand, which marks the course of the old Overhead Railway which ran parallel with the docks for 7½ miles (12.5km). It was pulled down in 1956. Cross the Strand by the traffic lights and head for the river. This is the area known as the **Pier Head (22).** The original stone pier is long gone and there is now a line of floating piers, which can cope with the rise and fall of the tides. It is from here that ferries leave for various points on the far side of the River Mersey and further afield to the Isle of Man, Belfast and Dublin. There have been ferries crossing the Mersey since 1207 and for several centuries they were operated by the monks of Birkenhead Priory. The crossing was always hazardous due to the strong tides and frequent fogs. This changed when steam ferries were introduced towards the end of the 19th century. It was thought that the ferry trade would decline when the Mersey tunnel opened, but many of the ferries not only survive, but flourish with the addition of the tourist trade.

Turn to look inland at the range of superb buildings for which Liverpool is justly famous. The first is the **Royal Liver Building (23)**, the offices of the Royal Liver Friendly Society. The building, which was completed in 1911, was designed by W. Aubrey Thomas (1859–1939). Its two towers are capped by the mythical Liver Birds, which are made of copper and are 18ft (5.5m) high. The birds should have been eagles, as on the seal presented to Liverpool by King John, but the seal was lost during the Civil War. Its replacement shows a bird which resembles the cormorant, commonly found in the Mersey estuary. The next building is the **Cunard Building (24)**, which was completed in 1916 in an Italianate style. It was the headquarters of the Cunard company founded by a Canadian, Samuel Cunard. The firm was famous for its large and luxurious transatlantic liners such as *Mauretania, Lusitania, Queen Mary* and *Queen Elizabeth*, which eventually reduced the Atlantic crossing to 3½ days. The advent of air travel was the death knell for the transatlantic ships and the last Cunard liner left Liverpool in 1966.

The third building in the row is the **Port of Liverpool Building (25)**, which has the role of port administration. It was built in 1907 and designed by Arnold Thornely. It is built in Portland stone and has three fine domes. Outside the building is a monument to Sir Alfred Lewis Jones (1845–1909) who introduced bananas to Britain, pioneered refrigeration in ships and founded the Liverpool School of Tropical Medicine.

The tour now approaches the **Albert Dock (26)** complex, which was built between 1841 and 1848 and opened by Prince Albert. It was one of the first enclosed docks in the world, with a water area of 7½ acres (3ha) and surrounded by five-storey warehouses which were claimed to be fire-proof. The whole complex was designed by Jesse Hartley (1780–1860), who was the Liverpool Dock Engineer. After World War II, the warehouses were used for bonded goods such as tobacco and rum, while the dock itself gradually silted up. In the 1980s the local authority decided to revitalize the area. The dock was dredged and the warehouses converted into museums, art galleries, shops and restaurants, so that by the end of the century the Albert Dock complex had become a major tourist attraction. It is quite possible to spend a whole day here, so the visitor must decide which attractions to visit or omit on this half-day walking tour.

At the entrance to the dock is the **Museum of Liverpool Life (27)**, based largely in the old river pilots' building. The museum traces the history of Liverpool and its people and the special culture of the area. Next on the left, in the arms of the Canning half tide dock, are a number of boats and sailing craft belong to the **Merseyside Maritime Museum (28)**. The main part of the museum is based in a warehouse on the north side of the dock. Its four floors contain displays on emigration, cargo handling and transatlantic slavery. Walk now along the side of Albert Dock to the **Tate Gallery (29),** home to the largest collection of contemporary art outside London. The London Tate Gallery was given to the nation by the sugar magnate Henry Tate who started his Tate and Lyall sugar business in Liverpool.

Now walk around to the far corner of the dock where the Tourist Information Centre is located. Note on the way the floating weather map in the dock. Go outside the line of old warehouses and turn right. This leads to the entrance of the **Beatles Story Museum (30)**. This traces the history of the famous Liverpool pop group and includes a mock-up of the Cavern Club. The tour concludes with an account of John Lennon's assassination (with the tune *Imagine* playing in the background) ensuring that few emerge dry-eyed into the giftshop. Continue from here anticlockwise around the dock, ending at the pub which was formerly the pumphouse operating many of the cranes using steam power.

Back into the City

Leave Albert Dock by the bridge between Canning and Salthouse Docks and cross Strand Street at the traffic lights. Turn slightly to the right and then immediately left into Canning Place. Both the dock and the street are named after George Canning (1770–1827), who was MP for Liverpool between 1812 and 1823. He was also briefly Prime Minister in 1827 but died shortly after taking office. Walk along Canning Place. At the traffic lights fork left into **Paradise Street (31)**. Despite its name this road was once a notorious part of the seaport, filled with brothels, drinking dens and gambling joints. Near to the crossroads is the Eagle public house, which is one of the few survivors of those times. Many emigrants would stay here before boarding their ships.

At the end of Paradise Street turn right into **Church Street (32)**, the main pedestrianized shopping street in the city. It was developed in the early 18th century and takes its name from the Church of St Peter, which has since been demolished. This busy street has branches of most of the country's 'high-street' shops and it was here that Frank Winfield Woolworth opened his first store in Britain in 1909. This is a favourite street for buskers. Look for the jovial statues of the Moores brothers, who have been important benefactors to the city in recent years. At the top of Church Street fork left into Parker Street, which leads on to Clayton Square. This was named after Sarah Clayton, a local colliery owner and coal merchant. At the end of Parker Street is Lime Street Station, where the walking tour ends.

The Cathedral Gate and Song School, Peterborough

WALKING THE
CATHEDRAL
CITIES OF
EASTERN
ENGLAND

LONDON: ST PAUL'S

Access: Nearby railway stations include Farringdon, City Thameslink, Blackfriars, Cannon Street and Liverpool Street. The most convenient tube station is St Paul's (Central line). London Transport buses 4, 8, 22B, 25, 26, 56, 141, 172, 501 and 521.

The first cathedral on this site dated from early Saxon times; made of wood, it was built in 604 for Mellitus, Bishop of the East Saxons, and founded by Ethelbert, King of Kent. It burnt down and was rebuilt several times.

When the Normans conquered Britain, Maurice, Archdeacon of Le Mans, was declared Bishop of London. Two years later, after the Saxon cathedral had fallen prey to fire yet again, he decided to build a new cathedral, one that would reflect the importance of the capital of the new Norman territory. This stone building, now referred to as Old St Paul's, was built in cruciform shape in the Gothic style, with the nave and choir of equal length and each having twelve bays. The third largest cathedral in Europe, and dominating medieval London, it had elements of Norman, Early English and Decorated design. Flying buttresses were prominent. The spire, one of the tallest ever built – it exceeded the present one by some 165ft (50m) in height – attracted lightning strikes on more than one occasion.

Old St Paul's became a popular meeting place and social centre, containing law courts, workshops and a marketplace. It also witnessed many important historic events. Prince Arthur was married here to Catherine of Aragon in 1501. During the Reformation it was, of course, stripped of images and crucifixes. Elizabeth I is said to have stood up here and shouted at a dean with whose sermon she disagreed. In 1588 a public notice was read on the steps giving news of the defeat of the Spanish Armada. Guy Fawkes (1570–1606) and the other Gunpowder Plot conspirators were hung, drawn and quartered on the cathedral steps. The poet John Donne (*c*1572–1631) was an active dean here.

By the mid-17th century the cathedral was in a sad state. The choir was used as stables by Cromwell's troopers, monuments were desecrated and windows were smashed. It was perhaps fortunate that the Great Fire of London razed old St Paul's to the ground in 1666, allowing a fresh start.

King Charles II was instrumental in the planning of the new cathedral, providing money himself and raising further funds by taxing coal coming into the city; additional cash came from a public appeal. In 1669, Sir Christopher Wren (1632–1723) was appointed architect; his design approved by the king, work began in 1675. The construction took thirty-five years, being completed in 1710, and spanned five reigns – those of Charles II, James II, William and Mary, Queen Anne and George I.

St Paul's is the only major English cathedral in Classical style, or 'Wrenaissance'. The building is dominated by the imposing dome, 102ft (31m) in diameter, surmounted by a lantern – Wren's uncle was Bishop of Ely, and the architect was clearly influenced by the octagon at that cathedral. The west end has a fine pair of Baroque towers.

Despite these Classical features, the plan and structure owe much to Gothic design. There is a wealth of flying buttresses, for example, although Wren concealed these by screens so that they are virtually invisible from the ground. The stone used comes from Portland in Dorset, and recent cleaning has emphasized the excellent carving, much of it by Grinling Gibbons (1648–1721). The west end approach is marked by a steep rank of steps, and this can cause problems on state occasions – as when the aged Queen Victoria found herself too infirm to enter the cathedral for her Silver Jubilee celebrations, which had to be held outside the cathedral while she sat in her carriage.

St Paul's survived the heavy bombing which London received during World War II and continues to be the main venue for state occasions like royal weddings, funerals and remembrance services. It no longer dominates the London skyline, however, being increasingly hemmed in by office blocks, but it remains an important national symbol and a major attraction for visitors from all over the world.

TOUR OF THE CATHEDRAL
Start: The west front.
Finish: The southwest door.

Before you climb the steps to the entrance, pause by the statue of Queen Anne, which makes a good observation point from which to view the **west front (1)**. Like the rest of the cathedral, this is built in two storeys, separated by a bold cornice. The Classical columns that dominate it are topped by a pediment containing a bas-relief of the conversion of St Paul. The statue itself is attributed to Francis Bird (1667–1731), as are the statues of the Apostles which appear at roof level around the building.

On each side of the building is a tower in Baroque style, with pillars, urns and cupolas; these two towers were the last parts of the cathedral to be built. One contains the clock and the other is the belfry. The clock, which has three dials, is known as Big Tom – it is of similar design and size to Parliament's Big Ben – and dates from 1893, although the present mechanism is more recent than that. The belfry's most used bell, Great Tom, dates from 1716 and is used for striking hours. The largest bell, Great Paul, is at 16 tons (17 tonnes) the heaviest swinging bell in the country.

Impressive as the west front is in daylight, do try to see it at night, when it is floodlit and incredibly beautiful.

A Famous Secretary of War and an Early Archbishop
Climb the steps and enter the cathedral through the side of the great west doors (the main doors are opened only on important state occasions).

Immediately on your left is the **Chapel of All Souls (2)**, which contains the Kitchener Memorial, dedicated to the servicemen who died in World War I. Lord Kitchener (1850–1916), whose face is still familiar from old recruiting posters, was Secretary of War from August 1914; he drowned when HMS *Hampshire* was mined off Orkney.

Next along is the **Chapel of St Dunstan (3)**, named after Dunstan (*c*909–988), a Bishop of London, during the days of the Saxon cathedral and later Archbishop of Canterbury. Note here the wooden entrance screen carved by Jonathan Maine and also the Richmond mosaic fresco behind the altar.

For further progress into the cathedral you have to pay an entrance fee – unlike the case in many other cathedrals, this is nothing new: St Paul's began charging in 1707, before the construction of the building was even complete! Choose here whether or not you want to pay also to visit the galleries.

The Military Connection

There is now a vista along the full length of the **nave (4)** towards the dome and high altar. In length the nave and the choir balance each other – it is this symmetry of the building which is so impressive. The large rectangular pillars have fluted pilasters with Corinthian capitals, while the arches, as elsewhere in the cathedral, are round-headed.

Proceed along the **north aisle (5)** and note on the right, filling an arch, the **Duke of Wellington Monument (6)**. This imposing memorial, completed in the 1870s, is composed of contrasting white limestone and black marble. The sculpture of Wellington (1760–1842) on his horse Copenhagen was added on top of the monument in the 20th century. The funeral of Wellington was a remarkable affair; some 13,000 mourners occupied the cathedral, which was draped with black cloth.

Passing the Lord Mayor of London's Vestry on the left, move on into the **north transept (7)** where the **font (8)** is found (unusually, as in most cathedrals it is at the west end). Carved by Francis Bird in 1727 in Italian marble, it is cream with subtle blue veins. On the opposite side of the transept, the **north transept chapel (9)** contains the colours of the Middlesex Regiment. The carved door shows a pelican pecking its own breast to succour its young – a recurring symbol in the cathedral.

The transept is dominated by Holman Hunt's painting *The Light of the World*. It dates from around 1900 and is the third version that Hunt painted. Also in the transept are two notable statues: a modern terracotta Virgin and Child by Josephine Vasconellos and a white marble figure by John Flaxman of Sir Joshua Reynolds (1723–1792), the artist and first president of the Royal Academy.

The Dome and the 'Box of Whistles'

Go next into the crossing and stand under the **dome (10)**. Believed to be the second largest dome in the world (after that of St Peter's in Rome), and estimated to weigh about 64,000 tons (65,000 tonnes), this is undoubtedly the great glory of St Paul's. Although Wren never went to Italy, he was obviously influenced by the great architects of the Renaissance such as Michelangelo (1475–1564), and he produced a dome which dominated the London skyline.

There are actually three layers to the dome: above the inner dome is a cone-shaped brick structure, followed by an outer dome of light wood covered with Derbyshire lead. The brick cone supports the beautifully designed Baroque-style lantern, which balances the Classical dome and the clearly Baroque west towers.

Back at ground level, note the marble floor, designed to represent a compass, in the centre of which is a circular brass grille, one of several around the cathedral constructed to allow hot air up from the original stoves in the crypt.

Also in the crossing are the lectern and the pulpit. These are totally different from each other in design. The lectern is in the form of a traditional brass eagle on a pedestal, likewise of brass, the whole done by Jacob Sutton in 1719. In contrast, the huge pulpit is of oak and limewood. It was installed in 1964 to celebrate the 250th anniversary of the opening of St Paul's. Interestingly, Wren's original pulpit had wheels and could be pushed around to allow sermons to be delivered in any part of the building.

The crossing is the best place to have an initial view of the **chancel (11)**, which is often out of bounds to visitors, and a convenient location to view the organ and the choir. The present **organ (12)** is not the original, which was built by 'Father' Shmidt and installed in 1695. What Wren used to refer to as a 'box of whistles' has been rebuilt and modified on countless occasions. There are today five keyboards, each with sixty-one keys, plus a pedalboard with thirty-two pedals. The organ has 138 stops. The casing, which you can see on both sides of the chancel, is unusual in that it is richly carved with animated figures, again by Grinling Gibbons.

Around the East End
The **choir (13)** once more shows Gibbons's artistry, in the beautifully worked stalls and the screen behind. Gibbons, the son of a London draper but brought up in Rotterdam, was responsible for most of the cathedral's interior wood carving and also some of the exterior stonework.

Here in the crossing you can also get your first view of the mosaic ceilings. By contrast with those of the dome, which are mundane, these are breathtaking,

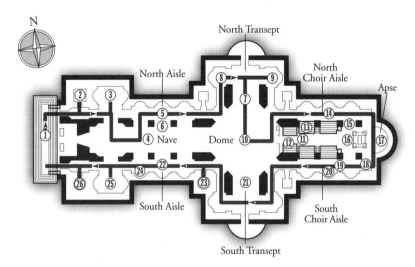

Key

1. West Front
2. Chapel of All Souls
3. Chapel of St Dunstan
4. Nave
5. North Aisle
6. Duke of Wellington Monument
7. North Transept
8. Font
9. North Transept Chapel
10. Dome
11. Chancel
12. Organ
13. Choir
14. North Choir Aisle
15. Tijou Gates
16. High Altar
17. American Memorial
    Chapel
18. Lady Chapel
19. South Choir Aisle
20. Effigy of John Donne
21. South Transept
22. South Aisle
23. Entrance to Galleries
24. The Light of the World
25. Chapel of St Michael and
    St George
26. Geometrical Staircase

particularly on the three saucer domes. Made in Whitechapel and dating from the late 19th century, they are the work of Sir William Richmond. The theme of the mosaics over the choir is wildlife – animals, fish and birds; in the apse over the high altar we see Christ flanked by cherubim and seraphim, while around the dome are prophets and evangelists. The impetus for the mosaics was provided by Queen Victoria, who in a letter to the bishop described St Paul's as 'most dreary, dingy and undevotional'. She herself never saw the completed mosaics, by then being too frail to climb the cathedral's entrance steps.

The **north choir aisle (14)** forms, with the south choir aisle and the apse, the ambulatory, or walk around the chancel. Otherwise the least interesting part of the cathedral, the north choir aisle is used as a display area. At its far end is a superb modern sculpture by Henry Moore (1898–1986) of the Madonna and Child. At this point stunning wrought-iron gates separate both aisles from the high altar; these are known as the **Tijou Gates (15)** after their maker, Jean Tijou, a French ironworker who from 1689 was almost continuously in Wren's employ. Both strong and intricate, the gates are considered Tijou's best work. The gilding was probably added later.

If you peer through the gates you can see the features of the east end of the chancel. Dominating the area is the **high altar (16)**, the third to occupy this spot. Wren's original was controversially replaced by a Victorian high altar, but this was bomb-damaged during World War II. The present altar, dating from 1958, is similar to a sketch Wren made for what he clearly intended to be a focal point in the grand design. A massive slab of Italian marble supports a cross 10ft (3m) high that is flanked by candlesticks of similar size. Over this is a canopy or baldacchino of carved oak, heavily gilded and topped with a statue of the risen Christ. At the side of the altar is the bishop's throne, with sumptuous carving that includes the arms of Bishop Compton (1632–1713), whose term of office stretched from the ruins of Old St Paul's to the completion of the new cathedral.

The whole of the apse is taken up with the **American Memorial Chapel (17)**. This end of St Paul's was badly damaged during World War II and completely restored afterwards. One of the architects involved was Stephen Dykes Bower, who was heavily concerned with work at Bury St Edmunds – see page 236. The chapel was dedicated in 1958 to the 28,000 US servicemen based in Britain who lost their lives during the war; their names are recorded in an illuminated roll of honour. Note the panels and stained glass, both of which have US themes.

At the corner of the apse and the south choir aisle is the minute **Lady Chapel (18)**, which dates from 1959. Some of the items here were retrieved from earlier features; the woodwork around the Virgin and Child statue, for example, came from Wren's first organ screen, and the oak altar table was his original high altar.

The **south choir aisle (19)** starts with the pair to the Tijou screen of the north choir aisle. Then follow two monuments of interest. On the chancel side of the aisle, a bronze of Bishop Mandell Creighton (1843–1901) rests on a plinth of green porphyry. Opposite is the marble **Effigy of John Donne (20)**, by Nicholas Stone (1586–1647); Donne was dean here for a number of years. This was the only figure from Old St Paul's to survive the Great Fire; it did so because it fell through into the crypt. Careful inspection reveals scorchmarks. Note, too, the statue of the Virgin and Child, once part of the Victorian altar screen.

The South Transept and the Galleries

The **south transept (21)** is distinguished by a number of white marble memorials, many with a nautical theme, such as those commemorating Lords Nelson (1758–1805), Howe (1726–1799) and Collingwood (1750–1819). Look also for those of Robert Falcon Scott (1868–1912) – Scott of the Antarctic –, J.M.W. Turner (1775–1851) and the prison reformer John Howard (1726–1790). Certainly the most impressive artwork in the south transept is the doorcase – yet another masterpiece by Grinling Gibbons. Also in the south transept is the entrance to the crypt (see below).

You now come to the **south aisle (22)**. Immediately on your left is the **entrance to the galleries (23)**. If you visit all the galleries you will have to negotiate over one thousand steps, so think carefully before you commit yourself!

The first gallery you reach is the **Whispering Gallery**, which runs around the interior base of the dome; it gets its name because a whisper against the wall can be heard on the opposite side of the gallery, some 140ft (42m) away. Try it if you like, but normally the place is too noisy for you to have any chance of success. A further spiral of steps brings you to the **Stone Gallery**, which goes around the dome's exterior and affords exceptional views over the rooftops of London. Masochists can tackle a further 150 steps up to the **Golden Gallery** at the base of the lantern; here you get even better panoramic views. It is an alarming thought that Wren was hauled up in a basket to this level two or three times a week to inspect the progress of his plans!

There are few outstanding works of fine art in the cathedral, but an exception is to be found in the south aisle once you've descended, doubtless breathless, from the galleries: *The Light of the World* **(24)** by William Holman Hunt (1827–1910), who is buried in the cathedral crypt. The (poorly lit) picture shows Christ knocking at a door, and has been described as a 'sermon in a frame'. In fact, this is a copy Hunt painted fifty years later of an original that hangs in Keble College, Oxford.

Next on your left is the **Chapel of St Michael and St George (25)**, dedicated to those who have been knighted for service to the Commonwealth.

Before you leave, by the southwest door, take a look at the **geometrical staircase (26)** designed by Wren and built and carved by William Kempster, with iron banisters by Jean Tijou.

TOUR OF THE CRYPT

Start and finish: The main entrance to the crypt, via the stairs in the south transept.

The main purpose of a crypt is as a burial place. However, although St Paul's boasts the largest crypt of any cathedral in Europe, there have been no burials here for some time, but as you will see there is an extraordinary number of tombs and memorials of the great and the good, with two tombs dominating – those of Nelson and Wellington. The architecture throughout is basic and the stonework has benefited from recent cleaning.

From the foot of the access steps, note the memorial to the British who died in the Falklands conflict of 1982, then turn right and go to the east end, where you will find the **OBE Chapel (1)**, dedicated to the holders of this award. This was

Crypt

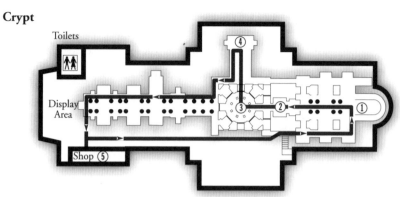

Key

3. Nelson's Tomb
1. O.B.E. Chapel
4. Treasury
2. Wellington's Tomb
5. Cathedral Shop

originally called St Faith's Chapel in recognition of a parish church demolished when Old St Paul's was extended in the 14th century. To the right are monuments to Reynolds, Wren and William Blake (1757–1827). Wren's tomb bears an inscription composed by his son: '*Lector, si monumentum requiris, circumspice*' – 'Reader, if you seek his monument, look around.'

The aisle to the south, often called Artists' Corner, has the tombs of or memorial slabs to painters like Reynolds, Turner and Sir John Millais (1829–1906).

Go down the central aisle to the **Tomb of Wellington (2)**: a rather severe block of brown Cornish porphyry inscribed 'Arthur Duke of Wellington' rests on a limestone plinth. The walls around the tomb have memorial plaques to field-marshals of World War II – Alanbrooke, Wavell, Dill, Wilson, Auchinleck, Gort, Montgomery, Slim, Alexander and Warwick.

Nearby, and immediately under the dome, is **Nelson's Tomb (3)**. After he died at Trafalgar in 1805, Nelson's body was preserved in a keg of rum and brought via Gibraltar to Britain. His funeral, in 1806, was a notable state occasion, with a flotilla of state barges and other craft sailing from Greenwich to St Paul's, where the procession inside the cathedral was led by the Prince of Wales, the future George IV.

Next turn right into the **treasury (4)**, which was opened by the Duchess of Kent in 1981. This contains a comprehensive collection of liturgical plate. Among the vestments on display the star exhibit is the Jubilee cope worn in the service to commemorate the 25th anniversary of Elizabeth II's coronation. The treasury's impressive steel gates are apparently very necessary – also among the display items are two ancient locks and keys which failed to prevent an audacious robbery in 1810. Near here are two scale models, one of Old St Paul's, the other showing an original design by Wren for the cathedral.

The west end of the crypt has little of permanent interest but is worth a quick look: it is used largely for informative displays. Also at the west end are the well stocked **gift shop (5)** and the toilets.

WALKING TOUR FROM ST PAUL'S CATHEDRAL

The tour looks firstly at the cathedral exterior and then follows a circular route taking in landmarks of the former printing, publishing and newspaper industries. Other features include Dr Johnson's House, the Old Bailey and some Wren churches.

Start and finish: The cathedral's west front.
Length: 1½ miles (2.4km).
Time: 1 hour, but allow longer if you want to visit the churches and other buildings.
Refreshments: Numerous pubs, restaurants and sandwich bars. Two pubs are strongly recommended – the highly atmospheric Ye Olde Cheshire Cheese, just off Fleet Street, and the unique Blackfriar near Blackfriars Bridge.

Before you start the walk proper, take a little time to stroll around the outside of the cathedral, going first along the south (Cannon Street) side.

This area is the **Churchyard** – not a graveyard but the precincts of the cathedral. Particularly in the days of Old St Paul's, this was a meeting place, a market, a place to preach and plot, the site of workshops and the haunt of prostitutes and thieves. In the 18th century, the Churchyard was the centre of the book trade. Today, the area is less frenetic and is a popular place for office workers to relax at lunchtime.

Look out for two statues. St Paul's Memorial Cross, in the northeast corner, dates from 1912 and stands on the spot where open-air sermons were preached. The other statue, more modern, shows the recumbent figure of Thomas à Becket (1118–1170).

Having circumnavigated the cathedral, walk up the broad steps into **Paternoster Square** (paternosters were strings of prayer beads). This area, flattened during the Blitz, was rebuilt in Modernist style as a pedestrianized square surrounded by office blocks. During the 1980s the architecture of Paternoster Square was the subject of a heated debate in which Prince Charles joined enthusiastically. The Corporation of the City of London has now decided to demolish the area and start again. For the moment, though, you needn't bother to explore the square – the office blocks are largely empty and there is little to see apart from one modern sculpture.

The Father of Fleet Street, and a Wren Church

Turn immediately left and walk down a sloping ramp into Warwick Lane. Cross the road and head up a short alleyway towards Amen Court – a private area, mainly offices and residences of cathedral staff. Just before you reach the gateway, turn left under a modern office block and then right into the forecourt of **Stationers' Hall**. This is the livery hall of the Stationers' and Newspaper Makers' Company, one of hundreds of livery companies descended from the craft guilds of the Middle Ages who administered apprenticeships and who were responsible for quality control. Many of the guilds became extremely wealthy and built extravagant halls for their lavish ceremonies. The officers of the guild wore elaborate uniforms or 'livery' – hence the name. Look on the front of Stationers' Hall for the plaque to Wynkyn de Worde (died *c*1535), the so-called Father of Fleet Street, who in *c*1500 set up his first printing press nearby.

Leave the forecourt along the alley by the Citizens' Advice Bureau and turn right on reaching Ludgate Hill. Lud Gate, one of six gates built in the old city walls, was finally pulled down in 1760.

A few yards to your right you'll see the unimposing entrance of the **Church of St Martin-within-Ludgate**. It is believed that a church was first built on this site about 1300 years ago, by King Cadwal, and some of the remains of that building may exist in the crypt of the building that stands here today. A medieval church (completed 1437) was destroyed in the Great Fire of 1666. The present church, built by Wren, was completed in 1684. Wren designed the spire to complement the view towards St Paul's; despite subsequent building it still carries out this function. St Martin's survived the Blitz intact, and its simple cruciform interior is today well maintained by several guilds and liveries. You can admire some more of Grinling Gibbons's carving while listening to the popular lunchtime concerts.

If you decide not to stop, keep going past the church until you cross **Old Bailey**, which runs inside and parallel to the old City walls. This street gives its name to the Central Criminal Court, which is 220 yards (200m) to your right from where you're crossing. Old Bailey was also the site of Newgate Prison, where large crowds turned up to witness public hangings.

Fleet Street and Environs

Cross Ludgate Circus and enter **Fleet Street**, named for a small stream, the Fleet, which rises on Hampstead Heath and which once marked the western boundary of the Roman city. For many years the Fleet was little more than a foul sewer. Wren attempted to tidy it up, canalizing the lower reaches and building four Venetian-style bridges – the foundations of one of these was recently discovered beneath Ludgate Circus. His scheme failed because habits die hard: people continued to use the Fleet as a receptacle for sewage, rubbish and dead dogs, along with entrails from Smithfield meat market. The stream was eventually covered up in 1766, reputedly after an inebriated butcher froze to death after becoming stuck in the mud. Also located here was the notorious Fleet Prison, where John Donne was obliged to spend some time, allegedly for marrying without his father-in-law's permission.

Fleet Street is, of course, famous for its connections with the newspaper industry. Printing came to the area with Wynkyn de Worde, who exploited the proximity of St Paul's and the inns of court. Two hundred years passed, however, before the first daily newspaper was produced here – the *Daily Courant*, a forerunner of *The Times*. The newspaper industry has now largely relocated to Docklands after an acrimonious dispute involving the print unions, whose craft had been rendered largely obsolete by new technology. Evidence of the industry remains, however. Look for the former *Daily Telegraph* building, with its Art Deco frontage – it is now occupied by a French bank – and the famous black-glass façade of the old *Daily Express* building. Opposite the latter is one of the very few of Fleet Street's remaining working links with the newspaper industry – the offices of the Reuters/Press Association news agency, housed in a sturdy stone building designed by Sir Edwin Lutyens (1869–1944) in 1935.

Continue west along Fleet Street until, on the right, you reach Wine Office Court, in which stands **Ye Olde Cheshire Cheese**. One of the most famous pubs in London, it dates from 1667, having been rebuilt after the Great Fire. The court is named for the excise office that was here until 1665. The pub is full of atmosphere – low ceilings, intimate corners, dark oak panelling – and provides excellent lunches and bar meals. It was the haunt of Samuel Johnson (1709–1784) and other literary

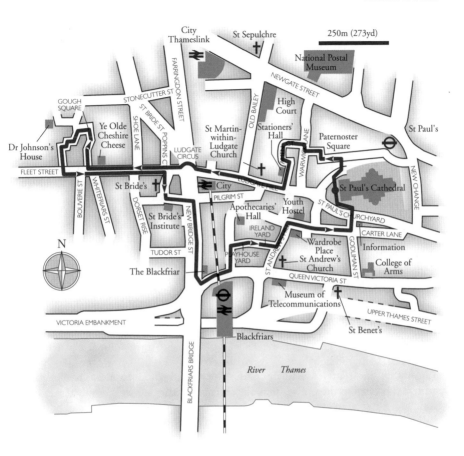

figures such as Alexander Pope (1688–1744), James Boswell (1740–1795), Lord Macaulay (1800–1859) and, more recently, Mark Twain (1835–1910).

Take the alleyway to the left of the tavern and fork left into Gough Square, a cobbled courtyard whose neo-Georgian buildings are mostly legal chambers. The one genuine 17th-century building is **Dr Johnson's House**, at 17 Gough Square; here Johnson lived from 1747 to 1759 while he compiled the first known dictionary of the English language. The house is full of memorabilia concerning both Johnson and his biographer Boswell. Look for the copy on display of the first edition of the dictionary. Don't miss the attic, where Johnson and six helpers compiled the dictionary.

Printing History

Leave Gough Square, pass through Johnson's Square and follow an alleyway back into Fleet Street. Cross the street and walk back towards St Paul's. Just before you come to the Reuters building, turn right to reach **St Bride's Church**.

Sometimes known as the 'printers' cathedral', the present church is the eighth to have been built on this site during the past 1500 years; its steeple (which is supposed to have inspired the tiered wedding cake) is the highest Wren built. Bombing badly damaged the church during World War II but also helped reveal the crypt, which has Roman mosaics, some medieval walls and the remains of previous churches. The crypt has a small chapel and a large display of artefacts discovered on the site. Alongside is a presentation of Fleet Street history. It was next to St Bride's that Wynkyn de Worde moved Caxton's printing firm in order to take advantage of the trade offered by the Churchyard book market and the law courts. Today there are frequent and popular lunchtime concerts in the nave of St Bride's.

Take the path alongside the churchyard to Bride Lane. Turn right and walk towards **St Bride's Institute and Printing Library**, which was opened by the Prince of Wales, the future Edward VII, in 1894 as a cultural centre. It stands on the site of the old Bridewell Abbey, and today includes a small theatre.

Blackfriars

Turn left at the institute, walk to New Bridge Street, turn right and head towards Blackfriars Bridge. You are now in the Blackfriars area, named after the Dominican monastery which existed here from 1278 until the Dissolution. This once-fashionable region is nowadays well off the tourist trail, but has a number of interesting buildings.

On the left, just before the bridge, is the unique **Blackfriar** pub, decorated in Art Nouveau style with a statue of a jolly black monk over the front door. Inside are friezes showing inebriated monks. This is a one-off – don't miss it.

Leaving the pub, go under the railway bridge and turn immediately left into Blackfriars Lane. Straight ahead is **Apothecaries' Hall**, dating from 1688 and arguably the most attractive of the City Livery Company buildings. The delightful courtyard is open to the public, but you can see the other attractions only if you have made a prior written application.

Just before you reach the hall, turn right into **Playhouse Yard**. Once the refectory of the monastery, the building here was converted into an indoor theatre, the Blackfriars Playhouse. William Shakespeare (1564–1616) was a partner in this theatre, which had three galleries and over six hundred seats, and functioned mainly in winter – summer performances were held in the open-air Globe Theatre, south of the Thames.

Fork right into **Ireland Yard**. On the left of the passageway was the Provincial Hall of the Dominican Monastery. After the monastery was dissolved in 1538, the Parish Church of St Ann Blackfriars was built on the site. The church was destroyed during the Great Fire and never rebuilt, the parish being amalgamated with the nearby St Andrew-by-the-Wardrobe. Gravestones can still be seen in the yard, which got its name from a haberdasher, William Ireland, whose shop was in the monastery gatehouse. Shakespeare is said to have bought the shop in 1613 and left it on his death to his daughter Susannah.

At the end of the yard, turn left into St Andrew's Hill and then immediately right into Carter Lane. On your left, the City of London Youth Hostel has an interesting pink and grey frontage. Immediately opposite is the delightful little courtyard of **Wardrobe Place**. This was where the Master of the King's Wardrobe, responsible for all the monarch's ceremonial robes, had his premises from 1359 until the Great Fire of 1666.

Continue along Carter Lane and take the next turning left, which brings you back to the west front of St Paul's, where the walk began.

LONDON: WESTMINSTER

Access: The nearest mainline railway terminals are Victoria, Charing Cross and Waterloo. The most convenient underground station is Westminster (District, Circle and Jubilee lines). Victoria Coach Station is five minutes' walk away. London Transport buses include 3, 11, 12, 24, 53, 77A, 88, 109 and 211. Most London open-top bus tours pass by and allow you to jump on or off.

Although strictly speaking not a cathedral (it claimed this title only during the period 1540–50), Westminster Abbey deserves inclusion for various reasons. First, as the 'nation's church' it has provided the venue for the majority of royal coronations and burials throughout its history. Second, though it was, like many of the great cathedrals, based on a medieval monastery, it survived the Dissolution of the Monasteries almost intact, probably because of its royal connections. And third, it is one of the main tourist attractions in Britain; there are as many as 15,000 visitors a day, so do not expect to find the usual tranquillity of an English cathedral!

To many who come to the abbey, the building seems somewhat like a gigantic mausoleum, the recent introduction of hourly prayers being little more than a token and the frequent admonitory notices – NO PHOTOGRAPHY, NO VIDEOS, NO LECTURES HERE, WALK ONLY ON THE CARPET, etc. – an irritation. There is, nevertheless, much of interest here if you can manage to visit the abbey at a quiet time, for the building is in many ways a religious and historical record of the country.

A number of stories tell of early religious buildings on the site of the present one, but none can be verified. What is certain is that a Benedictine monastery was set up here by St Dunstan (*c*909–988) in 960. When Edward the Confessor succeeded in 1042 the monastery was still small, having only twelve monks, but under his patronage it grew, and a large abbey was built in the French Romanesque style. The Bayeux Tapestry gives us a tantalizing glimpse of its architecture. The building, of cruciform shape, had arcades with tall, rounded arches, above which was a clerestory. A high tower had corner turrets. Edward was unable to attend the consecration in 1065, having become seriously ill; he died shortly afterwards and was buried by the high altar.

Edward was succeeded by Harold, who was defeated by William the Conqueror at the Battle of Hastings in 1066. On Christmas Day the same year William rode up the aisle of the abbey on horseback to be crowned king, thereby establishing the tradition of royal coronations in the building. Since then only two monarchs have not been crowned at Westminster – Edward V and Edward VIII.

The Confessor was canonized in 1161 and his shrine became a popular place of pilgrimage. In the next century his great admirer Henry III decided the shrine should belong in a more suitable building. He demolished the old abbey and constructed a new building in Gothic style, strongly influenced by Rheims

Cathedral in northern France. (The master mason was Henry de Reyns.) Work began in 1245 and, by the time money ran out in 1267, the apse, transepts and choir were complete, plus some bays in the east end of the nave. Materials used were varied. Much of the stone came from Reigate in Surrey, and many of the pillars were in Purbeck marble. The more ornate work was carved in stone from Caen, Normandy.

For over a century the Norman nave – and the parishioners who used it – saw little change, but in 1348 Simon de Langham (d1376), Archbishop of Canterbury, bequeathed some money to the abbey, and work recommenced under the patronage of Richard III. Progress was slow: not until 1506 was the west end reached. The height of the nave matched that of the east end, attaining over 100ft (30m); the nave was supported on the exterior by flying buttresses. The master mason was Henry Yevele, who kept closely to Henry de Reyns's original plan, so that the whole building seems to have been constructed as one.

An important later addition to the church was the Lady Chapel, at the east end, built in the time of Henry VII in Perpendicular style. Henry VII intended it to honour his uncle, Henry VI, but, as the latter was never canonized, it in the event became the last resting place for himself and his family.

The Benedictine monastery was dissolved on the orders of Henry VIII in 1540, and the abbey became the cathedral of the diocese of Westminster. For the next ten years there were two London cathedrals, the abbey and Old St Paul's – indeed, the abbey contributed money to the repair of the latter (hence the saying 'rob Peter to pay Paul'). Meanwhile the old abbey buildings became Westminster School, a public school which still exists today.

In the 18th century the two towers that dominate the west front were added by Nicholas Hawksmoor (1661–1736), a pupil of Christopher Wren (1632–1723). This completed the structure of the building. Today, the abbey is less a place of worship than a venue for large state occasions, while the great and the good of the nation are buried or commemorated within its portals.

TOUR OF THE ABBEY
Start and finish: The west end.

Viewed from the square outside, the overall impression of the **west end (1)** is of verticality, putting it firmly in the Perpendicular style. With its two dominating towers and its huge central window, this part of the abbey is largely the work, as previously mentioned, of Hawksmoor in the early 18th century. Unfortunately, the symmetry is ruined by the squat Jerusalem Chamber on the south side. In 1998 the ten niches over the door, which had been bare of statues since the Middle Ages, were filled with effigies of 20th-century martyrs. Some of the subjects are well known – e.g., Martin Luther King (1929–1968) – but others are less well so. None – and this has caused much debate – are English.

Walk through the main entrance and look back at the interior of the west end, dominated by the west window. The stained glass dates from 1735 and was designed by Sir James Thornhill (1675–1734). The top layer shows Abraham, Isaac and Jacob, while on the two rows beneath are fourteen other prophets. The lowest row of windows is made up of coats-of-arms, including those of Elizabeth I and George II.

Look next for the **Tomb of the Unknown Warrior (2)**. This takes the form of a simple black slab fringed by red poppies. The idea for such a memorial came from a British World War I chaplain and was taken up by the then Dean of Westminster. Working groups went to the six main battlefields and each brought back the exhumed body of an unknown British soldier. One corpse, chosen at random by the Director of the War Graves Commission in Flanders, was taken back to Britain. Here it was reburied at Westminster Abbey with full pomp on 11 November 1920. The three main allies on the Western Front all contributed to the memorial: an English oak coffin is surrounded by French soil and covered by a slab of Belgian black marble. Nearby is a memorial slab to Sir Winston Churchill (1874–1965).

Now look at the **nave (3)**. If you're accustomed to the long low vistas of most English cathedrals, Westminster Abbey's nave will remind you much more of a French cathedral. The general impression is of height and narrowness. In fact, at 102ft (31m) the nave is the loftiest medieval vault in England, and its proportions are what make it so visually satisfying: the main arcade, at 51ft (15.4m), forms half the height; the tribune, at 17ft (5.2m), is one-sixth of the height; and the clerestory, at 34ft (10.4m), makes up the remaining one-third. When you look at the nave from the outside you can see that this prodigious overall height is supported by three layers of flying buttresses. The architectural style largely represents a transition between Early English and Decorated (built later, but done to match the older part of the abbey). The windows at tribune level take the form of an equilateral triangle filled with three trefoil circles of bar tracery. Finally note the roof chandeliers, made of Waterford glass and installed to mark the abbey's 900th anniversary.

On the north side of the nave you find a pay desk. Unlike many English cathedrals, where paying for entry is a recent phenomenon, Westminster has been requiring an admission fee for centuries. The cloisters are free (but are best seen towards the end of the tour), while the chapter house, pyx chamber and Undercroft Museum, all run by English Heritage, require further payment.

The tour now continues along a set route – if you stray from it one of the numerous staff will promptly set you right.

Musicians, Fighter Pilots and the Virgin Queen

The first part of the north aisle is known as **Musicians' Aisle (4)**. Graves and memorials here include those of three of the abbey's organists – Henry Purcell (1659–1695), John Blow (1649–1708) and Orlando Gibbons (1583–1625). More recent memorials remember Ralph Vaughan Williams (1872–1958), Benjamin Britten (1913–1976) and Sir Edward Elgar (1857–1934).

The north aisle leads you to the **north transept (5)**, where there is an excellent rose window, again by Thornhill, displaying eleven Apostles – the one missing is, inevitably, Judas. The north transept, sometimes called 'Statesmen's Aisle', is cluttered with the marble statues of 19th-century politicians like Sir Robert Peel (1788–1850), William Pitt the Elder (1708–1778) and William Gladstone (1809-1898).

Go back towards the central aisle where, in the crossing and in front of the high altar, you'll find the **sanctuary (6)**, the focus of coronation ceremonies. The high altar and the reredos behind it were the work of Sir George Gilbert Scott (1811–1878) in the mid-19th century. Beneath the high altar is one of the abbey's most prized treasures – the Cosmati Pavement. Made by the Cosmati family from Rome, it was laid in 1268. In essence, it is a mosaic of coloured glass inlaid into Purbeck marble. Unfortunately it is in such a delicate state that it is usually covered by a carpet, being revealed only on state occasions.

The set route now takes you into the east end of the abbey. Look out on the right for the side of Henry III's tomb, which displays further Cosmati work, giving you a fair indication of what the pavement looks like. Regrettably, much of the mosaic work – up to the height of a raised arm – has been removed by souvenir hunters.

The north aisle is also the location of the **Tomb of Elizabeth I (7)**. This monument, in black and white marble and heavily gilded, shows a reclining effigy. Buried beneath Elizabeth is her half-sister Mary Tudor (Bloody Mary). The memorial was erected by James VI & I, who, aware of the ill-feeling between them, provided a Latin inscription which, loosely, reads: 'Consorts both in throne and grave, here rest we two sisters, Elizabeth and Mary, in the hope of one resurrection.'

The route now leads you to the apse at the extreme east end of the abbey and to the **Royal Air Force Chapel (8)**, dedicated to members of fighter squadrons killed in the Battle of Britain. The zigzag window contains modern stained glass by Hugh Easton showing some of the men who died plus the badges of the squadrons.

Tudor Tombs and the Confessor's Shrine

You now enter the main part of the east end, which is **Henry VII's Chapel (9)**. Completed in 1519, this is a riot of the Perpendicular and is justifiably considered the abbey's architectural showpiece. The fan-vaulted ceiling, with its circular designs, is particularly impressive. The choir stalls are intricately carved, with tall canopies over which is an extraordinary collection of nearly one hundred stone statues of saints. Above hang the banners of the Knights of the Order of the Bath, to whom the chapel is dedicated. The order goes back to the Middle Ages, and derives its name from the custom of bathing before receiving the knighthood – installation ceremonies being performed every four years, usually at the Tower of London.

While in the choir area, note the beautiful carved misericords under the seats.

At the other end of the chapel is the altar, actually a copy (but using two of the original pillars) of the first, 16th-century structure. The canopy has Henry's coat-of-arms; beneath it is a 15th-century Madonna and Child by Antonio Vivarini. Henry's tomb, which is also that of his wife Elizabeth, was made by the Florentine sculptor Pietro Torrigiani (c1472–1522), a pupil of Michelangelo (1475–1564) who fled to Britain after breaking his master's nose in a fight. Most of the other Tudor monarchs, princes and princesses are buried in the vaults under the chapel.

The official route now takes you over a glass 'bridge' into the abbey's most sacred core – the **Shrine of Edward the Confessor (10)**. This has been altered considerably over the years. In the days of the monastery it had three parts: a stone base decorated with Cosmati work; a gold feretory (bier) which contained Edward's coffin and a wooden canopy which could be raised or lowered in order to protect or reveal the bier. During the Reformation the shrine was dismantled and the feretory removed, although in the reign of Mary Tudor some restoration took place. What you see today is a rather battered stone base with remnants of the original decoration, on top of which rests the restored canopy. In front is a small, discreet altar. Proximity to the shrine was important in medieval times, so you'll find nearby the tombs and effigies of five kings and four queens, including Richard II and Edward III. Look for the grooves in the stonework where countless pilgrims have knelt.

The shrine is separated from the west end of the abbey by a 15th-century stone screen showing scenes from Edward's life. Also on this side of the shrine is the coronation chair of Edward I, which has been used at every coronation since. The gap beneath the chair once contained the Stone of Scone, the coronation stone of Scotland before it was looted by Edward in 1296. Scottish Nationalists briefly stole it back in the 1950s, and it was officially returned to Scotland in 1996.

Poets and an Inspiration to Poets
The official route now leads you, almost backtracking, to the **south aisle of Henry VII's Chapel (11)**, the site of the tomb of Mary, Queen of Scots, who was beheaded at the behest of Elizabeth I. Mary's body was brought here from Peterborough Cathedral by her grandson, James VI & I, and installed in this eight-poster tomb. Nearby is the tomb of Lady Margaret Beaufort (1443–1509), Henry VII's mother, known for her charitable works. Her effigy, showing her in old age, is by Torrigiani.

The south ambulatory now goes past the Chapel of St Nicholas (Santa Claus –

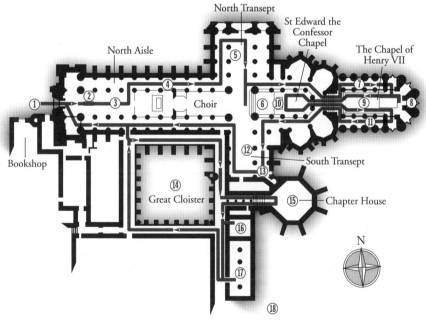

Key

1. West End
2. Grave of the Unknown Warrior
3. Nave
4. Musicians' Aisle
5. North Transept

6. Sanctuary
7. Tomb of Elizabeth I
8. Royal Air Force Chapel
9. Henry VII's Chapel
10. Shrine of Edward the Confessor
11. South Aisle of Henry VII's Chapel

12. South Transept
13. Poets' Corner
14. Great Cloister
15. Chapter House
16. Pyx Chamber
17. Undercroft Museum
18. College Garden

patron saint of children) and the Chapel of St Edmund, King of the East Anglians, before reaching the **south transept (12)**. The architecture here is pure Geometrical Decorated Gothic; the glass of the superb rose window is Victorian. Note the carvings beneath the window, in the angle of the arches and the 13th-century wall paintings. Look for the stairs next to the south side of the transept; these were part of the night passage from the monks' dormitory to the choir.

Also in the south transept is **Poets' Corner (13)**. The first to arrive was Geoffrey Chaucer (*c*1345–1400), who was buried here apparently because he lived near the abbey and had been clerk of works to the Palace of Westminster. No other poets were buried here for nearly two centuries, until Edmund Spenser (*c*1552–1599) was interred nearby. It is said that his contemporaries wrote elegies and threw them, with their pens, into the grave. There are now slabs, busts, statues and other memorials to a vast number of poets and writers, including Samuel Johnson (1709–1784), Robert Browning (1812–1889), Alfred, Lord Tennyson (1809–1892), Charles Dickens (1812–1870), Lord Byron (1788–1824), Ben Jonson (1572–1637) and W.H. Auden (1907–1973). In among them, strangely, is the grave of George Friedrich Handel (1685–1759), whose music was often heard at Westminster Abbey. It was at a performance of the *Messiah* here that George III mistakenly rose to his feet during the 'Hallelujah Chorus'; everyone else did likewise, so that the king would not be embarrassed. Thus was established the custom of standing whenever it is played.

Walk a few steps into the south choir aisle – where there is a monument to Admiral Sir Cloudesley Shovel (1650–1707) – and take the door into the **Great Cloister (14)**, which has remained intact since the time of the monastery and is still in good condition. In those days it would have been, in effect, a series of four long rooms with glass windows and rush floors. The north cloister, once a reading and writing area, is now a popular brass-rubbing centre. Young novice monks were educated in the west walk. The south side, which has the tombs of three early abbots, led to the refectory – a building destroyed at the Dissolution.

The Chapter House, Pyx Chamber and Undercroft Museum
The area to the east of here is administered by English Heritage, and a further admission fee is required. The charge is worth it, for this part of the abbey has few visitors and many interesting features.

The **chapter house (15)** was where the monks met to discuss daily business and for the reading of a chapter from St Benedict's Rule. It was used also as a parliament house by the Commons 1257–1547, much to the annoyance of the monks – who complained about the noise! Dating from 1250, it is octagonal, with a central column supporting delicate roof vaulting. Around the walls are traces of medieval painting, while the windows above contain modern clear glass interspersed with coats-of-arms; much of the Victorian glass was destroyed during World War II. Without doubt the most fascinating feature is the original decorated tile floor, which has survived through being covered for much of its life by a wooden floor. At the Dissolution the chapter house became property of the Crown, and remains so: the dean and chapter of the abbey have no control over it – hence the English Heritage involvement.

Go back from the chapter house, turn left and then left again into the **pyx chamber (16)**, which was also part of the monastic buildings. The simple stone altar and wall *piscina* (basin for the water used to wash the sacred vessels) suggest it was once a chapel; later it was certainly the monastic treasury. After the Dissolution it became Crown property, housing the pyx, a chest containing gold and silver pieces that were used annually as standards against which to test the coinage – this was known as the Trial of the Pyx. The large double door has six locks and is prevented from opening fully by a stone sill; these arrangements were apparently introduced after a burglary in 1303.

Exiting the pyx chamber, go left and left again into the **Undercroft Museum (17)**, a vaulted part of the monastery beneath the dormitory; it probably dates from *c*1070 and was almost certainly used as a *calefactorium* – a commonroom where the monks could keep warm. It became a museum in 1908.

A Roman sarcophagus on display probably dates from the 3rd century AD; the cross on the stone lid shows it was re-used in Saxon times for a Christian burial. Probably the most fascinating items are the wax death masks and funeral effigies, the figures dressed in original costumes so you get a good impression of what these people were really like. Among those represented are Charles II, Henry VII, a surprisingly diminutive Lord Nelson (1758–1805), Elizabeth I, William and Mary (the former standing on a stone so that his wife wouldn't tower above him) and Lady Frances Stuart, who was the model for Britannia on coins and whose pet parrot rests at her feet. Also shown are funeral armour, medieval stained glass and coronation regalia.

Close to the museum, via a dark passage and the Little Cloister, is the **College Garden (18)**. This was the infirmary garden where the monastery's physician grew the herbs with which he treated ailing monks. It is open to the public only on Thursdays, when it is a popular lunchtime venue for office workers – particularly in July and August, when bands occasionally play here.

Return through the cloisters back to the south aisle of the nave and on to the west end, where the tour began.

WALKING TOUR FROM WESTMINSTER ABBEY

This circular walk covers many aspects of the government of the country, including the Houses of Parliament, Whitehall, Buckingham Palace and one of the royal parks.

Start and finish: The west front of the abbey.
Length: 2 miles (3.2km).
Time: 1½ hours, but allow longer if you want to visit the church and museums.
Refreshments: Surprisingly few refreshment opportunities. The Cakehouse Restaurant in St James's Park can be pleasant in summer. The only two pubs of character are the Red Lion in Whitehall and the Two Chairmen in Dartmouth Street.

Leave the west front of the abbey and head across the grass to **St Margaret's Church**. Consecrated in 1523 and the third church to be built on the site, St Margaret's has long been known as the 'parish church of the House of Commons'. The architecture is almost entirely Perpendicular. The windows are of particular interest: one is dedicated to Sir Walter Raleigh (1552–1618), who is buried somewhere under the church (sans head, because that was claimed by his wife) and others are dedicated to John Milton (1608–1674) and William Caxton (*c*1422–*c*1491); the modern stained

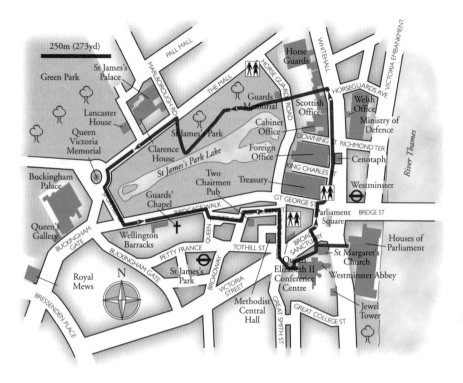

glass in a window in the south aisle is by John Piper (1903–1992).

The east end of the church is the most fascinating part of the building. It has a fine reredos and a window with stained glass that may be the original Flemish material which was part of the 16th-century church; such is the value of the glass that it was removed for safety during the two world wars. The window commemorates the marriage of Henry VIII to Catherine of Aragon.

Leave the church and walk along its side to Parliament Street (the south end of Whitehall), where there is a fine view of the **Houses of Parliament**, the clock tower of Big Ben prominent to the left. Although most people think only of the two debating chambers, there is much more to the Houses of Parliament – lobbies, bars, offices, libraries, over two miles (3km) of corridors, a police station, a travel agency; even an underground rifle range. Over 3000 people work in the building.

More correctly known as the Palace of Westminster, the original building burnt down in 1834, leaving only Westminster Hall and St Stephen's Chapel intact. The remainder of the extant parliament building was the work of Sir Charles Barry (1795–1860). Designed in ornate neo-Gothic style, it is undoubtedly the finest Victorian building in Britain and one of the best-known monuments in the world. Its honey-coloured stonework has recently been cleaned, so you see it in all its glory.

There are various ways of visiting the Houses of Parliament. For UK citizens probably the best is via one of the guided tours which MPs occasionally run for their constituents. To watch the proceedings in the debating chambers, join the queues for the public galleries. Note that the recesses, when MPs are on holiday, can be lengthy. When parliament is in session, a flag flies above the statue of Victoria on the south side of the building. You can also climb the tower of Big Ben and actually walk behind the clock face, and further entertainment can be had by strolling across to College Green, a favourite spot for publicity-conscious MPs to be interviewed by the media.

Now go back up one side of **Parliament Square** and cross the street by the pedestrian crossing. Laid out to give a vista of the Houses of Parliament, the square now resembles an extremely busy traffic roundabout. It contains the statues of five British prime ministers, including Disraeli (1804–1881) and Churchill, and of other notables such as Jan Smuts (1870–1950) and Abraham Lincoln (1809–1865).

Walk back down the other side of the square and into Parliament Street, which leads past the Treasury on the left and into **Whitehall**, a name synonymous with the bureaucrats who, behind the scenes, run the country.

Whitehall was named after the old Whitehall Palace, a royal residence in Tudor times that was destroyed by fire in 1698. In this building Henry VIII married Anne Boleyn, and here he died in 1547. The palace is said to have stretched for half a mile (800m) along the banks of the Thames and to have had nearly 2000 rooms. On its landward side were tennis courts, jousting yards, cockpits and other sporting venues. Today the broad avenue of Whitehall is occupied almost entirely by the offices of government departments.

First on the left is the large hulk of the Foreign Office, dating from the 1870s and built to a design by Sir George Gilbert Scott. Set back on the right is the Ministry of Defence, which contains in its bowels the old wine cellar of Whitehall Palace. Opposite is the Scottish Office (also known as Dover House), which has a porticoed entrance and a dome to its rear. Further north on the left is the Admiralty, whose splendid façade dates from 1726. The statues along Whitehall include Earl Haig (1861–1928), on horseback, Montgomery of Alamein (1887–1976), Lord Alanbrooke (1883–1963) and Raleigh.

In the centre of Whitehall, just opposite the Foreign Office, stands the **Cenotaph**, the focus of the annual Remembrance Day ceremony each November. The original memorial was designed in 1919 by Sir Edwin Lutyens (1869–1944) in plaster and wood, but it was replaced the following year by a more permanent structure in Portland Stone. It bears a simple inscription: 'The Glorious Dead.'

Just past the Cenotaph, on the left-hand side, is the short cul-de-sac of

The Cenotaph

189

Downing Street. The street is named after an Irish-born American, George Downing (*c*1623–1684), who came to Britain and became one of Cromwell's officials. He later supported the Restoration and by the time of his death he had built some fifteen houses in the street. No. 10 (including the large building behind it) was originally the home of the First Lord of the Treasury. An early holder of the post, Sir Robert Walpole (1676–1745), created for himself the role of Prime Minister and so No. 10 has since been the home of every PM except one. Next door, No. 11 has been the home of the Chancellor of the Exchequer since 1807, No. 12 is the office of the Chief Whip (interconnecting doors link all three), and the Cabinet Office is on the corner of Downing Street and Whitehall.

Downing Street was once open to the public, but when Margaret Thatcher was Prime Minister she had large wrought-iron gates erected at the entrance in a rather futile attempt to increase security.

A Royal Park and a Royal Palace

Continue along Whitehall until you reach the **Horse Guards building** on the left. Outside you'll see two mounted guards of the Household Cavalry (plus two unmounted guards), nominally to protect the building, which was designed by William Kent (1684–1748) in 1745. It actually contains little worth protecting, but the hourly changing of the two mounted guards is one of those curious English traditions which tourists arrive in flocks to see.

Pass through the archway (information boards here tell you about the guards regiments) and step into the open space called Horse Guards Parade. Once Henry VIII's jousting ground, this is now the square used each year for the Trooping of the Colour on the Queen's birthday.

Cross the parade ground and then Horse Guards Road, keeping the war memorial to the Household Division on your right, and enter **St James's Park**, one of London's royal parks. The land was acquired by Henry VIII, and the Court of St James was established. In 1603 James VI & I had a menagerie and a duck decoy here, and in 1660 Charles II had the park landscaped in a formal French style and opened it to the public. The first exotic birds, including pelicans, were introduced in 1667. Further informal landscaping was carried out in 1827 by John Nash (1752–1835) for George IV, and little has changed since. Today St James's Park is a popular lunchtime spot for office workers and tourists. Numerous kiosks sell snacks, and there is the popular Cakehouse Restaurant in the centre of the park.

Continue through the park with the lake on your left until you see a bridge. Turn right here and walk a hundred yards or so (100m) until you get to **The Mall**. This is the only London thoroughfare to resemble the boulevards of Paris. Look right to see Admiralty Arch, at the Mall's Trafalgar Square end, and left to see Buckingham Palace. Across The Mall are two royal palaces – St James's Palace and Clarence House. The former is the home of minor royals such as the Duke of Kent and Princess Alexandra, but for two centuries foreign ambassadors have been presented to the Court of St James here. Clarence House was the London home of the late Queen Mother.

Walk left up The Mall towards Buckingham Palace, in front of which is the impressive **Victoria Memorial**. Made of white limestone and installed in 1911 by Edward VII in tribute to his late mother, this is one of the better statues of her. The enthroned Victoria is accompanied by Truth, Motherhood and Justice. Above her are gilded figures proclaiming victory, while some distance from the main monument are groups of figures in black bronze depicting scenes from the Empire.

Behind the memorial is **Buckingham Palace**, renovated by Nash in the 1820s and the main home of the monarch since Victoria came to the throne. It dates from 1702, when the Duke of Buckingham lived here and was briefly owned by George III in the 18th century. Despite its lack of charm it is usually thronged with tourists hoping to get a glimpse of a royal personage. The Changing of the Guard, carried out here by the Foot Guards, takes place every morning May–Aug at 10:30. Since the 1992 fire at Windsor Palace and the subsequent need to raise money for repairs, Buckingham Palace has been open to the public on an experimental basis (daily 9:30–17:30 Aug–Sep; tickets from box office in Green Park at west end of The Mall). Note that only small areas of the palace may be seen and the queues can be long.

From the palace turn left into **Birdcage Walk** – the royal aviary used to be here. On your left is St James's Park and on your right is a series of buildings associated with the Guards. The first is the rather severe Wellington Barracks, where most of the guardsmen are billeted. This building also houses the Guards Museum. This is a good place to sort out the different Guards regiments and their uniforms. Next along Birdcage Walk is the unexpectedly modern Guards' Chapel, which replaced an earlier building destroyed by a V1 rocket in 1944.

An Historic Pub and Some Culture

At the first set of pedestrian traffic lights, turn right and then immediately left into **Queen Anne's Gate**, one of London's architectural gems. All the houses were built during the reign of Queen Anne and many feature ornately carved wooden canopies over the doors. Queen Anne's Gate is actually an amalgamation of two streets once separated by a wall; the position of the wall is now marked by a small, well eroded statue of Queen Anne – a far less grand affair than that outside St Paul's Cathedral (see page 171). The street has had a number of distinguished residents; blue plaques record Lord Haldane (1856–1928) and Lord Palmerston (1784–1865; he was born in No. 19).

At the end of Queen Anne's Gate turn left into Dartmouth Street, noting the **Two Chairmen** pub and possibly – who knows? – popping into it. The name derives from the sedan chair trade, which reached England in 1634. Each chair was operated by two 'chairmen', who would carry passengers between fixed points in the city – one being at the site of the Two Chairmen. Nearby are the Cockpit Steps, where cockfights were held in Henry VIII's time.

Carry on via Old Queen Street to Storey's Gate, named after Charles II's gamekeeper. Turn right into this street. It is flanked by two very contrasting buildings. On your left is the modern granite-and-glass **Queen Elizabeth II Conference Centre**, while on your right is the **Methodist Central Hall**. Built in 1912 in grey limestone – and in what can only be described as Edwardian Beaux Arts style – the latter is distinguished by its huge dark-grey dome. Its organ is claimed to be one of the best in the country. The United Nations Organization held its very first meeting here in 1946.

Now cross Victoria Street and return to the west front of Westminster Abbey, where the walk began.

LONDON: SOUTHWARK

Access: Nearby mainline railway stations include London Bridge and Cannon Street. The most convenient underground station is London Bridge (Northern line). Numerous London Transport buses serve the area: 17, 21, 22A, 35, 40, 42, 43, 45, 47, 48, 63, 78, 133, 149, 172, 188, 344, 501, 505 and 521.

At first glance this cathedral does not seem very inspiring, with flint and stone walls covered with the grime of centuries, and hemmed in by office blocks, a railway viaduct, a busy main road and a fruit and vegetable market. But do not be deterred: the cathedral and the district are rich in history, both ancient and modern.

There may have been activity at Southwark in Iron Age times, but it was during the Roman occupation that the first settlement of any size came into being. The Romans selected this spot as an ideal point for bridging the River Thames. The river was wider and shallower in Roman times, and a series of low marshy islands on the south bank allowed a wooden bridge to be constructed to link up with the city of Londinium (London), which lay on a low hill on the north bank.

Southwark, then, developed as a suburb of Londinium. Two roads from the south met here – Stane Street from Chichester and Watling Street from Dover – while the route across the causeway over the marshes is now Borough High Street.

After the Romans' departure there was a period of decline, but by the 10th century the new London Bridge had been built and Southwark was being listed as a 'burgh', a designation which usually meant fortifications, in this case to protect trade. The bridge was the effective head of navigation and Southwark developed as a commercial centre.

In 1106 the Normans, assisted by the Bishop of Winchester, William Giffard, built a church at Southwark, St Mary Overie ('over the river'). This church was serviced by the Augustine priory located on its north side. Giffard's successor, Henry de Blois, set his palace just west of the church, and subsequent bishops of Winchester continued to give patronage to it.

The Norman church was ruined by fire in 1212 and the cathedral now has only a few arches and doorways to remind us of this architectural period. Peter des Roches, then Bishop of Winchester, speedily began to rebuild the priory church in what has become known as Early English style, with long lancet windows and pointed arches. Work began in 1220; by 1270 the retrochoir, sanctuary, choir, aisles, tower and part of the nave were finished. Construction then stopped for fifty years, probably for financial reasons. In 1390, when the building was almost complete, yet another fire took its toll. St Mary Overie had to be rebuilt again, this time by Cardinal Henry Beaufort (1377–1447), an illegitimate son of John of Gaunt (1340–1399).

A further disaster occurred in 1469 when the vaulted stone roof of the nave fell in. It was rebuilt in wood; a few of the original carved stone bosses are on display at the west end of the present cathedral. An early 16th-century addition was the carved stone altar screen, donated by the then Bishop of Winchester, Richard Fox.

Meanwhile Southwark, being outside the jurisdiction of the City of London, became the playground of Londoners, who flocked across the river for bear-baiting and cockfighting and to visit the prostitute-ridden inns. A number of theatres were built here, including the Globe, where William Shakespeare (1564–1616) worked, the Rose and the Swan. Southwark has had connections with other great literary figures apart from Shakespeare, Geoffrey Chaucer (*c*1345–1400) and Charles Dickens (1812–1870) being among them.

During the Reformation the priory was dissolved and the building handed over to Henry VIII. St Mary Overie became the parish church of St Saviour, Southwark, incorporating the Chapel of St Mary Magdalene. Around this time Stephen Gardiner (1482–1555), the Bishop of Winchester, used the retrochoir for his consistory court. After his death it became a bakery and then a pigsty before falling into disrepair. The church survived the Civil War, but the Winchester Palace was badly damaged and quickly became a ruin. This marked the end of the patronage of the various bishops of Winchester.

The 17th and 18th centuries saw a number of improvements made to the structure of the church. The tower was completed in 1689 and in 1703 a wooden altar screen extended Bishop Fox's existing stone screen. In the 19th century there was much renovation and the Chapel of St Mary Magdalene was demolished. In 1841, the wooden roof was replaced and a temporary nave built.

The wharves and docks of Southwark and nearby Bermondsey thrived during the Victorian era and the borough became the centre of London's food industry. The railways also grew significantly, replacing the coaches which had run from Southwark's inns. London Bridge Station, opened in 1836, was the capital's first railway terminus.

With the reorganization of dioceses due to the enormous growth in population in the 19th century, Southwark was transferred from the see of Winchester to that of Rochester. It was clear, however, that a new cathedral was needed in South London and Southwark was the obvious place. Funds were raised to build a new nave that would be more fitting to cathedral status; the foundation stone was laid by the Prince of Wales, the future Edward VII, in 1890.

The church was given pro-cathedral status in 1897. In 1905 an Act of Parliament created the diocese of Southwark, making the parish church the Cathedral of St Saviour and St Mary Overie. The diocese has over three million inhabitants and is divided into three areas – Woolwich, Croydon and Kingston. Each has an area bishop.

Southwark suffered considerable damage during World War II, but the cathedral managed to survive. The last quarter of the 20th century saw the closure of the docks, as port activity migrated downstream to Tilbury. This gave a great opportunity to redevelop Thameside. The wharves have since been converted into apartments and office blocks, while historic buildings have been preserved; the final section of Riverside Walk was completed in 1994. Around the turn of the century, Southwark Cathedral underwent a £12 million redevelopment involving a new library, a courtyard garden, an exhibition centre and a restaurant. Clergy offices built in the 1980s have been knocked down to provide the cathedral with a riverfront setting. The renovations were 'opened' by Nelson Mandela in April 2001. Among all this redevelopment, Southwark Cathedral maintains its central position in the heart of the community.

TOUR OF THE CATHEDRAL
Start and finish: The west end.

The tour begins at the main entrance, just to the south of the **west end (1)**. On entering, look up to see the west window designed by Henry Holliday as part of the Victorian restoration. Beneath it on the floor is a memorial to the fifty-one victims, mostly young, who drowned when the *Marchioness* riverboat sank in the Thames near Southwark Bridge in August 1989. Against the rear wall, and seeming surprisingly large, are twelve roof bosses, all that remain of the 150 or so of the late 15th-century roof, which was taken down in 1930. Look out especially for the boss depicting the Devil swallowing Judas Iscariot. Also in this area is the hideous Victorian font in black marble, with a gold carved canopy by G.F. Bodley. The modern wooden font cover does nothing to improve its appearance.

Walk into the **nave (2)** to take in the view towards the chancel. The three levels of arcade, triforium and clerestory are nicely proportioned and topped by a simple vaulted roof. The pointed arches fit well with the Early English of the east end of the building; this is generally considered one of the better Victorian restorations of an English cathedral.

An English Poet and an American Benefactor
Cross into the **north aisle (3)**, noting the arch and recess built into the wall: part of what little remains of the Norman church built in 1106 and largely destroyed in 1206. The bases of the arch are, interestingly, 2ft (60cm) below the level of the present cathedral. Further east is the tomb of John Gower (*c*1325–1408), court poet to both Richard II and Henry IV and a friend of Chaucer. Gower was the first poet to write in English as opposed to Latin. The medieval wooden tomb is attractively coloured and canopied. The recumbent poet's head is resting on three books written in French, English and Latin, said to be his most highly regarded works: *Speculum Meditantis* (French), *Confessio Amantis* (English) and *Vox Clamantis* (Latin).

Nearby is a Norman doorway whose jambs may have been the entrance to the Norman chapter house. Step inside the doorway to see the illuminated bases – again the level is 2ft (60cm) lower than the present cathedral floor.

Walk into the **north transept (4)**, where there are monuments to Joyce Austin, Lionel Lockyer and Richard Blisse. Although the design of the transept dates from the 13th century, the walls are believed to have a Norman core. A curiosity here is the sword-rest against the north wall; it is dated 1674 and, unusually, is made of wood. It came from the Church of St Olave in Southwark, demolished in 1926.

Now amble under an unusual stilted arch into the north choir aisle and turn immediately left into the **Harvard Chapel (5)**, which has traces of Norman work. Originally the Chapel of St John the Evangelist, this was restored in 1905 and received a thorough renovation in 1975 thanks to funds from Harvard University. John Harvard (1607–1638) was born in Southwark in 1607, the son of a butcher. The cathedral's register shows that he was baptized in St Saviour's. He emigrated to

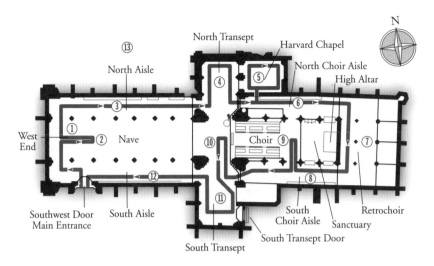

Key

1. West End
2. Nave
3. North Aisle
4. North Transept
5. Harvard Chapel
6. North Choir Aisle
7. Retrochoir
8. South Choir Aisle
9. Choir
10. Crossing
11. South Transept
12. South Aisle
13. Chapter House

New England, where he left his books and some money to a recently founded college at Cambridge, Massachusetts, which college later became Harvard University.

'Gentleman Portar to King James I'

Go back into the **north choir aisle (6)**, passing the organ (its case is in the south aisle) dating from 1897, with two tremolos, twenty-seven couplers, sixty-four speaking stops, and four manuals. Note the series of monuments on the aisle's north wall.

The first is the **Trehearne Monument**, showing John Trehearne, 'Gentleman Portar to King James I' and his wife and beneath them a family at prayer. It is claimed that Trehearne was one of the four parishioners who bought St Saviour's from James l in 1614. Next comes a wooden effigy of a knight, thought to have been carved between 1280 and 1300. It is possibly a knight of the Warenne family, who were benefactors of the priory. Opposite the effigy is the beautifully carved **Nonesuch Chest**, believed to date from 1588.

Perceived Heresies

You now come to the 13th-century **retrochoir (7)**, which measures four bays by three and is arguably the most fascinating part of the cathedral. The architecture is Early English almost throughout; particularly attractive is the blind tracery on the west wall. Memorials abound. One gruesome example shows a reclining figure, obviously a decomposing body in a shroud; this may have been one of the early priors. Note, too, the simple wooden modern sculpture in memory of John Robinson (1919–1983), the Bishop of Woolwich whose thought-provoking book *Honest to God* (1963) caused an uproar among more orthodox members of the Church of England.

The east end of the retrochoir is marked by four chapels dedicated, from north to south, to St Andrew, to St Christopher, to Our Lady, and to St Francis and St Elizabeth of Hungary. On the south wall of the retrochoir is the Rider Memorial Window, built around the turn of the century in preparation for the designation of the church as a cathedral. The spacious area of the retrochoir was used at times as a consistory court by the various bishops of Winchester; the trial of the Marian Martyrs took place here in the time of Bishop Gardiner. Gardiner must have been a man who easily ignored his conscience. He acted as Henry VIII's advocate to the Pope when the king wanted a divorce, yet years later, in the reign of Mary Tudor, he was suddenly a good Catholic who approved the brutal persecution of Protestants.

Proceed now into the **south choir aisle (8)**, which contains two notable memorials to former bishops. Immediately to your right is the tomb of Bishop Lancelot Andrewes (1555–1626). A flamboyant affair, dripping with gold leaf and coats-of-arms, it was restored by Sir Ninian Comper in 1930. Next to it is the monument to Bishop Edward Talbot, the first Bishop of Southwark in 1905–11.

Architectural Delights

Turn directly right into the **choir (9)**: another example of Early English at its purest, with a pleasing balance to the different levels. At ground level there are five bays. The piers alternate between octagonal and circular and lead to triple vaulting shafts. The triforium level has a row of pointed arches; the clerestory above has triple arcading.

Walk now towards the **sanctuary**, which is dominated by the superb altar screen. Built by Bishop Richard Fox or Foxe (c1448–1528) in 1520, it has three tiers of niches; the statues were added from 1905 onwards. The lower tier was gilded by Comper in 1930. Note also in this area the thrones for the bishops of the diocese.

Return to the south choir aisle and step into the **crossing (10)**. The tower is supported by four 14th-century piers. Gazing up at the painted wooden roof of the tower, your attention is inevitably drawn to the Great Chandelier, which was given to the church by Dorothy Applebye, a brewer's widow, in 1680. Its main symbolic features are a crown, a mitre and a dove. The tower has twelve bells, eight of which go back to 1424 and the remainder to 1735. In recent years, four have been recast.

Walk into the **south transept (11)**, usually full of chairs, making viewing difficult. The transept was rejigged by Cardinal Beaufort in 1420 – his coat-of-arms is on one of the shafts of the vaulting. There are also some busts of church benefactors.

The Bard of Avon

Finally you come to the **south aisle (12)**. The most notable feature here is the Shakespeare Memorial, dating from 1911. It shows the Bard reclining in thoughtful pose with a Southwark scene carved in relief behind him. Above the memorial is the Shakespeare Window, designed in 1954 to replace an earlier one destroyed during World War II. Shakespeare lived in Southwark parish from 1599, working at the Globe and other theatres. Arguably his four greatest plays – *Hamlet*, *Othello*, *Macbeth* and *King Lear* – were written in Southwark for the Globe. He returned to his birthplace, Stratford, in 1611 and died there five years later. His brother Edmund was buried in this church in 1607, but the site of his grave is unknown.

Alongside the Shakespeare Memorial is a small plaque in memory of Sam

Wanamaker (1919–1993), the US actor and director who was instrumental in the reconstruction of the Globe Theatre.

Return now to the west end, where the tour began. You'll almost certainly, however, wish to visit the new **chapter house (13)**. Composed of the same flint and limestone as the cathedral, and located on the site of the old medieval priory, this was opened in 1988 by Elizabeth II. Apart from the chapter room, the building includes a restaurant, bookshop, toilets and, on the upper floor, an art gallery.

WALKING TOUR FROM SOUTHWARK CATHEDRAL

The walk takes in a variety of riverside features, from HMS *Belfast* to old inns and the rebuilt Globe Theatre. Historic elements include the notorious 'Clink' Prison and the remains of Winchester Palace. En route you see plenty of examples of the way the riverside has been sympathetically redeveloped since the closure of the port facilities.

Start and finish: The cathedral.
Length: 2 miles (3.2km).
Time: 1½ hours, but longer if you want to visit the museums and places of interest.
Refreshments: Hosts of food outlets cater for the many office workers in the area. Modern riverside inns include the Horniman and the Founder's Arms, both on Riverside Walk; older establishments include the George in Borough High Street, the only galleried inn left in London, and the 18th-century Anchor Inn, the only survivor of the twenty-two inns which once lined Bankside.

Leave the cathedral's east end and climb the steps up to Borough High Street. Cross by the pedestrian crossing and head towards **London Bridge**.

The first bridge over the Thames was constructed by the Romans and made of wood. It was probably destroyed and rebuilt several times. The first stone bridge dates from 1176, and eventually houses, shops and a chapel were built on it; it had a draw-bridge and gate at the Southwark end. Until 1750, when Westminster Bridge was built, this was the only bridge across the Thames in London. The old London Bridge was demolished in 1831 and replaced with a stone, five-arched structure that stood slightly upriver from the present bridge. In 1967 it was bought by a US entrepreneur, dismantled and reassembled in Arizona. The latest London Bridge dates from 1973.

The New Reveres the Old

Turn down the steps on the downstream side of the bridge to **Riverside Walk**, the final Southwark section of which was opened in 1994. When the area was part of the Port of London, this was known as Hay's Wharf. Its old warehouses have been converted into apartments, offices, shops and pubs. On the left is the London Bridge City Pier, whence people take riverboats up to Westminster or down to Greenwich.

Walk onto the pontoon which leads out to **HMS *Belfast***. Launched in 1938, this cruiser saw distinguished service in World War II, taking part in the destruction of the *Scharnhorst* in the Battle of the North Cape and playing a supporting role in the Normandy landings. Recently repainted, it is now permanently moored at Southwark and you can see all of its seven decks.

Return along Riverside Walk. On the left is the **Horniman**, a modern riverside pub named after Thomas Horniman, the Victorian grocer who brought tea from many parts of the world to his warehouse on this site.

Turn left into **Hay's Galleria**, on the site of Hay's Dock, built by Sir William Cubitt (1785–1861) in 1856 and designed for the speedy 19th-century tea clippers. Hay's Galleria is a thriving example of the way the riverside has been regenerated. The Victorian architecture has been maintained and the former dock area covered with a glass roof. It has shops, restaurants and bistros on various levels; the development is dominated by a huge modern kinetic sculpture by David Kemp. Southwark Tourist Information Centre is on the basement level, next to the toilets.

Horrors!

Walk through the Galleria and out onto Tooley Street, to where the river's warehouses once extended. The name Tooley is believed to be corrupted from St Olave's Street, referring to the church demolished in 1926, itself named after King Olave of Norway, who was an ally of King Ethelred of England. Turn right in Tooley Street and head back towards London Bridge. On the south side of the street, under London Bridge Station, is the **London Dungeon** which, claiming to be the 'World's First Medieval Horror Museum', uses various frightening multimedia effects to present shows such as 'The Theatre of the Guillotine' and 'The Great Fire

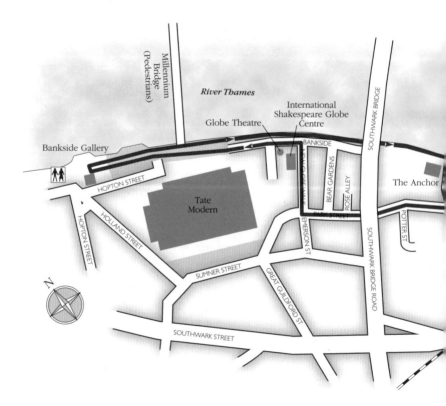

of London'. Not for the squeamish!

Fork left along Duke Street Hill, parallel with the arches of the railway, and turn left into Borough High Street, which marks the course of the old Roman causeway across the marshes. Turn briefly left into St Thomas Street, noting on the right the Bunch of Grapes, a Victorian-style pub which is full of atmosphere. On the left, at No. 9A, is The **Old Operating Theatre Museum**. This was rediscovered in 1956 in the roof of an 18th-century church and shows a genuine early Victorian operating theatre, with a wooden operating table and a number of simple instruments, which would have been used on patients without the benefit of today's anaesthetics. Also in this roof space is a herb garret, where the hospital apothecary cultivated his medicinal herbs.

On the north side of St Thomas Street are the extensive buildings of **Guy's Hospital**, founded by Thomas Guy (*c*1644–1724) in 1726. The son of a Thames boatman, he became a bookseller and publisher and, with the help of shrewd investments, became a wealthy man. He was a governor of St Thomas's Hospital, which once stood in the same road opposite Guy's (St Thomas's has now moved to Westminster). When he realized St Thomas's could not cope with the medical demands of the area he set up Guy's, leaving £220,000 in his will for its maintenance. He is buried in the hospital chapel.

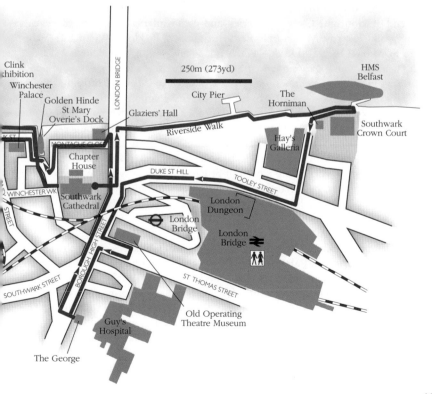

A Coaching Inn and Glaziers' Hall

Return to Borough High Street and turn left. After a hundred yards or so (100m) turn left into an alleyway where you'll find the long frontage of the **George**. Voted the 1995 Pub of the Year by the *Evening Standard*, the George is the only galleried pub left in London. Dating from 1676 and built on the site of an earlier inn, it originally stretched around three sides of a courtyard, but the north and west wings were demolished in 1899 to make way for railway buildings. It has been administered since 1937 by the National Trust. The George was one of a number of coaching inns in Southwark, each the starting point for destinations in southern England.

Cross Borough High Street and return towards London Bridge, passing on the left the cathedral and the appropriately named Barrow Boy and Banker pub. Immediately on the left and adjacent to the Thames is **Glaziers' Hall**. Built in 1808 as a warehouse, this had two floors and a Georgian façade added in 1850. It is the home of the Worshipful Company of Glaziers, who gained their charter in 1639. In more recent years it has become also the headquarters of the Worshipful Companies of Scientific Instrument Makers and Launderers.

Take the steps down from the hall into Montague Close, passing on the left the Mudlark pub. You now have an excellent view of the exterior of the cathedral (note the flying buttresses along the side of the nave) and the **chapter house**. Prominent outside is a modern sculpture of an armoured knight by Alan Collins.

Mercantile Connections

At the end of Montague Close is the brick-and-glass Minerva House, the offices of a banking group. Just past Minerva House turn right into Pickford's Wharf and further right to **St Mary Overie's Dock**, where a notice tells you that the dock is still 'a free landing place at which parishioners of St Saviour's parish are entitled to land goods free of toll'. Floating in the dock today is a replica of the *Golden Hinde*, the ship in which Sir Francis Drake (*c*1540–1596) became the first Englishman to circumnavigate the globe (1577–80). This replica is not just a mock-up: it too has sailed around the world, clocking up over 140,000 sea miles. Five decks of the ship can be seen.

Opposite the ship is the Old Thameside Inn, located in a former warehouse; outside tables overlook the river. Just to the side is a viewing platform from where you can see a superb vista of the city from St Paul's in the west to the Tower in the east. The buildings can be located on a scenic plaque unveiled by Sam Wanamaker in July 1988 as part of the Riverside Walk.

The Clink

Return inland to Pickford's Wharf and turn right into Clink Street. On the left are the ruins of **Winchester Palace**, the remains of the town house of the bishops of Winchester. The site was bought by Henry de Blois, Bishop of Winchester 1144–9, and it became the administrative centre for much episcopal business. As well as the palace there were gardens, courtyards and a prison (the notorious Clink). The surrounding estate reared sheep and pigs.

The palace was sold in the middle of the 17th century and warehouses built on the site. The excavated remains – they were first exposed in 1814 when a fire destroyed a mustard factory built on the site – show part of the inner north courtyard. The three doorways in the surviving wall – the west end of the main hall – led to the kitchen and domestic quarters, with a stone cellar below. The most important surviving feature is the elaborate but heavily eroded rose window. Probably dating from the early 14th century, it is constructed from Reigate Stone and its geometric design probably contained painted *grisaille* glass.

You are now in the part once known, ironically, as 'The Liberty of the Clink' – an area of some 70 acres (28ha) under the Bishop of Winchester's jurisdiction which was the red light district of the time. The population of the bishop's prison reflected the region's diverse activities: erring priests rubbed shoulders (if nothing else) with prostitutes. Opened in the 12th century, the prison was destroyed in 1780. It was one of a number of Southwark prisons, probably located here to be outside the City of London's walls. Conditions were appalling, with torture common and lack of food the norm. Many of the prisons contained mere debtors, incarcerated there until someone could bail them out. Charles Dickens's father spent time as a debtor in Marshalsea Prison, which was not closed until 1842. The King's Bench prison, on the east side of Borough High Street, was another well-known debtors' and military prison. The Horsemonger Lane gaol, built in 1791, was notorious for the public hangings outside its main gate, one of which was observed by Dickens.

Today's **'Clink Prison'**, located on the site of the original, aims to give you a realistic idea of the medieval conditions and hands-on experience of torture devices!

Theatreland

Now go under Cannon Street Railway Bridge, turn left and then immediately right into **Park Street**.

On your left is the site of the old Anchor Brewery, marked by a plaque listing the names of the various brewers who operated there. The best known was Barclay & Perkins, dating from 1787. They were taken over in 1955 by Courage, who closed the brewery down in 1980 – signally failing to appreciate the growing movement in favour of real ale. Southwark had been a brewing centre since the Middle Ages, when hops were brought from Kent and Hereford and stored in warehouses before being sold to the brewers. The Hop and Malt Exchange, dating from 1861, can still be seen in Borough High Street.

Continue along Park Street into what in medieval times was the theatre district. On the left, now hidden by hoardings, is the site of the original **Globe Theatre**. At the time of writing there is considerable controversy about the site, which is awaiting development. Academics want a full-scale archaeological survey, but this is being resisted by the Department of the Environment.

Pass the *Financial Times* building and go under Southwark Road Bridge. Immediately on your right is the site of the Rose Theatre, concealed under a modern office block whose owners are obliged to allow visitors to see the remains. The Rose was built in 1587 by Philip Henslowe (d1616). Its leading actor was his stepson Edward Alleyn (1566–1626), who performed in many plays by Shakespeare and by Christopher Marlowe (1564–1593). The Rose did not last long, however, being demolished when Henslowe's lease ran out in 1605. The other two theatres in Southwark were the Swan and the Hope, the latter having been converted by Henslowe from a bear-baiting arena.

Now turn right along New Globe Walk to the reconstruction of the **New Globe**. The first Globe Theatre opened in 1599 and was much larger than the other Southwark theatres, possibly holding as many as 3000 people. It burnt down in 1613 when the straw roof caught fire from a cannon shot used in a performance of *Henry VIII*. Legend has it that all escaped unhurt except a man whose trousers were ablaze; the flames were doused with ale! The Globe was rebuilt, this time with a tiled roof, and performances continued until the Puritans closed it in 1642.

The building of the New Globe was inspired by the late Sam Wanamaker. The design is as close as possible to what is known of the original building, and uses the traditional materials of the time – timber, wattle and daub, thatch, etc. The audiences sit on benches or stand in the yard in the open. Building was completed in late 1997 and the theatre is now the centrepiece of the International Shakespeare Globe Centre.

Bankside

You are now at **Bankside**. The original embankment was built to prevent the Bishop of Winchester's land from being flooded. On your left is a row of houses, Cardinal's Wharf. Among them is Cardinal's Cap Alley, which once led to the Cardinal's Cap Inn, popular with the Shakespearean actors. The inn was probably named after Cardinal Wolsey (*c*1475–1530 and briefly Bishop of Winchester in the early 16th century). A wall plaque at No. 49 Cardinal's Wharf states that Christopher Wren (1632–1723) lived there during the construction of St Paul's Cathedral.

Continue along Riverside Walk, noting on the left the hulk of **Bankside Power Station**. This was the last work of Sir Giles Gilbert Scott, grandson of the great Victorian architect Sir George Gilbert Scott (1811–1878). Sir Giles also designed the Bodleian Library, Waterloo Bridge and the chamber of the House of Commons. Bankside Power Station was built in 1948, with further additions and modifications in 1963. Later, the redundant power station was converted into an offshoot of the Tate Gallery. Known as the **Tate Modern**, it was opened in 2000 and has proved extremely popular with visitors. Visit its rooftop restaurant for spectacular views.

Move on to the **Bankside Gallery** in Hopton Street, near Blackfriars Railway Bridge. This small independent gallery is the home of the Royal Watercolour Society and the Royal Society of Painter–Printmakers. Most of the work is for sale.

Immediately opposite the Tate Modern is the blade-like **Millennium Bridge**. Opened in early 2000, it was closed almost immediately when it was found to be unstable. After extensive readjustments, the bridge re-opened in 2002.

Return eastwards along Riverside Walk until you see the **Anchor Inn** on the right. The only surviving inn of the twenty-two which once lined the river at Bankside, this has been in its time a chapel, a coffee shop, a brewery and a chandlery. Rebuilt in the 18th century, it is much older than it looks from the outside. Inside there is a minstrels' gallery, masses of oak beams and hiding places where customers could avoid the press gangs. Among the Anchor's customers have been Sir Joshua Reynolds (1723–1792) and Samuel Johnson (1709–1784).

Most of the Bankside inns were at one time or other brothels or 'stews' and, as the pubs came under the jurisdiction of the Bishop of Winchester, the prostitutes were known as 'Winchester Geese'. Henry VIII closed the stews in the mid-16th century.

From the Anchor, return along Clink Street to the cathedral, where the walk began.

CANTERBURY

Access: The M2 ends five miles (8km) short of the city; the M20, to the south, is the main route to the Channel ports. There are A-class roads from Margate, Maidstone, Whitstable, Herne Bay and Sandwich. National Express runs regular coaches from London, Gatwick and Dover. Buses to neighbouring towns are run by Stagecoach. Mainline trains from London stop at Canterbury East, five minutes' walk from the city centre. Canterbury West serves rural lines from Ashford and Ramsgate.

Few – if any – English cathedral cities have the attraction of Canterbury, the home of the mother church of the Anglican communion. The site of the most popular pilgrims' shrine in the country in the Middle Ages, Canterbury continues to attract visitors today; with the completion of the Channel Tunnel in 1994, a high proportion are now from the European mainland.

Archaeological work has confirmed there was a pre-Roman settlement on the site, but it was not until the 2nd century that the Romans began to build the formidable walled city, Durovernum Cantiacorum, which was to flourish for four centuries. Ironically, it was the Blitz which uncovered the great extent of Roman Canterbury, which had a huge D-shaped theatre, a forum and numerous temples.

At the fall of the Roman Empire during the early part of the 5th century the town was abandoned, although Danes and Jutes had small settlements in the vicinity. When St Augustine (d604) arrived in Britain at the end of the 6th century, full of Christianizing zeal, he found a thriving Kentish kingdom. He was well received by King Ethelbert and his wife Bertha and allowed to restore a church on the site of the present cathedral; Augustine became the first Archbishop of Canterbury. He later founded St Augustine's Abbey and Christ Church Priory at the cathedral; these two religious houses dominated Canterbury life for the next five centuries.

The martyrdom of Archbishop Thomas à Becket (1118–1170) in the Norman cathedral brought thousands of pilgrims to Canterbury over the succeeding 300 years and more. As a result of the building of inns and hostels for the pilgrims, the city began to expand outside the Norman walls. However, in the 1530s Henry VIII broke with Rome, dissolved the monasteries and removed Becket's shrine, and consequently Canterbury lost its prominence, particularly when the archbishop's seat was moved to Lambeth Palace in London.

Kent, however, began to receive religious refugees from mainland Europe. Among these were the Walloons, many of whom settled in the town and brought their textiles industry with them. There were English dissenters, too; it was in Canterbury that the Pilgrim Fathers planned the voyage of the *Mayflower*.

For the next three centuries Canterbury was, in essence, just a sleepy market town – even the Industrial Revolution did little to change this. The tranquillity was considerably disturbed, however, when in 1942 Canterbury became one of the targets of Germany's Baedeker Raids; in the fire-bombing of the city the cathedral remained relatively unscathed. The postwar years have seen the establishment here of the University of Kent and, more recently, the construction of the Channel Tunnel. Today, of Canterbury Cathedral's 2½ million annual visitors, more than half are believed to come from abroad.

As noted, the first cathedral was probably built *c*600, but later additions must have been impressive: excavations carried out in 1993 revealed the foundations of this building, one of the largest in the Western World at the time. The Anglo-Saxon cathedral suffered many indignities at the hands of marauding Danes, who on one occasion kidnapped and killed the archbishop. In 1067 the cathedral was almost totally destroyed by a fire which also swept through much of the town. The first of the Norman archbishops, Lanfranc (*c*1005–1089), rebuilt the nave within ten years and added a modest sanctuary. This work, in Romanesque style, was continued by his successor, St Anselm (1033–1109), who added the delightful staircase towers against the east transepts, the massive crypt and the quire above. Fire took a hand again in 1174, destroying the eastern end of the building. The crypt, which at that time contained Becket's tomb, was spared, as was the Norman nave.

By now the pilgrims were bringing considerable wealth to the cathedral, and it was decided that Becket's tomb needed a more worthy home. A French master-builder, William of Sens (d1180), was hired to rebuild the east end. Retaining the original outer walls and eastern towers, he constructed a new quire which pioneered the new Early English Gothic style in Britain. Unfortunately, William fell from the scaffolding and had to be replaced by William the Englishman, who completed the quire with the Trinity Chapel, where St Thomas's shrine was to be placed. The eastern end of the cathedral was finished off with the circular corona, giving this part of the building a 'continental' look that is unique among English cathedrals. The revenue from pilgrims also undoubtedly paid for the magnificent stained glass.

A succession of imaginative priors made some significant additions, such as the chapter house, with its stunning wooden wagon-vaulted roof, the stone choir screen and the great cloister, with its hundreds of bosses. Lanfranc's Norman nave was by now looking rather dated and in 1377 work began on its demolition. The designer of the new nave was Henry Yevele, fresh from triumphs at Westminster Abbey, who used the Perpendicular style to great effect. The final additions to the cathedral were the two west transepts and the west towers, all in Perpendicular style, followed in the 1490s by the dominating central tower, Bell Harry, the work of John Wastell.

Meanwhile the Priory of Christ Church and the neighbouring St Augustine's Monastery were facing hard times. Visited by Henry VIII's commissioners, the priory had to witness the spoliation of Becket's shrine and shortly afterwards, in 1540, the monks formally succumbed. Many of them, however, became members of the new cathedral foundation under the first dean, Nicholas Wotton.

There was a considerable amount of destruction during the Civil War, when Cromwell's troops inflicted enormous damage on the monuments and stained glass. The 17th and 18th centuries at Canterbury were, as with many English cathedrals, times of apathy and decay and it was not until the 19th century that the Victorians began to renovate. Fortunately, their efforts here were more sensitive than in many other similar buildings. A poignant, more recent scene was the visit of Pope John XXIII (1881–1963), who knelt in prayer with the then Archbishop of Canterbury, Robert Runcie (1921–2000) at the spot where Becket was murdered.

TOUR OF THE CATHEDRAL
Start: The Christ Church Gateway.
Finish: The southwest transept.

At the **Christ Church Gateway (1)** you must pay an entrance fee to gain access to the cathedral precincts and the cathedral itself. The gateway was built by Henry VII either to celebrate the marriage of his son Prince Arthur to Catherine of Aragon or as a memorial following Arthur's early death. (Arthur, the Prince of Wales, died aged 16. Catherine later was married to his brother, Henry VIII.) Perpendicular in style, it was restored in the 1930s. The many shields-of-arms are those of Henry VII's supporters, but the dominating feature is the copper-green statue of Christ, sculpted by Klaus Ringwald in 1990 to replace the original, lost to the Puritans in the 1600s.

Pass through the gateway and head towards the cathedral's Perpendicular **west end (2)**. With two bell towers and a large central window, the west end is hemmed in by buildings and does not have the 'presence' you'd expect from a cathedral. Enter the cathedral through the southwest porch, a richly carved Victorian addition, and step into the **nave (3)**. Designed and built by Henry Yevele between 1377 and 1405, the nave is a Perpendicular masterpiece. The first impression is of height: the tall, slender arcade has only a token clerestory above it and a triforium which is little more than a downward extension of the layer above. The main light comes from the aisle windows. The piers rise 80ft (24m) to a simple but pleasing *lierne* vaulting.

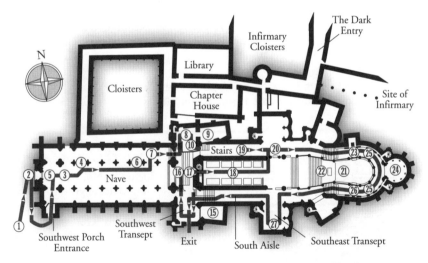

Key

1. Christ Church Gateway
2. West End
3. Nave
4. Font
5. West Window
6. Victorian Pulpit
7. Hales Family Monument
8. Martyrdom Chapel
9. Lady Chapel
10. No's 10-14 see map of Crypt
15. St Michael's Chapel
16. Bell Harry Tower
17. Pulpitum
18. Choir
19. Bible Windows
20. Chichele Tomb
21. Trinity Chapel
22. St Augustine's Chair
23. Tomb of Henry IV and Joan of Navarre
24. Corona
25. Miracle Windows
26. Tomb of the Black Prince
27. Modern Stained Glasss Windows

On the north side of the nave is the **font (4)**, which dates from Stuart times; smashed by Cromwell's men in the 17th century, it has been carefully restored. Made of marble, it has figures representing the twelve Apostles around its base. The cover is raised and lowered by a pulley system.

Turn around to face the **west window (5)**, which has some of the oldest stained glass in Europe, dating back to the beginning of the 13th century. At the centre of the bottom row you'll see Adam, expelled from Eden and dressed in an animal skin, busily digging. Above are Apostles, saints and 15th-century kings.

Two-thirds of the way along the nave, on the north side, is the **Victorian Pulpit (6)**, which is finely coloured and carved in wood. To its right, on the slightly raised floor, is a compass rose placed there in 1988 to symbolize the worldwide communion of the Anglican Church.

Money and Martyrdom

Cross into the north aisle, where (as in the south aisle) there are monuments set into the wall. Of particular interest is the **Hales Family Monument (7)**, placed here *c*1596. Sir James Hales was treasurer to the Portuguese Expedition of 1589 and the upper part of the monument, which is made of alabaster, shows his son being buried at sea, the weighted body dangling above the waves.

At the end of the north aisle the official route takes you into the most poignant part of the cathedral, the **Martyrdom Chapel (8)** in the northwest transept. It was here that Thomas à Becket was murdered on 29 December 1170 by four knights who believed they were obeying the wishes (and probably were) of Henry II. The spot where the deed was committed is marked by a simple modern altar, over which is a dramatically lit sculpture of swords and a cross. The north window of the transept is known as the Royal Window because of the fine stained glass showing a number of English kings.

Before leaving the transept, peep into the **Lady Chapel (9)**, just to the left of the altar. Sometimes known as the Deans' Chapel, it has some superb 15th-century fan vaulting.

Norman Capital in the Crypt

The Crypt

Now go to the right of the Becket altar through a dogtooth Norman arch and down the steps into the **crypt (10)**, which is generally agreed to be the finest in the country. Its western end is Romanesque, with rounded arches supported by stumpy pillars, every other one of which is carved. The capitals have some remarkable carving of animals and monsters, probably done *in situ*. In the centre of the crypt is the **Chapel of Our Lady of the Undercroft (11)**, which has 14th-century delicately carved screens and painted stonework.

Walk along the north side of the crypt towards the eastern end, built by William the Englishman and marked by the slightly pointed arches. Becket's body lay here from his Martyrdom in 1170 until it was taken to the Trinity Chapel above in 1220. At the extreme east end of the crypt is the delightful Jesus Chapel, which has good stained glass.

Return along the south side of the crypt, where the Chapel of St Gabriel is worth a look for its 12th-century wall paintings. On the

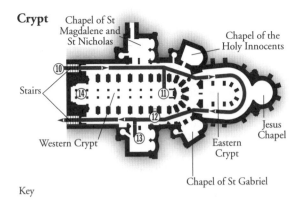

Crypt

Chapel of St Magdalene and St Nicholas

Chapel of the Holy Innocents

Stairs

Western Crypt

Jesus Chapel

Eastern Crypt

Chapel of St Gabriel

Key

10. From ground floor
11. Chapel of Our Lady of the Undercroft
12. Tomb of John Morton
13. Black Prince's Chantry
14. Cathedral Treasury

other side of the aisle is the flamboyant **Tomb of John Morton (12)**. Archbishop from 1486 to 1500, Morton was a zealous supporter of Henry VII's fiscal policy. Look at the gilded and coloured arch above the tomb, where the heads have been removed from all the statues, including those of the eagles! Almost opposite the tomb is the **Black Prince's Chantry (13)**, founded in 1363 by Edward III's eldest son, Edward the Black Prince, in return for the papal dispensation that allowed him to marry his divorced cousin Joan, known as the 'Fair Maid of Kent'. The chantry is now used on Sundays by the Huguenot community, with the service spoken in French.

Before you leave the crypt, notice on your right the **cathedral treasury (14)**, which contains the usual church plate and regalia, both from the cathedral and from churches in the diocese.

Warriors and Choirboys

Leave the crypt on the south side and climb the steps into the southwest transept. On its east side is **St Michael's Chapel (15)**, sometimes known as the Warriors' Chapel. Hanging from the walls are the colours and other mementoes of the Royal East Kent Regiment – the Buffs. Dominating the centre is a massive tomb with three effigies – those of the influential Lady Margaret Holland and her two husbands, the Earl of Somerset and the Duke of Clarence.

Outside the chapel, to the left, is a model of the sailing ship HMS *Canterbury*. Below it is the ship's bell, which is rung daily at 11:00 while one page of the memorial book to the dead is turned over.

Go into the crossing, climb the steps in front of the choir screen and look up into the lantern of **Bell Harry Tower (16)**. This was constructed between 1494 and 1504; beneath its stone veneer there are believed to be nearly a quarter of a million bricks. Designed by John Wastell, the lantern has some intricate fan vaulting interspersed with delicate carving. The central blue-and-white cathedral shield conceals a trapdoor through which stone was hauled up to complete the tower's exterior.

Turn towards the **choir screen** or **pulpitum (17)**. This was built at the time of Prior Chillenden in the early days of the 15th century, when it was the practice to separate the people in the nave from the monks in the choir. The screen has statues of six English kings: Henry V, Richard II and Ethelbert to the left of the door and Edward the Confessor, Henry VI and Henry VI to the right.

Step through the pulpitum door, which has 15th-century iron gates, into the **choir (18)**. Designed by William of Sens and completed by William the Englishman, the choir replaced the earlier Norman structure which was destroyed by the fire of 1174. Sens retained the outer Norman walls, but the interior is a pioneer work in the Early English Gothic style, with pointed arches. The Caen Stone piers are alternately octagonal and circular, rising to Corinthian capitals whence engaged shafts of Purbeck marble lead up to the base of the clerestory. The sexpartite vaulting is typical of the early Gothic in France, as in Notre Dame de Paris. The three levels of arcade, triforium and clerestory are in the classic proportion of 50:25:25, and are completely different from the nave, which was built later.

There is much to see in the choir, including the stalls carved by Roger Davis in 1682, the Victorian stone *cathedra*, the brass lectern (dating from 1663) and, at the east end, the simple high altar.

Leave the choir via the north side and walk into the north choir aisle. Immediately to the left are the world-famous **Bible Windows (19)**, whose stained glass is among the finest in Europe. A series of squares and circles depict Bible stories and miracles from both Old and New Testaments. In past centuries many of the congregation could not read, and they relied on pictorial features like stained glass and murals for their religious instruction.

More stained glass can be seen in the **rose window** in the nearby east transept. Opposite the transept is the magnificently gilded and coloured **Chichele Tomb (20)**. The tomb shows Archbishop Henry Chichele (*c*1362–1443) in his complete vestments; below this lies his *gisant*, or naked figure. Chichele founded All Souls' College in Oxford to commemorate those who died at the Battle of Agincourt.

Stroll now into the ambulatory, passing on the left St Andrew's Chapel, which has some recently restored medieval wall paintings. To the right is the **Trinity Chapel (21)**, completed by William the Englishman for St Thomas's shrine, which rested here from 1220 until 1538, when Henry VIII had it destroyed. The actual site of the shrine is marked by a burning candle, while to the west is an intricate marble pavement, the **Opus Alexandrium**, dating from the 13th century and probably made in Rome. Notice, too, the zodiacal pavement, laid down at the same time. Next to the pavement and immediately east of the high altar is the 13th-century **St Augustine's Chair (22)**. It is in this crude grey-green marble chair that archbishops are enthroned as primates of all England.

Tombs of Royalty

In prestigious positions alongside where Becket's shrine used to be are the only two royal tombs in the cathedral. Beside the north aisle is the **Tomb of Henry IV and Joan of Navarre (23)**. Carved in alabaster, possibly by Robert Brown, the effigies lie under a canopy showing the royal coat-of-arms. Henry IV, who spent much of his life fighting, was finally stricken by leprosy and died while praying at Westminster Abbey.

The ambulatory now takes us to the extreme eastern end of the cathedral and to the **Corona (24)**, a chapel added, like the Trinity Chapel but later, to house a Becket relic – in this case the top of the martyr's head, sliced off by one of the murderous knights. More recently rededicated to the Saints and Martyrs of our Own Time, it contains interesting 13th-century stained glass, some prominent shafts of Purbeck marble and the tomb of the last Cardinal Archbishop, Reginald Pole (1500–1558).

The ambulatory continues around the south side of the Trinity Chapel, passing a set of **miracle windows (25)** that show some of the events and miracles of St Thomas's times. Almost immediately opposite is the **Tomb of the Black Prince (26)**. Edward the Black Prince fought gallantly in his father's wars against France. During a campaign in Spain he contracted an illness which was to last until his death at the age of 46. His armoured effigy is of latten, but the blackening was apparently done in Victorian times. More recent evidence suggests that he never did wear a black armour, his nickname coming instead from his prowess on the battlefield. In the 1930s, accordingly, the black paint was removed to expose the original latten.

Above the tomb are copies of the Black Prince's battle accoutrements, such as gauntlets, helmet and vest. (The originals can be seen in a cabinet further along on the south side of the aisle.) Note on the tomb the Black Prince's shields; the one with the three feathers was taken on the field of battle and has ever since been the crest of the princes of Wales.

From one of the cathedral's oldest set of treasures let's move on to some of its newest. The **modern stained glass windows (27)** in the southeast transept were made by a Hungarian refugee, Ervin Bossanyi, in the 1950s. The east window denotes deliverance and salvation from evil while the west window represents peace among the nations of the world. The brilliance of the colours is stunning.

The tour concludes via the southwest transept and a covered way into the cathedral precincts.

WALKING TOUR FROM CANTERBURY CATHEDRAL

The walking tour is divided into two parts. The first, shorter walk is around the cathedral precincts and certain sections of the old Christ Church Priory. The second, longer walk leads you around the historic core of Canterbury, taking in the castle, old gates and walls, and a variety of domestic architecture.

Start and finish (shorter walk): The door of the southwest transept.
Start and finish (longer walk): The Christ Church Gateway.
Length: Shorter walk 660 yards (600m). Longer walk 2½ miles (4km).
Time: The shorter walk should take you ½ hour at most. The longer one takes 1½ hours, but you'll probably want more time than this in order to visit the museums and churches.
Refreshments: A good selection of food outlets. Ambience and good bar meals are provided by a number of historic pubs and coaching inns, including the City Arms (Butchery Lane), the 15th-century Three Tuns (Beer Cart Lane), the Pilgrims' Hotel (opposite the Marlowe Theatre – good blackboard menu) and the Cathedral Gate Hotel, which predates the nearby Christ Church Gate.

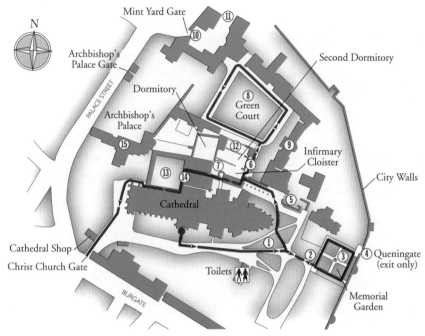

Key

1. Cathedral's External
   Features
2. Cemetery Gate
3. Memorial Garden

4. Quenin Gate
5. Infirmary Chapel
6. Dark Entry
7. Water Tower
8. Green Court
9. Deanery

10. Main Priory Gateway
11. Norman Staircase
12. Necessarium
13. Great Cloister
14. Chapter House
15. Archbishop's Palace

AROUND THE CATHEDRAL PRECINCTS

Walk eastwards onto the grassy area in front of the toilets, where there is a good view of the **cathedral's external features (1)**.

Note first the Bell Harry Tower, rising to 235ft (72m) and completed *c*1500 by John Wastell. The Perpendicular style gives it a strong verticality, enhanced by the corner pinnacles. Complementing the main tower is the St Anselm Tower, hard against the southeast transept. The base dates from Anselm's time, but the upper parts, with their interlocking Norman arches, were added in 1160. This tower has its twin on the north side of the cathedral, the pair having survived the fire of 1174. Lastly, note the Corona at the east end of the cathedral; from the outside it looks almost completely detached from the rest of the building. On the grass near the east end is a modern statue, *The Son of Man*, by David McFaul.

Walk eastward towards the stone wall, passing over what was once the priory fishpond. There are bee holes in the wall, reminding you that the monks produced much of their own food. Keep going until you reach the **cemetery gate (2)**, with its impressive rounded Norman arch and dogtooth decoration. It is believed to have been built *c*1160, in the time of Prior Wybert.

Pass through the gate into the **memorial garden (3)**. In the centre of the garden is a simple stone cross in memory of local soldiers who have died in times of war. The flint wall on the east side is part of the city walls and includes a large square bastion. An opening in the north corner leads to the **Queningate (4)**. This was the route that Queen Bertha, wife of Ethelbert, took through the city wall when she went to pray in St Martin's Church. Today it presents a convenient way to get to the ruins of St Augustine's Abbey – or, at least, it *would* be a convenient way were it not for the fact that you're not allowed back into the cathedral precincts through the Queningate.

So turn back and head across to a line of old stone arches marking the ruins of the **infirmary chapel (5)**. This chapel was provided for those monks who were too ill to attend the main mass. It was built *c*1150, but all that is left today are these Norman arches plus the occasional well carved capital and the remains of what must have been an impressive window on the north side.

A Haunted Alley

Walk past the spot where the infirmary itself stood and turn right into an alleyway known as the **Dark Entry (6)**. This is reputed to be haunted, late on Friday evenings, by one Nell Cook. The tale is that during the days of Henry VIII a canon who lived by the Dark Entry had a servant, Ellen Bean, who was secretly in love with him; because of her skill in the kitchen he called her Nell(y) Cook. In time the canon's 'niece' came to stay with him, and Nell's jealousy was roused when she found out they were lovers. So she put poison in the pie they had for supper, and the cathedral authorities kept the deaths secret for fear of the scandal that might erupt. Nell vanished, and it was not until many years later that it was discovered she had dispatched herself by eating the rest of the pie.

This was revealed, so the tale goes, when three masons uncovered a skeleton and an incriminating piece of pie-crust! The three masons were dead within the twelvemonth, one murdered and the other two hanged for the crime, and ever thereafter anyone who has seen the ghost of Nell Cook has likewise failed to live out the year.

Plumbing Matters

To reduce your chances of inadvertently sighting the ghost, look leftwards at the infirmary cloister, a grassy space once used for growing medicinal herbs. On its south side is the **water tower (7)** that once held the monastery's drinking water. The plumbing was evidently quite sophisticated. The water was taken from springs and put through settling tanks before coming to the monastery. From the water tower it was piped around the buildings; the dirty water was used to flush the monks' toilets.

Walk – briskly, if you're still worried about Nell Cook – along the Dark Entry, noting on your left the ruins of the old dormitories and on your right the Chequer Tower, all that survives of the priory's counting house. At the end of the passageway are the remains of the Prior's House and Prior's Gateway, the latter leading to the large grass-covered **Green Court (8)**. This was the business centre of the priory, and some the buildings around it have been sympathetically restored. Those still habitable are occupied by the King's School, one of the country's most highly respected public schools, whose foundation goes back to the time of Henry VIII. The buildings are not open to the public.

Turn right and walk round the square, passing on the right the old 12th-century bathhouse, now the **deanery (9)**. Ahead is a row of buildings; from right to left these were the granary, the bakery and the brewery. In the far corner stands the **main priory gateway (10)**. Behind this is the Mint Yard, the site of an old chapel which was the original building occupied by the King's School. To the right of the gate, is the **Norman staircase (11)**; it once led to a hall that was part of the prior's guesthouse.

Continue your circuit of Green Court. On the south side are the ruins of the **necessarium (12)** – the monks' lavatory – reputed to seat fifty-six. Under it a large drain flowed continually.

The Great Cloister Area

Turn right to go back through the Dark Entry and at its end go right again along another gloomy alleyway, past the water tower until you reach the **Great Cloister (13)**. Built in the late 14th or early 15th century, the present cloister is thought to be the fourth on this site. It is done in Perpendicular style; its fan vaulting is embellished with hundreds of roof bosses portraying the heraldic arms of people who contributed to the building of the cloister plus animals, monsters and religious symbols.

Turn left to find almost immediately the entrance door to the **chapter house (14)**, the only monastic building to have survived fully intact. Almost 100ft (30m) long, it is the largest cathedral chapter house in Britain. The present building dates from the early 14th century and stands on the site of a Norman chapter house. The magnificent wooden (bog oak) roof dates to 1400. Note the impressive prior's 'throne' at the east end. Today, the chapter house is used mainly for concerts.

Leave the chapter house and continue round the cloister. In the southeast corner is the door through which Thomas à Becket entered the cathedral before his murder. Just by the cloister's exit look back at the chapter house, where the superb Perpendicular west end window, with its Victorian glass, is framed by what appears to be a typical 'Dutch end'.

Outside the cloister you can get a glimpse, to your right, of the **archbishop's palace (15)**, built in the 19th century to replace one that burnt down in 1544; after a gap of almost 300 years, archbishops could once again reside at Canterbury.

Go back past the west end of the cathedral to the Christ Church Gateway, where this short walk ends. If you want, you can carry straight on into the longer walk.

BEYOND CANTERBURY CATHEDRAL

The Christ Church Gateway faces the **Buttermarket**, a small square which has always been at the centre of city life. The War Memorial in the middle marks the spot formerly occupied by a bull stake in the days when bull-baiting was popular. Leading off the Buttermarket is Mercery Lane, which has many old buildings with jettied walls; it was once full of pilgrims' inns and the shops of haberdashers and drapers. Note that many of the walls in Buttermarket are hung with 'mathematical tiles' to resemble bricks.

The Old Rush Market and the 'Leaning House'

Leave the Buttermarket by turning right into **Sun Street**, named after a pilgrim inn known as the Sun (now a shop); Charles Dickens (1812–1870) stayed at it when in

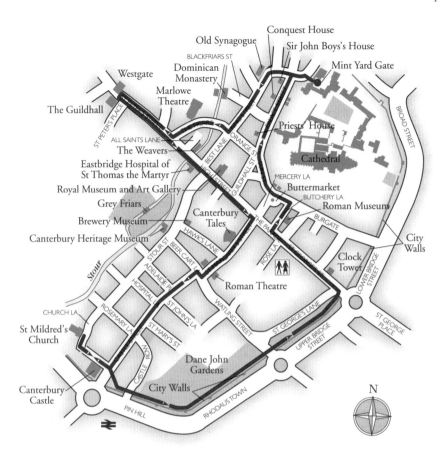

Canterbury. In medieval times Sun Street was the venue of the Rush Market – rushes were commonly used as a floor covering and for roofs.

Sun Street merges into **Palace Street**, named for the old bishop's palace, whose grounds stretched along its full length. This street is full of historic houses. The Pilgrim Fathers negotiated the hire of the *Mayflower* in a house on the right, now Beau's Creperie restaurant. Look on the left-hand side for the **Priests' House**, probably the oldest domestic building in Canterbury, a half-timbered Tudor building with jettied walls, carved beams and a grotesque in one corner. Further along on the left is **Conquest House**, another half-timbered house, now an antiques shop. It was in its 11th-century cellar that Becket's murderers are supposed to have plotted the deed. At the far end of Palace Street, on the corner with King Street, is **Sir John Boys's House**, now a bookshop. Sometimes known as the Leaning House, it was the home of Sir John Boys, a 16th-century lawyer and philanthropist. Note the crazy angles of the doors and windows and the fine carving on the timber posts.

Walk briefly to the right into The Borough to view the **Mint Yard Gate** of the former priory. The gate is a Victorian replacement of an earlier medieval gate, which was knocked down for redevelopment. The yard is named for an ancient coin mint discovered here. Inside the outer gate is the Almoner's Yard, where the poor of the town received alms from the priory. Further in is the main priory gate.

The Black Friars

Return now past Sir John Boys's House and fork left into King Street. If you look carefully on your right for a gap between the houses you should be able to spot the **Old Synagogue**. Behind pyramidal gateposts, the building is designed in Egyptian style, with prominent pillars and a balustrade. Built in the early 19th century, it is now owned by the King's School, who use it for music practice.

Further along King Street, stop at its junction with St Alphage Lane and Blackfriars Street. If you look left you'll find you have unexpectedly good views of the cathedral, while to your right are the surviving buildings of the **Dominican monastery**. The Dominicans, or Black Friars, came to Canterbury in 1221 and built a considerable complex of monastic buildings, of which only two survive. On the west side of the river is the old guesthouse or infirmary, while on the east side is the dining room, believed to date from the mid-13th century.

Walk to the end of King Street and turn right into The Friars. From the bridge over the Stour you get an excellent view of the friary. A little further along, on the right, you find the **Marlowe Theatre**, an unimposing building based in an old cinema. Christopher Marlowe (1564–1593), the author of *Doctor Faustus*, *Tamburlaine the Great*, *The Jew of Malta* and others, was born and educated in Canterbury; he died in a tavern brawl aged only 29. It has been claimed that he wrote some of Shakespeare's plays. The theatre puts on a varied programme, including music, dance and light entertainment. Opposite it are several convenient eating places.

Canterbury Tales

Continue to St Peter's Street (an extension of the High Street) and turn right, walking northeast towards the **Westgate**, which straddles an arm of the Stour. Of the eight gates around the city walls, this was the most important – it guarded the road to London, along which most of the pilgrims came – and has been rebuilt many times. The present Westgate dates from 1381 and was probably designed by Henry Yevele, also responsible for many parts of the cathedral. In the old days the Westgate contained a drawbridge and a portcullis, and was closed at night: pilgrims who did not reach the city in time had to sleep outside the walls – hence the many inns beyond the gate in St Dunstan's and London Road. It is claimed that the term to 'canter' originated when pilgrims spurred their horses on at 'Canterbury pace' to reach the city before the gate came down. The Westgate is now a museum, with displays concerning its time as a prison plus a comprehensive collection of Civil War weapons. There are superb views from the battlements.

Return along St Peter's Street towards the city centre. Just before you reach the bridge once more, make a quick diversion along **All Saints Lane**, a cul-de-sac on whose right-hand side is All Saints Court, a restored 15th-century half-timbered building with jettied walls and nicely carved grotesques on the support beams.

Return to St Peter's Street and look over the bridge at **The Weavers**, another half-timbered house, dating back to c1500. Flemish weavers worked here in the 16th and 17th centuries. A reproduction ducking stool protrudes out over the river.

Opposite is the **Eastbridge Hospital of St Thomas the Martyr**. Eastbridge was a hospital in the true sense of the word – i.e. it provided hospitality for poor pilgrims to the Shrine of St Thomas. Founded in 1180, it fell into decay but was refounded in 1342 by Archbishop John Stratford (d1348) and was probably busiest at the time when Geoffrey Chaucer (*c*1345–1400) was writing his *Canterbury Tales*. After Henry VIII ordered the destruction of St Thomas's shrine in 1538 there was another period of decline, but later archbishops arranged for the hospital to provide accommodation for the poor of the parish and it remains as almshouses today.

To the left of the entrance hall is a charming little chantry chapel. From here there are steps down into the Norman undercroft, which was used as a pilgrims' dormitory. Stratford decreed that only women over 40 (a good age at that time) should be appointed to be in charge, so that the pilgrims wouldn't be tempted! Stairs lead up to the refectory, built at the same time as the undercroft. The painting on the north wall, of Christ giving blessing, dates from the 13th century, having been hidden behind a chimney for many years. There is also a 'Minstrels' Gallery'; its panels are genuine late 16th-century, but the gallery was actually constructed in 1932. Finally, do not miss the 12th-century chapel, with its particularly fine wooden roof. Some of the sanctuary seats have misericords.

From the hospital, continue along the High Street. On your left is the imposing **Royal Museum and Art Gallery**, which is also the public library; it is sometimes known as the Beaney Institute, after its benefactor, a local doctor who made a fortune in Australia. The building is Victorian mock-Tudor. It is believed it may stand on the remains of the old Roman forum. The museum has a mixed collection of historical and archaeological artefacts and some military relics of the Buffs, while the gallery specializes in the work of the 19th-century local artist Sidney Cooper.

As you approach the modern part of the city, turn right into St Margaret's Street. On the right is **Canterbury Tales**, a theme museum based in the old St Margaret's Church. Chaucer's *Tales* are described with tableaux and realistic audiovisual presentations.

The crossroads at the end of St Margaret's Street marks the site of the **Roman Theatre**, believed to have been built *c*220 and to have thrived for the following 200 years. Traces of the foundations can still be seen in the basements of Alberry's Bistro and Slatter's Hotel.

All Saints Lane

Canterbury Castle

Continue southwest into Castle Street, which is lined with bistros, speciality shops and houses from all periods. On your left the Castle Gardens were once the churchyard of St Mary de Castro, long since disappeared. Eventually you get to **Canterbury Castle**, on your right. Construction of the castle began *c*1084. The finished structure consisted of a keep and a surrounding bailey, part of which included the Roman city walls. It was never a huge military success – it surrendered to the French Dauphin in 1216, to the Parliamentarians during the Civil War and was embarrassingly overrun by Wat Tyler's men during the Peasants' Revolt of 1381

All that remains today is the keep, which is the fifth largest in England. It acted as prison during the reign of Elizabeth I, while in this century it was a coal store for the local gasworks. There was an attempt to knock it down in the 18th century, but fortunately this got only as far as the top floor. The remains are now fully preserved.

You can make a short diversion here to **St Mildred's Church**, possibly the oldest parish church in Canterbury. Some 8th-century stonework can be seen in the south and west walls, and the south wall also has some reworked Roman tiles. St Mildred was the great-great-granddaughter of the Saxon King Ethelbert; after an education in Paris she became abbess of a convent at Minster-in-Thanet. Her body and relics were later acquired by St Augustine's Abbey in Canterbury.

Leave the church and walk back past the castle and across the carpark opposite to the steps which lead up to the **city walls**. Originally built by the Romans, the walls fell into decay before being rebuilt by the Normans. At their maximum extent they covered some 1½ miles (2.4km) and had eight gateways plus bastions and towers. Parts of the wall were destroyed during the Civil War and other stretches were taken down in the 18th century. Today about half of the original wall still stands.

We are going to follow part of the wall, going initially past the **Dane John Gardens**, landscaped during the 18th century when public executions were held here. Dominating the gardens is the Dane John Mound, thought to have been a Romano-British burial mound – if this is true the mound predates the wall. There is a small memorial dated 1803 to the gardens' benefactor, Alderman Simmons, on the top of the mound, which is reached by a spiral footpath.

Carry on along the wall past the bus station – which before 1956 was the site of the cattle market – until you reach the large roundabout with subways. This was the site of St George's Gate, demolished in 1801 when the New Dover Road was built. Descend the ramp and cross the road carefully into the pedestrianized St George's Street. This part of the city is modern; it was rebuilt after the Blitz. On the right is the **Clock Tower**, the only part of the Church of St George to survive German bombs.

Continue along St George's Street until older buildings start to dominate, then take a right turn into the narrow Butchery Lane. On the right, halfway along, is the **Roman Museum**. The Blitz actually helped reveal the extent of Durovernum Cantiacorum, hidden as it was under present-day Canterbury. The museum has a wide range of Roman artefacts, some authentic dioramas of Roman trades and professions and the latest hands-on computer reconstructions. The highlight is the large Roman pavement, which is actually *in situ*. Highly recommended.

Leave the museum and continue along Butchery Lane. Turn left at the end into Burgate, which takes you back to the Buttermarket.

The modern altar on the east side of the crossing at St Paul's Cathedral, London. Note Grinling Gibbons's choir stalls and the organ, which stand behind it.

The newly cleaned western towers of Westminster Abbey. The lower part dates from the early 12th century, but the towers were finished by Nicholas Hawksmoor in the 1740s.

The great reredos in the sanctuary at Southwark Cathedral. This was paid for by Bishop Fox of Winchester in the early 16th century.

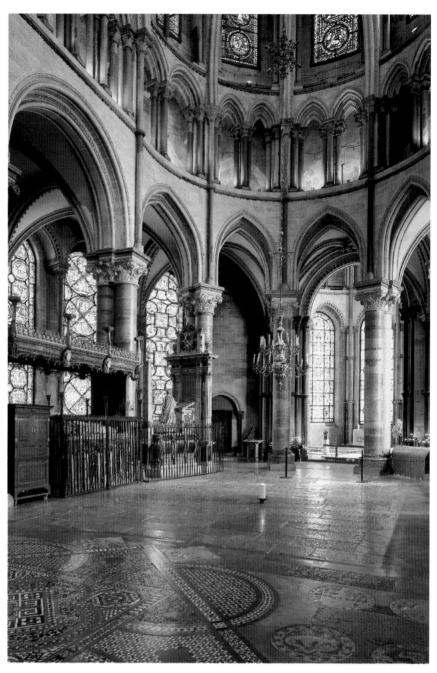

The Trinity Chapel, Canterbury Cathedral. In the foreground is the decorative porphyry pavement (c 12th century), and on the left is the tomb of Henry IV.

An elaborate early 14th-century doorway in the southeast transept of Rochester Cathedral, which leads through to the chapter room and cathedral library.

St Alban's Abbey, Hertfordshire, viewed from the southwest. It is notable for its Roman brick central tower. Grimthorpe's rebuilt transept is to its right.

Sir George Gilbert Scott's vibrant hammer-beam (angel) roof over the nave at Bury St Edmunds Cathedral, which was painted between 1948 and 1982.

Above: *St Paul's Cathedral at gallery lavel, looking right down the nave and chancel from the west end.*

Above: *The late 11th-century crypt at Canterbury Cathedral. Through the darkness, one can glimpse the late 14th-century chapel of Our Lady of the Undercroft.*

ROCHESTER

Access: Regular rail services from Victoria and Charing Cross (both about 45 minutes); station is ten minutes' walk from the cathedral. Regular coach services from Victoria Coach Station. M25, M20 and M2/A2.

The first religious building on the site of the cathedral at Rochester-upon-Medway may have been built by Christian soldiers at the settlement of Durobrivae, but evidence is scanty – although Roman building materials have been found in the walls of the old priory cloisters at the side of the cathedral.

Two hundred years later, in consequence of the evangelizing of Augustine (d604), King Ethelbert built a church at Rochester dedicated to St Andrew. Completed in the year of Augustine's death, this Saxon building could claim to be the second oldest cathedral in Britain. There is no trace today of this building above ground, but foundations have been revealed at the west end of the present nave.

It is believed the early Saxon building suffered continually from raiding Vikings. After the conquest of 1066, the Normans realized the strategic position of Rochester and built a large castle to guard both the river crossing and a new cathedral, begun in 1080 by the Norman bishop Gundulf (1024–1108), who laid out the west end, the nave and the quire. Gundulf also set up the Benedictine monastery, which is believed to have had around sixty monks by the time of his death in 1108. Work continued into the next century, being done in Early English Gothic style.

There is little of the Decorated period to be seen, although Bishop Hamo de Hythe's magnificent 14th-century chapter room doorway dates from this era. The important addition in the 15th century was the huge Perpendicular window in the nave. At the same time the original Norman windows in the clerestory were removed and replaced with larger ones, giving much more light to the nave. The building of the Lady Chapel in 1492 completed the cathedral.

When the monasteries were dissolved in the mid-16th century, Rochester's priory was speedily refounded as a cathedral and the prior became the first dean. Little remains of the monastery today, apart from a few of the cloister walls and some gateways.

During the 18th century several new buildings appeared in the cathedral precincts, including Minor Canon Row, Oriel House and the archdeaconry.

The following century was mainly concerned with restoration. There was serious subsidence in the south transept and an outward tilting of the quire, which were only halted by the construction of a large flying buttress close to the south door. The decrepit spire was pulled down, not to be replaced for sixty years. The removal of a pulpit in 1840 had the bonus of revealing part of a 13th-century wall painting. The ubiquitous Sir George Gilbert Scott (1811–1878) was involved in many of the Victorian renovations, replacing the roofs of the transepts, putting in some 'Early English' windows and designing a new high altar.

Today, work at the cathedral mainly concerns cleaning and restoration, with fund-raising a perpetual problem. The formation of the Rochester 2000 Trust and grants from English Heritage have helped in this conservation work, so that visitors (estimated annual figure: 200,000) see a busy and well cared-for cathedral.

TOUR OF THE CATHEDRAL
Start and finish: The west front.

Start by viewing the **west front (1)** of the cathedral from the outside – a good viewpoint is from the grassy slopes of the castle opposite.

The west front has recently been cleaned up, showing the Romanesque façade in all its glory. The overwhelming impression is of vertical lines, from both the tall, narrow Norman arches, dating from *c*1160, and the great Perpendicular window dating from 1470. Of the four turrets, two are attached and the two larger ones detached. Only the south turret is original; the others are accurate Victorian reconstructions. All demonstrate blind arcading.

Undoubtedly the best feature of the exterior of the west front is the Norman doorway, which reminds us of the carved Romanesque doorways of French churches – indeed, it may well be the work of a French sculptor. To view it, cross the road to the small green embellished by a catalpa – a North American bean tree. The door's tympanum shows Christ in Majesty, seated in a *vesica*. On each side are angels and beasts. The elongated figures on the inner pillars represent Solomon and the Queen of Sheba and are unique in Britain.

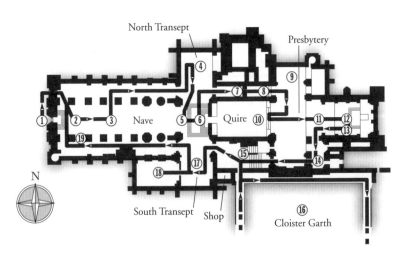

Key	6. Nave Altar and Screen	13. Sedilia
	7. Pilgrims' Steps	14. Chapter Room Doorway
1. West Front	8. North Quire Aisle	15. Crypt
2. Interior of the West Front	9. North Quire Transept	16. Cloister Garth
3. Nave	10. Quire	17. South Transept
4. North Transept	11. East End	18. Lady Chapel
5. Crossing	12. High Altar	19. Font

Enter the cathedral via the small door to the left. (Entrance is free, but a donation is welcome.) Immediately inside the door, look for the curved line on the floor that marks the position of the apsidal east end of the original Saxon cathedral built for Justus, the first Bishop of Rochester, in 604; Justus was one of Augustine's fellow missionaries.

You can now see the interior of the **west front (2)**, where two levels of Norman arcading on either side of the west door have been converted into a memorial to members of the Corps of Royal Engineers. The mosaic background to the names may not be to everyone's taste.

A Pious Baker and the Pilgrims' Steps

The **nave (3)** merits a lot of attention. Six bays of the original Norman survive, with subtle carved variations between each pier. At triforium level the symmetry continues, with two small arches within a larger one, all three being richly carved. The small Norman clerestory windows were, as we've seen, replaced by larger windows in the 15th century, bringing much more light into the nave. The wooden roof is not the original, fires having destroyed its predecessors on a number of occasions.

Proceed now along the north aisle of the nave into the **north transept (4)**, which is in Early English style with typical lancet windows. Against the main pillars, which are of cream limestone, rest thin pillars of Purbeck marble, a pattern repeated in other Gothic parts of the cathedral.

The north transept was the eventual location of the tomb – and later shrine – of William of Perth, a pious baker who stayed at the priory in 1201 en route to the Holy Land. He was murdered in the vicinity and his body brought back to the cathedral. Miracles at his tomb were soon reported and before long pilgrims started coming from all over the country. Unfortunately the shrine was destroyed in 1547, during the Reformation.

Walk now into the **crossing (5)**. The ceiling is made of plaster and dates from 1840; it was restored in 1992 with the original colours. Above it is the 12th-century bell tower; campanological details are given by a small notice on the wall at the corner of the north transept. Immediately ahead of you is the nave **altar and screen (6)**. The stonework has eight niches, four on each side of the central door, containing images of saints and other notables connected with the cathedral. On the left are St Andrew, King Ethelbert, Justus and Paulinus (d644), the missionary and first Archbishop of York; on the right Gundulf, William of Hoo, Walter de Merton (d1277) and John Fisher (1469–1535). Above the altar screen is the intricately painted organ case, restored by Sir George Gilbert Scott in the 1870s. This unfortunately obscures the view along the centre of the cathedral, making the nave and the quire two separate entities.

Move now to the left of the altar screen. On the left a small door marked PRIVATE leads to Gundulf's 12th-century bell tower. Carry on ahead to the **Pilgrims' Steps (7)**, whose stonework was worn away by countless pilgrims' feet visiting William's shrine; the steps are now covered with wooden boarding to prevent any further erosion. They lead you to the **north quire aisle (8)** and the original site of the shrine. At the end of the aisle is the **north quire transept (9)**, which features little of interest except a small patch of red-and-blue medieval tiled floor.

The Quire and the Dickens Memorial

Step into the **quire (10)**, which is Early English in architectural style. The choir stalls have little in the way of carving and lack misericords, but the wall decorations are interesting, with an alternation of the French fleur-de-lys and the English leopard. Look for the painting called *The Wheel of Fortune*, discovered in 1840 when the pulpit was moved; it is believed to date from the 13th century. Opposite is the **bishop's throne**, well carved and with a number of coats-of-arms.

You now arrive at the **east end (11)**. This area is notable for the lack of aisles or apse – so there is no processional walkway or ambulatory around the presbytery. The latter contains the **high altar (12)**, one of Sir George Gilbert Scott's less impressive contributions. To the south of the high altar is a **sedilia (13)** – seating for officiating clergy set in the stonework of the wall – built in the time of Bishop Hamo de Hythe in 1343.

Flanking the presbytery are two small chapels: one is the Oratory, the other contains the Charles Dickens Memorial. Dickens lived at various stages of his life in the Rochester area, and began modelling his fictional locations on parts of the city as early as *Pickwick Papers*. As we shall see when we walk around Rochester, this practice continued in his later novels, notably including *Great Expectations* (1860–61) and *The Mystery of Edwin Drood*. Indeed, it is thought that he was planning to use Restoration House (already featured in disguise in *Great Expectations*) in this last, unfinished novel, for the day before his death he walked into Rochester and was seen standing in thought for a time at its gate.

Not surprisingly, Rochester-upon-Medway likes its alternative title: 'The City of Great Expectations.'

The Chapter Room Doorway, the Crypt and an Outdoor Excursion

Behind the Dickens Memorial is arguably the most important architectural feature of the cathedral – the mid-13th-century **chapter room doorway (14)**, which would have been the monks' night entrance to the building. Carved in Decorated style, it shows standing figures representing the Church and the Synagogue. Higher up are the four Evangelists seated at desks, while at the apex of the arch is a human soul, apparently being rescued by angels. Altogether, a superb piece of carved stonework, which because of its interior position has escaped weathering. The oak door dates from the 19th century, but its carving is not of wood but of lead.

Now walk west and take the stairs down into the **crypt (15)**, which lies under the quire.

The oldest part of the cathedral, the crypt is laid out in seven aisles, with simple heavy vaulting. At the east end, the crypt chapel is dedicated to Ithamar (d655), the first English Bishop of Rochester. Also of interest here are the traces of medieval graffiti and wall painting.

Go back up the steps to the main body of the cathedral and walk out through the south door into the **cloister garth (16)**. Immediately on your left is the flying buttress constructed by L.N. Cottingham in the 19th century to support the quire. You can see some of the old cloister walls; a few of their Norman arches are interlocking.

Take a clockwise walk around the garth (garden). In the first corner are the remains of the old chapter house, built by Bishop Ernulf (1040–1124) in the early 12th century. Most of the stonework is at ground level. Note on the far side the 12th-century monastic dormitory doorway, the rough shafts of which are of Tournai marble from Belgium. Along the lintel is a heavily eroded tympanum showing Abraham about to sacrifice Isaac, while in the right-hand corner is a ram caught in a thicket by its horn.

In the opposite corner of the garth is the early-13th-century doorway that led to the monastic refectory and lavatory; it is made of Reigate Stone and Purbeck marble. On the lawn in the centre of the garth stands a modern sculpture, *Christ and the Blessed Virgin Mary* by John Doubleday.

Return through the south door and go leftward to the **south transept (17)**, completed in 1280 in Decorated style. Adjoining the transept is the **Lady Chapel (18)**, positioned here because the monastic buildings occupied the more usual site at the east end of the cathedral. It was completed in 1492 in late Perpendicular style. Its screen has more recently been moved through 90° so that the transept is less isolated.

Walk back along the south nave aisle, where the only item of interest is the Victorian **font (19)**. Located under one of the Norman arches, it is made of marble. The carvings around the side are by Thomas Earp and represent scenes of baptism from the Bible.

The tour ends at the west front, where it began.

WALKING TOUR FROM ROCHESTER CATHEDRAL
The walk visits historical features such as the Norman Rochester Castle and some remains of the old monastic buildings. There is also a wide range of Kentish domestic architecture on view. Other features have close links with Charles Dickens.

Start and finish: The west front of the cathedral.
Length: 2½ miles (4km).
Time: 1½ hours, but allow longer if you want to visit the two museums and the castle.
Refreshments: Excellent cathedral refectory. Rochester has a number of old pubs and coaching inns offering lunchtime food in historic surroundings. Recommended: the Norman Conquest, the Eagle Tavern, the King's Head Hotel and the Royal Victoria and Bull Hotel, all in the High Street.

Leave the west front and head north towards the High Street.

On your right is the **Church of St Nicholas**, dating from the early 15th century but rebuilt two centuries later. In 1964 it was declared redundant and became the administration office for the Rochester diocese. Although the building is not officially open to the public, visitors are treated in friendly fashion and there are some interesting items, including the stained glass at the east end.

Proceed under the arch of **Chertsey's Gate**. Formerly known as Cemetery Gate (it featured as Jasper's Gate in Dickens's *The Mystery of Edwin Drood*), it was one of the old gates into the monastery precincts. It dates from the early 15th century, but had a rather unfortunate black clapperboard house slapped on top of it in the 18th century. It is not open to the public.

Treasures of the High Street

Turn left into the semi-pedestrianized **High Street**. Without the constant noise of traffic, this has become a delightful part of the town, with a wide range of shops, inns and restaurants among a number of buildings of historical and architectural interest.

Immediately on your right is the **Old Corn Exchange**, dominated by a huge moon-faced clock. The building was erected in 1698, and was originally the butchers' market. Its frontage was revamped by Admiral Sir Cloudesley Shovel (1650–1707) in 1706. Shovel was a fascinating character. A naval officer, he represented the town in three parliaments under William III and one under Queen Anne; he is buried in the south choir aisle of Westminster Abbey (see page 186). The circumstances of his death were somewhat bizarre, if the tales are to be believed. He survived a shipwreck off the Scilly Isles, when his crew became drunk and incapable, but on being washed ashore was murdered by a fisherwoman for his emerald ring.

Further along on the left is **Two Post Alley**, which separates two fine examples of domestic architecture. On the left a drunkenly tilting Elizabethan building, covered with weatherboarding, has a bookshop at street level, while on the right is a particularly fine Georgian residence, once a printing office. Notice the elegant ornamentation between its first and second floors.

On your right is the **Guildhall**, claimed as the best 17th-century public building in the county. The exterior is certainly impressive, with imposing pillars, Georgian windows and a rooftop cupola on which is mounted a weathervane in the form of an 18th-century warship in full rigging. The interior is equally impressive, with some fine decorated ceilings above the main chamber and the staircase – another gift from Cloudesley Shovel. If by now you've become a Shovel fan and wonder what he looks like, you can see his portrait hanging in the main chamber.

The Guildhall has been a museum since 1979; it was reopened in 1994 after major refurbishment and now has some state-of-the-art displays. The route through it is an historical journey starting with geology and archaeology and passing through various periods to Victorian times. The highlight for many people is the two-tier gallery, which recreates one of the Medway prison ships from the Napoleonic War. The audiovisual effects leave little to the imagination.

Opposite the Guildhall is the **Royal Victoria and Bull Hotel**. This 18th-century coaching inn was originally just the Bull, but Princess Victoria had to make an emergency overnight stop here the year before she became queen, and so the name was proudly altered. Note the impressive coat-of-arms over the main gateway – not Victoria's, but that of George III and Queen Charlotte. Dickens used the hotel in his books: it was the Blue Boar in *Great Expectations* and in *Pickwick Papers* Mr Jingle describes it as 'a good house with nice beef'.

Finally in the High Street you'll find behind a mundane shop front at No. 4, just before the bridge, **Draper's Museum of Bygones**. Covering three floors, this has

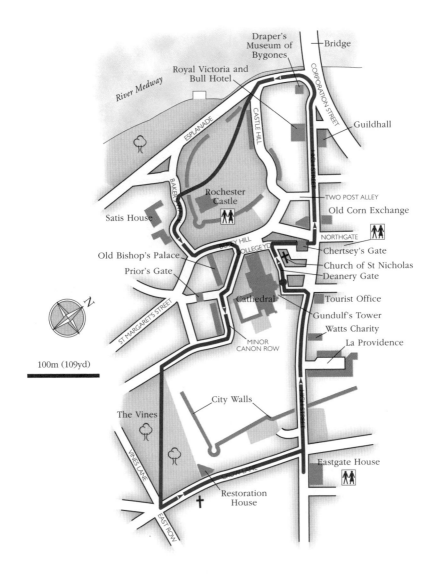

Draper's Museum of Bygones
Bridge
Royal Victoria and Bull Hotel
River Medway
CORPORATION STREET
ESPLANADE
CASTLE HILL
Guildhall
BAKER'S WALK
Rochester Castle
TWO POST ALLEY
Old Corn Exchange
Satis House
BOLEY HILL
COLLEGE YD
NORTHGATE
Old Bishop's Palace
Chertsey's Gate
Church of St Nicholas
Prior's Gate
Deanery Gate
N
Cathedral
Tourist Office
Gundulf's Tower
Watts Charity
ST MARGARET'S STREET
MINOR CANON ROW
La Providence
HIGH STREET
100m (109yd)
City Walls
The Vines
VINES LANE
Eastgate House
CROW LANE
Restoration House
EAST ROW

sixteen old shop sets such as a chemist, a toyshop, a haberdashery and a sweetshop. Absorbing to all ages, this is well worth a visit.

Rochester Castle

Ahead of you now is a **bridge complex** over the River Medway. This has been an historic crossing point since the Romans built the first stone bridge here to take Watling Street on its way to London. There been five others since; the present (steel) bridge was built in 1914 to carry two roads and a railway. Oddly, it is administered not by the Highways Authority but by the Rochester Bridge Trust, an ancient charity which pays for the upkeep.

Then turn left into the Esplanade. Ahead, on your left, is the entrance to **Rochester Castle**, via a mock Norman arch cut by the Royal Engineers in 1872. Walk up the steps through the 13th-century curtain wall. At their top is a cannon believed to have been fired in the Crimean War.

You are now within the grounds of the castle, originally fortified by the Normans shortly after the Conquest and initially consisting of earthworks and timber palisades. During 1088 Bishop Gundulf began the construction of a stone building, possibly the earliest masonry castle in the

Prior's Gate

country. It remained in the hands of the Archbishop of Canterbury until in 1215 it was besieged by King John. The siege was lasted two months and succeeded only when the king's forces undermined the southeast corner turret by burning its wooden props with the fat of forty pigs. The rebuilt turret was round rather than square, like the originals.

Today, all that remains of the castle are the curtain walls and the massive keep, which must be one of the best preserved pieces of Norman architecture in England. It is over 100ft (30m) high and has walls 13ft (4m) thick. Within the keep a circular staircase takes you to the battlements – a climb rewarded by superb views over the city and the river.

To the left of the castle and close to the toilets is a gap in the curtain walls which is probably the best spot from which to photograph the cathedral's west front.

Leave the castle grounds from the other side of the keep, where a small gate leads into Baker's Walk. Almost immediately opposite is a complex of buildings known as **Satis House**. The name comes from the Latin word meaning 'enough', said to have been Elizabeth I's comment on the hospitality she received when staying here in 1573. The buildings have changed considerably since then – the main building has a distinctly Georgian look – but Old Hall, to the left and once the east wing of the house, retains Tudor elements.

Ecclesiastical Dwellings

Turn left, in the direction of the cathedral, and then right into College Green.

Immediately on your right is the **Old Bishop's Palace**, a delightful 15th-century building of mellow brickwork. Bishop John Fisher, who was also chancellor of Cambridge University, lived here for thirty-one years before being put to death for refusing to acknowledge Henry VIII as head of the Church.

Just around the corner is the **Prior's Gate**, the best preserved of the three surviving 14th-century monastic gates. Today it leads pedestrians only into St Margaret's Street, where the Cooper's Arms was a favourite stop for pilgrims en route to Canterbury.

Turn left before you reach Prior's Gate into **Minor Canon Row**, a terrace of 18th-century houses built for the minor canons of the cathedral; originally there were six houses for the six minor canons, but a seventh was later added for the organist. The father of Dame Sybil Thorndike (1882–1976) was a canon at the cathedral, and so the actress lived here for several years.

The road now swings right past some of the buildings of the King's School. Just past the 18th-century Oriel House (note the fire insurance company marks on the wall) turn left into **The Vines**. This attractive public park was formerly the monks' vineyard. It is dominated by a row of plane trees, planted in 1880. A number were uprooted in the hurricane of 1987 and have been replaced. The trunk of one of the damaged trees has been carved into the figure of a Benedictine monk.

Secular Dwellings and the City Walls

On the far side of The Vines turn left into Crow Lane, where there is a variety of fine domestic architecture on view.

Immediately on your left, facing The Vines, is **Restoration House**. The name originated in 1666: this was the house, owned by Sir Francis Clarke, where Charles II stayed on the eve of his ascension to the throne. Dickens based the home of Miss Haversham in *Great Expectations* on this house, calling it Satis House – not to be confused with the real Satis House.

Continue down Crow Street until you once more reach the High Street. Turn right and immediately on your right, at No. 150, you see a magnificent half-timbered Tudor building with ground-floor shops. Dickens used this as the model for another building in *Great Expectations*, Uncle Pumblechook's shop.

Cross the High Street to **Eastgate House**, a timber and red brick mansion built in 1590 for Sir Peter Buck, once Mayor of Rochester. His coat-of-arms can be seen in one of the gables overlooking the High Street. In Victorian times the building was a boarding school for young ladies and well known to Dickens, who in *Pickwick Papers* called it Westgate House. It was the home of the city museum until in 1979, when it moved to the Guildhall. Eastgate House then became the **Charles Dickens Centre**. It was refurbished in 1996 and now uses high-technology visual aids to illustrate the author's life and times.

Dickens (1812–1870) was born in Portsmouth, but when he was 5 his father got a job in the Navy Pay Office at Chatham and the family moved to the Rochester area, staying here until Charles was 11, when the family moved again, this time to London. Here things went badly for them, and Charles's father spent some time imprisoned for debt at Marshalsea; Charles himself had to give up his schooling and take a hellish job in a rat-infested blacking warehouse. He escaped to take various more congenial jobs, although his great ambition at the time was to become an actor – an ambition which, to an extent, he achieved towards the end of his life when he gave highly dramatic readings from his works both in Britain and in the USA. By then he was living again near Rochester, at Gadshill, which he had coveted in childhood and which he had bought in 1856 as a country house.

By the time he moved permanently to Gadshill, however, his private life was in turmoil. In 1836, three days after publication of the first part of *Pickwick Papers* (1836–7), he had married Catherine, the daughter of his friend George Hogarth, editor of the *Evening Chronicle* and a highly respected man of letters. Charles and Catherine had nine children but she became increasingly infuriated by his adulterous relationship, begun about 1857, with a young actress, Ellen Ternan, and the couple separated in 1858. There was a huge scandal when the matter became public – the similarly unorthodox lifestyles of his contemporaries Wilkie Collins (1824–1889) and William Makepeace Thackeray (1811–1863) for some reason caused nothing like the same furore – and Dickens retreated with Ellen to Gadshill, which he made his home for the rest of his life, although hereafter he spent a large part of his time abroad. He died of a stroke at Gadshill while working at his desk on *The Mystery of Edwin Drood* (1870).

In the garden at the rear of Eastgate House is the Swiss chalet from Dickens's home at Gadshill; he used it as a summerhouse and also wrote some of his later works in it. Unfortunately, the chalet is not open to visitors.

Return westwards along the High Street to the **city walls**. The defensive walls in Roman times were merely earth ramparts, but the Normans replaced these with stone walls and four gates enclosing an area of nearly 25 acres (10ha). The best surviving stretches today are by the carpark on the north of the High Street and on the opposite side of the High Street, where a short length can be seen behind the window of the City Wall Wine Bar.

Continue west along the High Street, until you come, on the right, to **La Providence**, also called the French Hospital, and founded by the Huguenots. Today it provides apartments for elderly local people of Huguenot descent.

Further along on the right is **Watts Charity**, a Tudor building with a Georgian frontage. The charity was endowed by Richard Watts, an MP for the town in the 1500s, to provide board and lodging nightly for 'six poor travellers'. Echoing this phrase, Dickens called one of his famous Christmas stories 'The Seven Poor Travellers' (1854).

Next on the right is the Tourist Information Office, newly ensconced in plush surroundings. Cross the road here and walk into the War Memorial Gardens. Carry on towards the cathedral, where between the two north-facing transepts is the squat **Gundulf's Tower**. Once a free-standing bell tower, this was probably built after Gundulf himself had died. Today its main use is for choir practices.

Pass now through the **Deanery Gate**, a monastic inner gate dating from the 15th century, with original doors. Turn left at the end of the alleyway to reach the cathedral's west front, where the walk began.

ST ALBAN'S

Access: Within four miles (2.5km) of exits from the M25, M1, M10 and A1 (M). The former A5 (now A5183) and A6 (now A1081) run through the city. St Albans Station is on the Bedford–St Pancras line; no InterCity services, but the Thameslink service operates and also connects with Luton and Gatwick airports. Greenline coaches no longer stop at St Albans, but the 724 service linking Heathrow and Stansted stops en route at St Albans.

Both the city and the cathedral take their name from the 3rd-century St Alban, probably the first Christian martyr in Britain.

Alban resided in Verulamium, an important town in Roman Britain. He sheltered in his house a Christian priest fleeing persecution – Christianity was proscribed in the Roman Empire. Impressed by the man's devotions and prayers, Alban was eventually converted. He then helped Amphibalus (as Geoffrey of Monmouth named the priest) escape, disguising him in his own cloak. Brought before the Roman magistrates, Alban refused to deny his new faith and was condemned to death. He was beheaded on the hill outside the Verulamium city walls in *c*209, *c*254 or *c*304, depending upon which authority you believe. A church later built on the site soon became known for miracle healing. Pilgrims began come, the first documented visit being that of St Germanus of Auxerre (*c*378–448) in 429.

King Offa of Mercia founded a Benedictine monastery on the site in 793. After the conquest of 1066, the Normans decided to build a vast new church. The first Norman abbot, Paul de Caen, brought a master mason from Normandy to supervise the Saxon workmen. Although there was no building stone in the local area, there was abundant brick, tile and flint in the remains of the Roman city, and these materials were widely used in the new church. When dedicated in 1115 the church was the largest in England.

Meanwhile the monastery went from strength to strength. Its wealth ensured that the abbey church was continually extended and reconstructed. At its zenith, the abbey had over one hundred monks and three times as many lay helpers. Its abbots included Richard of Wallingford, Thomas de la Mare and the future Cardinal Wolsey.

In 1539, however, the monastery was dissolved as part of Henry VIII's campaign. Most of the buildings were destroyed (an exception was the abbey gateway at the top of Abbey Mill Lane) and the treasures were looted. The local people saved the church to use as their parish church, buying it for £400. The population was too small to cope with the upkeep of such a building, however, and over the next three centuries it inevitably deteriorated. In the mid-19th century serious efforts were made to restore it, and the eminent Sir George Gilbert Scott (1811–1878) was appointed architect. The dominating force in the restoration was the wealthy barrister Edmund Beckett Grimthorpe, 1st Baron Grimthorpe (1816–1905). He imposed many of his own ideas, most of them controversial, but his financial contribution was invaluable. The abbey church was proclaimed a cathedral in 1877.

The most recent addition is the chapter house, opened by Elizabeth II in 1982 and built of handmade bricks – to blend in with the Roman tiles found in the older parts of the cathedral – on the site of the original chapter house where monks assembled daily to read a chapter of the Benedictine Rule. During the excavation of the new building the remains of many of the early abbots were found; they have been reburied in the presbytery. The new chapter house includes a visitor centre, refectory, shop and theological library. Visitors may wish to visit the grave of Archbishop Lord Runcie (formerly Bishop of St Albans), which can be found in the North Churchyard.

TOUR OF THE CATHEDRAL

Start: The west door.
Finish: The new chapter house.

The **west end (1)** of the nave was reconstructed in Victorian Gothic style as part of the Grimthorpe renovations, and most experts today consider that it does not sit happily with the rest of the cathedral. The 19th-century work replaced what drawings show to have been an attractive Perpendicular construction, with a particularly eye-catching window. It was, however, in poor condition and the solution was to replace it completely with a design which was entirely Grimthorpe's. Inside his wooden draughtproof doors are windows and glass doors, with etchings which include the words of the Alban Prayer, 'I worship and adore the True and Living God who created all things'. The present glasswork dates from 1988 and is the work of David Pearce.

The **nave (2)** is impressive for its length (the second longest in England after Winchester) and for its variety of architectural styles. The eastern end, part of the original abbey church, displays typical round-ended Norman arches made largely of

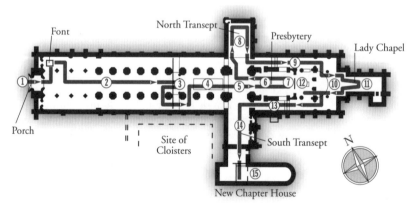

Key	5. Tower	11. Lady Chapel
	6. Presbytery	12. Chapel of
1. West End	7. High Altar	St Alban
2. Nave	8. North Transept	13. South Presbytery Aisle
3. Rood Screen	9. North Presbytery Aisle	14. South Transept
4. Choir	10. Retrochoir	15. New Chapter House

flint and bricks from the old Roman city and plastered to resemble stonework: the result is that the pillars are almost square. The pillars' west and south sides display a series of 13th- and 14th-century paintings showing saints and crucifixion scenes. The paintings were plastered over after the Reformation and rediscovered during the Victorian renovations.

The Norman columns are not duplicated on the south side of the nave as the originals collapsed during a service in 1323, killing two monks and a boy. They were replaced by five bays in Decorated style, made of 'clunch' from Tottenhoe in Bedfordshire, the work being finally completed in 1345. The triforium level is particularly ornate, and the sophisticated decoration of this style makes an interesting contrast with the more simplistic Early English work of the remainder of the western end of the nave.

The exterior of the nave on the south side shows some half-buried arcading, marking the site of the original abbey cloistering.

At the nave's eastern end is the 14th-century **rood screen (3)**, which effectively divided the public nave from the monks' choir and presbytery. The screen is of stone and noticeably asymmetrical. Its many recesses are now empty, the statues having been removed during and after the Dissolution in 1539. At the base of the screen, above the nave altar, is a 16th-century Spanish cross composed largely of crystal.

An English Pope and the Magna Carta

Next proceed via the south aisle into the **choir (4)**, where one of the stall nameplates is that of Nicholas Breakspear (1100–1159), who in 1154 became the only English Pope, Adrian IV. He had earlier been rejected by the abbey (where his father was a monk) because it was said that he was 'insufficient in learning'!

The present choir stalls are Victorian; the original monastic versions are thought to be those in the parish church in Leighton Buzzard. The wooden panels of the choir ceiling date from the late 14th century, with some Victorian restoration.

Go now into the crossing. The **tower (5)**, with its impressive Norman arches, is the oldest cathedral tower in England. Its walls, 7ft (2m) thick, are made of Roman tiles which were probably 800 years old when the Normans constructed the tower in the late 11th century! The decoration of the wooden tower ceiling consists of red-and-white roses of the houses of York and Lancaster, who fought each other twice at St Albans. These wooden panels are replicas of the medieval originals, which are still in place above them.

Over the ceiling, the ringing chamber contains a peal of twelve bells of widely varying ages, the oldest dating from 1699 and the most recent from 1935.

Move into the **presbytery (6)**, dominated by the **high altar (7)**, erected by Abbot William of Wallingford and dedicated in 1484. Its purpose was to exclude visiting pilgrims from the choir. The stone statues were removed during the Reformation, but Lord Aldenham provided new figures of magnesian limestone in the late 19th century. The distinctive reredos, sculptured in marble and paua shells from New Zealand, was designed by Sir Alfred Gilbert (1854–1934).

In the floor of the presbytery you'll find a slate slab below which eleven abbots and four monks are buried. Their remains were found during excavations for the new chapter house and reburied in the presbytery with full Benedictine honours. The inscription on the slab tells us that one of the monks was Robert of the Chamber, the father of Nicholas Breakspear. The 13th-century wooden ceiling was painted over in the 15th century, and the shields were added during 17th-century restoration. Interestingly, there are no stone vaulted ceilings anywhere in the cathedral: it appears funds were lacking at crucial times, so wooden ceilings had to suffice.

On the north side of the presbytery is the chantry chapel of the 16th century Abbot Ramryge. Look for his rebus – a play on words, in this case involving the ram motif. The chapel was restored in 1996.

From the presbytery, step back into the **north transept (8)**. The painting on the west wall shows, to scale, the abbey church and monastery as they were prior to Dissolution. (This knowledge is useful when walking around the city.) Nearby is a copy of the Magna Carta, compiled at the abbey before being presented to King John in 1215. Adjacent is a reconstruction of part of Abbot Richard of Wallingford's early-14th-century astronomical clock. Among the various busts is that of Lord Grimthorpe, while the tomb effigy is of the first Bishop, Thomas Legh Claughton. A 1995 addition to the north transept is Henry More's *Single Standing Figure*.

In 1999, fragments of the 12th-century shrine of St Alban were reassembled as the **Altar of the Persecuted** in the north transept. The architecture of the north transept is Norman throughout apart from the rose window, installed during the Victorian restorations. Architectural purists may bridle, but it's a fine piece of work. The stained glass in the window was a gift from Laporte Industries of Luton.

The Shrine of St Alban

Walk on into the **north presbytery aisle (9)**. The brass on the floor, for Abbot Thomas de la Mare (1349–1396), is believed to be of Flemish origin; since it does not record his death it may have been made during his lifetime.

On the south wall is one of the original panels from the ceiling of the tower. You can see the rear of the watching tower at the end of the aisle; you'll get a better view of it later, but notice here the carvings on the main beam, which show scenes of everyday life *c*1400. At the north end of the aisle are the stone remains of the Shrine of St Amphibalus, the mentor of St Alban.

From the **retrochoir (10)**, your next port of call, you get a fine view into the **Lady Chapel (11)**. Both were completed by Abbot Hugh Eversden *c*1320. After the Dissolution the Lady Chapel was walled off and a public passageway was made through the retrochoir. For the next 300 years the chapel was used as a boys' grammar school, with consequent wear and tear on its fabric. In 1870 the school was moved to the old abbey gateway and the chapel restored. There was a further renovation in 1958, when furnishings were added in memory of the Kent family.

Go now into the heart of the cathedral, the **Chapel of St Alban (12)**. In the centre is the Shrine of St Alban. The saint's relics, once contained in an elaborate stone pedestal, gained a reputation for healing, attracting pilgrims from far and wide. After the Dissolution the reliquary was taken by the Crown and the pedestal stone used for building material when the chapel was walled off. The pedestal was reconstructed in the Victorian renovation, and a more complete reconstruction, finished in 1993, was rededicated in the presence of the late Queen Mother.

Because of the value of the reliquary and the vast number of pilgrims which the shrine attracted, a wooden watching chamber on the north side of the chapel was constructed (*c*1400), from which monks could maintain a constant vigilance.

On the south side of the chapel is the vault of the only royal person to have been buried in the cathedral, Humphrey, Duke of Gloucester (1391–1447), the youngest son of Henry IV and Protector during Henry VI's minority. He was a personal friend of Abbot Wheat-hamptead, and on his death it was requested that he be buried as near as possible to the Shrine of St Alban.

Shrine of St Alban

Leave the chapel by the retrochoir, taking note of the small Chapel of the Four Tapers, now used by the Mothers' Union, and proceed into the **south aisle (13)**. On the right is the Chantry Chapel of Abbot William Wallingford (who built the altar screen), now reserved for private prayer.

Further along is a wall panel showing the martyrdom of St Alban. The painting probably dates from the 17th century and is thought to have originally been the central panel of the north transept ceiling.

Our tour ends at the **south transept (14)**, which merges into the **new chapter house (15)**. The south wall of the south transept was entirely rebuilt in Early English lancet style during the Grimthorpe restorations. The original Norman arches are retained in the triforium; their baluster shafts have been turned, and may be Saxon in origin. Some of the crescents above the balusters are filled with Roman tiles. One of the recesses in the transept walls was the original entrance to the cloisters. The wooden gallery and stairway are in memory of Bishop Greford Jones. The gallery is a new location for the Sanctus Bell, formerly at the west end of the cathedral.

A Norman arch leads the visitor into the new chapter house, which has a bookshop, an information desk, toilets and a highly recommended refectory.

WALKING TOUR FROM ST ALBAN'S CATHEDRAL

This circular walk visits some of the city's Roman remains as well as remnants of the once thriving abbey, plus a working water mill and an excellent museum. You can also see some varied domestic architecture in this Heritage Area of St Albans.

Start and finish: The west front of the cathedral.
Length: 2 miles (3.5km).
Time: 1¼ hours (allow longer if you want to visit the Verulamium Museum).
Refreshments: Excellent cathedral refectory. Numerous old coaching inns along the walking route provide excellent bar meals and pub lunches, notably the Fighting Cocks Inn (Abbey Mill Lane), the Tudor Tavern (George Street), the Rose and

Crown (St Michael's Street), the Blue Anchor, the Black Lion and St Michael's Manor Hotel (all in Fishpool Street). The last two offer accommodation.

Walk towards the **Abbey Gateway**, sometimes known as the Great Gateway. Built of flint and Roman tiles, it is the only surviving monastic building. It is believed to have been built in the early 1360s during the abbotcy of Thomas de la Mare (1349–1396). In 1381, during the Peasants' Revolt, it was besieged by insurgents, between 1553 and 1869 it was the local prison, and since 1871 it has formed part of the adjacent St Albans Boys' School.

Cockfighting
Go down Abbey Mill Lane towards the River Ver, at the side of which is the historic **Fighting Cocks Inn**, which claims to be 'probably the oldest licensed house in England' – a claim supported by *The Guinness Book of Records*. The name refers to the cockfighting which took place here during the 17th and 18th centuries (after cockfighting became illegal in 1849, it was briefly renamed the Fisherman). The main part of the inn is octagonal, and built on what is thought to have been a medieval pigeon house, rebuilt for human habitation *c*1600. An information plaque on the wall claims that the inn accommodated Oliver Cromwell (1599–1658) for one night, his horse being stabled in what is now the bar area.

Opposite the Fighting Cocks, on the far side of the Ver, are the **Abbey Mills**, which once provided water power to grind corn for the monastery. The present building dates from 1800 and is a silk-weaving mill.

Walk westward into Verulamium Park, dominated by a large ornamental lake dug out in the 1930s to replace the fishponds which had provided food for the monastery.

The Roman Legacy
Now you have a choice. The path along the river leads directly to St Michael's and the Verulamium Museum (see below). The longer route to the left of the lake goes there via various interesting features, including stretches of the **Roman wall** with the foundations of the London Gate. The walls are thought to have been built *c*200 to enclose about 200 acres (80ha) of the city. Follow the signs to take a leftward detour to the **hypocaust**, now housed in a brick building covering the remains of what was a large Roman townhouse, also dating from *c*200, with possibly as many as twenty rooms. The heating system, illustrated on wall panels, is well preserved.

Return to the path you left to visit the hypocaust and stroll along it to the carpark. This is the area known as St Michael's, in the heart of the old Roman city. Next to the carpark is the timber-framed **Glebe House**, a restored 16th-century building now the administrative and educational centre of the Hertfordshire and Middlesex Wildlife Trust. A small nature reserve nearby is open during the summer.

Cross the carpark to the attractive **St Michael's Church**, one of three churches founded by Abbot Ulsinus in 948 (the others being St Peter's at the northern end of St Albans town centre and St Stephen's, to the south of the city). St Michael's has had much restoration – the tower, for example, was replaced by Lord Grimthorpe – but there is original Saxon work in the windows of the nave, which is largely Norman. Look for the statue of Sir Francis Bacon (1561–1626), who lived at the nearby Gorhambury Estate. The churchyard was the location of the Roman basilica or town hall and the adjacent forum. It has been suggested that the basilica may have been as large as the present cathedral nave. Today, only one small part of the foundations can be seen, between the Verulamium Museum and the carpark.

Carry on to Bluehouse Hill, the main Hemel Hempstead–St Albans road, and cross by the traffic lights. Enter the gates of the Gorhambury Estate. Some fifty yards (50m) to your left is the **Roman Theatre**. This was not an amphitheatre for gladiatorial contests but a theatre with a stage for dramatic productions and possibly religious rites, and is the only fully excavated example of its type in Britain. It is thought the theatre was built *c*150, with a final rebuilding *c*300. The main excavations were carried out in the 1930s, with some reconstructions on the basis of available evidence. The remains of tradesmen's shops and an extensive villa have also been uncovered. An official guidebook is available at the kiosk.

Retrace your steps across Bluehouse Hill to the Roman **Verulamium Museum**. No ordinary stuffy museum this, but a lively display of everyday life in Roman Verulamium. There are interpretative displays, abundant Roman and Iron Age artefacts, plus realistic audiovisual presentations. Not to be missed!

Old Coaching Inns

Proceed now along St Michael's Street towards the Ver, passing two old coaching inns to your left. The first, the Six Bells, is built over the remains of the Roman

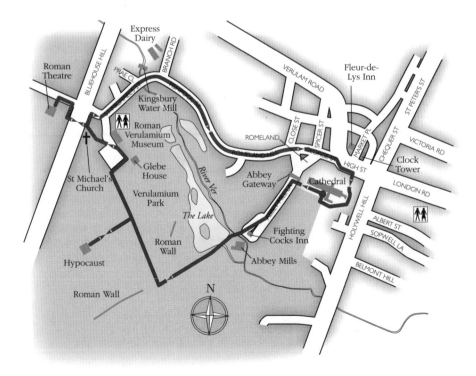

baths, which were destroyed during the Iceni revolt led by Queen Boudicca in 60–61. The carpark of the second pub, the Rose and Crown, is thought to lie above the old Colchester (or northeast) Gate to the Roman city.

After crossing the Ver you see on your left **Kingsbury Water Mill**. On the green in front of the mill is a large block of Hertfordshire puddingstone, an example of the local conglomerate which used by the Romans as a millstone. There has been a water mill on this site since at least Domesday times, although the present restored mill dates from the 16th century. It is open to the public, and you can see the water wheel and milling apparatus along with a fascinating collection of farming implements. There are also a shop, an art gallery and a restaurant, which sells delicious waffles.

Architecture buffs may wish to make a diversion into Branch Road, where a hundred yards or so (100m) along is the **Express Dairy**, which is pure Art Deco in style.

The main route now proceeds into **Fishpool Street**, named after the series of monastic ponds once close to the site. There are some superb examples of domestic architecture from timber-framed Elizabethan through Georgian to Victorian, with jettied walls, pargeting and fascinating memorial wall plaques dating from World War I.

This street was once the main road from St Albans to the north, and is well provided with old coaching inns. On the corner of Branch Road is the Black Lion, a timber-framed inn dating from the 16th century but refronted in brick in 1720. Further along on the right is the St Michael's Manor Hotel, once the home of the Gape family, who played a leading role in the life of the town for several centuries. The oldest surviving part of the hotel dates from the 1500s; the imposing porch, with its Doric columns, is from the 19th century.

The only other surviving inn is the Lower Red Lion, on the left near the top of Fishpool Street. Here you find a triangular walled area known as **Romeland** – probably from 'room land', meaning an open space. Fairs were once held here, and it was on this spot that the Protestant George Tankerville was burnt at the stake.

Continue up the hill into **George Street**, a marvellous medieval street named after the former George Inn. Most of the buildings are now specialist shops. The jewel is undoubtedly the **Tudor Tavern**, with its half-timber work and jettied walls. It is now a steakhouse; you can dine in its first-floor hall, which dates from 1400.

Moving towards the town centre, the next item of historical interest is the **Clock Tower**, built 1403–12 and 77ft (23m) high. Its medieval belfry, probably unique in England, contains the large Curfew Bell, dating from 1335. The tower was restored in 1866 by Sir George Gilbert Scott. Near it a cross once marked one of the resting places of Eleanor of Castile's body on its journey from Harby in Lincolnshire to Westminster; the cross was demolished in the 17th century.

At the side of the Clock Tower is the narrow pedestrianized, historic French Row, which includes the **Fleur-de-Lys Inn**, thought to date from 1440. A wall plaque claims this was the site of a building in which King John of France was held prisoner after the Battle of Poitiers in 1356. The present building has an interesting yard, with a 17th-century balustraded staircase which may have led to a gallery.

Leave the Clock Tower area and walk down the alleyway opposite. This leads you to Sumpter's Yard, at the east end of the cathedral. Here packhorses once unloaded supplies for the abbey. Walk along the south side of the cathedral to the west end, where the walk began.

BURY ST EDMUNDS

Access: The A14, which bypasses the town to the north, links with the M11 and London. Other main roads connect with Thetford, Diss and Sudbury. National Express coach services from London Victoria: two coaches daily. Rail from Kings Cross (change at Cambridge) or from Liverpool Street (change at Ipswich). Both rail and coach journeys take about 2½ hours.

The cathedral at Bury St Edmunds is of the 'upgraded parish church' type, and thus not really within our scope. However, such is the historic interest of the town and in particular the ruins of the abbey that an exception has been made. Indeed, had the abbey church survived the Dissolution it would have compared favourably with the other East Anglian abbey cathedrals, Ely and St Alban's.

The site of the present cathedral was occupied by a church – St Denis's Church, built 1065–98 – in early Norman times. This was demolished in the next century and replaced by a new church dedicated to St James. (It is said that the abbot responsible – Anselm – had hoped to make a pilgrimage to the shrine of St James at Compostella in Spain, but was too busy!) Most of the present building, however, dates from 1510–30 and is largely attributed to John Wastell. He was a local mason; his other work includes King's College Chapel in Cambridge, the fan vaulting in Peterborough Cathedral (see page 267), the Bell Harry Tower at Canterbury (see page 204) plus a number of Suffolk parish churches. Most of the rest of the cathedral is either Victorian or Modern.

The motto of Bury St Edmunds is *Sacrarium Regis, Cunabula Legis*, which approximately translates as 'Shrine of a King, Cradle of the Law'. The history of the town explains it all. Bury originated as a Saxon homestead, Beodricksworth, where *c*630 King Sigebert of the East Angles founded a monastery. Later, in 869, King Edmund was killed by the Danes (either in battle or as a martyr) on one of their frequent raids on Eastern England. His body was buried near Diss, but some time later, after miracles had been attributed to them, his remains were brought to the monastery at Beodricksworth, which changed its name to St Edmund's Bury, and the shrine became a place of pilgrimage. In 1032, King Canute, who had conquered the whole of the country, granted the monastery abbey status. Later, at the time of the Norman Conquest, the abbey was fortunate in having a French Abbot (Baldwin) who was able to ensure there was no destruction by the invaders.

Baldwin also constructed the abbey gates and walls and laid out the grid plan of the town's roads. It was in his time that work commenced on the abbey church. His successor, Anselm, continued the work afterwards, but on a much grander scale. A serious fire (*c*1150) held up progress, but the great west front was completed during the time of Abbot Samson, who held office 1182–1211, and pictorial reconstructions suggest it must have rivalled the west front of Ely (see page 245).

During King John's troubled reign, a group of barons gathered together at Bury ostensibly to celebrate St Edmund's Day but in fact to swear before the high altar of the abbey church that they would force the king to sign the Magna Carta. This he eventually did in 1215, so leading to the town's claim to be the 'cradle of the law'.

Relations between the abbey and the town were rarely peaceful. In 1327 there were riots that lasted for most of the summer, culminating in the destruction of a considerable part of the abbey and the abbey gateway, the abbot being abducted. Once peace was restored, the townspeople were reprimanded and obliged to rebuild the gateway.

The abbey was at its most powerful during the 15th century. The abbey church was among the largest in the country – at 505ft (154m) long it was some 15ft (5m) longer than Norwich Cathedral – and its style influenced the architecture of the other East Anglian cathedrals. Both of Bury's medieval parish churches, St James (now the cathedral) and St Mary's, stood within the abbey walls. In 1533 Henry VIII's sister Mary was buried at the abbey (although her body was later moved to St Mary's – see page 239). Shortly afterwards came the Dissolution of the Monasteries, and Bury St Edmunds Abbey was surrendered to the king in 1539. The abbey precinct was later sold to local people and the buildings became in succeeding years a quarry for the townspeople, so that today the Barnack and Caen stone has all but disappeared, leaving only the flint core to show the outline of the abbey church and buildings.

The town continued to prosper, its wealth based on the wool industry. A few medieval secular buildings, such as the Guildhall, survive. The original street plan, too, is largely extant between Market Square and Angel Hill, next to the abbey grounds. Prosperity continued into the 18th century, as shown by the numerous impressive Georgian buildings – e.g., the Athenaeum on Angel Hill and the Manor House on Honey Hill, the latter built for the family of the Earl of Bristol. It was during this period, in 1711, that the nonconformist Unitarian Meeting House was built.

The area lacks coal deposits, so during the Industrial Revolution Bury St Edmunds suffered little of the ugly development seen elsewhere in the Midlands and North. Its main industries were brewing, watch- and clockmaking and those related to agriculture. Victorian terraces are hard to find, and there are many gems of domestic architecture in the central area of the town.

The parish church of St James, Bury St Edmunds, became a cathedral in 1914 when the Diocese of St Edmundsbury and Ipswich was created; the bishop resides in Ipswich. Plans for extending the building were drawn up shortly thereafter, but two world wars and constant shortage of funds have rendered progress slow. The porch and the first part of the cloisters were completed by 1961, while the new choir and crossing were finished in 1970 (marking the 1100th anniversary of St Edmund's death). In 1990, the new cathedral centre and song school were opened.

Controversy rages regarding the continuing lack of a decent tower for the cathedral. Stephen Dykes Bower, who died in 1994, left a £2 million legacy in his will for the completion of his designs, which included a new tower to complete the

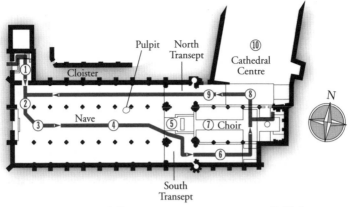

Key

1. Northwest Porch
2. West End

3. Font
4. Nave
5. Crossing
6. Lady Chapel

7. Choir
8. St Edmund's Chapel
9. Treasury
10. Cathedral Centre

present unfinished stump. This sum was insufficient, and the authorities made an application for funds to the Millennium Commission, who rejected the application for a new tower and spire as they regarded the design as 'insufficiently distinctive'. A more recent design was submitted in 1997 involving a tall tower without a spire, the work of Hugh Mathew, who was Dykes Bower's assistant for many years. This application was successful and work began immediately on the tower, with a completion date of January 2004. The funding will also involve the completion of the north transept, the building of two chapels (one linking the east end with the cathedral centre, the other in the crypt) and finally the completion of the east cloister.

Meanwhile, Bury St Edmunds is still a thriving market town and regional centre, with a particularly well preserved historic core. It prides itself on its cultural attractions and is well known for its flower displays, both in the Abbey Gardens and within the town itself.

TOUR OF THE CATHEDRAL
Start and finish: The northwest porch.

Although the cathedral is relatively small, it is certainly not without interest. Enter via the **northwest porch (1)** rather than the west door. Above the porch is the chapter house while to the north is a stretch of cloister; this complex was completed in 1960.

Go forward into the **west end (2)** and turn to note, above the porch on the inside, a cherub that once adorned the top of the old organ casing and was later retrieved from a Belgian antiques shop. If only the cherub could talk, so that it could tell us about all the adventures it had during its absence.

Dominating the west end is the **font (3)**. The base is medieval and the rest Victorian, the work of Sir George Gilbert Scott (1811–1878). The ornate font cover, designed by F.E. Howard, commemorates servicemen who fell in World War I. Both base and cover were painted and gilded in medieval fashion by the Friends of the Cathedral in 1960.

In the wall, flanking the font, are the two Reynolds memorials. Sir James Reynolds died in 1739, having been the town's MP and Chief Baron of the Exchequer; the other memorial is to his wife, who died in 1736.

The windows of the west end, though Perpendicular in style, are in fact Victorian. The glass too is Victorian, an exception being in the Susanna Window on the south side, opposite the porch, which is composed of fragments believed to be from the old abbey church.

Proceed into the **nave (4)**. Whereas the aisle roofs are original, the nave roof was designed by Sir George Gilbert Scott and completed in 1864. The hammer beams terminate with angels clutching shields which show either a scallop shell, the wallet and staff of St James, the Cross of St George or the crown and arrows of St Edmund. The colouring of the roof was begun in 1948 and took thirty-four years to complete. The nave roof's high pitch meant that Wastell's west end had to be modified – hence the Victorian windows. Note the kneelers in the nave; there are over a thousand of these, depicting local scenes or saints and made by parishioners in the diocese.

Walk on into the **crossing (5)**. The rest of the cathedral to the north dates from 1970 onwards. Scott's chancel was inadequate for the demands of a modern cathedral, so a new east end was designed by Dykes Bower (1903–1994). He created an illusion of transepts, although the real things could never be built because of the proximity of the churchyard. The high altar, retained from Scott's chancel, is backed by modern ornaments. Note, close to the lectern, the old chair with the date 1600 carved on it.

Carry on to the south side and into the **Lady Chapel (6)** via impressive wrought-iron gates designed by Dykes Bower and made by a local craftsman (a septuagenarian indeed, so his was some achievement). The chapel was furnished by the women of the parish.

The Choir and St Edmund's Chapel

Return to the crossing and enter the **choir (7)**. When this section of the cathedral was rebuilt to replace Scott's chancel an extra 36ft (11m) was added to the length of the building. Above the arches of the choir is a collection of shields representing the coats-of-arms of the barons who met at St Edmundsbury Abbey and agreed to force King John to sign the Magna Carta. The sedilia on the south side was resited there at the time of the extension. The *cathedra*, to the left of the altar, was designed by the same artist who produced the font cover; it has not, however, been coloured or gilded. The carving at the top of the throne depicts a wolf guarding King Edmund's decapitated head, as the well-known story of the saint describes.

The organ is an exceptional four-manual instrument with seventy-nine speaking stops. It is hoped to provide a suitable casing when funds allow.

On the north side of the choir is **St Edmund's Chapel (8)**, completed in 1970, the 1100th anniversary of St Edmund's death. As part of the pageantry, local schools produced banners showing a visual history of the saint's life. These are now mounted on the wall of the chapel. The glass in the chapel's east window has been reworked from a window, thought to date from 1832, formerly in the east wall of the south aisle. The ugly brick wall on the north wall of the chapel will be removed when further funds become available – a situation all too familiar to cathedral builders past and present!

The Treasury
Near the chapel gates is a broad staircase to the **treasury (9)**. An entrance fee is charged – drop your money into the early-19th-century poor box at the top of the stairs. As well as the cathedral's own valuable articles, the treasury contains gilt and silver plate from churches throughout the diocese.

Return now to the entrance porch, where a broad stairway leads down to the partially complete cloister and on to the **Cathedral Centre (10)**, completed in 1990 and housing a lecture hall, committee room, sacristy, song school and refectory.

WALKING TOUR FROM BURY ST EDMUNDS CATHEDRAL
The walk begins with St Mary's Church, which has a magnificent hammerbeam roof. On the way to the city centre, with its public buildings, private houses and museums, we explore the remains of the Abbey of St Edmund. Along the way we encounter two museums and see domestic architecture from many periods.

Start and finish: The west front of the cathedral.
Length: 2 miles (3.2km).
Time: 2 hours, but allow longer if you want to visit the two museums and St Mary's Church.
Refreshments: The Alwyne House Tea Rooms in the Abbey Gardens are particularly enjoyable on a summer's day. A number of old inns of character offer good lunchtime fare, notably the One Bull and The Angel Hotel (both in Angel Hill), the Queen's Head (Churchgate) and the Olde White Hart Hotel (Southgate Street). The two hotels also offer accommodation.

Leave the west front and turn left past the Norman Bell Tower and then along Crown Street.

A Church to Remember
After a hundred yards or so (100m) you reach **St Mary's Church**. Regrettably, this is not always open (see page 326 for details). Try to arrange the tour around the opening times, as St Mary's is a gem – in many ways more interesting than the cathedral.

A church existed on the site in early Norman times, although no evidence of it survives. The oldest parts of the church, the crypt and the Decorated chancel, date from 1290–1350; the rest was built in the first half of the 15th century. The glass throughout is Victorian. The last century and a half has seen considerable restoration, which continues.

The nave roof is of hammerbeam construction, with eleven pairs of life-sized angels; unlike that in the cathedral, it has not been painted. The earlier chancel roof

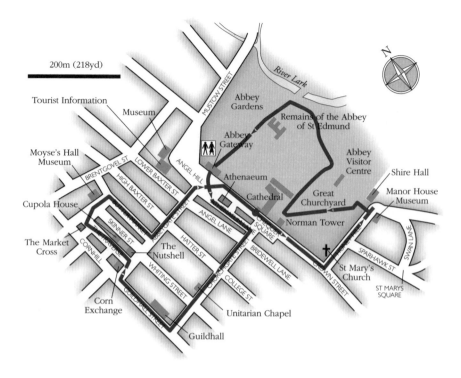

is of the wagon type, with some detailed bosses. There are five chapels or chantries; the North Chapel is the chapel of the Suffolk Regiment. St Mary's is also rich in monuments and brasses (mostly concealed under carpets).

There are two other features of interest. First, on the north side of the sanctuary is the grave of Mary Tudor, who was a sister of Henry VIII and, through her marriage to Louis XII, Queen of France. She was originally buried at the abbey, but at the Dissolution her tomb was transferred to St Mary's. Second, at the base of the tower in the north aisle is a 'squint' – a slit in the wall through which the sexton (who lived in the first floor of the tower) could observe the service and see when to ring the sanctus bell.

Leave St Mary's by the entrance porch and turn immediately left into Honey Hill. About 150 yards (135m) along on the right is the **Manor House Museum**. The building dates from 1738, when it was built for Elizabeth Hervey, wife of the first Earl of Bristol. It later had several owners before being sold to the St Edmundsbury Borough Council in 1988 and being converted into a museum, which opened in January 1993. It has displays of costume, fine art, and horology (watch- and clockmaking was a local industry), plus temporary exhibitions.

The Abbey of St Edmund

Cross Honey Hill and fork obliquely left into the **Great Churchyard**, believed to have been created in 1120–48. This was the town's burial ground, rather than the abbey's, and over the centuries was a popular meeting place. The path through it gives you a good view of the north side of St Mary's Church and in particular the Notyngham Porch, which sits rather unhappily against the wall. The porch is named after a local grocer who in 1438 left £20 for the building of a south and west porch. These were never built, but in 1440 a porch was constructed, entering the north aisle through a re-used Decorated style doorway.

To the right of the path is the flint charnel house, where bodies and bones were piled up.

The path leads you on to a grassy square facing the **west front** of the old abbey. Incorporated into the huge arches are a number of former dwelling houses which appeared after the Dissolution. There were three arches in all, and they would have been even more impressive in the days before the ground was raised 4ft (1.3m) to ameliorate flooding. The front was completed by Abbot Samson, who built octagonal towers at each end. The remains of the south tower are now the home of the Abbey Visitor Centre. Before you leave the west front green, don't miss the statue of St Edmund, the work of the local Suffolk sculptress Elisabeth Frink (1930–1993).

From here there is an informative way-marked route to take you round the remains of the Abbey of St Edmund; at each stop you're supplied with information and also given concise directions to the next point.

Stop (1) is at the back of the Abbey Visitor Centre; here you find a model of the abbey as it would have been at its prime in medieval times. Stops (2), (3), (4) and (5) concentrate on the ruins of the abbey itself, including the position of the Shrine of St Edmund. Particularly impressive are the huge supporting pillars at the one-time crossing. The remains consist almost entirely of just the flint and rubble cores of the pillars and walls, the building stone having been robbed by the townspeople over the centuries. Stop (6) looks at some of the other monastic buildings – such as the prior's house, the dormitory and the infirmary. Stop (7) is at the abbot's garden, from where the 13th-century Abbot's Bridge can still be seen. Stop (8) is in the middle of the ornamental gardens which mark the location of the Great Court, whence the abbot administered royal justice. This was surrounded by other busy abbey buildings – e.g., the kitchen, brewery, bakery, granary and workshops. Stop (9) is at the magnificent Abbey Gate; as we saw, the Norman original was destroyed in the town riots of 1327 and the townspeople had to build a replacement, completed *c*1340, next to the ruins. Note that today's tower does not quite line up with Abbeygate Hill opposite. The final stop (10) is back at the Norman tower, built in 1120–48 and now used as the cathedral's bell tower.

A Prosperous City

You're probably a little 'abbeyed out' by now, so carry on into the city centre, which has a street plan laid out in a grid pattern. As in many medieval towns, there are two squares – one for God and one for the people. The people's square is the marketplace, while God's is **Angel Hill**, a gently sloping open space leading down to the Abbey Gate.

Angel Hill has a wealth of historic buildings, including the house known as

Angel Corner, the Angel Hotel and the building which now houses the Tourist Information Office. By far the most fascinating building here, however, is the **Athenaeum**, a late-18th-century assembly house which has been serving that purpose for the townspeople ever since its completion. It has a fine ballroom, said to have been designed by the Adam brothers.

Take the alleyway, Angel Lane, on the right-hand side of the Athenaeum known. Turn right at the end into Churchgate Street. A couple of hundred yards (180m) along on the right is the **Unitarian Chapel** or **Meeting House**. Built in 1711 as a Presbyterian chapel, this is regarded as one of Britain's finest nonconformist chapels. Recently restored, it is well worth a visit. Note the double-decker pulpit.

Continue to the end of Churchgate Street and turn right into Guildhall Street. A few yards down it, on your right, is the **Guildhall** which was the St Edmundsbury Council Chamber until 1966. The central part of the building was built in the late 15th century, but a doorway inside the main porch is considerably older. The two wings were added in 1807.

Keep going along Guildhall Street until you get to the junction with Abbeygate Street. Immediately opposite is the **Corn Exchange**, an imposing building with a huge six-column portico and arched windows and pilasters on each side. This still operates as a corn exchange on market days. The ground floor is largely shops, while the upper storey is now a concert hall.

Go to the right of the Corn Exchange into a pedestrianized street, The Traverse. On the corner is the **Nutshell**, which claims to be the smallest pub in Britain. Admittedly it is far from unique in this, but certainly you couldn't swing a cat inside its single, minute bar, and often the drinkers have to resort to the pavement instead.

As you walk along The Traverse you'll notice the late 17th-century **Cupola House** on the right, built by well-known local apothecary Thomas Macro. It has a cupola, a belvedere and a second-floor balcony that projects over the street.

Market Square

The next building on the left is the impressive **Market Cross**, completed in 1780 and generally regarded as the city's most attractive post-medieval building. Designed by Robert Adam (1728–1792), it originally had a theatre on the first floor and an open market on the ground floor. The theatre later moved to its present site in the Corn Exchange and the first floor was made a concert hall; it has also functioned as the town hall. Today the ground floor consists of a number of commercial premises and the upper floor has become an art gallery.

Step now into Market Square which, despite the parked cars and garish shopfronts, still retains an historic air. The gem here is undoubtedly **Moyse's Hall**, one of the few surviving Norman domestic buildings in the country and certainly the oldest in East Anglia. The two rounded window arches you can see from the outside are typical of the period, while the interior is even more impressive. Moyse's Hall has had an interesting history, being successively a workhouse, a police station, a gaol and, during Victorian times, a railway parcels and enquiry office. Today it is a museum, concentrating on the historic and archaeological aspect of the area.

Leave Market Square via the Buttermarket and, on reaching Abbeygate Street, turn left. You will soon be back at Angel Hill and the west end of the cathedral.

ELY

Access: Ely is a focal point in the Fenland road system. It is situated on the A10, with easy access from the M11 via the Cambridge bypass. National Express coaches run from London to Cambridge; thereafter use the local Cambus services. Ely is a major junction on the recently electrified Kings Lynn–Liverpool Street line; there are connections with Norwich, Peterborough, Ipswich and the Midlands, and a new service to Stansted, the nearest international airport. The railway station is on the south of the city.

Ely derives its name from the Fenland setting. The place was once known as Elig or Elge, meaning 'island of eels', which were, and still are, prolific on the waterways of the Fens.

Ely owes its existence to St Etheldreda (d679). One of four daughters of Anna, ruler of East Anglia, she was twice unsuccessfully married, eventually fleeing her second husband to set up an abbey on land she had inherited on a low hill at what is now Ely. This was believed to be in 637. There was a small settlement about a mile (0.5km) to the north called Cratendune. On the founding of the abbey, the inhabitants abandoned their village and resettled close by.

In 870 the abbey, along with many others in East Anglia, was destroyed by raiding Danes. It was another century before Benedictine monks reestablished a monastery on the site. Meanwhile the remains of St Etheldreda had become a pilgrims' shrine; it is recorded that King Canute came to Ely with gifts of gold and jewels for it. The monks founded a school – at which Edward the Confessor received part of his early education.

During the Norman conquest, Ely and the Fens were a stubborn pocket of Saxon resistance, led by Hereward the Wake. Eventually William the Conqueror himself was obliged to come to the area in an attempt to overcome the rebels, an aim eventually achieved only with the help of treacherous monks.

The cathedral, to replace the old Saxon church, was begun soon afterwards, in 1083, under the stimulus of early abbots such as Simeon. The east end was completed by 1106, followed by the north and south transepts, the nave (1130) and the northwest and southwest transepts. The central and west towers are thought to have been finished *c*1189. The final result displays the full range of Norman/Romanesque architecture, particularly well seen in the southwest transept. The stone used was almost entirely Barnack limestone, brought by water from Lincolnshire.

In the interim, in 1109, the monastic church was made a cathedral and the existing abbot, Herve le Breton, became the first bishop while remaining the head of the monastery. Because of this dual role, there is no *cathedra* at Ely. (The bishop, as abbot, would have occupied a place in the stalls on the south side of the choir, while the prior had a similar seat on the north side.)

There have been only six additions to the cathedral since Norman times. In 1215 the Galilee Porch was completed at the west end in Early English style under the direction of Bishop Eustace. His successor, Hugh de Northwold, demolished the Norman east end and built a presbytery of six bays, again in Early English style; completed in 1253 largely at his own expense, this presbytery was able to cope with the increasing numbers of pilgrims to the shrine of St Etheldreda. When the cathedral tower collapsed in 1322 it was replaced by the famous stone octagon topped by a wooden lantern, unique in British cathedral architecture.

Before the tower fell, work had started on the Lady Chapel, and after some delays it was completed in 1349. The final additions were the two chantry chapels at the east end – Bishop Allcock's Chantry was completed in the late 15th century and Bishop West's Chantry in c1534.

The monastery was dissolved in 1539 and, although the basic structure of the cathedral had been completed, many of the images, statues and shrines were destroyed at this time, including St Etheldreda's shrine. However, Henry VIII swiftly refounded the cathedral and school.

Oliver Cromwell (1599–1658) lived in Ely for a number of years before he became Lord Protector of England. In his capacity as MP and governor of Ely he had the cathedral closed for some seventeen years. The house in which he lived is now the Tourist Information Office. The 17th century also saw the first attempt at draining the Fens, an endeavour supervised by the Dutch engineer Sir Cornelius Vermuyden (c1595–c1683). Cromwell was initially opposed to this work as he believed it would deprive the Fenmen of their livelihood, but in fact the drained land was fertile and Ely became a flourishing market centre.

By the 18th century (as noted by Daniel Defoe in 1724) the cathedral was in bad shape. A thorough survey of the fabric was begun by the architect James Essex in 1750, and over the next twenty years a considerable amount of repair work (rather than restoration) was carried out.

Until the mid-19th century, produce to and from Ely was still waterborne and the Waterside area of the city sprouted hythes and warehouses to deal with the goods. All this changed with the arrival of the railway in 1845, linking Ely to Norwich and London. A new railway station built two years later gave further impetus to the south side of the town.

The general neglect of the cathedral continued, until in 1839 Dean George Peacock arranged for Sir George Gilbert Scott (1811–1878) to embark on a thorough restoration. This lasted thirty years and to a large extent returned the cathedral to its former magnificence. The city of Ely was meanwhile developing agriculture-related industries such as brewing and jam making, and a large corn exchange was built in the marketplace. In the 1920s the first sugarbeet factory appeared just outside the town.

In 1938 the Lady Chapel, which had been used as a parish church, was handed back to the dean and chapter and thereafter underwent a comprehensive cleaning and refurbishment. By the mid-1950s it was clear that a considerable amount of restoration was needed, and in 1986 a public appeal was launched to finance the work. Several million pounds were raised and restoration proceeded in all parts of the cathedral. The decision to charge an entrance fee did not meet with universal approval, but Ely is a small city – just over 12,000 inhabitants – and additional resources are needed to fund the ongoing restoration work.

Ely remains a market town, but the brewery, corn exchange and sugarbeet factory have all gone. A western bypass and a pedestrianized shopping centre have improved the quality of life, and there is a new emphasis on leisure and tourism based around the riverside and the cathedral – the 'Ship of the Fens', as it is sometimes called.

TOUR OF THE CATHEDRAL
Start and finish: The west end.

The **west end (1)** is best viewed from the Palace Green, where the lopsided nature of this part of the cathedral is clearly seen. The west end is unique among British cathedrals in that it has a west tower, originally with two transepts. One of these, the north, fell down some time during the 15th century and was never replaced. Despite this absence, the west front presents one of the finest Norman façades in the country, with numerous tiers of blind arcading. The west tower was completed *c*1200 and was later topped with a stone spire. This was replaced in the 14th century with an octagonal capping, which until 1801 had a lead-coated wooden spire.

Enter the cathedral through the **Galilee Porch (2)**. Built 1200–1215, in the time of Bishop Eustace, this is a two-storey structure in Early English style with delicate shafts of Purbeck marble. Once you're through the doors of the Galilee Porch you find yourself under the **west tower (3)**. The patterns of the tiled floor form a labyrinth; the distance from the entrance to the centre is 215ft (66m), the exact height of the tower.

Step now into the **southwest transept (4)**, which includes St Catherine's Chapel. This area shows the full range of Romanesque architecture, starting with the classic rounded Norman arches, through interlocking and dogtooth to the pointed transitional windows at the top. The restoration programme in this area is now complete. Before you leave note the stone font, which shows the symbols of the four Evangelists.

From the Nave to the South Transept
To go into the rest of the cathedral you have to pay. Having done so, proceed into the **nave (5)**, which dates from 1110–30. It gives the impression of being long, well lit and narrow, largely because the pulpitum – which separated monks from public – was pulled down during the repairs of James Essex in the 18th century. The proportions of the arcade, triforium and clerestory are exceptional. (The triforium is not blind and is probably better referred to as a tribune.) The wide galleries are best appreciated from the Stained Glass Museum, which occupies the south side at this level. Despite the strong Barnack limestone pillars, there is no vaulting. The wooden ceiling was boarded in during the Scott renovations in 1858 and painted by Henry Styleman le Strange from Hunstanton. His designs were based on those at St Michael's Church at Hildesheim in Germany. Unfortunately, le Strange died before finishing; the work was completed by his friend Thomas Gambier Parry from Gloucester.

Move now into the **south aisle (6)**. Two doors led from here into the cloisters (which did not survive the Dissolution). The south (monks') door served as a processional entrance to the cathedral and is richly carved, but lacks a tympanum. The **prior's door**, viewed from the exterior, is one of the most notable features of the cathedral. It is thought to date from 1150 and is significant for the elaborate stone carving in the pillars and rounded arch. The tympanum is filled with flat figure carving (the sculptors of the time had not yet mastered carving in the round) portraying, among other subjects, Christ in Majesty supported by archangels. Note, too, the particularly gruesome corbel heads. Following recent restoration, the prior's door has been enclosed to protect it from further weathering.

While in the south aisle look for **Ovin's Stone**, the base of a Saxon Cross commemorating Ovin, Etheldreda's steward. It was discovered in the 18th century in the village of Haddenham, where it had been used as a mounting block.

The **south transept (7)**, one of the oldest parts of the cathedral, houses two of its most modern additions – two sculptures, both gifts: *Mary Magdelene Meeting her Risen Christ* by Davis Wynn and *Christus* by Hans Feibusch. On the east side of the south transept is the **Chapel of St Dunstan and St Ethelwold**. These two Benedictine monks revolutionized monastery life and music at Glastonbury. The chapel contains an interesting mosaic icon.

The Octagon and Lantern Tower

Walk on to the crossing, where you can appreciate the **Octagon and Lantern Tower (8)**. The original Norman tower collapsed in 1322, remarkably without loss of life. The sacrist of the time, Alan de Walsingham, decide to replace it with something completely different. The remains of the four tower pillars were removed and he took one bay from each of the two transepts, the nave and the choir, to leave a vast central space linked by arches set at 45° to each other, giving an irregular octagon unique in British church architecture. The capitals on the eight pillars (binoculars are useful here) depict scenes in the life of St Etheldreda.

Roofing the Octagon, which is 74ft (22m) wide, was clearly a problem. A stone vault was out of the question. The solution was a lantern tower built of wood faced externally with lead. It took fourteen years to build, under the direction of the master carpenter William Hurley. The vertical timbers, 63ft (19m) long and 3ft 4in (1m) thick at the base, were made from oak trees brought from Chicksands, Bedfordshire. The whole structure is remarkably successful, flooding the cathedral with light and marred only by the uninspiring Victorian glass. There are occasional tours of the Octagon, Lantern Tower and the cathedral roof – definitely not to be missed.

The Choir and Presbytery

Proceed into the **choir (9)**. Its first three bays were destroyed when the central tower fell, and were rebuilt in Decorated style. The stalls are 14th-century and were originally located beneath the octagon. The canopies are richly carved – look for the Victorian additions, done by a Belgian artist from Louvain, showing Old Testament scenes on the south side and New Testament scenes on the north. There are also some misericords of note.

Walk up three steps into the **presbytery (10)**. Originally the east end of the choir had a Norman apse, but Bishop Hugh de Northwold (in office 1229–54), worried by the increasing number of pilgrims visiting the Shrine of St Etheldreda, demolished the east end and extended the cathedral by six bays with his fine presbytery made of Barnack limestone and Purbeck marble in Early English style. The proportions reflect those of the nave. Dogtooth ornamentation, deeply cut carving, tierceron-ribbed vaulting and strongly carved bosses and corbels make this one of the gems of British Gothic architecture.

The Shrine of St Etheldreda itself was destroyed during the Reformation, but the spot is marked by a commemorative slate. It is not the only thing missing. As we've noted, you can seek in vain for a *cathedra*. However, to the right of the high altar are two modern wooden 'thrones', which were occupied by the Queen and Prince Philip at the distribution of Maundy Money.

Former Bishops
Turn next into the **south choir aisle (11)**, on whose floor you'll find a brass of the notorious Bishop Goodrich, who at the time of the Reformation was responsible for much of the destruction of statues, stained glass and ornaments here, and was later rewarded with the post of Lord Chancellor of England.

The **east end (12)** of the cathedral has two fine chantry chapels. In the south aisle is **Bishop West's Chapel**, completed *c*1538, a year prior to his death and just before the Dissolution. A wealthy man and on occasion Henry VIII's diplomatic envoy, West travelled widely in Europe, and the Italian influence in his chapel, with its early Renaissance ceiling, is clear to see. There are no figures in the numerous niches, and probably never were, reflecting the trend away from overadornment.

To reach the second chantry chapel, Bishop Allcock's Chapel, you must pass through the **Chapel of St Etheldreda**, dedicated in 1957 to those local people who lost their lives in World War II. **Bishop Allcock's Chapel**, facing the north aisle, was built 1488–1500 of soft chalky Cambridgeshire clunch, which was carved

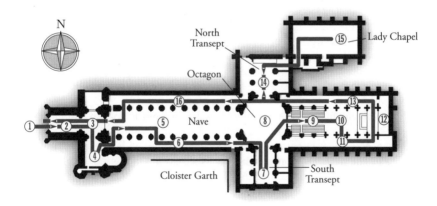

Key	5. Nave	11. South Choir Aisle
1. West End	6. South Aisle	12. East End
2. Galilee Porch	7. South Transept	13. North Choir Aisle
3. West Tower	8. Octagon and Lantern Tower	14. North Transept
4. Southwest Transept	9. Choir	15. Lady Chapel
	10. Presbytery	16. North Aisle

into ornate pinnacles. Here the numerous niches (in contrast to those in West's chapel) did indeed contain statues, but these were destroyed during the Reformation. Note the splendid late-Perpendicular fan-vaulted ceiling. Bishop Allcock's rebus, a cockerel standing on a globe (*all* and *cock*), can be seen in a number of places.

Proceed along the **north choir aisle (13)**, notable for a series of tombs and effigies of former bishops – successively Bishop Hugh de Northwold, Bishop Hotham, Bishop Kilkenny and Bishop Redman. Opposite the latter is a modern stained-glass window dedicated to the men of Bomber Command, stationed near Ely during World War II. Nearby is a spiral staircase leading to the organ loft. The case was designed by Sir George Gilbert Scott; the organ itself has recently undergone a £50,000 restoration and is claimed to be one of the finest in the country.

You can now step into the **north transept (14)**, on the east side of which are two chapels. The **Chapel of St Edmund**, killed by the Danes in 870; some 12th- or 13th-century frescoes on the north wall depict his martyrdom. This chapel was restored at the end of the 19th century, when the alabaster reredos was added. The adjacent **Chapel of St George** is dedicated to the men of Cambridgeshire and the Isle of Ely who lost their lives in World War I.

The northwest corner of the transept was rebuilt by Christopher Wren (1632–1723) in 1700. While the interior of the door is in Norman style, the exterior is of Classical design. Also in this corner of the transept is a model of the lantern tower, giving a good idea of the construction problems involved.

The Lady Chapel

A corridor in the northeast corner of the north transept leads into the **Lady Chapel (15)**. Most cathedral chapels dedicated to the Virgin Mary are at the east end, but here a monks' burial ground made this position undesirable. Work started on the chapel in 1321 but, because of the 1332 collapse of the west tower and its subsequent rebuilding, was not completed until 1349.

This is England's largest Lady Chapel, 46ft (14m) wide, spanned by impressive fan vaulting and containing numerous carved bosses. It was designed by Alan de Walsingham, but the work was directed by a monk called John de Wisbech (who died during the Black Death). The story goes that the work was financed by a hoard discovered by Wisbech while he was digging on the site.

After the Reformation, the chapel was used as one of Ely's parish churches; it was returned to the cathedral authorities only in 1938, after which extensive restoration took place. Most people entering the chapel are astounded by the amount of light provided by the huge Decorated windows. Needless to say, the stained glass and the plethora of statues did not survive the Reformation, but the large-scale restoration from 1986 includes a small area of original glass. Our successors, however, may have mixed feelings about the names of supermarkets and other firms etched into the glass in acknowledgement of their donations to the restoration fund!

Below the windows is a blind arcade, with the head of each arch bending forward in what is known as a nodding ogee. The clunch stone is richly carved into foliage, which is not to everyone's taste – Alec Clifton-Taylor once compared it to a parsley bed!

The acoustics of the Lady Chapel are something special. The celebrated Six-Second Echo makes conversation difficult but is superb for singers. Choirs come from all over the world to sing here, and you may be lucky enough to catch one should you be here at lunchtime.

Return to the north transept and proceed into the **north aisle (16)** of the nave. You can see here one of several huge Victorian Gurney stoves used to heat the cathedral. Originally they used solid fuel, but they were converted to gas in 1982.

Towards the western end of the aisle is a large bell. This once hung in the tower of St Nicholas Church, Feltwell, but, as it had been dedicated to St Etheldreda (probably *c*1500), it was given to the cathedral.

Go to the end of the north aisle, and from there on to the west end, where your tour finishes.

Before leaving the cathedral, visitors may wish to see the Stained Glass Museum, which is located in the South Triforium. Access is via the southwest transept and a narrow spiral staircase. You might also like to try your hand at brass rubbing. This takes place in the north nave aisle, next to the shop.

WALKING TOUR FROM ELY CATHEDRAL

Two connected walks are described below. The shorter one looks only at the area of the college – the collection of former monastic buildings by the cathedral. The longer one continues from the college to take in some of the city's other historic buildings and its riverside life.

THE COLLEGE WALK

Start and finish: The west front of the cathedral.
Length: ¼ mile (0.5km)
Time: No more than 15 minutes.
Refreshments: Space in the cathedral refectory is at a premium; the cathedral-run Almonry is a better bet.

Leaving the west end of the cathedral, turn right into a grassy area known as **Cross Green (1)**. This was the site of the former Church of the Holy Cross, which acted as a parish church from the mid-14th century until 1566. The green was a burial ground for some time. Opposite is **Steeple Gateway (2)**, once the entrance to the burial ground and possibly the route pilgrims took to the monastery. The gateway has a Tudor framework built over a 14th-century undercroft.

Further along the path is the **sacrist's gate (3)**, through which tradesmen came to the monastery; it is believed to have been built in 1325. Nearby is the **bell tower (4)**, sometimes known as Goldsmith's Tower – the prior's goldsmith had a workshop here. All the buildings round here formed the offices and stores of the sacrist to the monastery.

Next to the sacrist's gate is the **Almonry (5)**. The building once contained a school and its dormitories, and dates from the 12th century. The almoner was that official of the monastery who distributed alms to the poor. Nowadays, the Almonry is a restaurant run by the cathedral; in summer you can eat in the charming walled garden.

Medical Matters and More

Go to the east end of the cathedral along a path which gives good views of the Lady Chapel and, on the south side, the remains of the cloister walls. Turn into **Firmary Lane (6)**, which used to be roofed over and was the monastery's infirmary. The arches forming the bays can still be seen in the walls.

The first building on the left is **Powcher's Hall (7)**, named after an early prior. It was used as a 'bloodletting house' where monks were bled using leeches – a practice thought at the time to be healthy (and which has once again found favour in recent years in the treatment of hypertension).

Opposite is the **canonry (8)**, which still retains some 12th-century features. Further on the left is the **Painted Chamber (9)**, built in 1335 as a residence for Alan de Walsingham. On the opposite side of Firmary Lane is the **Black Hostelry (10)**, used to accommodate visiting Benedictine monks (who wore black habits).

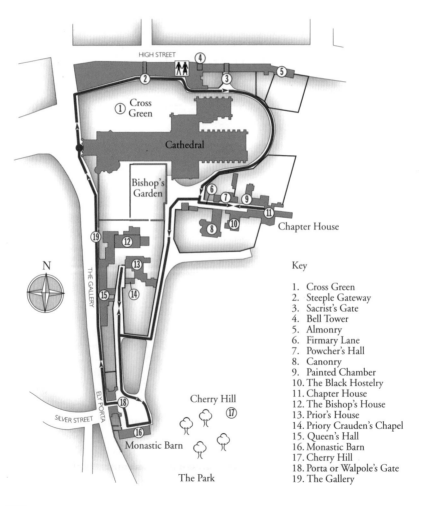

Key

1. Cross Green
2. Steeple Gateway
3. Sacrist's Gate
4. Bell Tower
5. Almonry
6. Firmary Lane
7. Powcher's Hall
8. Canonry
9. Painted Chamber
10. The Black Hostelry
11. Chapter House
12. The Bishop's House
13. Prior's House
14. Priory Crauden's Chapel
15. Queen's Hall
16. Monastic Barn
17. Cherry Hill
18. Porta or Walpole's Gate
19. The Gallery

Today, it continues to offer bed and breakfast; dress optional. At the end of the lane is the **chapter house (11)**. Once the chapel of the infirmary, it is now the administrative centre of the cathedral.

Return along Firmary Lane and turn left. On your right is a further group of old monastery buildings, the first being the **bishop's house (12)**. Formerly the great hall of the monastery, it was later the deanery. It was rebuilt in the 14th century, but retains a 13th-century vaulted undercroft. Next comes the **priory (13)** or prior's house, also rebuilt in the 14th century and now used by the King's School.

At the end of the priory garden, turn right into a lane which leads back to **Prior Crauden's Chapel (14)**. This gem of Decorated architecture, dating back to 1324, has some medieval wall paintings and a fascinating tiled floor showing Adam and Eve with the serpent. Although it is now used as a chapel by the King's School, you can look around if you collect the key from the chapter house (weekday office hours) or from the headmaster's house (weekends).

Opposite the Chapel is the **Queen's Hall (15)**, built to provide accommodation for Queen Philippa, wife of Edward III, and now the house of the headmaster of the King's School.

Returning southwards along the lane, you are confronted by the impressive **Monastic Barn (16)**, a brick-and-timber building now converted into a dining room for the King's School. At its west end is the wooded **Cherry Hill (17)**, which marks the site of a Norman 12th-century motte and bailey castle.

Outside the College

You now leave the area of the college through the **Porta** or **Walpole's Gate (18)** (named after the 14th-century prior). This was the main gateway into the Benedictine priory. On the ground floor was the porter's lodge, while other parts of the building housed the prior's prison. The Porta, like most of the other college buildings, is regrettably not open to visitors.

From the Porta turn right and proceed along **The Gallery (19)**, named after the bridge which once led from the bishop's palace to the cathedral. This brings you back to the west end of the cathedral.

THE CITY WALK

Start and finish: The west front of the cathedral.
Length: 3 miles (4.8km).
Time: About 1¼ hours, but allow longer if you want to visit the two museums.
Refreshments: Few ancient inns en route apart from the Lamb Hotel in Lynn Road, a 13th-century coaching inn (accommodation). The Cutter Inn, on the riverside, can also be recommended.

Walk across to Palace Green. On the south side is the **Bishop's Palace**, an imposing brick-and-stone building begun in the 14th century and not completed until 400 years later. Prior to its construction the Bishops of Ely used as many as ten different palaces or manor houses scattered around the south of England. In its time the palace has been a convalescent home for servicemen, a school for handicapped children and a private residence. It is currently a Sue Ryder home.

Opposite the palace is a private house, The Chantry, built on the site of Bishop Northwold's Chantry Chapel. At the far end of the green is a **cannon** captured from the Russians during the Crimean War and given to the city by Queen Victoria in 1860.

Church and Commonwealth

Close to the cannon is **St Mary's Church**, a fine parish church dating from the time of Bishop Eustace in the 13th century and displaying a variety of architectural styles: the columns in the nave are Norman, the north door is Early English, and the spire and tower are Decorated. A curiosity is the tablet set in the southwest wall commemorating those executed for taking part in the Littleport and Ely famine riots of 1816. The church is usually open, although many of its more valuable artefacts are removed for safety during the week – a sad comment on modern society. A nursery school is tucked away at the rear.

Carry on to **Oliver Cromwell's House**, a beautifully restored half-timbered building some 750 years old. Cromwell lived here for eleven years, and two of his daughters were born here. The house was once the vicarage for St Mary's, and has also been a public house; it is now owned by the District Council and is used as a Tourist Information Centre. An audiovisual presentation describes many aspects of Cromwell's life.

Cross the road into St Mary's Street, noting the Old Fire Engine House, now a restaurant. Walking along the street you'll find on your left **Bedford House**, which was the headquarters of the corporation responsible for much of the drainage of the Fens. Note the coat-of-arms over the door – the Latin motto loosely translates as 'dryness pleases'!

Just past the end of the street is the 14th-century **Lamb Hotel**; many of the pilgrims to St Etheldreda's shrine would have been clients.

Cross into the High Street, which formed the northern boundary of the college. Close to the sacrist's gate is the **Ely Museum**, opened in 1974. Its present displays concern the archaeology and social history of the area, including the drainage of the Fens.

Continue along the High Street until you reach Market Square. Now you're in the main shopping area of Ely. Market day is Thursday and the square is the venue for the May Fair and for the Etheldreda Fair, held in October.

The Waterside and Riverside Areas

Continue past Market Square down Fore Hill and into **Waterside**. This area, once semi-derelict, has in recent years undergone some gentrification, a number of buildings having been restored with the help of the Ely Preservation Trust.

Keep going until you reach the river. The **Riverside** area, formerly known as Broad Hithe, is where goods were unloaded in the days when the Ouse formed the region's main transport artery. Many of the old warehouses remain, although their usage has changed; a particularly good example is the three-storey antique centre. The attractive Riverside Walk has been known in part as the Quai d'Orsay since 1981, when Ely was twinned with the French town of this name, just outside Paris.

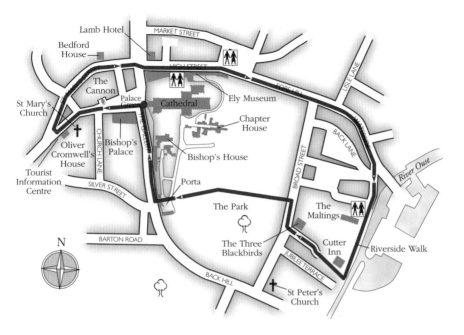

Among the historic buildings in this area are the **Cutter Inn** – named after not a boat but the men who 'cut' the arm of the River Ouse nearer the city – and the **Maltings**, formerly Harlock's Brewery and now sympathetically converted into a conference centre.

The recreational aspects of the area are clear to see. There is a flourishing pleasure-boat hire yard on the town side of the river, while the marina at Babylon, on the far side of the Ouse, has space for two hundred craft. Two boathouses provide rowing facilities for the King's School and Cambridge University.

By Way of The Three Blackbirds

To leave the Riverside area, take the footpath at the side of the Cutter Inn. This leads into a side street at whose end is **The Three Blackbirds**. Dating from the end of the 13th century, this house is probably the oldest secular building in Ely. Once belonging to a wealthy merchant, it was a public house in the 19th century. It has more recently been restored by the Ely Preservation Trust and converted into three dwellings.

Turn right into Broad Street. About fifty yards (50m) along, turn left through an ornamental gateway into the **Park**, which occupies the area between the college and Broad Street. The Park is owned by the dean and chapter of the cathedral, and originally contained the prior's vineyard and a number of fishponds, filled in at the middle of the last century.

Take the path up the hill, noting the old castle mound to the left; there are fine views of the cathedral to the right. Eventually you come once more to the Porta. Turn right here into The Gallery and return to the west end of the cathedral.

NORWICH

Access: The nearest motorway (M11) is over fifty miles away (30km), but the city is the focal point of a network of A-class roads and trunk roads, linking it with all the major towns of East Anglia; allow at least 2½ hours from London, a little longer from the Midlands. National Express: five coaches a day from London Victoria to Norwich; one coach a day from Birmingham. Local bus services are largely run by the Eastern Counties Company. InterCity trains run from Liverpool Street to Norwich's Thorpe Station, a ten-minute walk from the cathedral and city centre. Norwich Airport, on the city's northern outskirts, has flights to other English cities, scheduled continental passenger services and tourist charter flights.

The ancient core of the city of Norwich is located on a double bend of the River Wensum a little to the north of its confluence with the River Yare. Early settlement concentrated around the lowest fording point of the river, where there were nearby gravel terraces. These terraces have yielded flint axeheads which have been dated to the Palaeolithic, but it was not until Neolithic times that man began to seriously influence the form of the landscape as agriculture came to occupy the drier terraces.

The Romans preferred to develop their headquarters at nearby Caistor (Venta Icenorum). Their presence improved communications in the area, which helped Norwich grow as a route centre.

Saxons and Angles, originally arriving as raiders, now occupied the area and added their typical placenames to the area. A group of Middle Saxon villages near the Wensum coalesced to form a market town which took its name from one of them, Northwic. During this period numerous churches were built, with typical Saxon round flint towers. By late Saxon times development was still largely north of the river, centring on what is now Magdalen Street. The first defences – simple earth walls and ditches – were built, mainly as a protection from raiding Danes.

Huge changes came soon after the Norman invasion in 1066. William the Conqueror quickly put his stamp on the city and by 1075 the castle had been built. Of motte and bailey design, it stood on an artificial hill, replacing over ninety late-Saxon houses. The original building was of timber, but in 1120 work began on a new stone keep some 66ft (20m) high and faced with Caen stone.

The Normans also began the construction of a cathedral, following the transference of the see of East Anglia from Thetford to Norwich in 1094. At the same time work began on a Benedictine monastery for some sixty monks. The building materials used for the cathedral were local flints and white Caen limestone, shipped across the Channel, up the River Wensum and finally by a small canal from the river at Pulls Ferry to the site. Limestone also came from Barnack in Northamptonshire.

The cathedral was consecrated in 1278. The original roof and the tower, both wooden, were destroyed by a fire in 1463. Later in the 15th century a vaulted stone roof and a stone spire were added, along with the presbytery, which had exterior flying buttresses to support it. By now Norwich had become a cosmopolitan settlement, the Anglo-Danish population augmented by French, Bretons, Flemings and Jews.

Already by medieval times Norwich had become one of the wealthiest cities in the country. The population, which may have numbered 10,000, sustained over one hundred trades, of which weaving was the most important. The city was not without its problems, however. There was an intolerable gap between rich and poor, and conditions for the latter were generally dirty and unhealthy; the Black Death probably claimed as many as two-thirds of the population. Fires were a constant problem – eventually it was decreed that thatch roofs were to be replaced by tiles.

The gap between the urban poor and the wealthy families continued into the Tudor age, but overall prosperity was increased by the influx of refugees from the Netherlands. These so-called 'strangers' were mainly weavers but brought many other trades to the city.

There were no great upheavals when the monastery was dissolved in 1538 – the prior became the first dean and former monks became canons – except that the Lady Chapel was demolished. During the Civil War Norwich remained largely loyal to parliament. Although the city was outside the main area of fighting the war was a strain on resources and disrupted the woollen and other trades. The cathedral did not escape unscathed: rioting Puritans destroyed some of the artefacts.

Georgian times saw the woollen industry lose much of its influence to the textile towns of the North, but other industries continued to prosper. Georgian development remained within the city walls, but this changed in the 19th century, which saw Norwich's most spectacular expansion. By 1871 the population reached 80,000, swollen by farm labourers looking for work in the city and the development of the factory economy. The growth industries were now leather, brewing, soap-making, papermaking and a host of agriculture-related trades. The coming of the railways provided a great stimulus to economic development, while at the same time the lack of coal in the area prevented the ugly growth typical of the industrial cities of northern England.

The 20th century was marked by the coming of the tram car in the city centre. The suburbs had by now moved outside the walls. While World War I did not physically affect Norwich, one in nine of its servicemen were killed; most famously, the heroine Edith Cavell (1865–1915), a nurse from Norwich, was executed by the Germans for helping Allied prisoners escape. (A mountain in Alberta has been named after her by a grateful Canada.) During World War II the city experienced over forty air raids: 340 people were killed, 30,000 houses damaged and seven of the city's medieval churches destroyed. The cathedral was hit by a number of incendiary bombs.

The 1950s and 1960s saw major redevelopment, and unfortunately many of Norwich's historic buildings were demolished. By the 1970s sense prevailed, and the city's heritage became paramount. City authorities now work closely with charitable trusts, English Heritage and local groups such as the Norwich Society to ensure historic buildings are preserved.

Major recent changes have included the founding of the University of East Anglia, with its prestigious Sainsbury Centre for the Visual Arts, the opening of the Norwich regional airport at Horsham St Faiths, and the building of a new southern bypass. The city continues to develop as a regional centre for shopping, administration, sport, television and tourism.

The main activity at the cathedral has been a rolling restoration programme, while an important postwar addition has been the construction of the Visitor Centre, occupying the ancient monastic guest quarters over the cloisters.

TOUR OF THE CATHEDRAL
Start and finish: The west end.

The large Perpendicular window of the **west end (1)** has Victorian glass and is flanked by vertically grooved pillars, matching those on the tower – which, completed in 1145, is the tallest Romanesque tower in England. The Alnwick Porch, on the West Front, has recently been enhanced with two new statues, one of St Benedict and one of Julian of Norwich. The door beneath the window is usually closed, so enter through the Norman arch on the west end's north side.

Go into the **nave (2)**, completed *c*1120. The arcade and the triforium above it

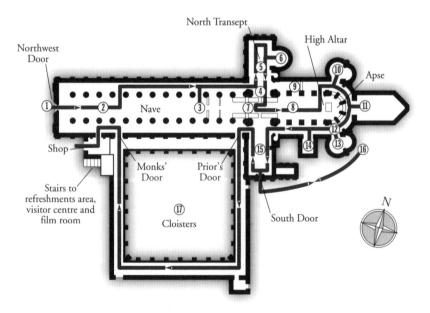

Key		
	6. St Andrew's Chapel	12. Stone Effigy
	7. Choir	13. St Luke's Chapel
1. West End	8. Presbytery	14. Bauchon Chapel of Our Lady
2. Nave	9. Reliquary Arch	of Pity
3. Pulpitum	and Treasury	15. South Transept
4. Crossing	10. Jesus Chapel	16. Grave of Nurse Edith Cavell
5. North Transept	11. St Saviour's Chapel	17. Cloisters

consist of rounded Norman arches. Look for two pillars with a spiral design; these are thought to have been prefabricated at the quarries at Caen. The clerestory was added in Perpendicular style in the late 15th century, in the time of Bishop Lyhart, and his rebus may be seen at the head of some of the pillars below it. At the same time a stone vaulted roof replaced the earlier wooden one, destroyed by fire. The vaulting is in tierceron, onto which *lierne* ribs have been added for purely decorative effect. The ribs on each side of the ridge produce alternating star and lozenge-shaped patterns – an effect continued throughout the choir, presbytery and transepts. There are around 1,100 bosses on the rib joints – over 300 have been recoloured and gilded in recent years. (Binoculars are useful for inspecting the bosses.) Despite the disparity in age between the Perpendicular clerestory and roof and the Norman arcade and triforium, the whole effect is oddly satisfying.

Flemish lectern

Move along to the other end of the nave, to the stone screen or **pulpitum (3)**, which with the ritual choir forms the last three bays of the nave; it divided the people's nave from the monks presbytery. Step to the side of the pulpitum and walk into the **crossing (4)**, where a small altar has been placed for services. The main item of interest here is the lectern, which is Flemish and dates from 1380. Made of brass, it depicts a pelican feeding her young from her own breast.

From here, walk into the **north transept (5)**. Note the private door for the bishop to reach his palace. On the east side of the transept is **St Andrew's Chapel (6)**, the first of a number of chapels based on a double circle plan. This chapel is reserved for private prayer and meditation. The window is 13th-century, with later glass. The modern statue of the Madonna is by John Skelton, who was brought up in the city of Norwich.

The Choir and Presbytery

Now head eastwards and turn into the **choir (7)**. It has stalls originally designed for the Benedictine monks, but recently renovated. Some stalls are kept open for visitors, so you can look at the misericords. One depicts an owl being mobbed by birds and a second shows a schoolmaster beating a small boy while others look on apprehensively.

Move further east into the **presbytery (8)**, which continues the architectural scheme of the nave. The Norman arcade and triforium and the Gothic clerestory and vaulting give a height to the east end which is unusual in Britain - the comparison with some continental cathedrals is inevitable. The presbytery contains the bishop's throne which, unusually for an English cathedral, is placed behind the high altar. The main part of the throne is a simple medieval wooden chair. It rests on two ancient stones, all that is left of a stone seat brought to Norwich when the see was moved from Thetford in the 11th century.

Return to the north presbytery aisle, turn right and approach the **reliquary arch and treasury (9)**. This was designed to display the cathedral treasures to pilgrims passing below as they went in procession round the ambulatory. Today the treasury contains not only cathedral artefacts but silverware lent by other churches in Norwich and the county. To reach it, pay a small fee (the proceeds go to charity) and climb the spiral staircase. Apart from its interesting silverware, the treasury is the best place in the cathedral to view the medieval wall paintings.

Returning to ground level, spend some time looking at the Erpingham Window, which contains a good collection of medieval glass from a variety of local sources, reassembled and leaded by the company of Kings of Norwich in 1963.

Continue around the ambulatory. On your left you will see the **Jesus Chapel (10)**, dating from 1096 and cleverly restored. It has the remains of wall painting which probably covered most of the building. The prize feature of the chapel is the picture *The Adoration of the Magi*, painted in 1480 by Martin Schwarz. We are now in the apsidal east end of the cathedral, which was the site of the Lady Chapel, demolished during the Reformation. It was replaced in 1930 by **St Saviour's Chapel (11)**, which is the regimental chapel of the Royal Norfolk Regiment, the honours of which drape the walls. The painted panels behind the altar come from the redundant Norwich church of St Michael-at-Plea.

Further along the ambulatory you'll notice in the wall a **stone effigy (12)** of what appears to be an early bishop giving his blessing with one hand and holding his pastoral staff in the other. The effigy was once thought to be of the cathedral's first bishop, Herbert de Lesonga, who died in 1119. Modern dating techniques, however, have cast doubt on this, as it is believed to have been made around 1100. It probably represents St Felix, who brought Christianity to East Anglia.

The Despenser Reredos

We now come to **St Luke's Chapel (13)**, formerly dedicated to St John the Baptist and nowadays used as a parish church for the parishioners of St Mary in the Marsh. This chapel contains the Despenser reredos, said to have been donated by Bishop Despenser in 1381 and showing five scenes on painted glass panels. Claimed to be the greatest artistic treasure in East Anglia, this survived the Reformation only through being turned upside-down and used as a table top! The chapel is also the home of a rather battered medieval font, showing the Seven Sacraments.

Next you come to the **Bauchon Chapel of Our Lady of Pity (14)**, named after the monk who built it in the 14th century. It has also acted as a consistory court. Don't miss its bosses; these tell the tale of an empress saved by the Virgin after being falsely accused by her brother, who had tried to seduce her.

The Grave of a Heroine

Leave the ambulatory at the chapter room (not open to the public) and go into the **south transept (15)**. The south wall of this was entirely refaced at one stage to remove the traces of a 14th-century prison that used to be inside the building. Notice the Taylor Ramsden Window, which has 17th-century French glass in

16th-century Flemish style.

To visit the **Grave of Nurse Edith Cavell (16)**, leave the south transept by the south door and turn left towards the east end of the cathedral. The simple grave is located between St Luke's and St Saviour's chapels on what was once the ancient burial ground of the monks. Prayers are said at her grave each Remembrance Day.

Return through the south transept and turn left through the **prior's door** to enter the cloisters. This door, which dates from c1310, is one of the most charming aspects of the cathedral and it is fitting that it leads to the largest cloisters of any English cathedral. Above its arch are seven figures in a radial arrangement. Behind them are gables, alternate ones in ogee form and liberally decorated with crockets.

The present **cloisters (17)** were built after the original Norman ones had been destroyed in a riot between the Norwich citizens and the cathedral staff in 1272. They are beautifully vaulted and have a fine collection of bosses, which have been skilfully recoloured and gilded. These bosses give a sociological account of medieval life and merit close attention. You may be glad of the movable mirror-topped tea trolley placed here to assist viewing. Look also for the monks' lavatorium (washing place) in the southwest corner and the various coats-of-arms which are scattered around.

Leave the cloisters by the monks' door in the northwest corner and return to the south aisle of the nave. Here you can visit the **Cathedral Shop (18)**, which sells a variety of books, cards and other gifts. The tour concludes at the west end door.

WALKING TOUR FROM NORWICH CATHEDRAL

The amount of historic interest within the old city walls of Norwich is immense, and several walks of interest could be chosen. The figure-of-eight walk detailed below aims to give a general impression of the city's heritage. It includes a riverside walk and a look at a few of the city's medieval churches, some excellent museums and some specialist shopping areas.

Start and finish: The Cathedral Close at the west end of the cathedral.
Length: 2½ miles (4km).
Time: 2 hours; allow longer if you want to visit the museums.
Refreshments: The cathedral refectory is recommended for light snacks and coffee. Traditional pubs along the route offer bar meals, notably the Adam and Eve (Bishopsgate), the Red Lion (Bishop Bridge), the Louis Marchesi (Tombland), named after the man who founded the Round Table movement, the Wig and Pen St Martin (Palace Plain) and the Maid's Head Hotel (Tombland).

Norwich's **Cathedral Close** claims to be the largest of any English cathedral. It consists of an area of grass and trees, with statues of both the Duke of Wellington (1760–1842) and Lord Nelson (1758–1805). It is surrounded by buildings in a variety of architectural styles, including the Carnary Chapel (1316) and the Bishop's Palace to the north of the cathedral.

There are three gates to the Close, two by land and one by water. The oldest is St Ethelbert's Gate, to your south, built by the citizens of Norwich as a penance following the riots of 1272. The Erpingham Gate, to your north, was built in 1420 by Sir Thomas Erpingham who fought in the Battle of Agincourt (1415). A statue of him is in a small niche above the arch of the gateway.

If you're short of time, you can omit visiting sites 1–8 and start your walk from the Erpingham Gate (see page 259).

An Executed Rebel

Leave the Upper Close by St Ethelbert's Gate and take the roadway through the Lower Close, where there are some gems of domestic architecture. Note on the left the line of stables marking the course of the canal built to bring Caen stone to the cathedral site and eventually filled in during the 18th century. Eventually you come to **Pull's Ferry**, named after the last ferryman to ply his trade in this area. The present watergate dates from the 15th century, and the ferry house itself is probably 16th-century.

Take the Riverside Walk westwards, to your left. After a couple of hundred yards (180m) you reach **Bishop Bridge**. This three-arched stone bridge dates from *c*1340 and is the only surviving medieval bridge in Norwich.

If you feel energetic you can cross Bishop Bridge and take the road up the hill past the gasometers to **Kett's Heights**. There you'll be rewarded by a superb view across the city to the cathedral, castle and beyond. The hill is named after Robert Kett, a farmer from Wymondham, who in 1549 used the area as headquarters for his army of some 20,000 men protesting about the enclosure of common land. They were eventually defeated and Kett was hung in chains from the walls of Norwich Castle until he died.

Back on the Riverside Walk, pass behind the Red Lion pub and, after another

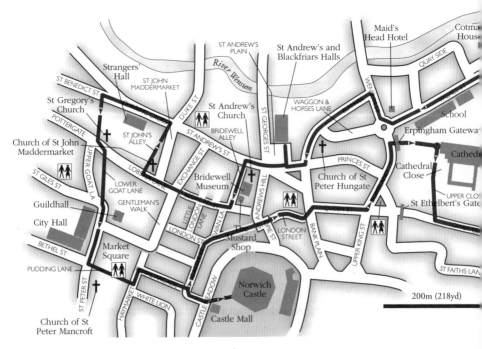

two hundred yards (180m), you'll reach **Cow Tower**, at a bend in the river. For many years cows sheltered in this somewhat decrepit building, which dates from *c*1378 and was at one time part of the city's defences. It is built of flint and brick; if you can get inside you will see evidence of original roof vaulting. From here there is a good view of the cathedral tower and spire; the cathedral's original wooden spire fell in 1362 and was eventually replaced by a stone spire which, at 315ft, is the second tallest in Britain (after that at Salisbury).

Continue along the Riverside Walk for a further three hundred yards (270m) until you arrive at a new flint wall. Fork left here and pass through the wall to find in front of you the **Adam and Eve pub**. Claimed as the oldest pub in Norwich, the Adam and Eve was named after a wherry (one of the famous Norfolk sailing barges which plied the Wensum) and was a favourite wherrymen's inn. The brick-and-timber building dates from 1249 and has classic Dutch ends. There was a brewhouse on the site for over 700 years.

A City of Many Churches

Opposite the Adam and Eve are the new law courts. Further on, on the right, is the **Church of St Martin at Palace**, in whose graveyard many of Kett's men are buried.

There were once fifty-seven churches within the city walls of Norwich. Thirty-one remain, and of these only ten are used for worship. Sixteen of the redundant churches are cared for by the Norwich Historic Churches Trust, which restores and preserves these buildings – St Martin at Palace among them. The church – fittingly, because of its proximity to the probation office and law courts – is used today as a probation day centre.

In the small square opposite the church is **Cotman House**, once the home of John Sell Cotman (1782–1842), best-known of the 19th-century Norwich School of landscape artists.

Proceed now along **Palace Street**. To the left, set back from the road, is the **Bishop's Palace Gate**, thought to have been built *c*1436. This fine flint and stone gateway is unusual in having twoarches, a large one for carriages and a smaller one for pedestrians. On the right is the Maid's Head Hotel, a 12th-century coaching inn.

You are now nearly back at the Erpingham Gate. (If you decided to miss the first part of the walk, this is where you join it.)

Turn right at the mini-roundabout and proceed into Wensum Street. After fifty yards (50m) turn left into **Elm Hill**, one of the best-known historic streets in Britain.

At the corner of Elm Hill and Wensum Street is another redundant church, the **Church of St Simon and St Jude**, one of the oldest in the city. It contains a number of monuments to the Pettus family, who provided numerous mayors of Norwich. It was saved from demolition by the Norwich Society in the 1920s and is now used as an outdoor centre by the Scouts and Guides.

Opposite the church is Roaches Court. At the end of its alleyway is a small quay from where boats leave for river cruises and trips to the Broads.

Continue up the cobbled surface of Elm Hill, admiring the timber-framed houses, many with jettied walls and pastel washes over the plaster. Most of the buildings date from the 16th and 17th centuries, the earlier houses having been destroyed by fire. One building which survived was **Pettus House**, home of Sir John Pettus, who was knighted by Elizabeth I and mayor of the city in 1608. The upper storey windows have original leaded diamond glass. It is interesting to remember that in the 1920s Elm Hill was so run-down that it was on the point of demolition, being saved only by the efforts of the Norwich Society and the casting vote of the mayor.

A Church Museum and the Black Friars

At the top of Elm Hill is a small cobbled square. Fork left here and continue to Princes Street. Note on the corner the Briton's Arms coffee shop, which dates from the 14th century and was once a béguinage – a centre for a religious sisterhood whose members were not bound by strict vows and could return to the world if they chose.

Opposite the coffee shop is another redundant church, the **Church of St Peter Hungate**. Its Perpendicular windows reach almost to the roof, and there is a quaint stair-turret between the tower and the porch. Inside is a sensational hammerbeam roof with gilded ends. St Peter Hungate is now a museum and brass-rubbing centre.

Coming out of the museum, turn right along

Elm Hill

Princes Street until on your right you come to an open space, St Andrews Plain. The feature here is the combined building of **St Andrew's and Blackfriars Halls**, originally the choir and nave of the Convent Church of the Blackfriars. The Dominicans – the Black Friars – arrived in Norwich in 1226 and built their first church here between 1326 and 1413.

Looking at the building (largely constructed by Sir Thomas Erpingham) from here on Princes Street, St Andrew's Hall is the one on the left. It has an arcade of six windows in Decorated style with a handsome clerestory above; between each pair of windows is the Erpingham arms. The superb hammerbeam roof was a gift from the Paston family, whose coat-of-arms is seen in the 15th-century doorway.

The former choir, Blackfriars Hall, was once the chapel of the local guilds and later became the church of the Dutch population. Today both halls are used as meeting places for the citizens of Norwich and provide facilities for exhibitions, banqueting, conferences, concerts and speech days.

To the north of the halls are the remains of the friars' cloisters, dormitory, refectory and crypt. The first three are now used by Norwich School of Art, while the crypt has become a popular coffee bar.

Church and State
Cross St Andrews Street, noting on the left **St Andrew's Church**. Still open for worship, St Andrew's is the second largest church in Norwich (after St Peter Mancroft – see below). The windows are in Perpendicular style and are topped by a clerestory containing close-set windows. The sturdy flint tower has diagonal buttresses. The small graveyard obviously suffered when St Andrews Street was widened for trams at the start of the 20th century. The church is usually open and well worth a visit. Although the fittings are mainly Victorian, it has some of the most interesting church monuments in the city, particularly those to the Suckling family.

Step now into **Bridewell Alley**, a narrow pedestrian thoroughfare full of specialist shops. On the left is the **Bridewell Museum**, which is larger than it appears as its buildings occupy all four sides of a courtyard. Built *c*1325, it was originally a merchant's house. It was lived in by William Appleyard, first Mayor of Norwich. In 1583, it was bought by the city and turned into a 'bridewell' – a prison for petty criminals. In the 1800s it was successively a tobacco factory, a leather warehouse and a shoe factory. Today, it houses an exhibition of the typical industries of Norwich.

At the end of Bridewell Alley, turn right into Bedford Street, and cross Exchange Street into the short Lobster Lane. On the right is the **Church of St John Maddermarket**, once hemmed in – as its name suggests – by the houses of dyers.

This is one of the most fascinating churches in Norwich. The windows at both arcade and clerestory level are clearly Perpendicular. But it is the ground plan that causes controversy: this is a short, squat church, and a Decorated window at the east end has led to the theory that a now demolished chancel might once have been there.

As it is, inside the church one feels hemmed in by the surrounding screens and gallery constructed of dark wood. Look for the small, but delightful, chapel on the north side and for the monuments to former mayors of Norwich in the south aisle. No longer open for worship, St John Maddermarket is preserved with all its furnishings intact by the Redundant Churches Fund.

Leave the church and turn down St John's Alley, under the tower. The Maddermarket Theatre, on the left, operates in a former Roman Catholic chapel. At the end turn left into Charing Cross. Twenty yards (20m) along on the left is **Strangers' Hall**. Originally a merchant's house from *c*1320, with 15th-, 16th-, 17th- and 18th-century additions, its name almost certainly comes from the Dutch refugees who lived here during the 1500s. The home of at least three mayors and sheriffs of the city, it now functions as a museum of Norwich domestic life. It has a paved courtyard and twenty rooms, many panelled, and furnished in the styles of different historical periods. There are displays of shop signs, toys, costumes, domestic utensils and vehicles (including the lord mayor's coach, still used on civic occasions).

Leaving Strangers' Hall, turn left along Charing Cross, past the Hog pub, to **St Gregory's Church**, described as a humbler version of St Andrew's. Take the alley beside the church and walk into the small grass square to the south which gives you the best view of the church's architecture. Note the curious two-storied porch with a clock and pinnacled niche over the door. Behind this is a sturdy flint tower, while stretching away to the right are an arcade and clerestory in Decorated style.

Inside, the best features are the impressive Perpendicular window at the east end and the octagonal font with its panelled stem. Of the many monuments, the finest, dating from 1659, is that to Francis Bacon (1561–1626) in the southeast corner of the nave. St Gregory's is now the Pottergate centre for music and the arts.

Market Square, and a Church That's Not a Cathedral

Cross the small green and go over Pottergate. This area, as the name suggests, was the centre of the pottery industry in Saxo-Norman times.

Move now into Lower Goat Lane, at the end of which is Market Square. Immediately to the left is the **Guildhall**, an impressive building of knapped flint and stone built 1414–35 and claimed as the largest medieval city hall outside London. It is particularly attractive from the lower east side, where the area beneath the clock has a chequerboard pattern of lozenges and triangles made of contrasting freestone and flint. Apart from its civic functions, which were carried out here for over 500 years, the Guildhall contained a prison in its undercroft and also functioned as a courthouse. Today it houses the city regalia and is the home of the Tourist Information Centre.

Proceed along the west side of Market Square. From the steps of the **City Hall** you get a fine view across the market, located here since early medieval times, and over to the castle. The city hall was built 1932–8 of brick and has a classical entrance with six tall pillars. Its clock tower is a notable local landmark.

On the south side of Market Square is the **Church of St Peter Mancroft**, the largest church in Norwich; not surprisingly, many people mistake it for the cathedral. St Peter's was built between 1430–55 and is almost entirely in the Perpendicular style. Externally, the massive tower dominates, but the arcade and the close windows of the clerestory are perfectly proportioned. One's first impression inside is of the light, streaming in through the clerestory. The tall and remarkably slender pillars support a heavy hammerbeam roof.

There is much to see at St Peter's, but the finest feature is the superb east window. The original glass was blown out by an explosion during the Civil War, but enough was collected to fill the 42 panels. The St Nicholas Chapel in the north transept houses the Mancroft Heritage Exhibition. Many of the furnishings are Victorian, but do note the brass commemorating Sir Peter Rede, dating from 1568.

Turn down from St Peter Mancroft into Market Square, past the attractive old Sir Garnet Wolseley pub, which dates back to the 14th century although the name, referring to the military leader Viscount Garnet Wolseley (1833–1913), is obviously much more recent. The south side of the market area, Gentlemen's Walk, was in the 19th century a fashionable area for promenading.

Turn into **Royal Arcade**, a delightful Victorian shopping thoroughfare designed by the Norwich architect George Skipper in 1899. With its glass roof, hanging lanterns, soft green tiles and beautiful friezes, Royal Arcade is a delight. Don't miss the Mustard Shop. Apart from selling a wide range of mustard, this contains memorabilia tracing the history of Colman's Mustard.

At its end is a lane called Back of the Inns. Here you have another choice of routes. To the right is the glass-topped **Castle Mall**, a pedestrian shopping precinct controversially built into the side of the Castle mound. Alternatively, if time is short, you can turn left and proceed back towards the cathedral.

Norwich Castle and Tombland

Most people, however, prefer to cross Castle Meadow and climb the steps to **Norwich Castle**.

The Normans built the original wooden castle on an artificial mound at the time of the conquest in 1067. This was replaced by the present stone structure probably in 1120–30. It was constructed of flint and mortar-faced stone – the same Caen stone shipped by sea from Normandy that was used in the cathedral. Norwich Castle was a 'Royal Castle' – it was held for the king by the Constable in Residence. This situation was maintained until 1806, when George III gave the castle to the county of Norfolk. It housed a garrison and its keep was the city's gaol.

In 1887 the castle was converted into a museum, opened in 1894 by the Duke and Duchess of York. There are sections on local history, geology and archaeology, plus an gallery specializing in works by the Norwich School of painters, particularly John Crome (1768–1821) and John Sell Cotman (1782–1842). Other local painters represented are Sir Alfred Munnings (1878–1959) and Edward Seago (1910–1974).

Retrace your steps from the castle back towards Royal Arcade, turn right into Castle Arcade, and walk along this until you reach London Street, one of the city's main pedestrianized shopping streets. At its top turn left at Bank Plain and then immediately right into Queen Street, at the bottom of which is the area known as **Tombland**; the name means 'empty land'. This was the site of the old Saxon marketplace. After the Norman cathedral was built the market continued, and there were numerous disputes between the cathedral and the citizens about who should claim the market tolls. This led to the infamous riot of 1272.

Tombland today is lively and full of interest. Look for Augustine Steward's House, occupied by Kett's rebels in 1549, and the 17th-century house with the figures of Samson and Hercules guarding the door. Pubs, restaurants and even nightclubs abound in this active part of the city.

Use either Erpingham Gate or St Ethelbert's Gate to return to the Cathedral Close, where the walk ends.

PETERBOROUGH

Access: The A1 runs just to the west of the city and the A47 passes through it. National Express coaches run to Peterborough twice daily from Victoria. InterCity trains operate hourly from Kings Cross.

The Bronze Age site at nearby Flag Fen shows that people have lived in the Peterborough area for at least 3000 years, and the Romans had a settlement just upstream from the present city centre. According to the Venerable Bede (*c*673–735), a Mercian nobleman, Saxulf, founded the first abbey at the site in 655. Modern scholars believe it was Peada, the Christian King of Southern Mercia (reigned 655–6), who founded the abbey, probably in 654, with Saxulf as first abbot. The Abbey of Medeshamstede, as it was then called, was consecrated by Deusdedit, then Archbishop of Canterbury. Unfortunately, this first abbey was destroyed and its monks slaughtered by marauding Danes in 870.

A second abbey was built on the site in the 10th century by King Edgar (or Eadgar), and this was later fortified by earthworks. This abbey church too was fated, burning down in 1116. Traces of the Saxon buildings have been discovered under the present south transept. The only Saxon remains above ground are the Hedda Stone in the New Building and another stone set into the wall of the south transept.

The first Norman abbot, Turoldus, imposed by William the Conqueror, had been able to claim his abbey only after a pitched battle with Hereward the Wake. The abbot at the time of the fire was John de Sais, and it was he who in 1118 began the construction of the present building, beginning with the apse at the east end. It was to be a long time before the work was finished.

The stone came from quarries owned by the abbey at Barnack, to the northwest of Peterborough, being brought by barge here to the site along the River Nene. (This cream-coloured limestone, which had also supplied the material for the first two abbeys, can be seen in other East Anglian cathedrals.) By 1140, all the building to the east of the crossing had been completed. The transepts and the crossing were done by 1160. The nave, the work of Abbot Benedict (in office 1177–93), was, thankfully, executed in the earlier Norman/Romanesque style, so that much of the interior has architectural purity. However, the western transepts, constructed *c*1200, have a small element of Early English design; this is the only part of the building with high stone vaulting (the aisles have simple low vaulting – some of the earliest in England). The high roof of the nave (built *c*1220) and the presbytery (15th century) are both of wood.

Two western towers were intended. The north one was completed *c*1270, but the south tower was never built. Instead, a unique west front was built in Early English style dominated by three huge arches. The central, narrower arch after a while began to tilt outwards, and so *c*1380 a porch was added (in the Perpendicular style) to prevent further movement. Also in the 14th century a series of small spires was added.

The completed building (minus the porch) was consecrated by Robert Grosseteste (*c*1175–1253), Bishop of Lincoln, in 1238. Further 13th-century developments included the addition of tracery in the Norman windows of the nave and the construction of a Lady Chapel to the east of the north transept.

The final major addition to the cathedral was the New Building, completed in 1508, to the east of the apse. It contains some delicate fan vaulting and is thought to be the work of John Wastell, who also designed King's College Chapel at Cambridge. The abbot at the time was Robert Kirkton and his rebus, consisting of the initials 'AR' followed by a kirk and a tun, may be seen in a number of places.

At the time of the Dissolution, Peterborough was fortunate in having John Chambers as its abbot. Anticipating the Dissolution, he spent a considerable amount of time with Henry VIII's commissioners to ensure that, when the abbey was dissolved in 1539, it became reestablished as a cathedral. When this came about, three years later, he was made the first bishop. His diocese was taken largely from that of Lincoln and included the soke (jurisdictional area) of Peterborough, Northamptonshire and Rutland. Henry's benevolence may have been prompted by the fact that his first wife, Catherine of Aragon, was buried in the cathedral. Fifty years later another queen, Mary, Queen of Scots, was buried at Peterborough; later her son, James VI & I, had her body removed to Westminster Abbey.

During the Civil War a detachment of Cromwell's soldiers caused great damage to the cathedral in 1643, destroying the stained glass, statues, choir stalls and high altar – the cloisters and Lady Chapel were so badly ruined they were later demolished. As a result the nave, lacking in stained glass and monuments, has a certain pristine quality today which emphasizes the purity of the Romanesque architecture.

During the 18th century the cathedral slipped into a certain amount of decay, so it was left to the Victorians to mount a comprehensive renovation programme. This included the provision of replacement stained glass, the best of which can be seen in the south transept. Much of the renovation work was completed by J.L. Pearson. One problem he had to deal with was the large crack that appeared in the central tower in 1883. His solution was to dismantle the tower completely and rebuild it using the same stones. He planned also to rebuild the east and west crossing arches in their original Romanesque style, but this proposal was unfortunately rejected. Pearson's other work included the Cosmati floor of the presbytery and the ciborium over the high altar; he designed the choir stalls, the *cathedra* and the pulpit; he removed the stone screen east of the crossing, thus giving us an uninterrupted view along the length of the cathedral; and with G.F. Bodley, around the turn of the century, he partially restored the west front. The work was very sympathetically carried out, and the results are much less objectionable than at many of the other cathedrals the Victorians 'improved'.

The cathedral survived major damage during the two world wars. A notable and spectacular recent (1975) addition has been the hanging nave rood, done in aluminium and gilt. New figures, carved by Alan Durst, have been placed on the west front. In 1988 there was a major appeal to mark the building's 750th anniversary, while ongoing repair work continues with the help of the Friends of Peterborough Cathedral. The repair work was hampered in November 2001 when an arsonist caused several million pounds' damage to the cathedral.

The city of Peterborough's first great expansion came when the railways brought new industry in the 19th century, adding engineering, railway repairs and textiles to the traditional agricultural industries. The growth of local brickmaking also dates from these times, being a response to the demand for new houses for the factory workers.

The 20th century saw Peterborough's second great expansion, when in 1967 it was designated a New Town. The population grew from 80,000 in 1967 to 114,000 at the time of the 1981 census. As a New Town, Peterborough attracted workers from all over the country, so new estates and industrial parks quickly appeared. High-technology firms are rapidly replacing the old, heavier industries.

Peterborough has had a chequered administrative history. Originally it was the main centre of the soke of Peterborough under the jurisdiction of Northamptonshire. Later it was part of Huntingdonshire, which was itself swallowed up by Cambridgeshire, in which county Peterborough remains today. From Victorian times it has been a municipal borough. It is now a thriving city, pleasantly combining old and new, and an important regional shopping and entertainment centre, with a wide range of leisure activities. Its cathedral has become the focal point of a new tourist industry.

TOUR OF THE CATHEDRAL
Start and finish: The west front.

The **west front (1)** is best viewed from the Cathedral Green, although photographers may find they have difficulty in retreating far enough for a good shot.

The west end was originally planned to have two transepts and two towers, to complete the Romanesque style of the building. Two transepts and one tower were completed by about 1270, but then the initial idea was scrapped and a new design followed. The result, in the prevailing Gothic style, is one of the most dramatic examples of cathedral architecture in England (although not without its critics). The dominant features are the three huge, recessed arches, some 85ft (26m) in height; the central arch is narrower than the others. The arches are flanked by square towers and topped by triangular gables with attractive rosettes. Both the main arches and the blind arcading on the front of the towers are pointed in the Early English style. The numerous small spires were added in the 14th century.

Two features detract from the overall symmetry. First, the west tower, left over from the original design, peers unhappily over the front – even had the second tower been built the overall effect would have been far from pleasing. Second, the Perpendicular porch, added in 1380 to fill the base of the central arch (which was showing a tendency to lean outwards), though in itself not unattractive, looks out-of-place in the overall scheme.

Nevertheless, the west front is a magnificent sight. Although the architectural features dominate, look carefully at the 13th-century sculptures in the corners of the arches (binoculars may come in handy for this); those portrayed include Peter, Paul and Andrew, to whom the cathedral is dedicated, plus an assortment of Apostles and kings. Some of the figures are modern, done by Alan Durst – such as the one of Elizabeth II.

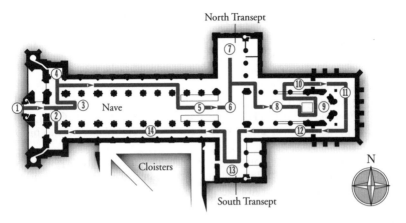

North Transept

Nave

Cloisters

South Transept

N

Key

1. West Front
2. West End
3. Nave
4. North Aisle

5. Choir
6. Crossing
7. North Transept
8. Sanctuary
9. Apse
10. Tomb of Catherine of Aragon

11. New Building
12. South Presbytery Aisle
13. South Transept
14. South Nave Aisle

Gravedigger by Royal Appointment

Enter through the porch – a plaque shows where the present queen has distributed Maundy Money. Once inside, look back at the **west end (2)** of the nave.

On either side of the door are portraits of Robert Scarlett, the Elizabethan gravedigger who during a long career buried both Mary, Queen of Scots and Catherine of Aragon, plus countless Peterborough denizens. The painting to the right of the door is poorly preserved, but the one on the left clearly shows a bearded man carrying a shovel with, in his other hand, a bunch of keys. A dog whip hangs from his belt – Scarlett was also the caretaker of St John's Parish Church in the town square. A simple stone on the floor indicates his grave. It is marked 'R.S.' and dated 1594.

Nave and Choir

Move on into the main body of the **nave (3)**, passing a desk where you can get a small guide to the cathedral and where you will certainly be encouraged to make a donation to the upkeep of the building.

The vista along the length of the cathedral from this point is impressive: the architecture is largely Romanesque from end to end and your view is uninterrupted by a screen. The lack of monuments and stained glass adds to the effect. Although the building of the cathedral was carried out by a series of abbots, the purity of the Romanesque was maintained and Barnack stone was used throughout the long period of building. The arcade, tribune and clerestory levels harmonize pleasingly. Some of the principal arches have billet moulding, while at the tribune level chevron patterns may be seen. Between each bay an engaged shaft stretches from floor to ceiling, which to a certain extent counterbalances the long, narrow nave.

The roof of the nave is wood, and was painted *c*1220. The design consists of a series of ornamental diamond or lozenge shapes containing pictures with topics such as the Lamb of God and the Apostles. There's a mirror so that you can look at the ceiling without getting a crick in your neck; there's also a slot machine you can stick a coin in to light the ceiling up so that you can see it better.

The hanging rood overhead is worth attention as well; it takes the form of a wooden cross, painted red, and a gilded aluminium figure of Christ. The motto is *Stat crux dum volvitur orbis* ('The Cross stands while the earth revolves'), reminding us of the permanence of the cathedral amidst the turbulence of the history that surrounds it.

Move back now to the northwest corner of the **north aisle (4)**, where you can look at a 19th-century lithograph of the painted nave ceiling. Nearby is the 13th-century **font**, made of Alwalton marble. It was retrieved from a canon's garden in Victorian times, from which period the supports date. Here you can also see one of many iron Gurney stoves, installed by the Victorians to keep the cathedral warm; originally these were coal-burning, but they have now been converted to gas.

Rejoining the north aisle, walk up the cathedral to the **choir (5)**. The stalls were designed by Pearson and carved in the 1890s by Thompsons of Peterborough. Note the 15th-century brass-eagle lectern, made in Tournai in Belgium and donated by Abbot William Ramsey (in office 1471–96). The double-branched candlestick it originally had was vandalized by Cromwell's soldiers.

Lantern, Lady Chapel and Sanctuary

Walk through the choir into the **crossing (6)** and look up into the lantern of the central tower. The first tower was built largely in the time of Abbot William de Waterville (in office 1155–75), but by the 14th century the rubble core of the piers had settled and it became dangerous. It was therefore demolished, being replaced by a shorter tower that used the original stones (the crossing arches were in Decorated style). The whole tower was again rebuilt by Pearson during the Victorian restorations.

From here go into the **north transept (7)**, which currently houses an exhibition, 'The Story of Peterborough Cathedral'. Both transepts show superb Romanesque work, with only some tracery added to the original Norman arches. The wooden ceilings are also partly original, and did not suffer from the Victorian renovations. The stained glass, however, is Victorian – and not particularly distinguished. Note the reassembled workings of the cathedral clocks, removed from the northwest bell tower in 1836.

On the east side of the north transept was an entrance to the Lady Chapel, which was demolished in the 17th century, the building materials being sold off to provide funds to repair the main building.

Behind a series of arches (corresponding with the chapels in the south transepts) is the new location of the treasury, formerly above the porch in the west front. A voluntary contribution at the entrance enables you to see a collection of ancient bibles, some of the original works of William Tyndale (*c*1494–1536), who translated the Bible into English, and the usual collections of silver and pewterware.

Leave the north transept for the **sanctuary (8)**, or presbytery, noting en route the effigy of Abbot Benedict (in office 1177–1193), done in Alwalton marble; it is one of a fine series of Benedictine effigies originally in the old chapter house. The sanctuary was completed in 1140 and has similar architectural features to the nave.

The wooden ceiling, however, is from the 15th century, and imitates a stone vault. Its hundred-plus bosses can be better seen by illuminating the ceiling – there's another slot machine by the southwest pillar of the tower.

At ground level the sanctuary is more modern. Pearson designed the complicated Cosmati floor, made of Italian marble, and built the ciborium, which covers the high altar – most unusual in an English cathedral. The pillars of the ciborium are of Italian marble, while the elaborate stonework in the upper part is in alabaster from Derbyshire. Pearson was also responsible for the *cathedra* here.

The Tomb of a Queen

At the far end of the sanctuary you come to the **apse (9)**, something of a rarity in English cathedrals though much more common on the European mainland. This was the first part of the cathedral to be built, being started by Abbot John de Sais in 1118. While the height of the apse is visually pleasing, the later insertion of Decorated windows is unfortunate.

A pair of 17th-century Flemish tapestries show Peter healing a lame beggar in the Temple and Peter being rescued from prison. The ceiling painting is by Sir George Gilbert Scott (1811–1878), and is based on a similar painting of medieval age which was destroyed by Cromwell's soldiers.

Retrace your steps a little way and then turn right to find yourself in the south presbytery aisle. Here you'll find the **Tomb of Catherine of Aragon (10)**. Catherine, the daughter of Isobel and Ferdinand of Spain, was the first wife of Henry VIII. After she'd been married to Henry for over twenty years without producing a son, she was expelled from court while Henry arranged a divorce of dubious legality. She spent her last days at Kimbolton, 20 miles (32km) south of Peterborough, where she died in 1536. Henry, by now married to Anne Boleyn, could not afford to have her buried at Westminster Abbey, so she was buried here. Her tomb is a simple stone backed by a fine piece of wrought-iron. She was a well loved queen, and flowers are still frequently left on her tomb.

There are two banners over the tomb: the royal coat-of-arms of 16th-century England and the royal arms of Spain with, at the lower edge, Catherine's personal emblem (also the emblem of Granada), a pomegranate.

The New Building

Continue along the south presbytery aisle until you reach the **New Building (11)** (also called the **Eastern Building**, the **Lady Chapel** and the **retrochoir**, which can lead to confusion). It was built in 1496–1508 during the time of Abbot Robert Kirkton, whose rebus, involving the letters 'AR', a kirk and a tun, can be seen under the windows. The architectural style used throughout is Perpendicular, and the crowning glory is the magnificent fan vaulting.

Although there is no documentation, the New Building is clearly the work of John Wastell. There are two interesting modern sculptures here. In the northeast corner is a statue of St Peter, carved in wood by Simon Latham, Artist in Residence in 1991. In the southwest corner is a sculpture of Our Lady of Lamentations, carved in Beer stone by Polly Verity in 1992.

Of much greater antiquity is the Hedda (or Monks') Stone, thought to be a Saxon shrine dating from *c*780. It has twelve carved figures, seemingly Christ, the Virgin Mary and ten Apostles. The regularly spaced shallow holes in it are something of a mystery.

Benedictine Tombs

Walk along the **south presbytery aisle (12)**, looking out for further Benedictine tombs. The first is the rather battered tomb of Abbot John Chambers, the last abbot (in office 1528–39) and first bishop (1541–56). Then follow the tombs of Alexander of Holderness, John de Sais and two unknowns.

The next feature of interest is the former burial place of Mary, Queen of Scots, directly opposite that of Catherine of Aragon. Mary's tragic and convoluted story is well known. After she was beheaded at Fotheringay, 10 miles (16km) west of Peterborough, on 8 February 1587, she was buried in Peterborough Cathedral. When Elizabeth I was succeeded in 1603 by James VI & I, Mary's son, he immediately had his mother's remains transferred to Westminster Abbey (see page 185).

Keep going until you can turn left into the **south transept (13)**, which dates from *c*1150, like the north transept, and has similar architectural features. On the west wall is a Saxon sculpture showing two figures, possibly a bishop and a king, under a palm tree. It was found during the Victorian restorations and is believed to date from *c*800.

The east side of the transept has three chapels. The northernmost, **St Oswald's Chapel**, is dedicated to St Oswald, King of Mercia 634–42. Known for his generosity to the poor, he was killed in the Battle of Oswestry, but his right arm was miraculously preserved. It was brought to the abbey in 1060 and was its principal relic until the Reformation, when it disappeared. A rarity in this chapel is its watch tower, whence a duty monk kept an eye on the relic.

Next is the **Chapel of St Benedict**, dedicated to the founder of the monastic order; it has some well preserved blind arcading on the south wall. Third is the **Chapel of St Kyneburga, St Kyneswitha and St Tibba**; these were the three sisters of Peada, King of Southern Mercia, who founded the first monastery *c*654. The chapel has recently been restored by the women of the diocese. The screen along the entrance of the three chapels shows some evidence of medieval decorative painting.

Leave the transept and step into the **south nave aisle (14)**. A small plaque on one of the pillars commemorates Nurse Edith Cavell (1865–1915), killed by Germans during World War I for helping French and British prisoners escape. Cavell, buried at Norwich Cathedral, was a pupil at Laurel Court School in the Peterborough Cathedral precincts. At the far end of the aisle is **St Sprite's Chapel**, restored thanks to money raised by former students of St Peter's, a teacher training college ¼ mile (400m) from the cathedral, in memory of a former principal. Note the regimental colours and the statue of the 12th-century Abbot Martin de Bec, in whose time the transepts were built.

Finally return to the west front.

WALKING TOUR FROM PETERBOROUGH CATHEDRAL

Peterborough is both an ancient city and a New Town. The figure-of-eight walk looks first at the cathedral's exterior and the remains of the old abbey and cloisters, then moves into the modern city, where elements of Georgian and Victorian architecture sit comfortably alongside 20th-century developments.

Start and finish: Minster Yard, at the west front of the cathedral.
Length: 2½ miles (4km).
Time: 1½ hours, but allow longer if you want to visit the museum.
Refreshments: Numerous fast-food outlets in the Queensgate Shopping Precinct. For more ambience, try some of the ancient pubs and former coaching inns, including the Tut and Shrive and the Wortley Almshouses (both in Westgate) and the Alderman (Cross Street). The Bull Hotel (Westgate), another possibility, offers accommodation.

The grassy area in front of the cathedral, Minster Yard, has three notable gateways around its perimeter. On the south side the **Bishop's Gateway**, known in monastery times as the Abbot's Gateway, leads to the bishop's palace. It was largely built in the early 13th century, although some of the windows may be older. Above the arch is the Knight's Chamber, built *c*1300. There are statues on both north and south sides; apparently original, these portray Edward I, an abbot, a prior and Peter, Paul and Andrew. The buildings to either side of the gate date back to medieval times although later alterations are obvious; they were once the abbot's offices.

On Minster Yard's west side, towards the city, is the **Cathedral Gate**, built *c*1180, in the time of Abbot Benedict. It is basically Norman (note the blind arcading, similar to that in the cathedral), but on the town side was faced in Perpendicular style

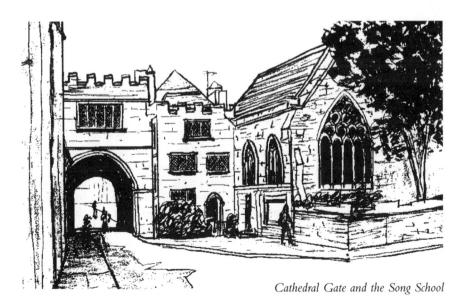

Cathedral Gate and the Song School

273

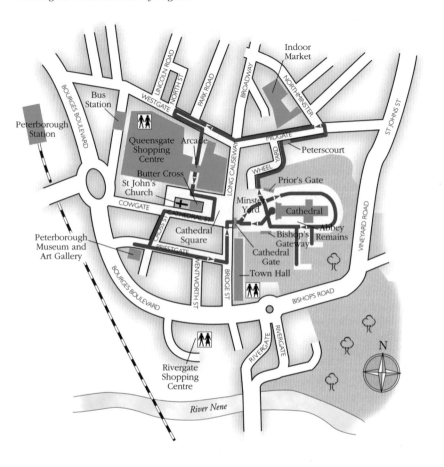

in the 14th century. On the upper floor is the Norman Chapel of St Nicholas, while the arch itself was once fitted with a portcullis you can still see the grooves in the wall on either side. The building on the right was once the abbot's gaol. Further right is the present Song School, occupying the chancel of the Chapel of St Thomas the Martyr – the chapel's nave and aisles were demolished in the 15th century to provide building materials for the St John's Church (see page 276) in Cathedral Square.

On the northeast side of Minster Yard is the **Prior's Gate**, built *c*1510 by Abbot Robert Kirkton – look for his weathered rebus. The gate, believed to have once led to the abbot's private deer park, now directs you to the deanery and chapter house. Its other side is of little architectural merit, so walk instead along the north side of the cathedral, noting on your right the Layfolks' Cemetery and, past the transept, the site of the former Lady Chapel.

Remains of the Abbey

From the east end of the cathedral, in the region of the Monks' Cemetery, there are fine views of the exterior of the rounded apse, which makes an interesting contrast with the New Building. Approaching the south transept, you find yourself among the **abbey remains**. Take the path southwards towards a group of buildings that mark the site of the monks' infirmary, which opened into the small Chapel of St Lawrence. The main buildings here today are the archdeaconry and Norman Hall, both built into the old arcades of the infirmary.

Return to the south transept area and take a narrow alley, Monks' Walk, southwards. On the left is the site of the monks' dormitory, built by Abbot Ermulf *c*1110. A century later Abbot Robert Lindsey glazed some of the windows and divided the building into cubicles for privacy. Although no dormitory survives today, it is believed an upper storey was connected to the south transept by night stairs.

On the opposite side of the wall of Monks' Walk is the site of the refectory, built by Ermulf and extended by Abbot John de Sais. It was replaced in Early English style by Abbot Walter of Bury St Edmunds *c*1240.

Continue to the end of Monks' Walk to what has been called the Monks' Stables but was originally the almoner's hall. (The almoner was responsible for handing out alms to the poor of the town, keeping the abbey accounts and collecting rents from the townhouses owned by the monastery.) The almoner's hall until recently housed the Cathedral Visitor Centre, with displays showing the history of the abbey and cathedral, but this exhibition has now moved into the north transept and the building is used by the local college.

Return once more to the south transept, to the left of which you'll find the remains of the old abbey cloisters. There are in fact three historical stages, Norman, Early English and Perpendicular. The oldest, found in the west wall, dates from the end of the second abbey (*c*1100) and is therefore older than the cathedral. The second period, from *c*1245, is found in the east bays of the south wall, when the arches were still unglazed. Finally the cloisters were completely rebuilt in 1525 in Perpendicular style, complete with panelling, tracery and stained glass on all four sides. Look for the lavatorium, where the monks washed their hands on their way to meals.

On the east side of the cloisters is the site of the chapter house, which was not in the traditional English polygonal shape but rectangular. The original building was Norman, built by Ermulf, but it was modernized in Early English style by Lindsey. Its effigies of 12th- and 13th-century abbots are now in the presbytery aisles of the cathedral.

Both the cloisters and the chapter house were pulled down after the Dissolution, most of the building material being sold.

The City Centre

Walk from the cloisters along the path to the west front of the cathedral and cross Minster Yard to its northwest corner, where you leave via Wheelyard, a thoroughfare marking the focus of the city's former wheelwrights' industry. Keep going towards a modern stone archway. Noting a stone head of Henry VIII set into the wall, take the path to the right of the arch.

The road now swings leftward to join Midgate, near the corner of which is **Peterscourt**, probably the finest Victorian building in the city. Built in 1860 to the design of Sir George Gilbert Scott, it was a teacher training college (St Peter's);

the modern block further along (now the offices of English Nature) marks the site of a small school for the students' teaching practice. A nearby curiosity is the milestone set in the wall showing the distances to London and Thorney.

Cross Midgate to the **indoor market**. Peterborough has had a market charter since 972, and for centuries the market was in Cathedral Square. It moved to its present position in 1979.

Turn and walk back along Midgate, noting on the right Hereward Cross, one of a number of indoor shopping complexes in the city. Go over Broadway and into **Westgate**, possibly once known as 'Webstergate' – the street of the weavers. Westgate today is a modern shopping street dominated by New Town buildings, but – remarkably – three old inns have survived. First, on your right, is the Bull Hotel, an old coaching inn; it probably dates from the late 17th century and may once have been the mansion house. Further along on your left is the Tut and Shrive, formerly the Royal Hotel. Once a Georgian residence, it is believed to have been built in 1730. The third inn is the Wortleys Almshouses, given to the city in 1744 by Edward Wortley Montagu, a local benefactor and MP. It is claimed Charles Dickens (1812–1870) based the workhouse in *Oliver Twist* on Wortley's Almshouses.

Walk back along Westgate until you're opposite the Bull again. Now enter the **arcade**, typical of those built in the 1920s. Full of specialist shops, it is now part of Queensgate, one of the largest covered shopping centres in the country, opened in 1982 by Queen Beatrix of the Netherlands.

Cathedral Square

Proceed straight through Queensgate to emerge along Cumbergate – an alley named after the combers who prepared wool for the weavers – to **Cathedral Square**. Although this has been much altered by the New Town developments, there are still a number of interesting buildings to give a flavour of the past.

Walk clockwise around the square. Immediately on your left, on the corner of Cumbergate, is the Miss Pears Almshouses, originally built in 1835 but much extended as a result of Miss Pears' will in 1903. It is now an Italian restaurant. On the east side of the square, the Cathedral Gate is flanked by the premises of two clearing banks, both imposing buildings.

On the square's south side is a curious building, designed in mock-Elizabethan style but built in 1911. You can see the cathedral arms in the gable; below are a number of brightly painted statues of men closely associated with the history of Peterborough, including King Peada, Henry VIII and Aethelwold (Bishop of Winchester, who refounded the second abbey *c*960). Unfortunately the overall effect is spoilt by the garish frontage of a fast-food chain. Further to the east, a small run of shops gives a good idea of what the square must have looked like in medieval times.

The centre of the square is dominated by two buildings. **St John's Church**, the parish church, was once sited east of the cathedral on marshy ground. After complaints by the townsfolk it was rebuilt in the early 15th century in its present position, using material from the original church as well as stone from the nave of the Chapel of St Thomas the Martyr, in Minster Yard. You can spot this latter material in the west door and in the arches supporting the tower. The nave has seven bays in Perpendicular style and the tower, too, is impressive, with large belfry windows, buttresses and parapets. The spire was removed during Victorian times, when many of the interior fittings were added.

The church is closed more often than not. If you wish to see the inside you may have to gatecrash a lunchtime concert.

The other building in the centre of the square is the **Butter Cross** (also known as the **Guild Hall** or **Market Cross**). Built in 1671 it basically comprises a large single-storey room supported by a number of arches. There is a clock in the gable on the east side, under which are the royal arms of Charles II. You can see four other coats-of-arms – those of Bishop Henslow, Dean Duport and two local families, the Montagues and the Ormes. A butter market was held here until 1926; the upper room has been used as a gaol, a magistrates' court and a schoolroom at various times in its history. Access is difficult except for pre-booked groups.

Priestgate and the Town Hall

Leave the Square via Cowgate (cattle for the local leather and boot and shoe industries were driven along here) and turn left into Cross Street, at the end of which is Priestgate.

Turn immediately right to see the **Peterborough Museum and Art Gallery** ahead of you. Originally built by Thomas 'Squire' Cooke in 1816, this was considerably enlarged in 1821. Later in the 19th century it was converted into a hospital. This, and a serious fire in 1884, mean there is little of the interior to remind us of gracious Victorian living.

The building has been a museum since 1931. Particularly impressive are the geology section – containing mammal bones and some from dinosaurs found in the local clay pits – and the social history section, showing domestic rooms from various decades of the 20th century. There is also an art gallery, whose exhibitions change regularly. Before you leave, look for the oil painting by Theodore Nathan Fielding in the entrance hall; this shows the marketplace in Cathedral Square as it was in 1795.

Leave the museum and proceed east along **Priestgate**, one of the oldest streets in Peterborough and an essential part of Abbot Martin de Bec's 12th-century town plan. Today it is an interesting mixture, with buildings varying from 16th-century to modern. The older buildings are on the south side; the one with a simple spire is all that's left of the demolished Trinity Chapel. Practically every property in Priestgate is now a solicitor's office – a remarkable example of functional clustering.

Your walk along Priestgate ends among modern office blocks that frame the **Town Hall** in the pedestrianized Bridge Street. The design of the Town Hall, built *c*1930, was by E. Berry Webber, who won a competition held for that purpose. The style is Neo-Georgian, and the entrance is through an imposing Corinthian portico. Step inside to see the wide Italian Renaissance-style staircase.

A few yards south along Bridge Street is the helpful Tourist Information Office.

Now go north along Bridge Street into Cathedral Square, then turn right through the Cathedral Gate to come back into Minster Yard.

SOUTHWELL

Access: Southwell is located on the A612, halfway between Nottingham and Newark. Pathfinder buses from Nottingham every twenty minutes, and some stop at Southwell en route to Newark. There are mainline stations at both Newark and Nottingham. The nearest airport is East Midlands Airport at Castle Donnington.

There is often confusion about the difference between a cathedral and a minster. A minster is best described as a subcathedral; in Southwell's instance the minster was in the diocese of York, along with Ripon and Beverley. It was administered by a college of prebendaries (or canons), who looked after local villages. All the canons had prebendal houses in Southwell. Unlike the case with many English cathedrals, there has never been an abbey on the Southwell site.

The minster has always been regarded as the mother church of Nottinghamshire. There has been a religious building on the site since Saxon times, and it is believed that Paulinus (d644) founded a church here *c*630. It was soon a place of pilgrimage, as the church contained the relics of St Edburga of Repton (fl 700). In 956, King Eadwig gave the manor of Southwell to the Archbishop of York, and succeeding archbishops remained the lords of the manor until the mid-19th century.

The present minster building was begun in 1108, and the Norman nave, transepts and towers remain today. The east end was rebuilt in the 13th century in Early English style, contrasting with the bulkier design of the west end. The octagonal chapter house, with its delightful carved stonework, was added in the late 13th century. The pulpitum, constructed of Mansfield stone, was built in 1290. The Perpendicular window in the west front was inserted towards the end of the 15th century.

Southwell survived the Reformation intact, largely because it was not an 'abbey church', but was not so fortunate during the Civil War. Cromwell's troops are believed to have stabled their horses in the nave and they inflicted considerable damage to the fabric, as well as wrecking the archbishop's palace. In 1711 a fire destroyed the roof, bells and organ. The spires on the western towers date from the 19th century, probably replacing earlier ones of similar design.

Southwell Minster became a cathedral with its own diocese in 1884; the imposing tomb of the first Bishop of Southwell, George Ridding, can be seen in the sanctuary. The centenary in 1984 was marked by the visit of Elizabeth II to distribute the Maundy Money.

TOUR OF THE MINSTER
Start: The west end.
Finish: The north porch.

To reach the **west end (1)** pass through the gate in Westgate, from where there is a superb view towards the west front along a path called The Broadwalk. This vista was not always free of obstructions; where today there is a grassy open space with some early-18th-century headstones, until the 1820s there were various buildings here including an alehouse, a limehouse, a shop and, remarkably, a pigsty! The west end was completed *c*1140. The rather 'flat' Norman façade, with typical round arches, has twin towers capped with pyramidal spires. The original spires were removed *c*1800 and the towers strengthened before restoration in 1880, giving the west end a somewhat Germanic look. The towers are known locally as the 'Pepper Pots'. The central Perpendicular window was inserted in the 15th century.

Old Architecture and New Sculpture

Move now to the north side of the exterior and enter the building through the **north porch (2)**, which consists of a series of round Norman arches with dogtooth and chevron decoration. A room over the porch (probably used by the Sacristan) has Norman windows and above it are two pinnacles, one of which serves as the room's chimney. The sides of the porch's interior contain a series of interlaced arches from the transitional Norman period. The door is equally impressive, its silver grey wood dating from the 14th century.

Walk into the **nave (3)**, which is dominated by solid Norman architecture. The arcade level has round drum pillars, replicated above, but with square columns, in the triforium. Above this is the clerestory, which has a row of smaller arches. The pattern of the three levels may remind you of a Roman aqueduct. The stonework supports a wooden wagon roof of Victorian age.

If you turn to the west end you'll see that the Perpendicular window is filled with subtle modern glass. This, the **Angel Window (4)**, was completed in 1996. (A brochure giving a detailed description is available in the bookshop.) If you look in the opposite direction you can see above the nave altar the hanging sculpture *Christus Rex* **(5)** by Peter Ball, made in wood, beaten copper and gold leaf and erected in 1987.

Move to the south aisle, where you'll find the **font (6)**, which has a descending dove on its lid. Dating from 1661, the font was the work of a local school of font carvers. The stained glass in the south aisle is Victorian and of little distinction.

Continue along the aisle and into the south transept. Here the most fascinating features are the **bread pews (7)**, ancient wooden seats where the needy of the parish waited for alms. Beneath the pews you can see small pieces of mosaic floor, possibly taken from a nearby Roman villa to form part of the floor of the original Saxon church. Also here are a modern wooden sculpture of the Madonna and Child by Alan Coleman and a small board showing the coat-of-arms of Charles II.

Turn now into the **crossing (8)**, where sturdy Norman columns and arches support the central tower. These arches – like those in the transepts – have well defined rope mouldings.

Dominating the crossing is the chancel screen or **pulpitum (9)**, which separates the Norman nave from the Early English chancel. Made like much of the rest of the minster of Mansfield stone, it is of Decorated style and probably dates from *c*1340. A slim central doorway is flanked by richly carved arches and canopies, with nearly 300 faces of men and animals. Unfortunately, the organ fills the space above the pulpitum completely, so there is no vista along the full length of the building.

Now walk into the south choir aisle and from here into the **quire (10)**, where the architecture is firmly Early English period, with rib vaulting, shafting on the pillars and lancet windows. Among the rich woodwork of the stalls are six 14th-century misericords.

Note the brass 16th-century eagle **lectern (11)**, which has an interesting history. It once belonged to Newstead Abbey, some 15 miles (24km) west of Southwell, and was thrown into the lake at the time of the Reformation. It was later recovered, cleaned and presented to the minster. Above the lectern is a fine brass 12-branch candelabrum dating from 1769.

Walk along the quire towards the high altar and, once you're about halfway there, look to your right to see two chapels. The east transept is occupied by the **Southwell Saints' Chapel** or **Chapel of Christ (12)**, with another modern sculpture by Peter Ball. Next to it, at the end of the south choir aisle, is the **Chapel of St Oswald (13)**, with an attractive reredos by Caröe. The altar front shows St Oswald's symbol of a raven, designed by John Piper (1903–1992). Oswald (d992), a Benedictine monk, was successively Bishop of Worcester and Archbishop of York.

The **sanctuary (14)**, just beside the latter chapel, gives you an opportunity to look at the east window, with its tall Early English lancets. Although the upper panes have Victorian glass, the lower ones are filled with 16th-century Flemish glass brought from Paris and given to the minster in 1818. In front of the simple high altar, which has a pair of 16th-century brass standard candlesticks, is a wooden altar rail by the 20th-century Yorkshire wood carver, Robert Thompson; you can have fun looking for the carved mice on the lower rails.

To the south of the high altar is a beautiful five-seater **sedilia (15)**, attributed to the same carvers as were responsible for the pulpitum.

Martyrs to War

Retreating from the high altar, turn right and go into the **Airmen's Chapel (16)**. Its main interest is the wooden altar made from the wreckage of planes shot down over France during World War I. Note, too, the highly original triptych and the Katyn Memorial donated by the Anglo-Polish Society to commemorate the Poles killed in Russia during World War II.

Outside the Airmen's Chapel, on the left as you emerge, is the imposing **Ridding Memorial (17)**, depicting Southwell's first bishop, who was also the 43rd headmaster of Winchester. The other small eastern transept is occupied by the **Chapel of St Thomas (18)**, which is devoted to private prayer. Now go along the north quire aisle and turn into a vestibule leading to the great delight of Southwell – the

Chapter House

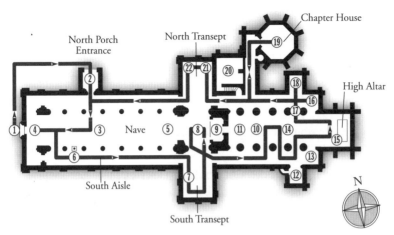

chapter house (19). Built at the end of the 13th century at a time when the Decorated style was beginning to evolve, it is the only octagonal English chapter house not to have a central supporting column; the absence of a central pillar allowed the construction of a superb star-vault, which has a bulky central boss. Entry is through an elegant double-arched doorway with contrasting plain pillars of Mansfield stone and pilasters of Purbeck marble. On both capitals and arches there is exquisite carving – almost entirely of plant and tree leaves found in the local area at that time: oak, ivy, hawthorn, buttercup, hop and whitethorn can be readily identified.

Inside the chapter house you'll almost certainly be impressed by the tall geometrical Decorated windows, which let light flood into the building; they are mainly plain glass with occasional fragments of medieval stained glass. Beneath the windows the arcades have shallow recesses with thirty-six wooden seats, one for each canon of the parish. Above them stone canopies with trefoil arches show more leaves and also heads, some damaged by Cromwell's men. Within one carved set of hawthorn leaves is a green man. This entity, although entirely pagan, is a frequently found motif in church decoration. The chapter house's 'Leaves of Southwell' are a national treasure and will not disappoint you.

A Prolific Bishop

Return along the vestibule and turn into the north transept. On the east side is the **Pilgrims' Chapel (20)**, which replaced an earlier semicircular apse. The chapel, which has had many uses during its history, is currently a place of prayer for all pilgrims who visit the minster. Although most of its accoutrements are modern, note the two *piscinas* (basins for the water used to wash the sacred vessels) and also the aumbries (wall cupboards where the communion plate was kept).

In the corner of the north transept is the striking alabaster **Tomb of Archbishop Sandys (21)**. His statue is held up by four angels, while the side of the tomb shows his two wives and eight children praying for him. Sandys (d1588) was Bishop of Worcester and later Archbishop of York.

In the opposite corner is a small doorway above which is a richly carved **Saxon tympanum (22)**, possibly from the old Saxon church. The carvings show David rescuing a sheep from a lion and St Michael fighting a dragon.

Leave the north transept and walk along the north nave aisle to the north porch.

WALKING TOUR FROM SOUTHWELL MINSTER

Southwell (often pronounced 'suth'll', but to most locals 'south well') is probably England's smallest cathedral city, and so this walk covers little more than a mile (1.6km). There are no museums or monuments; the tour concentrates on domestic architecture, particularly the prebendal houses.

Start: The north porch of the minster.
Finish: The Visitor Centre.
Length: 1¼ miles (2km).
Time: Half an hour.
Refreshments: The minster's refectory is popular. Other decent eating places are few and far between, but the Saracen's Head in Westgate has a good lunchtime menu and offers accommodation.

Standing at the **north porch** you have an opportunity to view some of the external features of the cathedral. Pass the octagonal chapter house and look out for the numerous carvings of heads, birds and foliage. Higher up you can see a variety of gargoyles and the flying buttresses supporting the nave. Note, too, the clerestory windows which, although arched on the interior, have a bull's-eye shape on the outside.

At the east end of the minster is a wide grassy area which once contained a well. This was blocked up in the 18th century after a clergyman fell down it and drowned.

Opposite the east end is the **Vicars' Court**, a series of fine Georgian houses on three sides of a garden. These were built towards the end of the 18th century to house the Vicars Choral. At the far end of the court is the most impressive building, The Residence, home of the Provost of Southwell.

Continue around the east end of the minster and along the south side. To the left are the ruins of the **Archbishop's Palace**. Rebuilt in the early 15th century, this was a favourite resting place of many of the archbishops of York. The building was largely destroyed by Cromwell's men during the Civil War and later local people pilfered much of the building materials. What remains is the remodelled great hall. Once a seminary for young ladies, it was reclaimed for the minster at the end of the 19th century. It is not open to the public.

Opposite the palace is the minster's **south door**, once used by the archbishop to reach the minster from his palace. The doorway is Norman in style with elaborate dogtooth carving, a pattern repeated in the window above it.

From the west end of the minster, take the diagonal path to a gap in the church-yard wall. Immediately to your left there is a view into the garden of **Bishop's Manor**, the residence of the Bishop of Southwell, framed by the ruins of the old palace. To your right is a single-storey building, the **Trebeck Memorial Hall**. Once the Choristers' Song School, it is now used by the general public for local functions.

Prebendal Houses
At the end of the path turn right into Bishop's Drive and then right again into Westgate. A little way along on the right, the minster's west gate acts as a frame for a good view of the west end. On the opposite side of the road you get your first glimpse of the prebendal houses, the residences of the secular canons – who often leased them out. Today most are in private hands. **Dunham Prebend** is largely hidden by trees, but there is a better view of the 17th-century **Rampton Prebend**, which has three gables and a pleasing symmetry. To its right is **Sacrista Prebend**, where the minster choristers live.

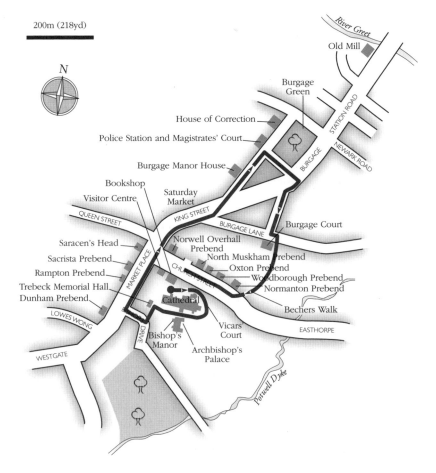

You now come to the **Saracen's Head**, an old coaching inn dating back to the late 14th century. The 'post and pan' half-timbered work on the front was revealed during repair work in 1978. The hotel has now taken over the assembly rooms next door, but their early-19th-century portico can be plainly seen. Further old coaching inns in this general area include the Crown, the Admiral Rodney, the Black Bull (now a shop) and the Wheatsheaf.

Walk north to the junction with Queen Street and King Street. Here a building has been demolished to reveal some fine half-timbered work.

Go rightwards into King Street, at whose top is an open space formed by the demolition of several houses. This is the site of the lively **Saturday market**.

Burgage Green

Ahead is the county library building. Pass to its left and the road will lead you to the attractive **Burgage Green**, full of shady lime and chestnut trees.

Immediately on your left is the elegant façade of **Burgage Manor House**. This building has had a varied and interesting history. Once the home of the mother of Lord Byron (1788–1824) – the poet often stayed here as a youth – it has also been a convalescent home, a girls' school and a youth hostel. Compare the beauty of the manor house with the ugly white Victorian residence opposite.

Set in the wall a few yards past the manor house is a Victorian letterbox. Also Victorian are the nearby **police station** and **magistrates' court** and, further on the left, the old **House of Correction**. The latter dates from the early 19th century and could house nearly 150 prisoners. Among its punishment equipment was a treadmill!

(If you'd like a longer walk, go to the lower part of the Green and take Station Road, which leads down to the River Greet, beside which is an old flour mill. The old railway track here is a nature trail. Then retrace your steps to rejoin the main walk.)

Back in Prebendary Country

Cross the green to its lower part, then go past the war memorial and along a lane towards the somewhat dilapidated Georgian **Burgage Court**, a once fine house in extensive grounds. Turn left along Burgage Lane and then immediately right down a pathway, Becher's Walk. After two hundred yards (180m) you reach Church Street.

(Here there is another option for the more energetic. Turn left and a few hundred yards until you see, on your left, a pub called the Bramley Apple. Four doors away, at 73 Church Street, is the small cottage where the first Bramley apples were grown. After you've covered this, return along Church Street to rejoin the main walk.)

You are now back in prebendary country. The first house on the right, set well back from the road, is the late-18th-century **Normanton Prebend**, which once had a tithe barn in its grounds. No. 31, now known as Ashleigh, was once the **Woodborough Prebend**; in the early years of the 20th century it was a girls' school. Next along is the **Oxton Prebend**, now called Cranfield House, a delightful Queen Anne building with pleasing symmetry. Now look for the **North Muskham Prebend**, formerly a boys' school and now occupied by solicitors' firms. Finally, to the west of the carpark entrance, is the **Norwell Overhall Prebend**, which is now a branch of the National Westminster Bank.

Just across the road is the Visitor Centre, which is where the walk ends.

LINCOLN

Access: Road access is usually via the A1 and the A46 from Newark in the south (the Roman Fosse Way), the A57 from Retford in the north, or the A15 from London. Rail links with London are via Newark or Peterborough on the main east coast line; local services connect with Nottingham and Sheffield. The nearest international airport, East Midlands, is some 45 miles (72km) to the west.

Celts, Romans, Anglo-Saxons and Vikings all had settlements at Lincoln. Some built churches and in late Roman times there was even a bishop, but the history of Lincoln Cathedral effectively goes back only to the arrival of the Normans in 1066.

William the Conqueror appointed Remigius, a Benedictine monk and one of his staunch supporters, to be bishop of a huge diocese which stretched from the Humber to the Thames. The first cathedral was at Dorchester-on-Thames, but William soon realized the strategic importance of Lincoln, where he had already built a castle, so in 1072 he commanded Remigius to build a cathedral there. Remarkably, the new building was complete within twenty years, although Remigius himself died just before the cathedral was consecrated.

This first cathedral was much shorter than the present building, with transepts, a tower (in the present position) and, at the east end, a semicircular apse. The roofs were almost certainly of timber, and in 1141 a fire seriously damaged the building. The third bishop, known as Alexander the Magnificent, was responsible for a partial rebuilding. He had travelled widely on the European mainland and was clearly influenced by some of the architectural developments he saw there. It is believed he vaulted the entire building in stone and was responsible for the Romanesque frieze and doorways on the west front, making what was probably the finest cathedral in the country at that time.

Unfortunately, what seems to have been an earthquake destroyed the greater part of the cathedral in 1185, and, though the west front and its towers could be retained, a major reconstruction was required. This task fell to Hugh, Bishop of Lincoln 1186–1200. A Carthusian monk from Avalon, near Grenoble, Hugh built the new parts of the cathedral in Early English style, with pointed windows and arches. The windows were larger and the walls were supported by flying buttresses. In addition to the normal transepts, a smaller eastern pair was added, while the east end was extended with chapels and apses so that the building broke through the line of the old Roman city wall. It is said that Hugh was often seen carrying a hod to help complete the building, but unfortunately he died before the nave was complete. Hugh (*c*1140–1200) was canonized in 1220, and the choir was named St Hugh's Choir.

More disasters were in store. In 1237 the central tower collapsed, destroying part of the choir. Its repair and the completion of Hugh's cathedral were largely the work of Bishop Robert Grosseteste (*c*1175–1253). By the time of his death, the chapter house had been completed and the east end enlarged, mainly to accommodate the hordes of pilgrims who flocked to visit St Hugh's tomb. In the 14th and 15th centuries, all three towers were raised and had spires added. This, it is believed, made Lincoln Cathedral the tallest building in the world at that time.

In 1548 the central spire blew down in a storm (the western spires remained until 1807, when they were demolished for safety reasons). Another disaster occurred in 1609, when part of the library was destroyed by fire. Its replacement, designed by Christopher Wren (1632–1723), was completed in 1675.

As with many cathedrals, the period from the 14th to the 18th centuries was a time of decay and neglect. Much destruction of statuary, glass and shrines took place during the Reformation, while further damage was committed by both sides during the Civil War. Not until the mid-18th century was there some attempt at restoration; this process has continued ever since, particularly in Victorian times, when much of the stained glass was replaced. Today, the Fabric Fund is responsible for raising the enormous amounts of money required to keep the structure of the cathedral in good shape.

The 1990s were not happy for Lincoln Cathedral. Problems began when the cathedral's copy of the Magna Carta was taken on a tour of Europe to raise money – and instead, a huge loss was made. A new dean was brought in, and that saw the start of some very public infighting among the factions at the cathedral – which the media delighted in reporting. Eventually, to bang some heads together, the bishop boycotted his own cathedral. In 1997, rightly or wrongly, the dean resigned, and hopefully peace will return.

TOUR OF THE CATHEDRAL
Start and finish: The west front.

The late Alec Clifton-Taylor described the **west front (1)** as an 'architectural hotchpotch'. Although there is a certain amount of truth in this, one cannot help but be impressed by the sheer size and uniqueness of the feature. Much of the early Norman fortress-like stonework remains along with the rounded arches, but the most imposing feature is the carved frieze over the doorways, dating from the time of Bishop Alexander. He is thought to have copied the idea from the cathedral at Modena, which he probably saw on his way to Rome. The frieze shows scenes from the Old Testament on the south side and from the New Testament on the north. As with many cathedral features, such as stained glass and murals, it was designed to tell a moral story to a congregation who were largely illiterate.

Above the frieze is a lofty set of tiers of arcades, culminating in a steep-angled gable and, at the ends, a pair of octagonal angle turrets with two small statues on the top. That on the south is of St Hugh, and the Swineherd of Stow – renowned for giving his life savings of sixteen silver pennies to the cathedral – is on the north, blowing his horn. Extensive maintenance on the west front was completed in 2000.

A Feeling of Space
Enter the cathedral not through the richly carved central doorway but via the southwest door. In the **nave (2)** you'll find a welcoming desk manned by

volunteers who will not demand an entrance fee but who will expect a donation.

The first impression of the nave is of height and narrowness. There are the usual three levels – arcade, triforium and clerestory – with the abundant trefoil decoration typical of the Early English period, topped by impressive tierceron vaulting with regular bosses along the ridge-rib. If there is a criticism of the overall design, it is about the proportions, both at the various levels and in terms of the vaulting, which seems to spring from too low a level. The stone used is cream-coloured local limestone with rich brown Purbeck marble, a combination used throughout the cathedral. Each of the main pillars, for example, is enriched by eight free-standing Purbeck marble shafts, linked to the pillars halfway up by annulets.

The nave is also mercifully free of memorials, which, with the absence of seating, adds to the feeling of space. Tomb slabs on the floor have all had their brasswork removed.

Cross over to the mid-12th-century **font (3)**, by the south aisle. It is made of dark Tournai marble and is on a base, added in Victorian times, of Ashford limestone from Derbyshire. The carving on the font's sides shows lions, dragons and griffins in combat, no doubt representing the struggle between good and evil.

The Dean's Eye and the Bishop's Eye

Walk down the south aisle. The stone benches built into the wall provided seats for frail members of the congregation (hence the saying 'the weakest go to the wall').

Soon you reach the **great transept (4)**. In almost every other English cathedral there are two transepts, north and south, but at Lincoln there are the great transept and two smaller eastern transepts (northeast and southeast).

Stand under the **crossing (5)** and look up at the lantern, with its stone vaulting. Above this is the tower, containing the main cathedral bell, Great Tom, put in position in 1835. The north and south walls of the great transept each have a fine rose window above lancet windows, dating from the 1220s. The rose window to the north, the **Dean's Eye (6)**, has plate tracery and a considerable amount of the original glass, which has the theme of the Last Judgement. The five lancet windows below have *grisaille* glass. The rose window on the south side, the **Bishop's Eye (7)**, replaced an earlier window *c*1330. It has bar tracery in the form of two immense leaves filled with fragments of glass of various ages and origins reassembled from other parts of the cathedral, giving a quite beautiful effect unique in English cathedrals. The four lancet windows below have medallions of 13th-century glass, again drawn from other parts of the cathedral.

On the east side of the crossing is the 14th-century stone **pulpitum (8)**, marking the west end of St Hugh's Choir. It has a profusion of carving – saints, animals, monsters and flowers – plus a series of ornate double-curved arches. Traces of red, blue and gold here and there on the stonework hint at the colourful scene that confronted medieval worshippers.

Walk into the **south side of the great transept (9)** – what would normally be called the south transept. Here there are a couple of memorials of interest. On the west wall are the remains of the **Shrine of John Dalderby**. Dalderby was Bishop of Lincoln in the early years of the 14th century. His relics, kept in a silver reliquary, attracted pilgrims, but were destroyed during the Reformation. At the far

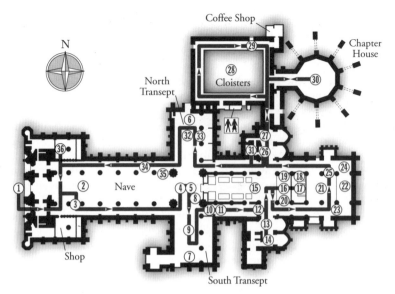

Key

1. West Front
2. Nave
3. Font
4. Great Transept
5. Crossing
6. Dean's Eye
7. Bishop's Eye
8. Pulpitum
9. South Side of Great Transept
10. South Choir Aisle
11. Shrine of Little Hugh

12. Trondheim Pier
13. Southeast Transept
14. Bishop Grosseteste's Tomb
15. St Hugh's Choir
16. Sanctuary
17. High Altar
18. Easter Sepulchre
19. Tomb of Remigius
20. Chantry of Katherine Swyford
21. Angel Choir
22. Great East Window
23. Eleanor of Castile's
    Visceral Tomb

24. Head Shrine of St Hugh
25. The Lincoln Imp
26. Damini Wall Paintings
27. Touch Exhibition
28. Cloisters
29. Wren Library
30. Chapter House
31. Treasury
32. North Side of Great Transept
33. Services' Chapel
34. North Nave Aisle
35. Tournai Marble Tomb Slab
36. Morning Chapel

end of the transept is a striking bronze statue of Bishop Edward King, who was tried (and acquitted) by the court at Canterbury for his High Church practices. The statue, which rests on a plinth of Dent marble, was originally meant to be outside in the cathedral grounds.

A Murdered Boy and Nineteen Murdered Jews

Leave the great transept and enter the **south choir aisle (10)** through a wonderfully carved 13th-century door. Purbeck shafts and vertical bands of roses and dogtooth decoration lead at about eye level to capitals showing angels and birds. The arch has a broad band of openwork foliage, reminiscent of the stonework in Ely's Lady Chapel (see page 248).

Immediately to your left is the ruined **Shrine of Little Hugh (11)**. In 1255 a young boy called Hugh was discovered dead in a Lincoln well, and the Jewish community was promptly charged with his ritual murder. After anti-Semitic riots, nineteen Jews were executed for this supposed crime and others were imprisoned. In an early example of ecumenism, the Benedictines intervened for the release of

The great Norman nave of Ely Cathedral viewed from the north side of the octagon. The monks' choir stalls would have been in the foreground during medieval times.

Norwich Cathedral, with its Romanesque tower and 15th-century spire, as viewed from the ruins of the Hostry hall off the west range of the cloister.

The burial place of Queen Catherine of Aragon, the first wife of Henry VIII, in the north choir aisle of Peterborough Cathedral.

The early 12th-century western arm of Southwell Minster in Nottinghamshire, with its impressive western doorway.

The western façade of Lincoln Minster, with its three great early Norman arches, similar to a Roman triumphal arch.

Outside the south transept of York Minster, a new statue of the emperor Constantine has been erected, revealing something of York's Roman history.

The beautiful Galilee chapel at Durham Cathedral, with its chevroned arches and monolithic Purbeck marble shafts.

Above: Detail of the fan vault in the 'New Building' at Peterborough Cathedral, by royal master mason John Wastell.

Above: The screen at the entrance to the choir at York Minster was made to house carvings of all the kings of England, from William I to Henry VI.

these innocents, who were nevertheless heavily fined. Later a small shrine was placed in the cathedral. The original canopy over it was destroyed during the Civil War. The legend of Little St Hugh is encountered in 'The Prioress's Tale' in Chaucer's *Canterbury Tales*.

Further along on the left are some late 15th-century wood carvings thought to be from Bavaria. On the right of the aisle is a stone screen, believed to be of the same age as the pulpitum.

At the end of the aisle, again on your right, is the **Trondheim Pier (12)**, one of a pair of unusual pillars (the other is in the north aisle). It consists of three strongly carved limestone shafts and, on the outside, complementary shafts of Purbeck marble, all rising to boldly carved leaf capitals. The only other known examples of this distinctive design are found in Trondheim Cathedral, Norway, which suggests that 13th-century stonemasons were more peripatetic than is generally realized.

Now you come to the **southeast transept (13)** and **Bishop Grosseteste's Tomb (14)**, which is in front of the Chapel of St Peter and St Paul. Grosseteste, Bishop of Lincoln 1235–53, was a distinguished academic, scientist and theologian, and first Chancellor of Oxford University. Known as a strict disciplinarian, he was highly thought of in his diocese. It is a surprise that he has never been canonized. His original chest tomb was destroyed during the Civil War; the modern slab replacement was rededicated in 1953.

St Hugh's Choir and the Sanctuary

Now cross the aisle into **St Hugh's Choir (15)**. The architecture here is clearly Early English, with pointed arches, lancet windows and the by now familiar combination of local limestone and Purbeck marble. The vaulting is tierceron in style (this was probably one of the first examples of the kind in Europe) and highly irregular, particularly along the ridge, so that this is commonly described as the 'crazy vault'.

It is the wooden choir stalls, however, that give St Hugh's Choir its unique atmosphere. They are luxuriant with pinnacles, canopies and outstanding carving; the numerous misericords have been dated at *c*1370. Name plates mark the seats of the canons of the cathedral, each allocated the first line of a psalm. The stalls were extended eastward in 1778 to accommodate the bishop's throne.

Other items of interest here include the Victorian pulpit, designed by Sir George Gilbert Scott (1811–1878), and the much older brass eagle lectern, which dates from 1667.

Now walk into the **sanctuary (16)**. Nominally part of the Angel Choir (see below), this is boxed off from it by a stone screen, most of which dates from a Gothic-style restoration done in 1769.

Dominating the area is the **high altar (17)**. Once a simple table, this has a stone reredos to match the surrounding screen. The tracery was once filled with artwork, later removed to give a better view of the east window. The northern screen features an **Easter sepulchre (18)** – more accurately, Christ's tomb, guarded at floor level by three seated soldiers.

The next three bays to the left contain what is believed to be the **Tomb of**

Remigius (19), the founder of the original cathedral at Lincoln. On the south side of the sanctuary is the narrow **Chantry of Katherine Swyford (20)**; she was mistress and later wife of John of Gaunt (1340–1399), an influential figure in Plantagenet times.

Burial in Parts

Walk back into the south aisle and round to the **Angel Choir (21)**, at the east end. Built primarily to cater for the pilgrims visiting the Shrine of St Hugh, it is one of the great successes of English Gothic, continuing the geometrical Decorated style of St Hugh's Choir, using local cream limestone and darker Purbeck marble. It gained its name from the profusion of angels carved in the stonework at triforium and clerestory levels.

Dominating the Angel Choir is the **great east window (22)**, with eight lights and 60ft (18m) high – a great technical achievement for its time, when bar tracery was in its early days of development. The Victorian glass is perhaps unworthy of the window.

There are four chantry chapels in the Angel Choir: going anticlockwise, the Russell Chantry, the Cantilupe Chantry, the Burghersh Chantry and the Fleming Chantry. All are worth a brief look.

Of more interest is **Eleanor of Castile's Visceral Tomb (23)**. Eleanor was queen and wife of Edward I – the marriage lasted thirty-five years and produced thirteen children. She died nearby at Harby, and Edward took her body in procession to London for burial, the twelve stops along the way being marked by the famous Eleanor Crosses. She was buried in Westminster Abbey, but her heart went to Blackfriars Church in London and her internal organs were returned to Lincoln. Her tomb here was destroyed in the Civil War; the present monument is a copy made in 1890.

We now come to the *raison d'être* of the whole Angel Choir – the **Head Shrine of St Hugh (24)**. The body of St Hugh was exhumed and transferred to a prepared shrine in 1280. Unfortunately, the head came off, and for a while two shrines existed. The Body Shrine has since vanished, but the Head Shrine is said to have been the third most popular place of pilgrimage in England. It was stripped of its jewels and other decorations by Henry VIII and later, during the Civil War, the head and its reliquary disappeared. What remains is probably just the base of a portable shrine (which could have been used in processions). In 1986, to celebrate the 800th anniversary of St Hugh's arrival in Lincoln, a bronze canopy was attached. Opinions differ widely as to its suitability – make up your own mind!

You can't leave the Angel Choir without looking at a feature which charms old and young alike – the **Lincoln Imp (25)**. The small carved figure above the pier nearest to the Head Shrine, sitting with his legs crossed, has horns, claws and a seemingly feathered body. The tale is that he was once alive, but behaved so badly the angels turned him to stone. The image has today become a good-luck symbol and is closely associated with the city.

Cloisters and Chapter House

Leave the Angel Choir, walk down the north choir aisle and turn into the northeast transept, marked on the west side by the second Trondheim Pillar. Immediately to your left are the **Damini Wall Paintings (26)** – four 12th-century bishops of Lincoln painted by the 18th-century Venetian artist Vincenzo Damini. They are probably restorations, as medieval paintwork has been discovered underneath. Further along on the left is the **Touch Exhibition (27)**, offering a tactile experience of building materials and other items for the benefit of the blind.

Now go through a vaulted passage, The Slype, to the **cloisters (28)**. They might be considered something of an extravagance, as Lincoln did not have a monastic foundation, but no doubt the canons, choristers and priests made as much use of them as monks would have done, with similar enjoyment. The vaulting in the cloisters is of wood, as are the delightfully carved bosses, many of which have been made with considerable wit.

The north cloister is obviously an odd one out among the other three; the original was pulled down in the 15th century to accommodate the dean's horses, so what you now see today is a 17th-century replacement designed by Sir Christopher Wren at the behest of Dean Honywood, who was donating his valuable collection of books to the cathedral and wanted them to have a proper home. This is now called the **Wren Library (29)** and incorporates at its eastern end the 100 or so manuscripts from the Medieval Library, which was destroyed by fire.

Leave the cloisters from the east side and enter the **chapter house (30)**. Built in the mid-13th century and measuring nearly 22 yards (20m) across, Lincoln's was the first cathedral chapter house to be polygonal – it has ten sides. The elegantly slender central pier supports a number of ribs which fan out into a tierceron vault, supported outside by flying buttresses and pinnacles.

The oak seat on the far side of the entrance was probably provided for Edward I when he called a parliament here in 1301 to declare his son (the future Edward II) the first Prince of Wales. Later, in 1536, the leaders of the Lincolnshire Rising who resisted the Reformation met here to hear Henry VIII's response to their demands. The stained glass chronicles other events in the building's history.

Servicemen Remembered

Return via The Slype and the northeast transept to the north choir aisle. Turn right. Immediately on your right is the **treasury (31)**, formerly the Medicine Chapel, which contains a collection of silver plate belonging to the cathedral and other churches in the diocese.

Further along the aisle, turn right into the **north side of the great transept (32)**. On its east side you find the **Services' Chapels (33)** – successively the Soldier's, Seamen's and Airmen's. A quick look in all three reveals some fine modern stained glass.

Walk back along the nave via the **north aisle (34)**, where there are two monuments of interest. The first is a Romanesque **Tournai marble tomb slab (35)**, once thought to be the tomb of Remigius but now believed to be that of Bishop Alexander. Nearer the west end is a more modern memorial to Bishop Kaye (1827–1853).

Just by this latter monument, turn right into the **Morning Chapel (36)**. Once used as a parish church, it is now the venue for Matins and, at other times, for private prayer. The obvious feature of architectural interest is the slender central pier of Purbeck marble.

Finally, leave the Morning Chapel and return to the west front.

WALKING TOUR FROM LINCOLN CATHEDRAL

The tour is in two parts. The first looks at that part of the city known as 'uphill', which is close to the Cathedral and has a number of historic buildings in a largely residential area. The second part looks at the 'downhill' section of the city, which is more commercial in character. The return walk to the 'uphill' area involves a steep climb; you might want to opt for a taxi.

Start and finish: The west front of the cathedral.

Length: 3 miles (4.8km).

Time: 2½ hours (because of the steep slopes). Allow more time if you want to visit museums, etc.

Refreshments: Excellent cathedral refectory. Plenty of choice in the city to suit all tastes and pockets. Old inns of character offering good pub lunches include: the Magna Carta (Exchequer Gate), the Lion and Snake (Bailgate), the Wig and Mitre (Steep Hill) and the White Hart (Bailgate). Waterside pubs include the Royal William (Brayford Wharf) and the Witch and Wardrobe (Waterside).

From the west front, cross the cathedral close and leave it via the **Exchequer Gate**; this fine stone gateway dates 1320. About fifty yards (50m) beyond the gate is a crossroads, with, on the corner, a fine, half-timbered house with jettied walls that is now the city's **Tourist Information Office**. The helpful staff here can provide you with much useful material.

Turn right into Bailgate, a street full of old coaching inns and good domestic architecture from various historical periods. The brick and stone circles you see in the roadway are believed to be the bases of Roman columns.

At the end of Bailgate is the stone-built **Newport Arch**, a 3rd-century gateway into the Roman city, claimed to be the oldest Roman archway in Britain under which traffic still passes. The Romans came to the area in AD48 and built a magnificent walled settlement on this site. A number of Roman sites can be visited in the upper part of the city, including sections of the city wall, an interval tower and an aqueduct.

An Elegant Mental Hospital

Just before the arch, turn left along Chapel Lane. When this runs into Westgate, go right for about a hundred yards (100m) until you reach a road junction. Turn left (south) into Union Road. A little way along on the right is a complex of buildings, the **Lawn Visitor Centre**.

The main building here is a stately-looking mansion with an imposing Classical portico. First impressions, however, can be deceptive, because the Lawn was built in 1820 as a lunatic asylum. The complex was reopened in 1990 as a tourist attraction.

Its features include a 5000 sq ft (465m^2) tropical conservatory, with a comprehensive collection of plants. There is also an archaeological interpretative centre, a fudge factory, an RAF museum and another rather gruesome interpretative centre depicting the history of treating mental illness, including some of the more barbaric methods used in Victorian times.

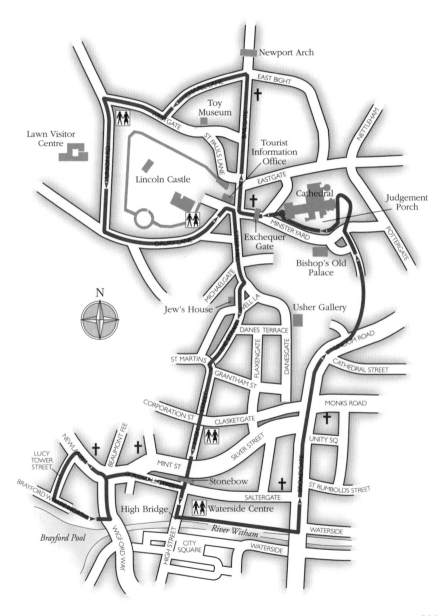

Lincoln Castle

Opposite the Lawn is the west entrance to **Lincoln Castle**. If you want to look at the castle from inside the walls, enter here. If you decide to give the castle a miss, continue south along Union Road and turn left into Drury Lane, which swings back round to the Tourist Information Office.

Built from 1072 on the instructions of William the Conqueror, the castle was constructed on the site of the original Roman castle and used some of its building materials. You can stroll along the ramparts to the **Observatory Tower**; the climb to its 19th-century turret is rewarded by stunning views over the cathedral, the city and the surrounding countryside.

Also don't miss the **Cobb Hall**, the section of the castle which acted as a prison until 1878 and where public executions were watched by enthusiastic crowds. You can also visit the rather depressing Victorian prison chapel, which has models of both chaplain and prisoners in their individual, coffin-like pews.

Leave by the east entrance (you will then find yourself back by the Tourist Information Office).

'Downhill'

Now head towards the 'downhill' part of the city by way of **Steep Hill**, the usual route for pilgrims as they plodded uphill to the Shrine of St Hugh at the cathedral. Today, Steep Hill is cobbled and pedestrianized, and has a range of pubs, historic houses and specialist shops.

The road continues into The Strait where, on the right, you can see one of Lincoln's most famous buildings: the **Jew's House**, dating from *c*1170 and almost certainly the city's oldest domestic building. The ornate entrance arch also served the adjacent Jew's Court, believed to have been the site of a synagogue. Once powerful in the community, the Jews were expelled in the latter part of the 13th century, after much anti-Semitic feeling. The two buildings were restored during the 20th century, and today the House is a restaurant and the Court a specialist bookshop.

The Strait leads on into High Street. Ahead of you is the imposing stone arch known as the **Stonebow**, located at the southern entrance to the old town. The present arch was built in the 15th century, replacing predecessors from Roman and medieval times.

Above it are the city's council chambers and the mayor's office, while to one side is the **Guildhall**, where, in a small museum, Lincoln's civic insignia are displayed. The Mayoralty of Lincoln was established in 1206 and is one of the oldest in the country. The insignia and other items include the city charter, dating from 1141, and the swords of both Richard II and Henry VII.

Brayford Pool and High Bridge

Pass through the Stonebow and turn right. Take the first left to reach **Brayford Pool**, located at the point where the River Witham makes a right-angled turn as it cuts through the Lincoln Edge. Here, too, the Fossdyke Canal leads off to join the River Trent to the west.

There has been a settlement at this place since Celtic times, and it was a busy port under the Romans, Vikings and Normans. The stone for the cathedral was unloaded here, while grain and wool were exported. The most important period for Brayford Pool was during the 18th and 19th centuries, when, despite being over forty miles (64km) from the sea, it was the fourth busiest port in England, with warehouses and industry lining the poolside. Today, pubs, prestigious hotels and the new university take pride of place. Sightseeing cruises leave the jetty near Wigford Way Bridge during the summer months.

Retrace your steps to the High Street and look to the right, towards a remarkable structure, **High Bridge**. The bridge is constructed of stone with a vaulted roof and dates from Norman times. Above it is a two-storeyed half-timbered building with gabled rooms in its tiled roof. High Bridge is thought to be the oldest bridge in the country still to bear buildings. Certainly it is the city's most photogenic spot!

Go down the steps at the nearer side of High Bridge and walk along **Waterside**. On the left of this redeveloped area is the new indoor Waterside Shopping Centre, home to more than forty retail outlets. Continue along past the **Central Market**, housed in a Grade II listed building. The square outside the market is a favourite spot for buskers.

You now arrive at Broadgate. Turn left. Here the hard walk back up the hill to the cathedral begins, and you might prefer to hail a taxi or jump on one of the open-topped buses which, between Easter and the end of October, ply this route back to the cathedral.

Assuming you're made of sterner stuff and want to walk back, follow Broadgate, which eventually becomes Lindum Road. Shortly after a rightward bend, take the fork left up a set of well used steps, the Greestone Stairs. These lead you to the south side of the cathedral close, Minster Yard.

Here you have an excellent opportunity to view the external features of the cathedral. Walk past the east end to the **chapter house**, where you can appreciate the full beauty of this building, with its conical roof and massive flying buttresses. The **east end**, by contrast, is rather disappointing from outside. The upper window seems too large and balances precariously on the tip of the window below, while the excess of crocketing on the numerous pinnacles gives an over-fussy impression.

So move hastily on to look instead at the exceptional southeast porch, or **Judgement Porch**, which demonstrates some of the cathedral's best carving, with some fine gargoyles. It was built in the mid-13th century, largely to offer an impressive entrance to the increasing numbers of pilgrims bound for the Shrine of St Hugh.

Finally, cross to the south side of Minster Yard and the **Bishop's Old Palace**, in the shadow of the cathedral. Although largely derelict, it has the remains of the banqueting hall, offices and the luxurious accommodation which housed many a visiting monarch. On the south-facing slopes of the palace is a vineyard, claimed as England's most northerly, the vines having been donated by Lincoln's twin town, Neustadt an der Weinstrasse in Germany. The ruins of the palace are administered by English Heritage, who, during the summer months, arrange medieval music recitals and other displays.

Leaving the palace, return by way of Minster Yard to the cathedral's west front.

YORK

Access: By road from the south via the M1 and A1(M); major road links in other directions using the A19 and A64. National Express coaches from London and other large cities, arriving at and departing from Roujier Street. Rail journey time from London is under two hours; there are also direct services from Edinburgh, Liverpool, Manchester and Birmingham. Two international airports – Leeds/Bradford and Manchester – are within easy reach. North Sea ferries arrive at nearby Humberside from Belgium and Holland.

The first building on the site of York Cathedral was not a religious institution but the northern headquarters of the Roman army. Constantine the Great, who later declared Christianity a permitted religion of the Empire, was proclaimed Emperor at York in 306. There was not much Christianity in the area, however, when Paulinus (d644) came to York in 625 with Princess (later St) Ethelburga (d647) in order to marry her to Edwin, the pagan King of Northumbria. Two years later Edwin was baptized by Paulinus in a small wooden church built specially for the ceremony.

That wooden building is usually regarded as the first York Minster. It was replaced *c*640 by a stone building dedicated to St Peter. This Anglo-Saxon cathedral was rebuilt and renovated several times before being almost completely destroyed by William the Conqueror's soldiers during the 'harrowing of the North'.

The first Norman cathedral was started by Archbishop Thomas of Bayeux *c*1080 and completed by the turn of the century. (Some of the stonework of this building can still be seen in the Foundations Exhibition below the present minster.) From 1200 onwards, the first Norman cathedral was gradually replaced by a Gothic-style building. Under Archbishop Walter de Gray, the transepts were rebuilt in Early English style. The south transept was not entirely successful, but the builders learned from their mistakes and the north transept is much more pleasing. The chapter house and its vestibule were added between 1260 and 1290.

The builders then moved on to the nave, which must have looked uninspiring compared with that by William of Sens at Canterbury. The replacement, one of the glories of English cathedral architecture, is in Decorated Gothic style; at the time of its completion it was one of the largest building spaces in Europe. This in itself caused problems: the planned stone vaulting was never put in place – the roof has always been wooden.

Attention was then turned to the east end of the minster. As this area was in constant use, the new work had to be completed around and over the existing structure. The style here is Perpendicular Gothic, but remains in keeping with the nave. The work began in 1361 with the Lady Chapel and proceeded westwards towards the choir. While this was going on, part of the central tower collapsed. The plan was to replace it with a new tower surmounted by a lantern and spire, but it soon became evident that the existing masonry would not support the weight, so this notion was abandoned.

By 1472, the minster was complete apart from the western towers, and the building was consecrated.

No new building works have been carried out since the 15th century. The minster escaped serious damage during the Reformation and the Civil War. There have been other difficulties, though, mainly as the result of fire: there were two serious conflagrations during the 19th century, one destroying the roof of the choir and the other the roof of the nave. A major problem was discovered in 1967, when it was found that the foundations were unstable; a large-scale civil-engineering operation strengthened the foundations with enormous concrete collars reinforced with steel rods, and as a by-product gave us improved archaeological knowledge of the Roman, Saxon and Norman building processes. In 1984 yet another fire, probably caused by lightning, destroyed the roof of the south transept, though fortunately the 16th-century rose window survived. A sum of £2½ million was quickly raised for the restoration, and the roof was replaced within four years using the traditional structure and materials of medieval craftsmen.

Today, some 2¼ million people visit York Minster annually. Few of them leave without being impressed by this magnificent building.

TOUR OF THE MINSTER
Start and finish: The west end.

Enter the cathedral through the door on the south side (wheelchair users should take the door on the north side). There is no entrance fee, but a donation is recommended. (There are entrance fees to visit the chapter house, the crypt, the foundations and the tower.)

Walk to the centre of the nave and look back at the **great west window (1)**. The tracery is in the 'flamboyant' Decorated Gothic style and contains a heart-shaped central feature – the window is often known as the 'Heart of Yorkshire'. It was glazed in 1338 by Master Robert Ketelbarn. The lower line of pictures shows eight of the cathedral's archbishops with, above them, the Apostles.

A Superb Nave
Move to the centre of the **nave (2)**, which is uncluttered with memorials so your eye is not distracted from the simplicity and elegance of the architecture. The lack of memorials may be because until 1862 the nave was not used for services, but instead for secular activities – even today it is often the venue for civic functions and degree ceremonies.

The nave provides one of the best examples of Decorated Gothic in the country. Architectural purists criticize the proportions – rather too broad for its height – undersized capitals, variable thickness of shafts, rather boring tracery in windows and lack of a stone vaulting. All this may be true, but the fact remains that this is an extraordinary nave, and its sheer majesty, elegance and spaciousness are almost awe-inspiring.

The roof is an exact Victorian copy of the original, destroyed by fire in 1840. The roof bosses, each about a yard (1m) across, show the life of Christ. One used to show Mary breast-feeding Jesus, but here the Victorians abandoned their fidelity to the original and depicted the Virgin instead bottle-feeding the babe!

The minster retains much of its original medieval glass. Two windows are of particular note. On the third bay to your right is the **Jesse Window (3)**, dating from *c*1310, which takes the form of a family tree with Jesse at the base of the trunk, the prophets sitting on the branches and the Virgin Mary and Jesus in the canopy.

On the sixth bay to your left is the **Bell Founder's Window (4)**, donated by Richard Tunnoc, a local Member of Parliament, in 1390. He owned the local bell foundry, and the window has bells everywhere – like a gigantic medieval advertising hoarding!

Before you leave the nave, look for the **Dragon's Head (5)**, which protrudes from the triforium. It is often claimed this was a hoist to lift the lid of the font but, as there are no records of a font ever having been in this position, the theory is dubious. It may be no coincidence that there is a small carving of St George on the opposite side of the nave at the same level.

The Five Sisters Window and the Chapter House

Walk along the north nave aisle into the north transept, built 1240–65. Note the Purbeck marble shafts on the columns – a typical feature of the Early English style. Dominating the transept is the **Five Sisters Window (6)**, named for the five lancets filled with green–grey *grisaille* glass. It is said to contain over 100,000 pieces of glass arranged in geometrical patterns. This was cheaper than a pictorial display, and it was probably thought that a benefactor would fund a replacement, but no such benefactor ever appeared.

Note the small patch of blue glass at the lower end of the central lancet. This is believed to be glass which survived from the original Norman cathedral.

One of the two chapels in the transept, St Nicholas's Chapel, contains the only surviving medieval brass in the cathedral. The transept's two clocks are of mild interest, though neither is of any great antiquity.

Turn along the vestibule that leads to the **chapter house (7)**. Built in the late 13th century in the Decorated Gothic style, the chapter house is octagonal and owes its feeling of spaciousness largely to the lack of a central column. The roof is wooden, although it looks like stone from below.

The tracery in the windows is strictly geometrical. Much of the glass, here as in the vestibule, dates from the 13th century. The overhanging canopies of the forty-four stalls have some fine free-flowing carvings featuring animals, heads and foliage. A Victorian restoration programme removed the remains of the medieval gilding and painting and installed the Minton floor.

The Choir, Sanctuary and Great East Window

Leave the chapter house via the vestibule and walk through the north transept into the crossing. Look up into the **central tower (8)**, built in the mid-15th century to replace one that collapsed in 1407. It rises to over 200ft (60m) and was in fact planned to go even higher until it was realized that the foundations would not stand any more weight. The wooden lantern is notable for its fine collection of gilded bosses (binoculars are useful here); the central boss, showing St Peter and St Paul, is at 4ft (1.5m) wide the largest in the minster.

Back at ground level, the **pulpitum (9)** dates from 1461. The central band shows the figures of the kings of England from William I to Henry VI. Note the particularly miserable expression on the face of William II.

Pass through the central doorway of the pulpitum, which has the only fan vaulting in the cathedral, and move into the **choir (10)**, where the style is now Perpendicular. The stalls are Georgian – a pyromaniac had destroyed the originals. Note the brass plaques under the stall canopies; these represent the parishes in the diocese, but apparently their real purpose was to hide the marks on the woodwork made by the Victorian canons' hair oil!

The archbishop's *cathedra* on the south side is balanced on the north side by the equally large wooden pulpit.

Move forward to the **sanctuary (11)**, which has a 20th-century high altar. From here you get a good view of the windows of St William (to your left) and St Cuthbert (to your right). Both date from the 15th century, but their styles contrast considerably. Also, this is the best place to view the great east window (see below).

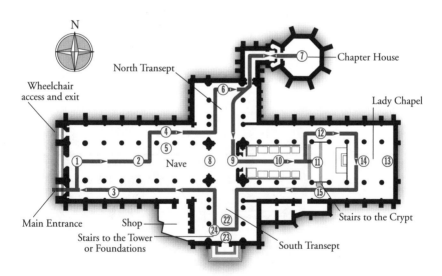

Key

1. Great West Window
2. Nave
3. Jesse Window
4. Bell Founder's Window
5. Dragon's Head
6. Five Sisters Window

7. Chapter House
8. Central Tower
9. Pulpitum
10. Choir
11. Sanctuary
12. North Choir Aisle
13. Great East
   Window

14. Lady Chapel
15. Stairs to Crypt
16–21. See plan of Crypt
22. South Transept
23. Rose Window
24. Stairs to the Tower
   or Foundations,
   see Foundations plan

Leave the sanctuary for the **north choir aisle (12)**, which is cluttered with a plethora of tombs and memorial tablets, the most imposing being the tombs of Archbishop Thomas Savage and Prince William of Hatfield (brother of the Black Prince and son of Edward III). The latter is the only royal tomb in the cathedral.

Walk along the north choir aisle to the east end, which is dominated by the Perpendicular **great east window (13)**. Dating from 1405–8 and the world's largest area of medieval stained glass, it tells the story of the Creation and the destruction. It is said that the glazier, John Thornton of Coventry, received a £10 bonus for finishing the work on time. Because of the internal stone screen which supports the glass, you get a better view of the window from the sanctuary than from here.

The east end is taken up with three chapels. Occupying the whole of the central space is the **Lady Chapel (14)**. The tombs in it include that of Archbishop Richard le Scrope (*c*1350–1405), who was beheaded for becoming involved in the failed rebellion against Henry VI. The screen rails are modern, the work of 'Mousey' Thompson of Kilburn, North Yorkshire – look for his trademark carved mice.

The other two chapels in the east end are St Stephen's, with a large Victorian reredos, and All Saints'.

The Crypt and Foundations

Leave the east end via the south choir aisle and go down some stairs to the right into the **crypt (15)**. In the Norman cathedral this was the space below a platform built to raise the high altar. It is divided into the eastern crypt and the western crypt (filled in during the 14th century and excavated after the 1829 fire).

From the entrance, turn right and into the eastern crypt. Here on your right you will see the **Doomstone (16)**, a 12th-century carved slab which probably came from the west front of the old Norman cathedral. On the east wall is the **York Virgin (17)**, a headless figure on a plaque, discovered after the 1829 fire; this Romanesque work had, remarkably, been used as rubble filling in the 14th-century east wall of the cathedral!

Close by is a **Roman column base (18)**, dating from the 4th century. It appears to

Crypt

Crypt

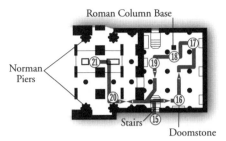

Roman Column Base

Norman Piers

Stairs

Doomstone

Key

15. Stairs from South Choir Aisle
16. Doomstone
17. York Virgin
18. Roman Column Base
19. Font
20. Norman Piers
21. Shrine of St William of York

Foundations

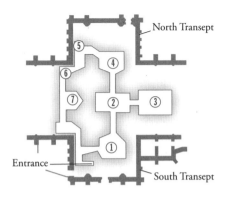

North Transept

South Transept

Entrance

Key

1–7. Chambers

be in its original position as part of the colonnade of the house of the commanding officer of the Roman legion here. Alongside it are red stud marks on the floor; these approximate to the eastern apse of the 11th-century Norman cathedral.

Against the south wall is the **font (19)**, the only one in the minster. It dates from the mid-15th century, but also has a modern cover which was designed by Sir Ninian Comper.

Now walk through into the western crypt, which is dominated by some massive **Norman piers (20)** carved with dogtooth and spiral patterns in the manner of those in Durham Cathedral (see page 310). The most important part of this area of the crypt is the **Shrine of St William of York (21)**. William (d1154) was Archbishop of York in the 12th century. After a period in exile he returned to the city to be greeted by thousands of people on the bridge over the River Ouse. Such was their weight that the bridge collapsed. Although the river was in flood, it is said that St William's prayers ensured not a single person drowned. His bones are contained in a Roman coffin with a medieval lid. Nearby are modern mosaics telling his story.

Also in the western crypt is the treasury, which has some impressive silver, but is otherwise of only moderate interest.

Go back up the steps to the south choir aisle, turn right and go left into the **south transept (22)**, the first part of the Gothic cathedral to be built and not generally considered an architectural success. It is dominated by the 13th-century **rose window (23)**, which was probably originally glazed with *grisaille* glass. The tomb of Archbishop Walter Gray, in whose time the south transept was built, can be seen close to the aisle.

The south transept was the scene of the disastrous 1984 fire, which was probably caused by a lightning strike. As part of the restoration programme, a new series of bosses was made – including six designed by children through television's *Blue Peter* programme.

From the corner of the transept, steps lead up to the tower (entrance charge). If you are claustrophobic or have no head for heights, miss out the tower and take the steps to the right which lead to the **foundations (24)**. This is basically space excavated in something of a hurry between 1967 and 1972 when the central tower seemed in danger of collapse. The foundations present a cross-section of the early history of the city and the cathedral, and are definitely not to be missed. The Roman, Anglo-Saxon and Norman remains discovered during the excavation can be seen in a series of chambers separated by the massive reinforced concrete walls that now support the tower.

Chamber One was at the ground level of the Roman basilica. The base of one of the pillars can be seen in its original position.

Chamber Two shows part of the foundations of the Norman cathedral. Some steps lead up to the treasury, which was probably visited from the western crypt.

Chamber Three has some large models demonstrating the relative positions of the various buildings.

Chambers Four and Five take us outside the boundary of the Norman cathedral.

Chamber Six returns to the Roman area, revealing a culvert that ran from north of the minster to the River Ouse. Also on view here is an interesting Roman military wall painting.

The route through *Chamber Seven* reenters the basilica. It was roughly at this spot that Constantine was proclaimed Caesar on the death of his father in 306.

Finally, leave the foundations by returning up the steps to the south transept. Walk back along the south nave aisle to the west door.

WALKING TOUR FROM YORK MINSTER

The route includes sections of the city walls, a stretch of the Ouse riverside and parts of the pedestrianized streets of the medieval core. Note that many of the placenames have Viking origins. Gates in the walls, for instance, are known as 'bars' (they barred entry as well as letting people through), while many of the streets include the word 'gate', which derives from the Norse 'gata' for street. The walk does not cover all the historic sites of the city (this would be impossible in such a short time), but detours are suggested.

Start and finish: The west front of the minster.
Length: 3 miles (4.8km).
Time: 2½ hours. Allow extra time depending on how many museums, churches and other attractions you want to visit.
Refreshments: A number of ancient inns on or close to the route provide pub lunches and bar meals, notably the Punchbowl and Ye Olde Starre Inn (both in Stonegate), the Hole in the Wall (High Petergate; it has a resident ghost), the Three Tuns (Coppergate) and the Golden Fleece (Pavement).

From the west front of the minster head to the right along High Petergate, named after the minster's patron saint; it follows the route of the Roman Via Principalis.

York

After about 150 yards (135m) you reach **Bootham Bar**, one of four original
gates in the city walls (the others are Micklegate, Monk and Walmgate). All once had
barbicans (fortified entrances); only that at Walmgate Bar survives. The gates also had
portcullises, and you can see the one under the arch at Bootham Bar. The original
Roman gateway, the Porta Principalis Dextra, lies beneath the present bar.

Immediately on your left through Bootham Bar you'll find toilets and the helpful Tourist Information Office. Across the road opposite Bootham Bar is a complex
of buildings around the Museum Gardens which would make a profitable detour for
any visitor with an extra half day to spend in the city. Immediately opposite the bar
is the City Art Gallery. To its left is the King's Manor, a Stuart building with
Charles I's coat-of-arms over the door. It is now part of the university. Nearby is the
Yorkshire Museum, which concentrates on archaeological treasures. Alongside the
museum are the ruins of St Mary's Abbey, which was dissolved in 1536.

A Walk on the Walls

Otherwise, climb the steps at the side of the toilets and go through the upper part
of Bootham Bar onto a section of the **city walls**. Built of the same magnesian
limestone from Tadcaster as the minster, the walls date from the 13th and 14th
centuries and rest on Roman foundations. They stretch for three miles (5km) and
almost completely encircled the medieval city, which had four times as many
inhabitants as does the same area today – though also rather
more filth and squalor.

Walk leftwards along the wall. On your right you
can see the Dean's Park and, above the shrubs
and trees, good views of the minster and of
the minster's library, a building which
was once a chapel of the medieval
archbishop's palace.

At the clearly signed
Robin Hood Tower, the
walls swing around to the
southeast, and finally
you come to **Monk
Bar**. This was the
most heavily fortified
of the gateways. The
portcullis still works,
but the barbican was
removed in Victorian
times. The upper floor
used to be a prison
in the 17th century,
and it is reputed that
heads would be hung
from the gate after
executions.

St William's College

303

An Ancient Church and a Roman Column

Descend the stairs into Goodramgate; about fifty yards (50m) along this street fork left. After a further hundred yards or so (100m) turn right through an iron gateway into the graveyard of **Holy Trinity Church**. This remarkable little building, undoubtedly the best of the many parish churches in York, is claimed to be the oldest church in England, and certainly records go back to 1080. It has a rare saddleback roof, some 17th-century box pews, a 15th-century font, Jacobean altar rails and much, much more. A little gem – don't miss it!

Head back along Goodramgate to the fork and cross over the road into College Street. On your right is the half-timbered **St William's College**, built in 1467 and named after the Norman archbishop. Formerly the royal mint for Charles I and college for the minster's priests, it is now an information and conference centre with an excellent restaurant and bistro. At the top right of the main entrance door you can spot one of 'Mousey' Thompson's little rodents. From the college, there is an excellent view of the minster's great east window in all its Perpendicular glory, while to the right is the chapter house with its external buttresses.

Walk now past the south side of the cathedral along Deangate and Minster Yard. On your left you'll see a **Roman column** which in the 4th century stood in the great hall of the 6th Legion. It was found in 1969 during the excavation of the minster's south transept, lying where it had collapsed. It was erected on this site by the York Civic Trust in 1971 to mark the 1900th anniversary of the founding of the city by the Romans.

This is a good spot to look at the architecture of the south side of the minster, notably the rather unfortunate south transept, with its strange relationships, lack of sculpture and three irritatingly steep gables over its door.

Minster Yard leads towards the west front of the minster. On your left is the simple little early-16th-century **Church of St Michael le Belfry**, said to be the only church in York to be built during a single architectural period. The interior has a plain, Presbyterian feel to it. There is some stained glass dating from the 1330s, but the church's main claim to fame is that Guy Fawkes (1570–1606) was baptized here; his birthplace, now Young's Hotel, is just across the road.

From the Shambles to a Viking Centre

Leaving the church, turn left into Low Petergate and go along it to King's Square, reputedly named after the Viking kings who lived hereabouts in the 7th to 10th centuries. From the right-hand corner of the square, enter York's most famous street, the **Shambles**.

Until the early 1930s, almost every building here was a butcher's shop; the street got its name from the 'fleshammels', ledges beneath the windows used to display the meat. Many of these ledges can still be seen, although the shops are now much more varied. Narrow and with overhanging walls and roofs, the Shambles remains full of medieval atmosphere.

At its end, turn right briefly into Pavement, the first street in York to be paved and the site of political executions; it once had stocks and pillories. Turn almost immediately left into Piccadilly where, on the banks of the River Foss (a tributary

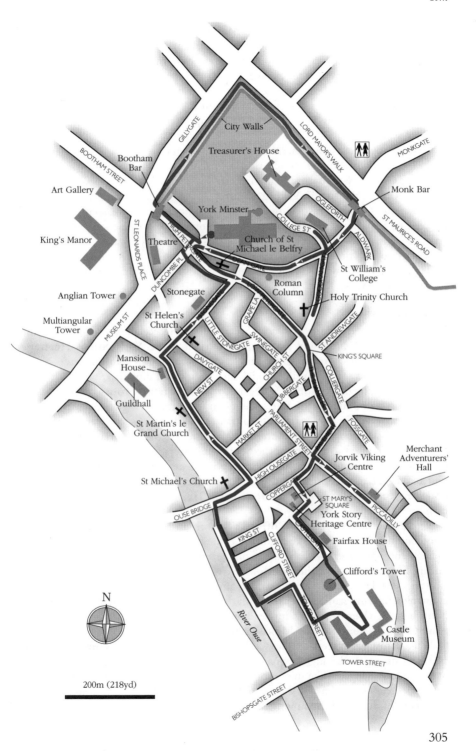

City Walls
Treasurer's House
Bootham Bar
Art Gallery
Monk Bar
King's Manor
York Minster
Theatre
Church of St Michael le Belfry
St William's College
Anglian Tower
Stonegate
Roman Column
Holy Trinity Church
Multiangular Tower
St Helen's Church
Mansion House
Guildhall
St Martin's le Grand Church
King's Square
Jorvik Viking Centre
Merchant Adventurers' Hall
St Michael's Church
York Story Heritage Centre
Fairfax House
Clifford's Tower
Castle Museum

GILLYGATE
LORD MAYOR'S WALK
MONKGATE
BOOTHAM STREET
ST MAURICE'S ROAD
OGLEFORTH
COLLEGE ST
ALDWARK
ST LEONARD'S PLACE
HIGH PETERGATE
DUNCOMBE PL.
MUSEUM ST
GRAPE LA
LITTLE STONEGATE
SWINEGATE
CHURCH ST
ST ANDREWGATE
COLLIERGATE
DAVYGATE
NEW ST
LOW PETERGATE
MARKET ST
PARLIAMENT STREET
STONEGATE
UBBERGATE
FOSSGATE
HIGH OUSEGATE
PICCADILLY
COPPERGATE
ST MARY'S SQUARE
OUSE BRIDGE
KING ST
CLIFFORD STREET
CASTLEGATE
TOWER STREET
River Ouse
BISHOPSGATE STREET

N

200m (218yd)

of the Ouse) to your left, you see the **Merchant Adventurers' Hall**. This half-timbered building was the Guildhall of the Merchant Adventurers Company of the City of York, founded 1357. For 500 years these were the most powerful people in the area. Their ships went as far afield as Russia and the Middle East, dealing in such commodities as wool, lead, timber, sugar, dyes and silks. Inside the building is a magnificent timbered great hall, festooned with the emblems of the various guilds. Below, in the undercroft, is a delightful little chapel, which today is a popular venue for local weddings.

Retrace your steps along Piccadilly to Pavement and turn left into Coppergate – nothing to do with copper: coopers (barrelmakers) worked here. On your right is All Saints Church, with its prominent lantern tower. Turn left into Coppergate Walk. On your right is the **Jorvik Viking Centre**.

When the foundations of a nearby modern shopping centre were being dug, remains of a Viking settlement were found along with a tremendous number of artefacts. This museum, built on the site, has won many awards. Visitors travel backwards on a 'time car' and then forwards through a reconstructed Viking settlement complete with sounds and smells. Be assured that this will be a highlight of your visit to York!

The Story of York

Walk through the modern St Mary's Square shopping complex, leaving it on the right-hand side. A little way along on your right is the **York Story Heritage Centre**, based in a redundant church. The exhibitions within trace York's development over the ages using models and audiovisual displays.

On leaving, turn left along Castlegate to reach **Fairfax House**, claimed, with justification, to be one of the finest Georgian townhouses anywhere in Britain. It was built in 1762 for the 3rd Baron Fairfax (1612–1671), victor over Charles I at the Battle of Naseby (1645). Although a staunch parliamentarian at this time, Fairfax later refused to march on the Scots, supporters of the Old Pretender (later Charles II), and retired from his military posts. Later he headed the commission sent to The Hague to organize the Old Pretender's accession to the throne. The house, restored in 1982–4 by the York Civic Trust, contains a fine collection of furniture, clocks and art.

At the end of Castlegate is **Clifford's Tower**, an artificial mound topped by a stone building. This was the keep for the castle built by Henry III. The mound was there before, however: William the Conqueror built a wooden tower on its top during his 'harrowing of the North'. This was burned down during anti-Semitic riots in 1190. The extant tower is named after Roger Clifford, one of its hereditary constables. Another name associated with the tower is that of Robert Aske, who was hung here in chains in 1537 for leading the Pilgrimage of Grace – the protest against the Dissolution of the Monasteries.

Walk across the green to the **Castle Museum**, housed in some old prison buildings in which the highwayman Dick Turpin (1705–1739) spent his last night before being hanged. The museum has a high reputation, and includes some authentic reconstructions of Victorian and Edwardian street scenes and shops – although you may find the innumerable school parties an irritation.

A Stroll by the Water and Two Fine Churches

Leave the Castle Green and, with Clifford's Tower on your right and St George's Field on your left, head towards the bank of the **River Ouse**. Turn right on reaching the river and walk along South Esplanade and King's Staith towards Ouse Bridge. This is a good place to pick up a river cruise; the floodlit ones in the evening are particularly recommended. Most trips last about an hour.

The east side of the river along here is mainly residential, with Edwardian and Victorian houses, but you'll see across the water that the west side, which once consisted largely of warehouses and riverside industry, is being redeveloped with expensive apartments, restaurants and hotels.

Leave the riverside at Ouse Bridge and turn right, into Ousegate. On your left is **St Michael's Church**, one of York's many redundant parish churches. The interior is mainly 12th-century; the tower was added three centuries later. The church has some notable 15th-century stained glass. In Victorian times, some 7ft (2m) of the south wall was removed in order to improve access to Ouse Bridge. St Michael's was refurbished in 1989 to serve as a Christian Centre.

Turn left into Spurriergate, which soon becomes the modern Coney Street. A fair way along on your left you'll come to **St Martin's le Grand Church**. Built in the 15th century, this was largely destroyed in an air raid in 1942, but the remains have a modern extension that imaginatively blends old with new. The most remarkable feature is a large painted clock jutting out over the street; on top of the clock is the figure of an 18th-century sailor, usually known as the **Little Admiral**, using a cross-staff sextant.

Old Public Buildings and an Old Public House

At the end of Coney Street, St Helen's Square was the site of the main Roman entrance to the city. On the square's southwest side are two important public buildings. The **Mansion House** was completed in 1730 and is still occupied by the Lord Mayor during his year in office. Next door is the stone **Guildhall**, best seen from the other side of the Ouse. Constructed in 1446 as a headquarters for the local craft guilds, it was damaged by bombs during World War II but has been sympathetically restored and is now occupied by York City Council.

Tucked into the corner of the north side of the square is **St Helen's Church**, which has a small lantern tower and some 15th-century glass.

Leave St Helen's Square to the left of the church and walk along **Stonegate**, one of York's fascinating pedestrianized streets. Full of speciality shops and old inns, Stonegate has some interesting architectural features. Note the Tudor building to the left whose jettied walls are covered in Minton tiles. Kilvington's shop to the right has a figurehead taken from one of the many ships abandoned at York when the Ouse gradually silted up. Further along is **Ye Olde Starre Inn**, licensed in 1644 and believed to be the city's oldest inn. Don't miss the Red Devil, sitting on top of a window on the right-hand side; it is believed to represent a printer's devil (or errand boy) – there were certainly print shops in Stonegate at one time.

Turn left at the top of Stonegate and walk along High Petergate until the west front of the cathedral is to your right.

DURHAM

Access: The A1, the usual route from the south, is of motorway classification for much of its length. The cross-Pennine A66 provides a scenic link with the Lake District to the west. There are luxury coach services from London and other centres. InterCity trains from London; journey time under three hours. The nearest international airports are at Newcastle and Teesside. Ferries run from Tyneside to Bergen, Stavanger, Amsterdam, Gothenburg and Hamburg. Within Durham, a City Courier minibus runs a shuttle service from the Market Square to the Palace Green outside the cathedral.

The historic core of Durham lies within an incised meander of the River Wear, an area known locally as the Peninsula. At the south end is the cathedral; protecting it at the north end is the castle, the seat of the prince–bishops who controlled the region from the Scottish border to the River Tees.

The cathedral owes its location to the story of St Cuthbert (*c*634–687), appointed Bishop of Lindisfarne in 685. On his death, not long afterwards, he was buried in the church on the island. Ten years later his coffin was opened and his body was found to be without signs of decay. This was hailed as a miracle, and his body was placed in a shrine.

Two centuries later, frequent Danish raids made it impossible for the monks to stay on Lindisfarne. The shrine was dismantled and St Cuthbert's body and other relics, such as the head of St Oswald and manuscripts including the Lindisfarne Gospels, were taken by the monks in their search for a new home. In fact, they wandered around northern England for over a century before finally settling at Durham, where initially they made a wooden shelter for the saint's body. This was followed by the stone-built White Church, which was to remain until Norman times.

In 1071 William the Conqueror built the castle at Durham in an effort to introduce some law and order into the area, and shortly thereafter he established the first of the prince–bishops, who were expected to be both religious leaders and military commanders. Meanwhile, the first Norman bishop, Walcher of Lorraine, had evicted the Congregation of St Cuthbert and introduced Benedictine monks.

His successor, William of Calais, demolished the White Church and the shrine so that a new cathedral could be built. This was begun in 1092 and by 1133 the choir, transepts and nave had been completed, all with stone vaulted roofs – unique at that time in northwest Europe. The stone used for the construction was quarried locally. (The Coal Measures have a number of sandstone strata and a particularly thick layer was used, which inevitably became known as the Cathedral Sandstone.) By this time a new shrine had been constructed for St Cuthbert behind the high altar. The chapter house was finished in 1140 and in the same year an attempt was made to construct a Lady Chapel at the east end; this was abandoned because of unstable ground, so it was built at the western end and known as the Galilee Chapel. The main entrance to the cathedral was now moved to the north side.

By the 13th century improved building techniques meant that some additions could be made to the east end. The Chapel of the Nine Altars was constructed to provide better facilities for the Benedictine monks to celebrate mass. At the Dissolution the monastery was dissolved, but in 1541 it was reconstituted as a cathedral. The last prior, Hugh Whitehead, became the first dean, and twelve canons were appointed to replace the monks. Fortunately, the monastic buildings survived almost intact – indeed they are the most complete of any English cathedral. A good deal of damage was done to the cathedral during the Reformation – the Shrine of St Cuthbert was broken up, among other things – and further damage was wrought during the Civil War: after the Battle of Dunbar, Cromwell housed some 4000 Scottish prisoners in the cathedral, and they tore up woodwork to make fires to keep themselves warm.

By the 18th century the fabric of the cathedral was in a bad state, so the usual Victorian renovation was much needed. Sir George Gilbert Scott (1811–1878) designed a new pulpit and choir screen. The great doors of the west end were opened up, but then blocked up again. Some of the windows in the nave were altered and filled with mediocre stained glass. There was some restoration of the tower as well, with the replacement of a number of statues, while parts of the former monks' quarters were renovated.

Today the cathedral looks in good shape, but it is a constant battle to raise the funds to maintain the building. In 1987 Durham Cathedral and Castle were designated a World Heritage site of architectural and historical interest.

TOUR OF THE CATHEDRAL
Start and finish: The north door.

Just before you enter through the **north door (1)**, take a look at the Sanctuary Knocker, which was provided for any fugitive who might happen to come seeking sanctuary inside. There were chambers above the door so that the monks could watch for such fugitives, who were granted thirty-seven days' refuge. During the 16th century more than three hundred people sought the sanctuary of St Cuthbert.

The inside of the door is much as it was when it was built in the 12th century, but the outer porch and chambers have been demolished. The present Sanctuary Knocker is not the original (which can be seen in the treasury) but the 20th-century bronze replica looks authentic enough.

Step inside the cathedral and, ignoring the nave for the time being, walk to the right into the **Galilee Chapel (2)**. If you're familiar with southern Spain the regularly spaced pillars of Purbeck marble and rounded dogtooth arches will immediately remind you of the Mesquita in Cordoba. Note the 12th-century wall paintings behind the altar; these are reputed to be of St Cuthbert and St Oswald but, as only their lower halves are represented, you need a bit of imagination.

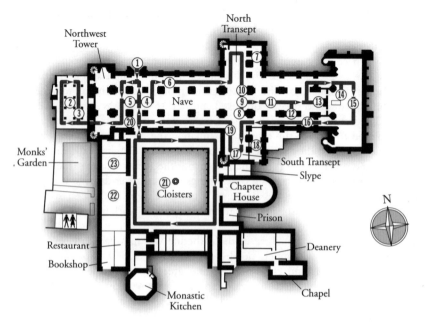

Key

1. North Door
2. Galilee Chapel
3. Tomb of the Venerable Bede
4. Nave
5. Font
6. North Nave Aisle
7. Gregory Chapel

8. Pulpit
9. Choir Screen
10. Lectern
11. Choir
12. Bishop's Throne
13. Neville Screen
14. Tomb of St Cuthbert
15. Chapel of the
    Nine Altars

16. Millennium Window
17. Prior Castell's Clock
18. Chapel of the Durham Light
    Infantry
19. Statue of Shute Barrington
20. Miners' Memorial
21. Cloisters
22. Treasury
23. Monks' Dormitory

Venerable Bones

On the south side of the Galilee Chapel is the **Tomb of the Venerable Bede (3)**. Bede (*c*673–735) was a notable scholar and wrote the first history of England, *Historia Ecclesiastica Gentis Anglorum* ('The Ecclesiastical History of the English People'). His bones were brought to Durham in 1022 and placed in the chapel in a magnificent shrine in 1370. Sadly, the shrine was destroyed in the Reformation, but the bones remain, marked by a simple black tombstone carved with a Latin inscription that can be loosely translated as: 'In this tomb are the bones of the Venerable Bede.'

Return now to the massive and awesome **nave (4)**, undoubtedly the most impressive piece of Romanesque architecture in Britain. The proportions are satisfying, with the arcade 2½ times the triforium. Both clerestory and triforium have galleries. It is, however, the pillars which dominate. They are nearly 22ft (6.6m) in both circumference and height, and alternate between plain and composite design. The round pillars are ornamented with diamonds, chevrons and vertical fluting (spiral designs appear only in the transepts and choir).

The arches have a strong dogtooth ornamentation, a pattern continued at triforium level. Above is the earliest British example of stone vaulting, and the dogtooth ornamentation is again prominent. The overall effect may not be elegant but it certainly has an austere strength.

At the west end of the nave is the **font (5)**, placed there by Bishop John Cosin (1594–1672) towards the end of the 17th century. By contrast with the simplicity of the font, its cover is one of the most ornate to be found in any English cathedral. Richly carved in dark wood, it stands on eight prodigiously tall pillars. Just in front of the font is a long, thin slab of black Frosterley marble, said to mark, in monastic days, the limit to which women were allowed to go.

Modern Aspects

Turn now to the **north nave aisle (6)**, where the main item of interest is a modern stained glass window, *Daily Bread*, designed by Mark Angus. It represents a vertical view of the Last Supper, and was donated by the staff of the local Marks & Spencer to commemorate the firm's centenary. Some find it inspiring; others, more conservative, compare it to a Marks & Spencer fruit and vegetable counter, and wonder whether it has a place in a Romanesque cathedral. It is certainly difficult to be neutral.

Walk to the north transept, where the architectural pattern of the nave is repeated, this time with spirally ornamented pillars prominent. On its east side is the **Gregory Chapel (7)**, which is reserved for private prayer. This chapel was restored in Victorian times and furnished by the Mothers' Union in 1992. Look for the aumbry – a small cupboard set in the wall by the altar; here items of the Sacrament were kept.

Move into the crossing. The black-and-white marble floor, dating from the 17th century, was brought here from the choir as part of the Victorian alterations. Also Victorian is the ornate marble **pulpit (8)**, designed by Sir George Gilbert Scott in a (failed) attempt to replicate the design of the nave. The marble and alabaster **choir screen (9)** is also Scott's work. The aim was to remove the organ screen and replace it with something to allow a continuous view towards the east end. Another failed attempt! The **lectern (10)**, again Victorian, shows, rather than the more customary eagle, a pelican feeding its young from its own breast.

The Choir and the Bishop's Throne

Pass through the screen into the **choir (11)**. The richly carved stalls here date from 1662, when they replaced medieval originals; the identity of the designer and carver are not known for certain. The misericords are certainly worth a look. At the end of the choir stalls is the **bishop's throne (12)**, undoubtedly the tallest in the country. Richly gilded and coloured, it was built for Thomas Hatfield, Bishop of Durham 1345–81, and includes his tomb in a chantry underneath the throne.

Continuing eastward, you come to the high altar, behind which is the superb **Neville Screen (13)**, donated by Lord Neville in 1380. Made of Caen stone, it was carved in London, shipped to Newcastle and finally brought by wagon to Durham. Its niches are now empty, an estimated 107 statues having been removed during the Reformation.

Just by the altar steps is a brass to the memory of Bishop Beaumont which must be one of the largest brasses in England. Unfortunately it is usually covered by a carpet.

St Cuthbert's Tomb

Turn into the north choir aisle and immediately climb the steps behind the altar screen to the **Tomb of St Cuthbert (14)**. His body used to lie here in an elaborate and bejewelled shrine; you can still see the grooves worn in the floor as the untold pilgrims who came here throughout the Middle Ages shuffled past. After the demolition of the shrine, St Cuthbert's coffin was buried at the site. A statue near the tomb shows Cuthbert holding the head of St Oswald (d642), King of Northumbria, which was buried with him.

In case you were wondering, the line of lead on the floor marks the original line of the apsidal east end of the cathedral.

Go back down the steps and into the extreme east end of the cathedral, the **Chapel of the Nine Altars (15)**. Under each of the nine lancet windows here there used to be an altar, separated from its neighbour(s) by a screen. Started in 1242 but not finished until 1280, the chapel shows the evolution of architectural styles during this period.

The rose window is much later, having been redesigned in the late 18th century. Note the thin shafts of black Frosterley marble with prominent sections of white fossil coral.

The Millennium Window and Prior Castell's Clock

Leave the chapel by the south choir aisle, where the main item of interest is the **Millennium Window (16)**. The glass was installed in 1995 to celebrate the 1000th anniversary of the building; donated by the Binks family of Thornley, County Durham, it was designed by Joseph Nuttgens of High Wycombe. The window shows the stages in the life of the cathedral and the surrounding area, beginning with St Cuthbert on Lindisfarne and ending with more modern features such as the Tyne Bridge, Stephenson's *Locomotion* and local coalmining – all delightfully enhanced when the sun streams in from the south.

Walk on into the south transept, which is dominated by **Prior Castell's Clock (17)**. Dating from *c*1500, this probably survived the Cromwell's Scottish prisoners because a thistle features prominently among the decoration. The Victorians (predictably) moved it about, but in 1938 the Friends of the Cathedral restored the clock and returned it to its original position.

On the east side of the transept is the **Chapel of the Durham Light Infantry (18)**, which replaced a medieval chapel after World War I. Colours from the various campaigns hang from the walls and a Book of Remembrance holds the names of those killed in battle.

At the exit to the transept is the **Statue of Shute Barrington (19)**. Barrington (1734–1826), Bishop of Durham from 1791 until his death, is arguably the most highly regarded bishop in the cathedral's history. In addition to his religious duties he was a patron of the arts and contributed much to agricultural development in the area.

Stroll down the south aisle, past the site of the Neville Chantry, until you reach the **Miners' Memorial (20)**. Erected in 1947 and appropriately made of black wood, thought to be 17th-century Spanish, this remembers Durham miners who lost their lives in the pits. The last coalmine in Durham closed in 1994, but the Durham Miners' Gala continues to take place annually.

Associated Buildings

Go through the door into the **cloisters (21)**. These were restored in 1827–8. The roof, however, is original and there are some fine bosses with 15th-century coats-of-arms.

Turn left and stroll round the cloisters in a clockwise direction. Many of the buildings you pass – including the chapter house, prison and monastic kitchen – are unfortunately not open to visitors.

On the opposite corner from where you entered is the prior's hall undercroft, in which is the Audiovisual Display Area. The restaurant and the bookshop are at the next corner you reach, and alongside them is the **treasury (22)**, which contains the relics of St Cuthbert, including his coffin, cross and vestments. The treasury was recently renovated with a grant from the Heritage Lottery Fund.

Past the treasury, go up some steps to the former **monks' dormitory (23)**. This could accommodate up to forty monks, each with a private cubicle. A blocked-up doorway at its cathedral end once led to the 'night stairs', the route the monks used to go into the cathedral for prayers at night. Today, the dormitory's most impressive feature is its beamed roof, around 600 years old and said to have required the wood from over twenty oak trees. Now used as a library and study centre for students, the dormitory also contains a collection of over seventy Anglo-Saxon stones – some originals, others moulds – mainly in the form of crosses.

Leave the cloisters and return through the nave of the cathedral to the north door, where the tour began.

WALKING TOUR FROM DURHAM CATHEDRAL

This walk circumnavigates the Peninsula and includes stretches of the Riverside Walk, the castle and parts of the university, plus the older section of the city. The whole site encompassing the cathedral, castle, Palace Green and the surrounding buildings has deservedly been recognized by UNESCO as a World Heritage Site.

Start and finish: Palace Green, just outside the north door of the cathedral.
Length: 2 miles (3.2km).
Time: 1½ hours, but allow longer if the castle is open.
Refreshments: The spacious cathedral restaurant is recommended. Surprisingly few pubs and inns of character, but you could try the Market Tavern (Market Place) or the Swan and Three Cygnets (next to Elvet Bridge). The Three Tuns (New Elvet) and the County Hotel (Old Elvet) provide more expensive food as well as accommodation.

Between the cathedral and the castle is a large grassy open space, **Palace Green**. Once called 'The Place', it was covered with houses until the 12th century, when these were pulled down as a health hazard. It is surrounded by buildings once closely connected to the cathedral but now largely used by the university.

On the east side are: Bishop Cosin's Hall, a late-17th-century mansion that is now a university hall of residence; the Bishop's Hospital, now the Students' Union building; the more modern infill of the Pemberton Building, used as a debating chamber; and the Queen Anne-style Abbey House, now occupied by the Department of Theology. Between the latter and the cathedral is the cobbled Dun Cow Lane, named after the animal which, legend tells us, decided the ultimate resting place of St Cuthbert's coffin. Note the carving nearby on the northeast transept of the cathedral showing a dun cow and a milkmaid.

The west side of the Green has: the 15th-century exchequer and chancery, once the mint and bishops' court; Bishop Cosin's Library (note his coat-of-arms over the door); the old University Library, built in the mid-19th century; the Diocesan Registry, now part of the library; and the Grammar School, built in the 1660s, once a private residence and now the University Music School.

Durham Castle

Looming over the northern end of the Green is the imposing **Durham Castle**. The building was started *c*1072 and is on the typical Norman 'motte and bailey' plan. Shortly after completion it was given to Bishop Walcher, and it was to remain in cathedral hands for 750 years, with the prince–bishops maintaining a combined religious and military rule. The castle successfully carried out its defensive role – despite frequent skirmishes with the Scots, there is no record of the building ever being taken.

As times became more peaceful and the castle no longer needed to be a fortress, the prince–bishops gradually converted it into a residence where they could entertain lavishly, and over the centuries the original Norman architecture became mixed with other styles. In the 1930s, Bishop van Mildert established the University of Durham, and the castle became University College. Shortly afterwards the Norman keep, by now little more than a ruin, was restored; sympathetic renovation of the building continues to this day.

If you take a tour of the castle you'll see much of the original Norman architecture, particularly in the gatehouse, interior doorways, gallery and chapel (which dates from 1080). Also of interest are the great hall, the bishop's dining room, the state rooms and Tunstal's Chapel.

St Cuthbert's Well and a Riverside Stroll

Leave Palace Green via a small alleyway (or vennel), Windy Gap, between the University Music School and the old registry. The vennel leads to the Upper Riverside Walk. Turn left on this and after about fifty yards (50m) you'll see a sign pointing down through the trees to **St Cuthbert's Well**. This has some stonework around it with a 17th-century inscription, now difficult to read. These days only a trickle of water emerges from the well, and it often dries up completely in the summer.

Continue down the path through the woodland, which is carpeted with pungent wild garlic in the spring, until you reach the Lower Riverside Walk. Turn left and, with the water close by on your right, follow this path to the old fulling mill (fulling is the scouring and thickening of fabric), now the **University Museum of Archaeology**. The displays inside chart the archaeological history of Durham and its surrounding area.

Walk further along the path to **Prebends' Bridge**, built in 1778 after an earlier footbridge had been swept away in a flood. There are superb views northwards along the wooded gorge toward Framwellgate Bridge, with the tips of the cathedral towers peeping above the trees. This vista inspired Sir Walter Scott

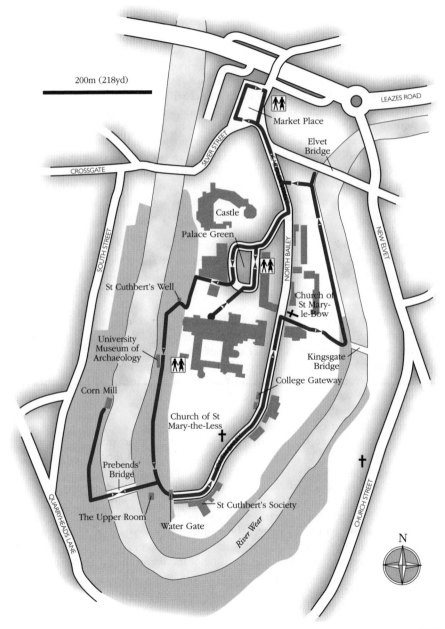

(1771–1832), and lines from his *Harold the Dauntless* are inscribed in a tablet on the wall of the bridge:

Grey towers of Durham,
Yet well I love thy mixed and massive piles.
Half church of God, half castle 'gainst the Scot.
And long to roam these venerable aisles
With records stored of deeds long forgot.

Cross the bridge and turn right along the path to a **corn mill**, on the other end of the weir from the fulling mill. The two mills were originally the Prior's Mills, and the profits from them paid for work in the cathedral. You can't go into the corn mill, but the terrace with picnic tables on its north side, with a view across the river and the weir and up the slopes to the cathedral, provides great photo-opportunities!

Return to Prebends' Bridge, cross the river again, and make a short detour to the right to a group of dead elm trunks carved to represent the Last Supper. Called the **Upper Room**, this is the work of Colin Wilbourn, the first Artist in Residence at Durham Cathedral (1986–7). Twelve trunks denote both the twelve Apostles and the arches of the room, while the thirteenth tree has an integral seat representing Christ's place, and here you can sit – an extraordinary experience.

A City of History
Go back once more to Prebends' Bridge, turn right and walk up the hill to the **Water Gate**. Also known as **Bailey Gate**, this was constructed in 1778, shortly after Prebends' Bridge, and made a gap in the city's walls through which carriages could travel to the south.

Pass through the gate into **South Bailey**, a road which runs along the east side of the cathedral and merges eventually into North Bailey. The street was named after the area between the inner and outer walls of the castle, the Baileys. This has always been a fashionable area of the city, and provides some wonderful examples of domestic architecture. On the right, for example, is the **Home of St Cuthbert's Society**, which dates from the early 18th century and has a stunning moulded doorway with a shell-hood above.

Next, on the left, is the **Church of St Mary-the-Less**, built in the 12th century but heavily restored in early Victorian times. This charming little building, once the parish church of South Bailey but now the chapel for St John's College, retains its Norman windows and a dogtooth arch over the main door.

Further up the hill, again on your left, is the **College Gateway**, the old monastery gatehouse, dating back to the 16th century. The gateway is vaulted and has some interesting bosses, one of which has the arms of Prior Castell, responsible for the gate's construction. If you peer through the gateway you'll see College Green (also known as the Cathedral Close), surrounded by monastery buildings which were handed over to the cathedral at the time of the Reformation. In the centre of the Green is an octagonal well house, built (it is believed) *c*1750.

Continue past the gateway. The road now becomes North Bailey. On the left is a fine view of the east end of the cathedral. Almost opposite, on your right, is

St Mary-le-Bow Church, which probably occupies the site of the original wooden church where St Cuthbert's body was sheltered when first brought to Durham. The church was named after the arch or 'bow' which crossed the bailey. The arch and attached tower collapsed in 1637, demolishing much of the nave of the church, but it was speedily rebuilt using local taxes. The church finally closed in 1967, and ten years later it was converted into a Heritage Centre and Museum offering audiovisual displays and opportunities for brass rubbing.

Go down Bow Lane, by the side of the church, until you get to **Kingsgate Bridge**. This footbridge was provided as a link for students between the colleges and the administration blocks on the east side of the river. It was designed by the Danish architect Ove Arup, who produced the original design for Sydney Opera House. Walk onto the bridge for views north along the gorge towards Elvet Bridge and south to see the tower of St Oswald's Church rising above the trees on the far side of the river.

Return to Bow Lane and take the steps down the right-hand side of the bridge to the level of the River Wear. Turn left along the path, Fearon Walk, and walk along the riverside to **Elvet Bridge**. The original bridge, built *c*1160, was badly damaged in a serious flood in 1771. It was extensively rebuilt in 1805, doubling its width with dry arches and massive buttresses on the upstream side. There are shops over the dry arch on the east side; on the city side, one of the first buildings you see was once a prison. Since the building of the New Elvet Bridge to the north in 1975 to relieve traffic in the city centre, the old bridge has been reserved for pedestrians.

Market Place and Saddler Street

Turn left at the bridge, climb up the steps and fork right into **Market Place**. Always busy with shoppers, tourists and students, Market Place is the social and economic hub of the city. The market first received its charter in 1180, but most of the buildings around the square date from Victorian times, with some impressive bank fronts.

The Church of St Nicholas on the north side (to your right as you enter the square) dates from 1888 and is Victorian Gothic in style. Alongside is the Town Hall complex, with Guildhall and Art Gallery. Behind these are the indoor markets.

Dominating Market Place are two statues. Next to the church is the equestrian statue of the 3rd Marquess of Londonderry, a leading political figure in Victorian times. On the south side of Market Place is a more modest statue of Neptune which once stood over a wellhead in the square. This latter statue was given to the city in 1729 by George Bowes MP to represent the scheme to link Durham to the sea by improved navigation along the River Wear. After spending half a century exiled to a local park, Neptune was renovated and returned to Market Place in 1991.

Leave Market Place the way you entered it, via what was once called Fleshergate, the butchers' quarter. Mustard was ground at a mill behind No. 73 until *c*1900, though nothing remains to be seen today. Go past the steps down to Elvet Bridge and fork right into **Saddler Street**, named after Sir Richard Saddler, whose 16th-century house is probably the oldest residence in a street whose delightful domestic architecture may cause you to pause and browse for a while. During the 18th century this was also Durham's theatreland. At the head of Saddler Street is the site of the North Gate, demolished in 1820.

Here fork right into Owengate, a cobbled street that leads back to Palace Green.

FURTHER
INFORMATION

Visitors to English cathedrals are welcome to attend public services, but should bear in mind that access to parts of the buildings may be restricted at such times. They should also be aware that the naves of cathedrals are frequently used for events such as concerts and ceremonies. At such times the buildings may be closed to visitors.

The information below gives contact details for each cathedral. Also listed are opening hours, access details and an indication of any entrance charge required for each cathedral and any nearby places of interest. The official cathedral web site is also shown.

WESTERN ENGLAND

EXETER
Cathedral
www.exeter-cathedral.org.uk
Toilets are located in the cloisters and in the refectory. **The cathedral shop**, just off the south quire aisle, sells guidebooks (in English, French and German), souvenirs and gifts. **The refectory** in the cloister room sells light meals Mon–Sat 13:00–17:00. Both shop and refectory are closed Sundays. Excellent wheelchair access, with ramps to virtually all areas.
Underground Passages
Guided tour every half-hour preceded by a video presentation. Exhibition. Open Easter–Oct Tue–Sat 10.00–17.00, Nov–Easter Tue–Fri 14.00–17.30, Sat 10.00–17.00. Admission charge.
Royal Albert Museum
Open Tue–Sat 10.00–17.30. Admission free to Exeter residents; small charge to others.
St Nicholas' Priory
Open Easter–Oct Mon–Sat 13:00–17:00. Admission charge.
Tuckers' Hall
Open Jun–Sep Tue, Thu and Fri 10:30–12:00. For the rest of the year Fri only 10:30–12:30.

WELLS
Cathedral
www.wellscathedral.org.uk
A **giftshop** and a **refectory** occupy the west cloister. It is no surprise to see that they are linear in shape! **Toilets** may be found in the Camery Gardens, with facilities for the disabled in the west cloister.
Wells Museum
Open daily 10:00–17:00 (summer) and 11:00–16:00 (winter).
Bishop's Palace
Open on a somewhat irregular basis Apr–Oct.

BATH
Abbey
www.bathabbey.org
The nearest **toilets** are located inside the entrance to the Roman Baths (turn left and go down the stairs). There is **wheelchair access** to most parts of the abbey, which has few interior steps. A small **bookshop** just off the south aisle sells a variety of gifts, music and books.
Abbey Vaults
Open 10:00–16:00 Mon–Sat; closed Sun. Modest entrance fee.
Museum in Sally Lunn's
Open during restaurant opening hours.
Museum in the Octagon
Open Mar–Dec 11:00–17:00 Mon–Sat; 14:00–17:00 Sun.
Postal Museum
Open Mar–Dec 11:00–17:00 Mon–Sat; 14:00–17:00 Sun.
Museum of Costume
Open 10:00–17:00 Mon–Sat; 11:00–17:00 Sun. Admission free.
Museum of East Asian Art
Open Mon–Sat 10:00–18:00 , Sun 10:00–17:00. Admission charge, with concessions.
Museum in No 1 The Royal Crescent
Open 10:30–11:00. Closed Mondays.
Roman Baths Museum
Open in summer 09:00–17:00, winter 09:00–18:00; torchlit visits on August evenings 20:00–22:00. Visitors are given easily used `wands' or autoguides, which give commentaries in six languages. Entrance charge.

SALISBURY
Cathedral
www.salisburycathedral.org.uk
Open daily Apr–Sep 07:00–20:15 and Oct–Mar 07:00–18:30. **Toilets**, including those for the disabled, may be found adjacent to the chapter house. Self-service **coffee shop** and **giftshop** alongside the north cloister. Salisbury is a **wheelchair-friendly** cathedral, with ramps throughout the building. For details of the **Friends of Salisbury Cathedral** tel (01722) 555120.
Salisbury and South Wiltshire Museum
Open Mon–Sat 10:00–17:00; Sun in Jul and Aug 14:00–17:00. Entry charge. Tel (01722) 332151.
Museum of the Royal Gloucestershire, Berkshire and Wiltshire Regiment
Open Apr–Oct daily 10:00–16:30; Nov, Feb and Mar Mon–Fri 10:00–16:30. Closed Dec–Jan. Entry charge. Tel (01722) 414536.
Mompesson House
Open Apr–Oct 12:00–17:30; closed Thu and Fri. Tel (01722) 335659.

WINCHESTER
Cathedral
www.winchester-cathedral.org.uk
The modern **Visitor Centre** is in an attractive walled garden just to the southwest of the cathedral. It has a spacious **restaurant**, with outside tables. A range of imaginative lunches are cooked on the premises. Next to the restaurant are **toilets**, with full facilities for the disabled. A comprehensive **giftshop** in the Visitor Centre sells books, music and souvenirs. There is **wheelchair access** to all parts of the ground floor of the cathedral; use the main entrance.
Guildhall
The gallery is open daily during office hours.

City Mill
Open in summer Wed–Sun 11:00–16:45.
Winchester College
Guided tours available during the summer, starting at the Porters' Lodge at 14:00 and 15:15.
City Museum
Open daily 10:00–19:00, Sun 14:00–17:00. Admission free.
Peninsula Barracks/Regimental Museums
Opening times vary. Free admission to all five museums.

CHICHESTER
Cathedral
www.chichestercathedral.org.uk
There is a **refectory** in the Bishop Bell Rooms in the cloisters, where **toilets** may also be found. The **wheelchair entrance** is in the southwest corner of the building (disabled visitors may have to vary the route described in the text). There is a **giftshop** in the ground floor of the bell tower. For details of the **Friends of Chichester Cathedral**, contact The Royal Chantry, Cathedral Cloisters, Chichester, PO 19 1PX.
Pallant House
Open all year Tue–Sat 10:00–17:30. Closed Sun, Mon and bank holidays. Modest entry fee, with concessions.
City Museum
Open 10:00–17:30 Tue–Sat. Entrance free.
Guildhall Museum
Open Jun–Sep only, Tue–Sat 13:00–17:00. Entrance free.

OXFORD
Cathedral
www.chch.ox.ac.uk/cathedral
There is no eating place at the cathedral or in the remainder of Christ Church. **Toilets** can be found on the west side of the cloisters. The **bookshop** is in the chapter house. Christ Church Cathedral is open daily 09:00–17:00, Sun 13:00–17:00 – note one peculiarity: cathedral time is five minutes behind standard time.
Christ Church Picture Gallery
Open Mon–Sat 10:30–17:30, Sun 14:30–17:30. Small entrance fee.
Botanic Gardens
Open Apr–Sep 09:00–17:00 and Oct–Mar 09:00–16:30 (greenhouse times may vary). Entrance free.
St Mary the Virgin Tower
Open 09:00–17:00 all year round. Entrance fee.
Bodleian Library
Open to the public 09:00–17:00. Entry to the Divinity School and Duke Humphrey's Library is by guided tour only during the summer months.
The Oxford Story
Open Apr–Oct 09:30–17:00; Jul and Aug 09:00–18:30; Nov–Mar 10:00–16:00. Admission charge.
Carfax Tower
Open Mar–Oct 10:00–17:30 and Nov–Feb 10:00–15:30. Admission charge.

GLOUCESTER
Cathedral
www.gloucestercathedral.uk.com

The spacious **refectory** and the **toilets** (including for the disabled) are located on the west side of the cloisters. There is a **bookshop** situated in the southwest corner of the nave and another in the Cathedral Close. There is good **wheelchair access** in the main body of the cathedral, though not for the Gloucester Cathedral Exhibition. For details of the **Friends of Gloucester Cathedral** contact the Chapter Office, tel (01452) 528095.

Folk Museum
Open Mon–Sat 10:00–17:00; Sun (Jul–Sep only) 10:00–16:00. Modest entrance fee. Wheelchair access to the ground floor only.

Soldiers of Gloucester Museum
Open Tue–Fri 10:00–17:00. Modest admission charge.

National Waterways Museum
Open daily 10:00–18:00, with reduced hours in winter. Sizeable admission charge, but with concessions.

Museum of Advertising and Packaging (Robert Opie Collection)
Open daily 10:00–18:00, with reduced hours on Sun and in the winter. Admission charge, with concessions.

East Gate Viewing Chamber
Open May–Sep 10:00–13:00 and 14:00 and 17:00, Sat only.

HEREFORD
Cathedral
www.herefordcathedral.co.uk
The **Mappa Mundi/Chained Library** are open 10:00–16:15 in the summer and 10:00–15:15 in the winter. Closed Sun in the winter. Admission charge. The **giftshop** and **refectory** are located in the East Cloister. There are **toilets** including those for the disabled in Chapter House Yard.

City Art Gallery, Museum and Library
Open all year Tue–Sat 10:00–17:00; also Sun 10:00–16:00 during the summer. Entrance free.

Cathedral Cruises
40min river boat cruises leave hourly from 11:00 between Easter and October.

The Old House
Open Tue–Sat 10:00–17:00; also Sun during the summer. Admission free, although donation welcome.

Cider Museum
Open Apr–Oct daily 10:00–17:30; Nov–Mar Tue–Sun 11:00–15:00. Entrance charge, with concessions.

WORCESTER
Cathedral
www.cofe-worcester.org.uk
Open daily 07:30–18:00. The **giftshop** is located to the west of the cloisters. There is a small **tearoom** on the east side of the cloisters. **Toilets** (including for the disabled) are on the north side of College Green. **Wheelchair access** throughout the cathedral except in the crypt. Details of the **Friends of Worcester Cathedral** from the Secretary, 10a College Green, Worcester, WR1 2LH.

Royal Worcester Porcelain Company
Open 09:00–17:00 daily, not Sun. Tours of the factory on weekdays at regular intervals starting at 10:25. Clearance shop, a seconds shop and an interesting museum.

Civil War Centre
Open daily Mon–Sat 10:00–17:00; Sun 13:30–17:30. Entrance fee, with concessions.

Museum of Local Life
Open daily 10:30–17:00, closed Thu, Sun, Bank Holidays. Wheelchair access limited.
The Greyfriars
Open Apr–Oct 14:00–17:00. Entrance fee, except for NT members.

COVENTRY
Cathedral
www.coventrycathedral.org
The cathedral is open daily 09:00–17:00. Note that the **Visitor Centre** and **Benedict's Coffee Shop** have restricted winter opening. There is a **giftshop** on the north side of the old cathedral. **Toilets** are available in the Visitor Centre, and there is **wheelchair access** throughout the cathedral.
Museum of British Road Transport
Open daily (except Christmas Eve, Christmas Day and Boxing Day) 10:00–17:00. At time of writing, entrance was free. Small restaurant and giftshop.
St Mary's Guildhall
Open only in the summer. Check current opening times with the Tourist Information Office.
Herbert Art Gallery and Museum
Open Mon–Sat 10:00–17:30; Sun 14:00–17:00. Entrance free.

LICHFIELD
Cathedral
www.lichfield-cathedral.org
No entrance fee, but donation recommended. The **cathedral cafeteria** is on the south side of the close, and has public **toilets**. There are two cathedral **giftshops**, one in the south aisle of the cathedral and the other in a house on the west side of the close. There is **wheelchair access** to most parts of the cathedral, but not to St Chad's Head Chapel. For details of the **Friends of Lichfield Cathedral**, contact the Friends' Office, 19A The Close, Lichfield, Staffs. WS13 7LD, tel (01543) 306120.
Heritage Centre
Open daily 10:00–17:00 all year round. Admission fee also covers entry to the Samuel Johnson Birthplace Museum. Concessions available.
Samuel Johnson Birthplace Museum
Open daily 10:30–16:30; closed Sun during winter. Admission fee also covers entry to the Heritage Centre. Concessions available.
Erasmus Darwin Centre
Open Tue–Sat 10:00–16:30, Sun 12:00–16:30. Closed Mon except Bank Holidays. Admission charge, with concessions.

CHESTER
Cathedral
www.chestercathedral.org.uk
The **giftshop** and **toilets** are in the west cloister. There is good **wheelchair access** to most parts of the cathedral. The **Friends of Chester Cathedral** can be located at their e-mail address: friends@chestercathedral.org.uk.
Grosvenor Museum
Open Mon–Sat 10:30–17:00, Sun 14:00–17:00. Admission free. Only limited access for wheelchair users.
Chester Visitor and Craft Centre
Open Mon–Sat 09:00–17:00. Admission free.

Dewa Roman Experience
Open 09:00–17:00 daily. Admission charge.

LIVERPOOL
Anglican Cathedral
www.liverpoolcathedral.org.uk
Open daily 08:00-18:00. Admission free, but donations invited. **Wheelchair access** throughout. There are **toilets** at the Vistors' Centre and also near the Chapter House. The Visitors' Centre includes a SPCK **Gift Shop** and an excellent **Refectory** that has gained Egon Ronay recommendations. The **Tower** is open to the public Mon–Sat 11:00–16:00. Tickets are available from the shop. The first tower lift also leads to the **Elizabeth Hoare Embroidery Gallery**, where there is a fine collection of Edwardian and Victorian ecclesiastical embroidery.
Metropolitan Roman Catholic Cathedral
web site: www.liverpool-rc-cathedral.org.uk
Mount Pleasant, tel (0151) 709 9222. Open daily 08:00-18:00. Admission free, but donations welcome. **Wheelchair access** except to crypt.
Liverpool Museum and Planetarium
Open Mon-Sat 10:00-17:00, Sun 12:00-17:00. Admission fee. Extra charge for planetarium.
Merseyside Maritime Museum
Open daily 10:00-17:00. Admission fee. **Full wheelchair access.**
Museum of Liverpool Life
Open daily 10:00-17:00. Admission fee. **Full wheelchair access.**
Tate Gallery
Open Tues-Sun 10:00-18:00, closed Mon. Admission free, but charge for special exhibitions. **Wheelchair access** throughout.
Walker Art Gallery
Open Mon-Sat 10:00-17:00, Sun 12:00-17:00. Admission fee. **Wheelchair access** throughout.
Western Approaches Museum
Open Mar-Oct Mon-Thu and Sat 10:30-16:30. Admission fee. No wheelchair access.
The Beatles Story Open daily Mar-Oct 10:00-17:00, Nov-Feb 10:00-17:00. Admission fee.

EASTERN ENGLAND

LONDON: ST PAUL'S
St Paul's Cathedral
www.stpaulscathedral.org.uk
Open daily 08:00–1730, except Sun 08:30–1600. For pre-recorded information messages, tel 020 82364128. Wheelchair access throughout the ground floor. Toilets in southwest corner of crypt. No cathedral refectory, but plenty of food outlets in surrounding streets.
Dr Johnson's House
Open daily May–Sept 10:00–17:30 and Oct–May 11:00–17:00. *Entrance fee.*

LONDON: WESTMINSTER
Westminster Abbey
www.westminster-abbey.org

Open: the nave and the cloisters (which are free) are open daily 09:00–16:45. The rest of the Abbey (which has an *entrance fee*) is open Mon–Fri 09:00–16:45 and Sat 09:45–14:45, 15:45–17:45. There is an additional *entrance fee* to be paid to visit the Chapter House and Pyx Chamber (run by English Heritage), which are open daily 10:30–16:00. For information, contact the Chapter Office, tel 020 72225152. Wheelchair access over most of abbey, although large visitor numbers can make things difficult. Bookshop outside west door. You will search in vain for toilets.

Houses of Parliament
Open to visitors: 14:30–22:00 Mon–Thurs; 10:00–14.30 when house is sitting. To attend Prime Minister's Question Time a special ticket is needed; tel 020 72194272. Closed most public holidays.

Guards Museum
Open daily 10:00–16:00. *Entrance fee.*

Southwark Cathedral
www.dswark.org/cathedral
Open 09:00–18:00 throughout the year. For information, contact the Vergers Office, Southwark Cathedral, London Bridge, London SE1 9DA, tel 020 74072939. The Friends of Southwark Cathedral may be reached via the Secretary, tel 020 74073708. Wheelchair access throughout cathedral. Toilets in chapter house, which also houses a commercially run restaurant.

HMS *Belfast*
Open daily 10:00–18:00 summer, 10:00–17:00 winter. *Entrance fee.*
Tel 020 74076434. Disabled access difficult.

London Dungeon
Open daily 09:30–20:00 Jun–Sep, 10:00–17:30 Oct–May. *Entrance fee.*

Old Operating Theatre Museum
Open daily (not Mon) 10:00–16:00; closed 15 Dec–5 Jan. *Entrance fee.*

Golden Hinde Replica
Open daily 10:00–17:00. *Tickets* can be bought at the office opposite the ship.

The 'Clink Prison'
Open daily 10:00–18:00 Oct–Apr. 10:00–21:00 May–Sep. *Entrance fee.*

New Globe Theatre
Open daily 10:00–17:00. *Entrance fee.*

Bankside Gallery
Open during exhibitions 10:00–17:00. *Entrance fee.* Bookshop.

Tate Modern
Open Sun–Thurs 10:00–18:00, Fri–Sat 10:00–22:00. *Entrance charge for special exhibitions only.* Bookshop.

Canterbury Cathedral
www.canterbury-cathedral.org
Open 08:45–19:00 Easter– Sep, 08:45–17:00 Oct–Easter. For information, contact The Cathedral Office, The Precincts, Canterbury, Kent, tel 01227 762862. For information about the Friends of Canterbury Cathedral, tel 01227 471000. No cathedral refectory. Pay toilets, with facilities for the disabled, are located on the south side of the precincts. Bookshop in southwest transept. Larger gift shop close to Christ Church Gate. A permit is needed for photography within the cathedral.

Westgate
Open Mon–Sat 11:00–12:30 and 13:30–15:30. *Entrance fee.* No toilets or wheelchair access.
Eastbridge Hospital of St Thomas the Martyr
Open Mon–Sat 10:00–17:00. *Entrance fee.* No disabled access.
Royal Museum and Art Gallery
Open Mon–Sat 09:00–17:30. *No entrance fee.* Disabled access to ground floor only.
Canterbury Tales
Open: opening and closing times depend on day and time of year. High *entrance fee.* Shop
and restaurant. Tel 01227 454888.
St Mildred's Church
Open Apr-Oct. No entrance fee.
Roman Museum
Open Mon–Sat 10:00–17:00, Sun during Jun–Oct 13:30–17:00. Small *entrance charge.*
Disabled access. Tel 01227 785575.

ROCHESTER
Rochester Cathedral
www.rochester.anglican.org/cathedral
Open daily 07:00–18:00. For information, contact the Cathedral Office, tel 01634 843366.
The Friends of Rochester Cathedral, tel 01634 832142. Cathedral refectory and toilets in
deanery. Wheelchair access to cathedral via north door.

Guildhall
Open daily 10:00–17:30. No entrance fee.
Draper's Museum of Bygones
Open daily 10:00–17:00. *Entrance fee.*
Rochester Castle
Open daily 10:00–18:00 Apr–Sep, 10:00–16:30 Oct–Mar. *Entrance fee* for the keep.
Eastgate House/Charles Dickens Centre
Open 10:00–17:30; last admission 1645. *Entrance fee.*

ST ALBAN'S
St Alban's Cathedral
www.stalbanscathedral.org.uk
Open daily 08:00–17:45 winter, 08:00–18:45 summer. No entrance charge, but donation
expected. For information, contact The Administrator's Office, Cathedral and Abbey
Church of St Albans, Sumpter Yard, St Albans, Herts. AL1 1BY. The Friends of the
Cathedral are located at the same address. Full facilities for the disabled, who should enter
by east end door. Excellent refectory, open 10:30–16:30.

Hypocaust
Open Mon–Sat 10:00–17:30, Sun 14:00–17:00. No entrance fee.
Glebe House Nature Reserve
Open Mon–Fri 10:00–16:00 summer, Sun 12:00–16:30.
St Michael's Church
Open 14:00–17:00 Easter–Oct.
Roman Theatre
Open daily 10:00 to 17:00 (dusk in winter). *Entrance fee* (reduced for children).
Verulamium Museum
Open Mon–Sat 10:00–17:30, Sun 14:00–17:00. *Entrance fee* (reduced for students

and OAPs).
Kingsbury Water Mill
Open Mon–Sat 11:00–18:00, Sun 11:00–17:00. *Entrance fee.*
Clock Tower
Open weekends Easter–Sep, also bank holidays, 10:30–17:30.

BURY ST EDMUNDS
Bury St Edmunds Cathedral
www.stedscathedral.co.uk
Open 09:00–17:00. For information, contact The Cathedral Office, Abbey House, Angel
Hill, Bury St Edmunds, Suffolk, tel 01284 754933. The Friends of the Cathedral may be
reached at the same address. Coffee shop in Cathedral Centre. Toilets near Abbey
Gateway and in Cathedral Centre. Shop near entrance porch. Wheelchair access
throughout cathedral.

St Mary's Church
Open: times posted on west door; at time of writing they are: Sun/Mon 14:00–16:00, Wed
09:00–14:00, Fri 10:00–12:00, Sat 11:00–14:00; closed Tue and Thu.
Manor House Museum
Open Mon–Sat 10:00–17:00, Sun 14:00–17:00. *Entrance fee.* Tearoom attached.
Abbey Visitor Centre
Open daily from 10:00; closing time depends on season. *Entrance fee.*
Moyse's Hall
Open Mon–Sat 10:00–17:00, Sun 14:00–17:00. No entrance fee.

ELY
Ely Cathedral
www.cathedral.ely.anglican.org
Open Mon–Sat 07:00–19:00 and Sun 07:30–17:00 summer, Mon–Sat 07:30–18:00 and Sun
07:30–17:00 winter. The Stained Glass Museum (located in the south triforium and
approached via the west tower) is open daily 11:00–16:30. For information, contact The
Chapter Office, Ely Cathedral, Ely, CB7 4DN, tel 01353 667735. The same telephone
number will also reach The Friends of Ely Cathedral. Small refectory at west end of north
nave aisle; cathedral also runs Almonry Restaurant in High Street. Limited toilet facilities in
refectory; main toilets on Palace Green and near sacrist's gate (facilities at latter for
disabled). Ground floor of cathedral has ramps for wheelchairs. Shop next to refectory.

Oliver Cromwell's House
Open 10:00–18:00 summer, 10:00–1715 winter. *Entrance fee.* Oliver Cromwell Exhibition.
Tel 01353 662062.
Ely Museum
Open Tue–Sun 10:30–13:00 and 14:15–17:00 summer, Tue–Sun 11:30–15:30 winter; also
open Bank Holiday Mondays. *Entrance fee.* Unsuitable for the disabled (the museum is
largely on the first floor and there is no lift).

NORWICH
Norwich Cathedral
www.cathedral.org.uk
Open daily 07:30–18:00 mid-Sep–mid-May, 07:30–19:00 mid-May–mid-Sep. For
information, contact the Visitors Office, Norwich Cathedral, Norwich, NR1 4EH. The

Friends of Norwich Cathedral may be reached at 12 The Close, Norwich, NR 1 4EH. Refectory up steps outside shop and over cloisters. Toilets under steps leading to refectory. Good wheelchair access to cathedral; use south transept door.

Cathedral Shop
Open Mon–Sat 09:15–17:00.
St Peter Hungate Museum
Open Mon–Sat 100:00–17:00. No entrance fee.
Bridewell Museum
Open Mon–Sat 10:00–17:00. *Entrance fee.* Ticket affords reduced charge for other museums.
The Mustard Shop
Open during shop hours. No entrance fee.
Church of St John Maddermarket
Open daily 10:00–16:00. No entrance fee.
Strangers' Hall
Open Mon–Sat 10:00–17:00. *Entrance fee.*
Guildhall
Open 09:30–18:00. No entrance fee.
Norwich Castle
Open Mon–Sat 10:00–17:00, Sun 14:00–17:00. *Entrance fee.* Tours of battlements and dungeons at weekends and bank holidays. Coffee bar and shop.

PETERBOROUGH
Peterborough Cathedral
www.peterborough-cathedral.org.uk
Open Mon–Fri 08:30–17:15, Sat 08:30–17:45 and Sun 12:00–17:45 May–Sep; Mon–Fri 08:30–17:15, Sat 08:30–17:15 and Sun 12:00–17:15 Oct–Apr. For information, contact The Chapter Office, Peterborough Cathedral, Laurel Court, The Minster Precincts, Peterborough, PE1 1XS. The Association of the Friends of Peterborough Cathedral may be contacted at the same address. Refectory and bookshop in Cathedral Close. Toilets at rear of refectory. Wheelchair ramps throughout cathedral.

Peterborough Museum and Art Gallery
Open Tue–Sat 10:00–17:00. *Entrance fee.*
Tourist Information Office
Open Mon–Fri 09:00–17:00, Sat and bank holidays 10:00–16:00.

SOUTHWELL
Southwell Minster
www.southwellminster.org.uk
Open daily 08:00–18:00. Information may be obtained from the Minster Office, Trebeck Hall, Bishops Drive, Southwell, Notts. NG 25 0JP, which will also supply details of The Friends of Southwell Cathedral, tel 01636 812649. Modern complex on southwest of cathedral houses spacious refectory, toilets and shop. Visitor Centre, with small audiovisual room, is next door in a former bank.

LINCOLN
Lincoln Cathedral
www.lincolncathedral.com
Open Mon–Sat 07:15–18:00 and Sun 07:15–17:00 winter, Mon–Sat 07:15–20:00 and Sun

07:15–18:00 summer. For information, contact the Communications Office, Lincoln
Cathedral, Lincoln, LN 2 1PZ, tel 01522 544544. Details of the Association of Friends of
Lincoln Cathedral may be obtained from 4 Priory Gate, Lincoln, LN2 1PZ. Coffee shop
on northeast side of cloisters. Toilets on south side of cloisters. Shop in southwest corner
of nave. Wheelchair access throughout cathedral.

Lawn Visitor Centre
Open 10:00–17:00 Easter–Sep, Oct–Easter 10:00–16:00. No entrance fee. Pub. Restaurant.
Grounds ideal for picnics.
Lincoln Castle
Open Mon–Sat 09:30–17:30 and Sun 11:00–17:30 summer, Mon–Sat 09:30–16:00 and Sun
11:00–16:00 winter. *Entrance fee.*
Sightseeing Cruises from Wigford Way Bridge
Summer months only. Contact Cathedral City Cruises, tel 01522 546853.
Bishop's Old Palace
Open Thu–Mon 10:00–18:00 (summer only). *Entrance fee* with concessions.
Tel 01522 527468.

YORK
York Minster
www.yorkminster.org
Open 07:00–20:30 summer, 07:00–17:00 winter. For information, contact the Visitors'
Department, St. Williams College, 4–5 College Street, York, YO1 2JF, tel 01904 557216.
Details of the Friends of York Minster can be obtained from the same address. No toilets
or restaurant in cathedral itself, but plenty of facilities nearby. Ramps for wheelchair
users in most parts of cathedral – enter through north door of west front. Shop next to
south transept.

Merchant Adventurers' Hall
Open Mon–Sat 08:30–17:00 Mar–Nov, 08:30–15:30 Dec–Feb. *Entrance fee.*
Jorvik Viking Centre
Open 09:00–17:30 Apr–Oct, 09:00–15:30 Nov–Mar. *Entrance fee* with concessions.
York Story Heritage Centre
Open Mon–Sat 10:00–17:00, Sun 13:00–17:00. *Entrance fee.* A combined ticket may be
obtained for this museum and the Castle Museum.
Fairfax House
Open Mon–Thu 11:00–17:00, Sat 11:00–17:00, Sun 13:30–17:00. *Entrance fee.*
Castle Museum
Open Mon–Sat 09:30–17:30, Sun 10:00–17:30 Apr–Oct, Mon–Sat 09:30–16:00, Sun
10:00–16:00 Nov–Mar. *Entrance fee.*
Guildhall
Open Mon–Fri 09:00–17:00. No entrance fee.
St Helen's Church
Open daily 10:00 to dusk. No entrance fee.

DURHAM
Durham Cathedral
www.durhamcathedral.co.uk
Open daily 09:00–17:30. For information, contact The Chapter Office, The College,
Durham, DH1 3EH, tel 0191 384 5266. For details of The Friends of Durham Cathedral,

contact the Secretary at the same address. Restaurant in undercroft in southwest corner of cloisters. Toilets nearby, with facilities for disabled. Shop near restaurant.

Durham Castle
Open daily 10:00–12:30 and 14:00–16:00, 22 Mar–30 Sep. *Entrance fee.* Tel 0191–374 3800.
University Museum of Archaeology
Open daily 11:00–16:00; reduced hours at weekends and in winter. Small *entrance fee.*
Heritage Centre and Museum
Open Sat–Sun 14:00–16:30 Apr–May, daily 14:00–16:30 Jun and Sept, daily 11:00–16:30 Jul–Aug. Small *entrance fee.*

BIBLIOGRAPHY

Most cathedrals have official guidebooks, usually approved by the dean and chapter, which can be obtained in cathedral shops.

Clifton-Taylor, Alec *The Cathedrals of England,* London, Thames & Hudson, 1967
A classic and very readable.

Ditchfield, R.H. *An Illustrated Guide to the Cathedrals of Great Britain,* London, J.M. Dent, 1902
Out of print, so scour the second-hand bookshops.

Howarth, Eva *Crash Course in Architecture,* Brockhampton Press, 1994

Morris, R. *Cathedrals and Abbeys of England and Wales,* J.M. Dent, 1979

Morris, Richard and Curbishley, Mike *Churches, Cathedrals and Chapels*, London, English Heritage, 1996

For teachers, but useful for younger readers. *Pitkin Guide Cathedral Architecture,* Pitkin, 1992
Pictorial account of English cathedral architecture.

Pitkin Guide - Dissolution of the Monasteries, Pitkin, 1995

Smith, Edwin and Cook, Olive, *English Cathedrals,* The Herbert Press, 1989
Fascinating largely photographic volume.

Cook, G.H., *The English Cathedral Through the Centuries,* The Herbert Press, 1961
Out of print, but can often be found in second hand bookshops.

Tatton-Brown, T. *Great Cathedrals of Britain,* BBC Books, 1989

Tatton-Brown, T. *The English Cathedral,* New Holland, 2002

Wilson, C. *The Gothic Cathedral,* Thames and Hudson, 1990

INDEX